SAVAGE PRESERVATION

Savage Preservation

*The Ethnographic Origins of
Modern Media Technology*

BRIAN HOCHMAN

UNIVERSITY OF MINNESOTA PRESS

MINNEAPOLIS • LONDON

The University of Minnesota Press gratefully acknowledges financial assistance provided for the publication of this book from the Georgetown University Graduate School of Arts and Sciences, the Georgetown University Film and Media Studies Program, and the Georgetown College Office of the Dean.

Portions of chapter 3 were published in "Hearing Lost, Hearing Found: George Washington Cable and the Phono-Ethnographic Ear," *American Literature* 82, no. 3 (2010): 519–51. Copyright 2010 Duke University Press. All rights reserved. Reprinted by permission.

Published by the University of Minnesota Press
111 Third Avenue South, Suite 290
Minneapolis, MN 55401-2520
http://www.upress.umn.edu

Library of Congress Cataloging-in-Publication Data

Hochman, Brian.
    Savage preservation : the ethnographic origins of modern media
        technology / Brian Hochman.
    Includes bibliographical references and index.
    ISBN 978-0-8166-8137-2 (hc : alk. paper)—ISBN 978-0-8166-8138-9 (pb : alk. paper)
    1. Ethnology—Fieldwork. 2. Anthropology—Fieldwork. 3. Mass media—
Technological innovations. 4. Mass media—Social aspects. 5. Technology—
Social aspects. 6. Technology and civilization. I. Title.
    GN346.H64 2014
    303.48'3—dc23

                                                    2014002047

Printed in the United States of America on acid-free paper

The University of Minnesota is an equal-opportunity educator and employer.

20 19 18 17 16 15 14   10 9 8 7 6 5 4 3 2 1

for
Hillary

CONTENTS

The Passamaquoddy Experiment

If the plastic arts were put under psychoanalysis, the practice of embalming the dead might turn out to be a fundamental factor in their creation. The process might reveal that at the origin of painting and sculpture there lies a mummy complex. The religion of ancient Egypt, aimed against death, saw survival as depending on the continued existence of the corporeal body. Thus, by providing a defense against the passage of time it satisfied a basic psychological need in man, for death is but the victory of time. To preserve, artificially, his bodily appearance is to snatch it from the flow of time, to stow it away neatly, so to speak, in the hold of life. It was natural, therefore, to keep up appearances in the face of the reality of death by preserving flesh and bone. The first Egyptian statue, then, was a mummy, tanned and petrified in sodium. But pyramids and labyrinthine corridors offered no certain guarantee against ultimate pillage.

Other forms of insurance were therefore sought.

—André Bazin, "The Ontology of the Photographic Image"

I n March 1890, an ethnologist at Harvard University named Jesse Walter Fewkes left his home in Boston for a four-day research expedition to Calais, Maine, one of the easternmost points in the continental United States. The purpose of the trip was to document the language and music of the Passamaquoddy tribe, who had for centuries called the region surrounding Calais home. According to Fewkes, the Passamaquoddy were the "purest-blooded race of Indians . . . in New England," a marooned nation within a nation.[1] Yet their way of life appeared to have reached a dire crossroads as the century drew to a close. "There are stories, rituals, songs, even the remnants of languages which once extended over great States, which are now known only to a few persons," Fewkes explained in the pages of *Science*. "These persons are in some instances old men and old women, with whose death they will disappear forever from the face of the earth if some record is not now made of them. Many have already been lost forever, even in the last twenty years, and some are fated to disappear in the next decade."[2] Time was perilously short. The Passamaquoddy, Fewkes claimed, were "rapidly losing their former character."[3] Soon they would fade into the misty recesses of history.

Fewkes's contemporaries harbored similar concerns. For many Americans who came of age in the decades following the Civil War—for many who had witnessed a nation violently fulfill its manifest destiny in the West and begin to set its sights on territories overseas—cultural groups like the Passamaquoddy were fated to pass away. In 1890 the myth of the vanishing Indian was as widespread as it was flawed, already something of a hallowed cliché.[4] But Fewkes's efforts among the Passamaquoddy added an unexpected twist to the tale. On his trip to Calais he brought paper for taking notes and pencils for drawing diagrams as well as a diary that he planned on using as the basis for a series of published articles.[5] He also brought a phonograph, a rotary treadle, and a box of wax cylinders.

Perfected only a few years prior, the cylinder phonograph was no ordinary tool of the ethnographic trade. But when Fewkes arrived in Calais, he met two Passamaquoddy tribal elders, Noel Josephs and Peter Selmore, who were eager to see if his newfangled recording machine could preserve the "old customs" for posterity.[6] The three men worked together for several days, proceeding mostly by trial and error. While Fewkes cranked the cylinders, cautiously putting needle to wax and converting sound into history, Josephs and Selmore took turns talking directly into the bell of the phonograph horn. They recorded six Passamaquoddy tales, six Passamaquoddy songs, and a number of routine conversations in the Passamaquoddy language.[7] They also recited the Passamaquoddy numerals from one to twenty, the days of the week, and an extended list of words and phrases that corresponded to the vocabulary schedule provided in the U.S. Bureau of Ethnology's *Introduction to the Study of Indian Languages* (1877).[8] All told, Josephs and Selmore filled thirty-five of the forty cylinders that

Fewkes brought with him. "I might fill many hundreds," Fewkes conceded in a letter home, "but the present work is only an experiment and I must limit my work to a superficial examination of the subject."[9]

When Fewkes returned to Boston, he began writing a series of journal articles that promoted his experimental recordings and defended the value of modern sound technology. He predicted that the phonograph was destined to find its most lasting social use in the ethnographic arena, preserving the dying sounds of disappearing cultures the world over. "Now is the time to collect material before all is lost," he insisted. "The phonetic methods now in use are good, but phonograph records are easier to make and more satisfactory." For Fewkes, the Passamaquoddy could only live on in grooves and spirals, on wax rather than on paper. He concluded that "[Thomas] Edison has given us an instrument by which our fast-fading aboriginal languages can be rescued from oblivion, and . . . posterity will thank us if we use it."[10] History would prove his predictions both right and wrong.

Fewkes's trip to record the Passamaquoddy in March 1890 offers us a compelling image, celebrated in the annals of media history as the first known use of the phonograph in the context of ethnographic fieldwork.[11] Like many of the famous "firsts" on which we rely to distinguish revolutionary moments of media change, the Passamaquoddy experiment performs important ideological work in the present, upholding the relationship between technological invention and cultural use as natural, even necessary, when the historical record tells a far less tidy story. In truth, the cylinder phonograph wasn't an easy or obvious solution to the problem of the vanishing Indian. Early recording machines were unreliable and difficult to operate, nowhere more so than in remote field locations. ("A portable form of the phonograph is very much needed for this kind of work," Fewkes later complained.[12]) Wax cylinders were notoriously prone to deterioration, deforming when exposed to heat and wearing out when subjected to excessive use.[13] And then there was the issue of cost: in 1890, the cylinder phonograph was a prohibitively expensive piece of equipment, an exorbitant purchase for any scientist working on a shoestring budget.[14] After taking stock of the technology's possibilities and shortcomings—after weighing the miracle of sound reproduction against the material realities that constrained its cultural application—the majority of Fewkes's contemporaries in the growing field of anthropology had actually dismissed the phonograph as "too imperfect to be of value."[15]

It's easy to overlook all of this. Accustomed as we are to living in a world in which technologies of all sorts seamlessly store and deliver the content of culture, the contingencies of Fewkes's interest in the phonograph generally remain lost on us today. The disorienting fact of history is that the Passamaquoddy experiment wasn't an inevitable product of the "acoustical marvel" of modern sound reproduction, as nineteenth-century commentators had first deemed it.[16] In context, Fewkes's phonographic errand into the wilderness was a hedged bet, a calculated response to the gathering scientific consensus that human groups differed according to behaviors and beliefs, with the variations among them determining their ability to survive and progress over time. Like the photographic image before it, and like the cinematic image to come, the cylinder recording had a future in the United States, according to Fewkes, because it offered a "practical and efficient" way for the civilized to prevent the savage from vanishing into obsolescence.[17] The sentiment was more of a wish than a reality, but for Fewkes this much was certain: the promise of media and the problem of race were inextricably linked.

This book explains why men and women like Fewkes understood new technologies like the phonograph in these terms, examining the surprising connections between thinking about race and thinking about media in late-nineteenth- and early-twentieth-century America. During this period, writers and anthropologists believed that historical forces had pushed the world's primitive cultures to the brink of extinction. They also believed that films, photographs, and phonograph recordings—modern media in their historical infancy—were uniquely suited to capture and preserve primitive life before it disappeared forever. *Savage Preservation* uncovers how the modern impulse to record cultures directly influenced audiovisual innovation, experimentation, and use in the United States, tracing the parallel histories of ethnography and technology during this crucial period of transition: from the photographic documentation of American Indian sign languages in the Great Plains, to the phonographic collection of Afro-Creole slave songs and spirituals in New Orleans, to the cinematic portrayal of tattooing rituals in colonial Samoa. My central contention is that the ethnographic rush to document the world's peoples—of which Fewkes's trip to Calais is but one small example—helped many Americans come to terms not just with the global realities of human difference, but with the audiovisual technologies that increasingly served to mediate them. New media like photography, phonography, and cinema provided tools to popularize the discipline of anthropology in the United States. At the same time, the anthropological crusade to record race and culture provided both an ideological framework and a material occasion to experiment with the social possibilities of new media. In the end, the project of cultural preservation catalyzed debates that would shape the contours of media culture in twentieth-century America—debates about permanence and obsolescence, progress and stasis, truth and fiction, the primitive and the modern. In short, the origins of modern media in the United States are distinctly ethnographic.

Critics and historians typically associate the American mythology of vanishing races and disappearing cultures with the history of salvage ethnography, an intellectual paradigm that took shape in the human sciences during the nineteenth century and flourished in a variety of cultural locations well into the twentieth.[18] In the broadest of terms, salvage ethnography constitutes the set of ideas and practices out of which efforts like Fewkes's emerged. Because many of the world's peoples appeared to be on the verge of extinction, the argument went, scientists and artists alike were obligated to document (or "salvage") them before they passed on. At bottom, the architects of the salvage paradigm insisted that certain populations were incapable of progressing beyond the primitive social state. It was the duty of the civilized to record primitive life in the face of its certain demise.

As James Clifford has noted, the logic of salvage ethnography reduces culture to little more than a "disappearing object" to be collected, classified, and preserved. The work of the anthropologist, in turn, becomes something of a "last-chance rescue operation," documenting the soon-to-vanish traditions that constitute the authentic core of cultural identity.[19] This line of reasoning rests on two foundational assumptions. The first is that variations in mankind create variations in manners, customs, and capacities. This is an assumption that *cultures exist*, a uniquely modern way of understanding the bewildering variety of the world's peoples. Although many thinkers had expressed similar sentiments before, this idea became increasingly common during the nineteenth century, when ethnologists, philologists, and philosophers all came to believe that the human species was fragmented into a series of groups whose members shared distinctive patterns of thought and behavior.[20] Whether the existence of these groups resulted from more essential human variations—variations in racial origins, for instance, or variations in environmental contexts—remained a matter of intense debate. But the invention, and gradual acceptance, of an anthropologically oriented concept of culture in this period meant that the state of man was irreducibly marked by difference.

The second assumption at the foundation of salvage ethnography is that human variations are distributed unevenly, thus rendering cultural groups unevenly fit to survive over time. This is an assumption that *cultures conflict*, an idea that also gained institutional traction during the nineteenth century, even if its intellectual roots lie in an earlier historical moment.[21] During this period, thinkers on both sides of the Atlantic began classifying the world's peoples according to a three-tiered scale of historical development: "savagery," "barbarism," and "civilization." Fueled by the rise of evolutionist cultural theory, which posited that groups in lower social states (savagery, barbarism) were ceding to groups in higher social states (civilization) as time moved forward, developmental models of human difference increasingly made cultural extinction seem inevitable and irreversible, part of the natural order of things.[22] Charles Darwin captured something of this viewpoint when he posited in 1871 that "when civilised nations come into contact with barbarians, the struggle is short."[23] Certain cultures disappeared, in other words, because they were unable to adapt to changing historical circumstances, putting them at an inherent disadvantage in the ongoing fight for evolutionary survival.

Cultures exist, cultures conflict: it goes without saying that the foundational assumptions of salvage ethnography remain at odds with what we know to be true today. From our contemporary vantage point, cultures look more like moving targets—flexible webs of affiliation and difference that respond, resist, and adapt in the context of broader social pressures. While a group's customs, behaviors, and beliefs may change over time, waxing and waning with the course of history, what we tend to identify as "culture" today is neither as fixed nor as monolithic as the architects of the salvage paradigm assumed it to be. During the late nineteenth and early twentieth centuries, by contrast, the pervasive belief in the imminent disappearance of authentic primitive cultures made the ethnographic project of preservation and recovery seem like a vital necessity. Writers and anthropologists championed the salvage endeavor as a scientific opportunity and a moral imperative, very often turning a blind eye to the realities of survival and change that surrounded them. As the American ethnologist Lewis Henry Morgan cautioned in 1877, "while the fossil remains buried in the earth will keep for the future student, the remains of [primitive] arts, languages, and institutions will not. They are perishing daily, and have been perishing for upwards of three centuries. . . . These circumstances appeal strongly to Americans to enter this great field and gather its abundant harvest."[24] More than three decades later, indigenous cultures persisted around the globe, complicating the narratives of modernization and disappearance that had motivated thinkers like Morgan (and like-minded experimentalists like Fewkes). Yet the compulsion to record and preserve somehow still remained pressing. "Primitive life is disappearing with ever-increasing rapidity," wrote Franz Boas in 1910. "Unless work is taken up at once and thoroughly, information on the earliest history [of man] . . . will never be obtained."[25] Boas's colleague Edward Sapir expressed similar sentiments a year later: "Now or never is the time in which to collect from the natives what is still available for study. What is lost now will never be recovered again."[26]

As I demonstrate in the chapters that follow, however, even as the turn-of-the-century project of cultural preservation naturalized primitive races as the "disappearing objects" of human history, it also established audiovisual media as the permanent records of their remains. In so doing, the history of salvage ethnography would seem to recall an aging fable about the origins of modern media that the film theorist André Bazin first proposed in a 1945 essay "The Ontology of the Photographic Image," quoted in the epigraph. Writing at the end of World War II, Bazin claimed that all media were linked in their ability to satisfy a "mummy complex" deeply rooted in the mind of man—a basic psychological need to cheat death, restore loss, and preserve the living world in the face of time's passage.[27] Like linens and chemicals protecting the sanctity of a decaying corpse, the technologies of photography and cinema, in particular, seemed to provide both a "defense against the passage of time" and a recognizable trace of past experience "in the hold of life."[28] According to Bazin, audiovisual media constitute modernity's signature addition to a genealogy of preservation through artificial means that stretches back to antiquity. In this sense, the world's first medium of recording was a mummy, embalming the image of man against the ravage of time.

As a comprehensive account of the social functions that audiovisual media perform, Bazin's thesis has a number of obvious shortcomings. (Consider, for instance, its calculated disregard for technologies of communication and connection, like radios and telephones.) Yet the primary aim of this book is to demonstrate that the fable of the mummy complex has a special applicability in the late nineteenth and early twentieth centuries, when the salvage ethnographic imperative led many writers and anthropologists to regard new media devices as privileged repositories of the world's disappearing cultures. During this period, a host of social and intellectual transformations seemed to confirm that certain groups were fated to die out with the passage of time. Also during this period, the emergence of audiovisual storage technologies offered new ways to embalm the cultural wreckage that civilization seemed to be leaving behind in its wake.[29] When turn-of-the-century Americans looked to the phonograph to record the songs of the Passamaquoddy, or to motion pictures to recover the tattooing rituals of colonial Samoa, they necessarily brought these two historical trajectories together. In so doing, I argue, they helped to create modern understandings of media.

In considering the convergence of thinking about race and thinking about media in the late nineteenth and early twentieth centuries, *Savage Preservation* has two main objectives. First, and most broadly, this book reveals connections among a network of U.S. historical figures—some well known, others forgotten—who left a legacy on twentieth-century media culture that has long gone unrecognized: from literary luminaries such as George Washington Cable and Gilbert H. Grosvenor; to professional anthropologists such as John Wesley Powell, Garrick Mallery, Franz Boas, and Jesse Walter Fewkes; to photographers such as Eadweard Muybridge, Franklin Price Knott, and Fred Payne Clatworthy; to filmmakers such as Hugh Lenox Scott, Richard Sanderville, and Robert and Frances Flaherty. Despite the fact that the majority of these figures considered themselves to be part of a coherent cultural project, even corresponding with each other about matters of method and practice, scholars have traditionally addressed their work as though it occurred in disciplinary isolation. John Wesley Powell and Franz Boas, for instance, are often viewed narrowly as the institutional architects of professional anthropology in the United States. Yet their specialized scientific theories actually had a lasting influence on popular novelists such as George Washington Cable, whose earliest attempts at fiction writing developed out of his own amateur ethnographic research on Afro-Creole music in New Orleans.[30] Likewise, Robert and Frances Flaherty are frequently mentioned in the same breath as many of the photographers and filmmakers listed earlier. But their cinematic efforts have never been examined, for instance, in the context of Fewkes's Passamaquoddy experiment, which ended up establishing many of the benchmarks by which later ethnographers could rationalize the use of audiovisual media for scientific purposes.

This study corrects these sorts of historical biases, employing an approach that draws extensively on the field of media archaeology. Media archaeology is a specialized method of studying media culture that looks to the messiness of the technological past to denaturalize the superficial certainties of the present.[31] Instead of viewing media history as a linear progression of landmark technological innovations and differentiated media traditions, media archaeologists emphasize convergences, contingencies, and roads not taken. As Thomas Elsaesser explains, the primary lesson of the archaeological approach to media history is that "it was a whole range of very different technologies at different points in time, with very different agendas, which have contributed to changing our idea of the audiovisual media."[32] From the perspective of the media archaeologist, Robert and Frances Flaherty have been cordoned off from figures such as Fewkes, the intellectual pioneer of audio ethnography, not just because their work violates conventional standards of anthropological science but because they chiefly employed the medium of motion pictures—a symptom of our ongoing tendency to quarantine histories of visual technology from histories of sound technology. Similarly, to borrow Elsaesser's terminology, our impoverished understanding of the relationships among figures such as Powell, Boas, and Cable suggests that it is far easier to discern the "family trees" that misleadingly isolate intellectual fields and media traditions than the "family relations" that in fact connect them.[33]

In what follows, by contrast, the history of Indian language documentation sits alongside the history of serial photography, dialect novels alongside cylinder recordings, ethnographic films alongside mass-market magazines, anthropological science alongside popular culture. Though this trajectory may seem methodologically chaotic, the distinctions between media forms and cultural fields that seem like second nature to us now actually made little sense to the historical subjects who were struggling to understand them at the time. During the late nineteenth and early twentieth centuries, American writers and anthropologists regarded audiovisual media as interchangeable tools in a larger ethnographic toolbox, providing novel solutions to debates about perception, permanence, and difference that had long plagued the salvage endeavor. Moreover, divisions between science and entertainment, anthropology and popular culture, were not nearly as rigid in this period as they might seem today. A brief history of the term *documentary*, a keyword often associated with the history of the salvage project, should illustrate these points, while also demonstrating the need to adopt more archaeologically informed perspectives in the study of media history.

By all accounts, our modern-day understanding of the term *documentary* dates back to February 1926, when the filmmaker John Grierson first singled out the "documentary value" of Robert and Frances Flaherty's salvage ethnographic film *Moana* (1926), a text that occupies much of my interest in chapter 4. "*Moana*, being a visual account of events in the daily life of a Polynesian youth and his family, has documentary value," the original usage reads.[34] Most film historians agree that Grierson's initial deployment of the term stems from the French word *documentaire*, which in the early decades of the twentieth century generally pertained to travel films set in exotic locations.[35] Yet, in the 1926 version of the documentary, which Grierson and his acolytes later codified as "the creative treatment of actuality," many of the hallmarks of our current appreciation of the documentary concept also appear to be in place: the reproduction of daily life unadorned by fiction; the desire for methodological consistency and historical significance; and, above all, the use of visual technologies like film to achieve such ends.[36]

Before 1926, however, Anglophone uses of the term *documentary* had a slightly different connotation, cohering instead around issues of written historical evidence and archival preservation: "the nature of or consisting in documents," according to the *Oxford English Dictionary's* historical definition.[37] In other words, when Anglophone speakers used the term *documentary* before Grierson, they usually meant that something was worthy of committing to historical memory and therefore worthy of writing down. This is a meaning that in fact extends as far back as the early 1800s; indeed, Grierson may have also had it in mind in his review of the Flahertys' film. As Philip Rosen has pointed out, this earlier sense of the documentary as historical evidence reflects a more unstable understanding of the concept— one that came into crisis when nineteenth-century innovations in photography, phonography, and cinema began to lay competing claims on the storage of cultural information.[38] Before 1926, according to Rosen, the parameters of the documentary depended not just on these sorts of technological changes (an expanded sense of what counts as writing and historical evidence, for instance) but on a range of cultural responses to the promises and uncertainties that those changes signified at the time. This notion of the documentary had wider connotation than we would likely accept today, beholden as we are to Grierson's more limited use of the term.

The research for this book began by asking what a media-archaeological history of the documentary might look like, a history that takes into account the technologically malleable sense of the documentary concept that had currency in the years before Grierson's formative efforts in the late 1920s and early 1930s. What is revealed by adopting a methodology that regards the documentary as a fluctuating set of technological practices, both visual and nonvisual, rather than as a static set of generic conventions? How does history change if we view the documentary as a "recording tendency," as the writer and editor Richard Watson Gilder described it in 1897—as an evolving orientation toward writing and audiovisual technologies themselves?[39] Asking such questions about the late-nineteenth- and early-twentieth-century period forced me to adopt a more capacious sense of what qualifies as "documentary," "ethnographic"—and even "media"—to understand how turn-of-the-century subjects understood the changing world around them. In following the archival trail, a number of neglected historical actors and institutions unexpectedly came to occupy center stage, and a number of geographical "contact zones" turned out to play a crucial role in their emerging story.[40] As we will see, the ethnographic origins of modern media lie not only in Thomas Edison's Menlo Park and in the Lumière brothers' Paris, but also in places like Calais, Maine, Congo Square, and the tiny Samoan village of Safune, on the outer fringe of the nation's global reach.

The second objective of this book is to demonstrate that ideologies of race and difference are absolutely necessary to the story of media history in the United States—a story that we too often tell in neutral terms of research, development, and social use. Ethnographic encounters with disappearing cultures played a key role in the development of audiovisual media during the late nineteenth and early twentieth centuries, so much so that race and media began to share something of a reciprocal logic in this period: just as much as the presence of audiovisual media structured prevailing beliefs about race, the mythology of race structured prevailing beliefs about audiovisual media. This is a contention that both extends and revises a time-honored scholarly consensus surrounding media technology's role in what critics and historians have termed *racial formation,* a social process first identified in the discipline of sociology during the 1980s and later addressed in a wide range of critical approaches to American cultural history. For Michael Omi and Howard Winant, the architects of this account, racial formation refers to the "sociohistorical process by which racial categories are created, inhabited, transformed, and destroyed" over time.[41] On its most basic level, a racial formation perspective views race and identity as fluid constructions rather than fixed designations, primarily determined by "social structure and cultural representation" and wholly dependent on historical context.[42] According to this account, racial difference is neither essential nor illusory. Instead, race constitutes a historically flexible set of "projects" that define social phenomena along racial lines.[43]

Within the racial formation framework, media technologies and media representations—both ethnographic and fictional—function as preexisting nodes in the wider network of projects that make race intelligible in the social sphere. For instance, novels and recordings are commonly said to "produce" race for mass audiences; images and broadcasts are likewise thought to "construct" difference in the service of racial formation.[44] These sorts of narratives have of course paved the way for a wealth of scholarship in a variety of academic fields, and they have afforded us a nuanced understanding of how racial ideologies and practices operate at particular moments of historical time. Yet the racial formation framework also tends to obscure one of the cardinal rules of historical media studies since the 1970s: that new technologies are far from "self-acting forces" that function independently of human intervention and cultural negotiation.[45] The fact that media can "represent," "produce," or "construct" racial common sense, or even contribute meaningfully to the broader project of racial formation, is by no means an unconditional given. Technologies do not become media outside of history.[46]

Here, again, it is helpful to think of Fewkes, who followed up on the Passamaquoddy experiment by hauling a cylinder phonograph into the arid deserts of Arizona and New Mexico to record the music of the Hopi and Zuni nations; or of Robert and Frances Flaherty (the subjects of chapter 4), who were initially forced to use a cave as a darkroom while developing rushes of ethnographic film footage in a remote region of colonial Samoa; or of Fred Payne Clatworthy (the subject of chapter 5), who in the very same period carried thousands of delicate autochrome transparency plates around the world to photograph cultural life in full color. In all of these cases, phonography, photography, and cinema provide both problems and solutions, a fitting testament to the amount of intentional work—at once physical, ideological, and cultural—required to transform the raw materials of technology into media that effectively produce and preserve culture. As Brian Larkin has pointed out, "the meanings attached to technologies, their technical functions, and the social uses to which they are put are not an inevitable consequence but something worked out over time in the context of considerable cultural debate."[47] *Savage Preservation* is ultimately about this work and those debates: about why it was that men and women like Fewkes, Clatworthy, and the Flahertys would choose to lug fragile, expensive, and untested equipment into the field rather than papers and pencils, the far more established (and far less strenuous) alternative. Time and again, as we will see, the unruly logic of race played an important role in their decisions, in ways that work against the idea that media determine the realities and fictions of difference in the absence of historical contingency.

This isn't the only story to be told about race and media in this period, of course. In the context of the salvage ethnographic project, the narrative that currently holds sway is a narrative of agency—a narrative of adaptation, resistance, and survival.[48] There is good reason for this. The fifty-year period under consideration here (from 1875 to 1925, roughly) was a period in which native peoples actively began to pursue strategies of sovereign self-determination in the burgeoning global economies of sound and image.[49] Though the anthropologists and writers who serve as the protagonists of this book may have believed that groups like the Passamaquoddy were destined to die out in theory, the vanishing races of the salvage paradigm were hardly vanishing in practice. At a time when their collective future seemed outwardly imperiled, native peoples sat for photographs, talked to phonographs, and performed in films, and they had their own motivations for doing so. They carved their own paths, in other words, and the distinctive forms of life that they fashioned along the way still persist today—a simple fact of history that exposes the fatal inadequacy of the salvage ethnographic paradigm as a way of understanding the vagaries of culture. From this vantage point, the anthropological texts, recordings, and images that form the basis of my account look less like technological memorials to cultural extinction and more like the documentary products of cross-cultural exchange. Indeed, as Elizabeth Edwards reminds us, the ethnographic encounter is always structured by two "parallel realities": the reality of the observer and the reality of the observed, neither of which can be entirely reconciled or reduced to the other.[50]

The story that I tell in these chapters could very easily be told along these lines. Yet if at times I seem to hold the problem of agency in abeyance in my case studies, it is not without careful consideration. The agency narrative is at this point well known, and its potential shortcomings have already occasioned a great deal of scholarly debate.[51] More important for my purposes here, contemporary interest in the recovery of agency—a residual product, perhaps, of the same sorts of biases that limited nineteenth-century native studies to the recovery of authenticity—has had the adverse effect of obscuring some of the most enduring and troublesome legacies of the salvage ethnographic project. From John Wesley Powell and Franz Boas to George Washington Cable and Gilbert H. Grosvenor, the vast majority of the figures considered in this book wielded extraordinary cultural power. It is tempting to dismiss this power as merely illusory or imaginary, as the result of a flawed worldview that was easily subverted at the time and left behind once we knew better. But this power was real, and it was not incidental. It put American anthropologists and writers in contact with cultural groups living in remote locations; it afforded them the means, technological and otherwise, to offer what they mistakenly believed to be the last word on the lives of indigenous peoples the world over; and it even gave them direct lines to influence federal policy. In the process, their efforts shaped understandings and uses of media technology in ways that scholars haven't sufficiently scrutinized.

As we will see, despite indigenous assertions of agency—or perhaps especially because of them—ideas about human difference gave turn-of-the-century anthropologists and writers cause to authorize the technological changes that surrounded them. The project of cultural documentation created pressing ethnographic needs that audiovisual technologies seemed uniquely fit to satisfy: while the diversity of Native American languages exposed the limitations of phonetic writing and serial photography (chapters 1 and 2) and the sounds of the African American voice indirectly helped to enhance the phonograph's scientific objectivity (chapter 3), the inability to document indigenous skin and dress through existing photographic processes provoked major shifts in cinematic technology and early color media (chapters 4 and 5). Thus, whereas conventional scholarly wisdom suggests that media technologies merely work to construct popular ideas about race and cultural difference, this book demonstrates that the reverse has also been true. During the late nineteenth and early twentieth centuries, encounters with race and cultural difference actually helped to construct the authority of new media technologies, both as socially intelligible inventions and as reliable archives of the real. Race produced media, in other words, even as media produced race.[52]

The chapters of this book trace a broad narrative arc from the specialized theories of race and technology that American ethnologists first formulated in the 1870s to their popular adaptations in U.S. media culture in the 1920s.[53] Readers familiar with the history of the salvage project in the American context will doubtless notice some canonical absences in my account of this extended period: the writings of Frank Hamilton Cushing; the phonograph recordings of Alice Fletcher, Frances Densmore, and Alan Lomax; the photographs and films of Edward Sheriff Curtis—the list could go on.[54] Also underrepresented here are the powerful critiques of the ethnographic enterprise that indigenous writers and activists launched in the early decades of the twentieth century, already well documented in the existing body of scholarship.[55] The principle of selection for my case studies was governed less by the goal of comprehensive historical coverage than by my own archival encounters with what Charles Acland has termed "residual" media objects, all of which seemed to suggest new stories and alternative histories: from phonetic alphabets and sign photographs to wax cylinder recordings, early films, and full-color autochrome transparencies.[56] In this way, this book performs a salvage operation of a different sort, rescuing artifacts of the turn-of-the-century ethnographic enterprise that have failed to withstand the basic test of time. I address this irony more fully in the book's postscript.

The first two chapters of *Savage Preservation* examine the parallel narratives of race and technology that proliferated in the second half of the nineteenth century, when American writers and ethnologists explicitly began measuring the progress of man by the yardstick of media. In chapter 1, I consider John Wesley Powell's attempts to create a phonetic alphabet for Native American languages at the U.S. Bureau of Ethnology, an effort that reflected a new understanding of the importance of media technology to the development of human societies. This idea, a core tenet of so-called "evolutionist" cultural theory, posited that the ability to record and communicate language in writing—the ability, in other words, to *mediate*—was an essential prerequisite for racial progress and survival. Powell was instrumental in promoting evolutionism in the 1870s and 1880s. Yet his commitment to the doctrine led him to reject alternative methods of cultural self-preservation that Indians themselves had pioneered over the course of the nineteenth century, and the biases of his worldview in fact lived on in the theories of media and communication that Marshall McLuhan and Walter Ong would popularize in the second half of the twentieth century, long after evolutionist thinking supposedly waned.

In chapter 2, I examine the career of Garrick Mallery, a little-known ethnologist who worked under Powell to compile a comprehensive record of Plains Indian "sign talk," a highly developed system of sign language communication that had for centuries flourished among Native American tribes who spoke in different tongues. For Mallery, as for many of his contemporaries, the sign language of the Plains Indians represented a disappearing vestige of mankind's first and most primitive medium of communication, evidence of the earliest developments that had separated humans from animals. Working from this theory, Mallery compiled a number of landmark ethnographic studies in the early 1880s, many of which overtly experiment with forms of graphic representation that borrow from the work of Eadweard Muybridge, whose contemporaneous innovations in serial photography suggested new ways to preserve sign talk—a language based not on the sounds of speech but on the movements of the body. Chapter 2 concludes with an account of the ethnographic films of Hugh Lenox Scott and Richard Sanderville (Chief Bull), whose shared interest in resurrecting Mallery's documentary project in the 1930s helps us to understand why modern media technologies like chronophotography and film seemed to hold enduring promise as agents of cultural preservation in this period.

Chapter 3 explores a range of texts that attempt to salvage African American and Native American music at a time when phonographic technologies increasingly appeared to have authority over documentary sound preservation. I begin with George Washington Cable's *The Grandissimes* (1880)—a dialect novel that frequently signals its own inability to reproduce the vernacular sounds of New Orleans's Afro-Creole community—to illustrate the written word's inadequacies as a cultural sound archive. For Cable, as well as for like-minded contemporaries such as Franz Boas, the auditory limitations of the print medium represented a symptom of a far more basic problem: humanity's inability to comprehend objectively, on its own terms, the realities of racial and cultural difference. In the 1890s and 1900s, two American ethnologists, Jesse Walter Fewkes and Benjamin Ives Gilman, eventually attempted to solve this problem by turning to the newly invented phonograph, a machine that promised a form of listening and writing wholly uncontaminated by the cultural biases of the ear and the pen. Chapter 3 ultimately demonstrates that the phonograph's cultural authority evolved out of ethnographic encounters with the sound of race. It was only after American writers and anthropologists began to recognize the cultural politics of listening that the new technology of mechanical sound reproduction made the old medium of the written word seem insufficient.

Chapters 1, 2, and 3 of *Savage Preservation* focus on the specialized theories and technologies that shaped the nascent science of anthropology in the United States. In the book's final two chapters, I turn to the mass cultural domains of film and magazine photography, where the salvage paradigm's archetypal myths about vanishing races were popularized in the early decades of the twentieth century. Perhaps no two figures did more to reshape the salvage paradigm for American audiences than the husband-and-wife filmmaking team of Robert and Frances Flaherty. As I demonstrate in chapter 4, expectations about the visual representation of race indelibly shaped the making of the Flahertys' landmark film *Moana* (1926), a dramatic reconstruction of indigenous life in colonial Samoa that eventually became the first motion picture to be labeled "documentary" in the modern sense of the term. *Moana*'s most lasting cinematic achievements—most important, its pioneering use of color-sensitive "panchromatic" film stock—emerged out of the Flahertys' preoccupation with depicting Samoan skin color realistically. By uncovering *Moana*'s tumultuous production history, I reveal that the Flahertys' controversial version of salvage ethnography constituted a direct response to ongoing anthropological debates about racial difference, even on the most basic level of motion picture technology.

Chapter 5 considers the forgotten history of early ethnographic color photography, focusing on *National Geographic Magazine*'s unprecedented investments in color image reproduction during the 1910s and 1920s. Throughout the nineteenth century, photographers, chemists, and engineers searched for reliable ways to capture visual images in color, yet none of their technical discoveries were deemed suitable for everyday use. The dream of full-color photography was only realized in the form of the "autochrome," a rare early-twentieth-century picture format with the ability to capture the colors of nature on transparent glass plates. Despite the fragility and unpredictability of the autochrome process, which severely limited its commercial fortunes, *National Geographic* pursued color work at all costs because it offered the chance to record the most colorful and recognizable artifacts of indigenous cultures—clothing, handcrafts, and art—in a way that standard monochrome photography could not. The ethnographic desire to preserve the disappearing colors of culture thus powerfully shaped the development of modern color media in the early decades of the twentieth century. If not for the pioneering efforts of *Geographic* colorists such as Franklin Price Knott and Fred Payne Clatworthy, who were directly inspired by the vanishing race theory, the autochrome would have likely fallen into obsolescence as quickly as the color processes that preceded it.

Savage Preservation concludes with a postscript that follows a number of the book's central archival materials into recent history, exploring how native peoples have begun to reinterpret neglected turn-of-the-century media artifacts in the service of cultural persistence. To be sure, the vanishing races of the late nineteenth and early twentieth centuries have in many cases outlived the analog media technologies that were originally thought to memorialize their disappearance. A century removed from the work of John Wesley Powell and Garrick Mallery, George Washington Cable and Robert Flaherty, phonograph recordings and celluloid films are actually what threaten to fall into historical obsolescence, despite the strident claims to authority and permanence initially made on their behalf.

In closing, a brief caveat on terminology and a note on the title of this book are in order. It is customary in academic writing to undermine outmoded language with the use of scare quotes. Words such as *primitive* and *savage*—as well as their antonyms, *modern* and *civilized*—are typically placed in quotation marks not only to signal their historical contingencies but also to dissociate the writer from the worldview that they imply. The same goes for the vocabulary of late-nineteenth- and early-twentieth-century anthropologists, who regularly made use of stock terms such as *native* and *aboriginal* to describe indigenous peoples with diverse histories, *race* and *nation* to categorize cultural groups with far more flexible affiliations, and *man* and *mankind* to generalize about the human species regardless of gender. I have elected to forgo the convention of using scare quotes throughout this book, however, except when referring to original source materials. I have also tried to resist the impulse to substitute contemporary terminology for outdated language. My intention in doing so isn't to naturalize the authority of the figures who are studied here, or to suggest an uncritical stance toward their ideas and actions. On the most basic level, this was a stylistic choice. At times it seemed as though just about everything that wasn't a direct quotation needed to be rendered in scare quotes, which would have certainly taxed the patience of even the most generous reader. Yet it is also important to remember that the ideas about race and culture that had currency in this period were extraordinarily influential, so much so that we still feel their weight today. As such, I have also strayed from academic convention to offset any false distance that the passage of time affords.

As for my title, on one hand, the phrase *savage preservation* seems to capture the central claim that I advance in these pages—that many of the core
ideas and uses we have come to accept for audiovisual media emerged, at
least in part, out of the scramble to preserve disappearing primitive cultures
during the late nineteenth and early twentieth centuries. Yet the phrase
savage preservation has a much darker resonance, as well, and I hope that
my title will simultaneously evoke the distinctive forms of cultural violence
that the anthropological project of preservation clearly helped to reinforce.
Jim Crow, the Dawes Act, and the Open Door; segregation, genocide, and
empire: though my case studies address these historical developments in
passing, I want to underscore that they provide the essential backdrop for
the story that follows. To borrow a resonant turn of phrase from Thomas
Pynchon, it is only by recognizing such contexts that we can begin to
recover the hidden history of exclusion on which the "secular miracle" of
media—seemingly universal, seamless, and ongoing—in fact depends.[57]

1

Media Evolution

Indians, Alphabets, and the
Technological Measures of Man

On the evening of February 3, 1885, almost twenty-three years after losing his right arm in the Battle of Shiloh, the American ethnologist John Wesley Powell opened his annual address to the Anthropological Society of Washington by acknowledging the inevitability, and the price, of human progress. "It is a long way from savagery to civilization," Powell began, alluding to the narratives of cultural development that European and American intellectuals had popularized in the decades prior. "In the attempt to delineate the progress of mankind through this long way, it would be a convenience if it could be divided into clearly defined stages."[1] For thinkers like Powell, human history could be understood as the progression of three such stages—savagery, barbarism, and civilization—but the new science of anthropology had failed to grasp the mechanisms that enabled human groups to advance from one stage to the next. The primary object of ethnographic inquiry was thus

to set forth the characteristics of savage art as distinct from barbaric art, and the nature of the change; to explain savage institutions and barbaric institutions, and how the lower class developed into the higher; to set forth . . . the characteristics of savage language and barbaric language, and the origin of the change; to show the nature of the opinions held by savages and the opinions held by barbarians, and to explain the reason of the change from one to the other; and finally to explain savage and barbaric intellections, and to show how savage methods of reasoning were transformed into barbaric methods of reasoning.[2]

Change, transformation, development: wherever the world's peoples were located on the "long way" to civilization, cultural evolution's most advanced stage, what was certain was that history was moving forward. It was only a matter of time before the races of mankind left savagery and barbarism behind.

For all of its teleological certainty about the course of human history, Powell's address also conceded a few inconvenient truths about the future to come. Certain cultural forms, even entire populations, were fated to disappear as mankind moved up the evolutionary ladder—this was the price of progress. Racial groups that lagged behind in the savage and barbaric states were vanishing rapidly and threatening to die out. According to Powell, this was no historical accident. Cultural disappearance was part of the natural order of things, an unfortunate by-product of a basic "tendency toward homogeneity" among human groups the world over.[3] "Arts compete with one another, and progress in art is by the survival of the fittest in the struggle for existence," he went on to explain. "In like manner, institutions compete with institutions, languages with languages, opinions with opinions, and reasoning with reasoning; and in each case we have the survival of the fittest in the struggle for existence."[4] Three years later, addressing the same constituency in Washington, Powell summarized his position in slightly more ominous terms: "That which has been is not now, and that which is never will be again. . . . Old institutions decay as new institutions take their place. Old languages decay and are forgotten because new and higher languages are learned. When civilization meets with savagery or barbarism it always teaches it a new language."[5]

That Powell would choose to adopt language loss as his primary metaphor for inevitability of cultural extinction is significant: Americans had long associated the progress of civilization with the disappearance of indigenous forms of speech. The myth of the disappearance of native languages was in fact age-old—at least as old as the American colonies, probably older—and the idea motivated a wide range of salvage ethnographic projects from the seventeenth century onward.[6] In the North American context, the earliest efforts to document indigenous languages were chiefly motivated by the missionary impulse. During the 1600s, religious leaders such as Roger Williams (*A Key into the Language of America* [1643]) and John Eliot (*The Holy Bible: Containing the Old Testament and the New Translated into the Indian Language* [1663] and *The Indian Grammar Begun* [1666]) compiled Native American vocabularies to further the civilizing mission and facilitate the diffusion of the biblical Word into the New World.[7] Yet by the American Revolutionary period—and well into Powell's own day, as his remarks in the mid-1880s make clear—the future of the Indian seemed less certain. The coexistence of savagery and civilization seemed far less tenable. This ideological shift had the effect of redirecting the aim of native language studies from translation to preservation, religious conversion to historical collection. Heralding the arrival of the modern preservationist paradigm was Thomas Jefferson's *Notes on the State of Virginia* (1787), which famously posited the extinction of the American Indian as a foregone conclusion, urgently appealing for the systematic documentation of native languages in the name of historical understanding and national self-definition. "It is to be lamented . . . very much to be lamented, that we have suffered so many of the Indian tribes already to extinguish, without our having previously collected and deposited in the records of literature, the general rudiment at least of the languages they spoke," wrote Jefferson in what would come to be regarded as a founding document in the field of historical linguistics. "Were vocabularies formed of all the languages spoken in North and South America, preserving their appellations of the most common objects in nature, of those which must be present to every nation barbarous or civilized, with the inflections of their nouns and verbs, their principles of regimen and concord, and these deposited in all the public libraries, it would furnish opportunities to those skilled in the languages of the old world to compare them with these, now, or at any future time, and hence to construct the best evidence of the derivation of this part of the human race."[8]

Jefferson's oft-cited "lament" for Indian languages is noteworthy here for two reasons, and both help to situate Powell's interest in the relationship between cultural evolution and language loss at the end of the nineteenth century. First, Jefferson's statement testifies to the remarkable durability of the vanishing race myth. Here, as early as 1787, Indians are already threatening to "extinguish," a necessary casualty of historical progress.[9] Second, and perhaps more important, Jefferson's call for an organized Indian linguistics also implicitly figures the Native American voice as a historical artifact that stores and communicates hidden information about the evolutionary past: "Were vocabularies formed of all the languages spoken in North and South America . . . it would furnish opportunities to those skilled in the languages of the old world . . . to construct the best evidence of the derivation of this part of the human race." This notion of language as a vehicle of history first took shape in the Enlightenment philosophies of Locke, Rousseau, and Herder—by the end of the nineteenth century, it had achieved the status of intellectual orthodoxy.[10] When Powell addressed the Anthropological Society of Washington in 1885, he had already argued in a variety of venues that "the condition of primitive man is . . . discovered in the study of languages."[11] Indeed, as the founder of the Smithsonian Institution's Bureau of American Ethnology, he had institutionalized the idea on a national scale. Just one month after Powell's Washington lecture, the prominent American ethnologist Daniel G. Brinton championed the very same principles in an address to the Pennsylvania Historical Society: "The affinities of [Native American] speech, properly analyzed and valued, are our most trustworthy guides in tracing the relationship and descent of nations. . . . We can turn them, like the reflector of a microscope, on the secret and hidden mysteries of the aboriginal [primitive] man, and discover his inmost motives, his impulses, his concealed hopes and fears, those that gave rise to his customs and laws, his schemes of social life, his superstitions and his religions."[12] By committing Indian languages to the permanence of the page, nineteenth-century American ethnologists thus believed they could shed light on the shadowy recesses of mankind's primitive past. If Powell was right that civilization was in the process of teaching savagery a "new language" over time, the native tongues that were being left behind appeared to offer answers to basic questions about the origins of human communication, even the origins of humanity itself.

To historians of anthropology, linguistics, and American Indian affairs, this is an eminently familiar story.[13] Yet in this chapter I attempt to resituate its cultural significance, arguing that ideas about the decline of Native American languages provided a crucial framework for ideas about the rise of modern media. This may seem like an unorthodox historical claim. To be sure, Powell's evolutionary theory of language loss is not overtly about "media," at least in the ways we typically conceive of the term today. But the problem of vanishing Indian languages in fact directly influenced how nineteenth-century Americans like Powell understood both the history and the future of human communication technology. Salvage ethnographic encounters with the "barbarous tongues" of Native Americans generated new ideas about orality and literacy, obsolescence and permanence, the primitive and the modern—all of which would become key terms in the twentieth century's burgeoning empire of media and communications. In the United States, the Indian linguistics of Powell and his contemporaries might even be said to have inaugurated the field of media studies itself.

The difficulty we have in recognizing the importance of encounters with Native American languages to modern media history stems both from the uncertainty among nineteenth-century subjects about what it was that media were, and from our own inability to rid ourselves of the biases at the center of their worldview. As John Guillory has shown, the modern "media concept" is a relatively recent invention, only gaining popular traction in the context of the technological sea changes of the late nineteenth century.[14] Prior to this period, philosophers and ethnologists treated language as a "medium" *avant la lettre*. Language constituted the first medium, the most primitive medium—the medium that both communicated the stuff of thought and stored hidden information about the prehistoric past. As the accounts of Jefferson, Brinton, and Powell all suggest, this line of thinking offered a crucial rationale for salvaging Native American speech: preserving the disappearing languages of the world meant preserving a potential key to the black box of early human history.

As Guillory rightly points out, however, the invention of the phonograph and motion pictures at the end of the nineteenth century threw this older, more abstract understanding of the media concept into question, gradually forcing European and American intellectuals to view media with strict material reference to storage, reproduction, and communications technologies, the written word chief among them.[15] Ethnocentric accounts of Native American life and history helped to establish this more modern sense of the media concept, as well. Because Native Americans allegedly lacked Western technologies of writing, they appeared to embody living vestiges of an unlettered and unmediated past that civilized societies had long ago left behind. In the nascent discipline of anthropology, in particular, the absence of alphabets and other reproducible technologies of inscription increasingly served to explain not just why Indian languages seemed to be disappearing over time but also why Indians themselves had failed to evolve out of the primitive social state.

Ultimately, nineteenth-century ethnologists drew on these two competing understandings of media—language as the "medium" of thought and history, writing as the "medium" of reproduction, communication, and progress—to make sense of their documentary encounters with Native American languages. To be sure, this conceptual instability reflects the novelty of the late-nineteenth-century media environment. The period's leading ethnologists found themselves fascinated by media of all sorts, in both the "old" and the "new" senses of the term, yet they generally lacked a coherent vocabulary to distinguish between them and explain their relative cultural significance. In the long run, their confusion had the effect of obscuring the discipline of anthropology's contributions to the conceptual apparatus of media and communications studies. Yet, as I demonstrate in this chapter, the anthropological impulse to distinguish between races and cultures in evolutionary terms in fact hastened the consolidation of the modern media concept that still holds sway today: a model based on reproducible written inscription rather than spoken language, and a model that represents innovations in writing technology as catalysts for historical progress.

Nowhere is this transition more visible than in the work of John Wesley Powell, who spearheaded a massive federal effort to document Native American languages as the nineteenth century drew to a close. In this chapter, I use Powell's work during this period—his attempt to invent a phonetic alphabet for Indian speech, in particular—as a focal point for examining the ascendancy of "evolutionist" cultural theory, a body of thought that explicitly identified the written mediation of language as a pivotal component of racial development. For evolutionists like Powell, the development of writing technologies like the phonetic alphabet reflected innate differences among human groups, serving as the most reliable ethnological index of man's evolutionary attainment. As we will see, this is a way of looking at history that cleared conceptual space for the emergence of the modern media concept because it helped to identify not just which languages and cultures were fated to win out in the struggle for evolutionary existence but which storage, reproduction, and communication technologies were crucial in ensuring their survival. This is also a way of looking at history that would stubbornly persist in twentieth-century media and communications theory, long after the evolutionist account of culture had supposedly waned.

Writing Progress

John Wesley Powell stands at the center of far-reaching transformations in U.S. federal policy, scientific practice, and anthropological thought that took place during the second half of the nineteenth century. As Wallace Stegner pointed out sixty years ago, perhaps no American played a greater role in the realization of the nation's manifest destiny in the West—in the charting of its geography, in the mastery of its natural resources, and in the understanding of its indigenous populations—and perhaps no American figured more centrally in the emergence of professional ethnology in the decades following the Civil War.[16] Powell's biography is therefore well known.[17]

After sustaining life-threatening wounds while fighting for the Union Army, Powell rose to national prominence in the late 1860s when he successfully undertook several treacherous geographical surveys of the Colorado River region, filling in one of the last blank spaces on the great map of the American West.[18] In the decade that followed, he wrote a landmark series of scholarly articles on the natural environment of the western territories ("The Cañons of the Colorado," "An Overland Trip to the Grand Canyon," and "Physical Features of the Colorado Valley," all published in 1875), while turning his attention to the lives and customs of the native peoples who lived there.[19] Convinced that his research had immense practical value in the administration of federal Indian affairs, Powell began petitioning for the creation of a government-sponsored institution that would centralize the study of indigenous life throughout North America. Congress agreed in 1879, and he served as the director of the ethnographic organization that resulted—the Bureau of Ethnology (later rechristened as the Bureau of American Ethnology, or BAE)—until his death in 1902, overseeing its emergence as one of nineteenth-century America's most influential cultural institutions.[20]

Widely publicized in newspapers across the United States and later serialized in the nation's leading monthly magazines, Powell's western expeditions captured the attention of the American public during the 1860s and

1870s. But it was his interest in institutionalizing the nascent discipline of ethnology at the BAE—illustrated in far less glamorous publications such as *Introduction to the Study of Indian Languages* (1877) and *Indian Linguistic Families of America North of Mexico* (1891)—that left his longest-lasting mark. For Powell, organized anthropological inquiry was key to the democratic future of the United States. Understanding how Native Americans responded to forces of "acculturation" (a term Powell in fact coined in 1880) seemed to improve federal Indian policy and hasten the progress of the nation as a whole.[21] "In pursuing . . . ethnographic investigations," he wrote in the introductory section to the BAE's *First Annual Report* (1881), "it has been the endeavor as far as possible to produce results that would be of practical value in the administration of Indian affairs, and for this purpose especial attention has been paid to vital statistics, to the discovery of linguistic affinities, the progress made by the Indians toward civilization, and the causes and remedies for the inevitable conflict that arises from the spread of civilization over a region previously inhabited by savages. I may be allowed to express the hope that our labors in this direction will not be void of such useful results."[22]

Setting aside, at least for a moment, the fact that Powell's mission statement reveals a contradictory connection between the preservative efforts of the BAE's ethnographic project and the culturally destructive effects of nineteenth-century U.S. Indian policy, what is crucial to note here is that Powell believed that language constituted the essential baseline for any politically "useful" inquiry into the history of Native American life.[23] "With little exception," he continued in the BAE's *First Annual Report,* "all sound anthropologic investigation in the lower states of culture exhibited by tribes of men, as distinguished from nations, must have a firm foundation in language. Customs, laws, governments, institutions, mythologies, religions, and even arts cannot be properly understood without a fundamental knowledge of the languages which express the ideas and thoughts embodied therein."[24] Powell had inherited this position from several generations of political philosophers and linguists working in Europe and America. But his approach to the documentation of Native American languages was most immediately indebted to William Dwight Whitney and Lewis Henry Morgan, two widely acclaimed nineteenth-century American scholars who had established convergent theoretical models for understanding language's role in shaping human history. It is worth outlining their claims to situate both Powell's language preservation project at the BAE and the new ideas about human evolution that motivated it.

On one hand, William Dwight Whitney's *Language and the Study of Language* (1867) channeled Enlightenment philosophy to advance the argument that the history of languages was intimately bound up with the history of cultures.[25] Speech, Whitney insisted, was not some primordial human endowment, fixed and unchanged since the dawn of time. On the contrary, languages had histories—histories as diverse as the world's peoples, reflecting the unique social relations out of which they emerged. What this meant, in essence, was that languages carried vital information about the cultural past. Changes in vocabularies and speech patterns, for instance, potentially bore witness to changes both in the organization of societies and in the historical relationships between them.

As Whitney explained in the opening pages of *Language and the Study of Language,* the special connection between language and history had profound implications for understanding the world's primitive peoples— American Indians, among others—who were allegedly trapped in an early stage of human development, without access to written records that would otherwise shed light on their collective past. "Language furnishes the principal means of fruitful inquiry into the deeds and fates of mankind during the ages which precede direct historical record," Whitney continued. "It enables us to determine, in the main, both the fact and the degree of relationship subsisting among the different divisions of mankind, and thus to group them together into families, the members of which must have once set forth from a common home, with a common character and a common culture, however widely separated, and however unlike in manners and institutions, we may find them to be, when they first come forth into the light of written history. . . . It [language] is, in brief, a volume of the most varied historical information to those who know how to read it and derive the lessons it teaches."[26] Here we see the natural extension of Jefferson's idea about language as a medium of human antiquity. For Whitney, native speech can be "read" and deciphered, like an ancient text or an archaeological artifact, to unlock the primitive past's secrets.[27]

On the other hand, Lewis Henry Morgan's widely read *Ancient Society; or, Researches in the Lines of Human Progress from Savagery through Barbarism to Civilization* (1877) incorporated Whitney's ideas into a much broader narrative about the historical progress of the human species. In Morgan's view—the view that would eventually become known on both sides of the Atlantic as "evolutionism," initially formulated in the mid-1860s by British thinkers like John Lubbock and E. B. Tylor—humans proceeded from common origins and developed at different rates toward a perfectible social ideal, passing through a successive series of stages in the process.[28] "The history of the human race is one in source, one in experience, one in progress," Morgan claimed, outlining the evolutionary narrative of cultural history. Over time, "savages, advancing by slow, almost imperceptible steps, attained the higher condition of barbarians . . . [and] barbarians, by similar progressive advancement, finally attained to civilization." Yet, in the process, certain "tribes and nations have been left behind . . . some in barbarism, and others in savagery."[29] For evolutionists like Morgan, all of the world's peoples were traveling on the same road toward the ideal social state, but certain racial groups had been waylaid at different stops on the journey: some earlier ("savagery," "barbarism"), some later ("civilization").

According to Morgan, language served as one of many cultural indicators of a racial group's place on the evolutionary timeline. The more complex a group's belief system or subsistence method, the more advanced its level of evolutionary maturity. Likewise, the more "organized" and "refined" the language (the more speech patterns were consistent among individuals who shared a common tongue, for instance, or the more words in a given linguistic system expressed distinct ideas), the higher the "culture-stage" of the people who spoke it. For Morgan, who had spent the better part of the 1850s and 1860s conducting field research among the Plains Indian nations, Native American life provided a handy case in point for his theories about evolutionary progress. Because Indian belief systems and subsistence methods seemed rudimentary when compared to Western norms— and because Indian languages seemed unorganized and unrefined when compared to languages like English—"it follows that the history and experience of the American Indian tribes represent, more or less nearly, the history and experience of our own remote ancestors when in corresponding conditions [of savagery]. Forming a part of the human record, their institutions, arts, inventions and practical experience possess a high and special value reaching far beyond the Indian race itself."[30] In Morgan's view, then, Indian languages appeared to bear the unique imprint of a primitive state of human development. Studying them within the evolutionist paradigm led to answers not merely about their origins in the savage state (as Whitney had hoped) but about their relative capacity for progress toward the civilized ideal.

Both Whitney and Morgan played a crucial role in Powell's intellectual development (*Language and the Study of Language* and *Ancient Society* are cited extensively throughout his early essays), and this line of influence has long preoccupied historians of anthropology and linguistics.[31] Yet Powell's writings during the 1870s, 1880s, and 1890s, composed during his extended tenure at the BAE's Washington headquarters, also diverge from the thinking of his predecessors. For Powell, cultural evolution depended not just on the capacity to express complex ideas in language but on the ability to store and communicate them in written form—on the ability to "technologize" cultural information, to borrow Walter Ong's terminology.[32] In Powell's account, disparities in human attainment are attributed to a variety of factors, but above all else progress toward the civilized ideal hinges on the development of writing, on the development of what I will call the *media function*. As Powell argued in "Human Evolution" (1883), the first in the trilogy of writings on evolutionism that included his 1885 Washington address "From Savagery to Barbarism" and its 1888 sequel "From Barbarism to Civilization," "language is the agency by which men have been interrelated through the communication of thought. In the course of its evolution gesture-speech has gradually been replaced by the more highly organized oral speech; and finally written language has been based thereon by representing to the eye symbols of that which is spoken to the ear. To a very large extent, in its earliest history, language was addressed to the eye. It then became chiefly addressed to the ear; and at last the eye and ear alike become the passive organs of speech."[33] For Powell, in other words, language is the glue that binds together cultures, but it isn't until the invention of writing technology that progress toward the civilized state truly commences. To be savage and primitive is to be without writing, without media. To be civilized and modern is to be lettered. From the ear-centered world of orality to the eye-centered world of literacy, Powell believed that the development of human consciousness, the human senses, and even human history itself depends entirely on the presence of the media function.

This was a familiar refrain, of course. European writers and thinkers had for centuries offered variations on Powell's basic point about the historical value of the written word. As Walter D. Mignolo has shown, fifteenth- and sixteenth-century explorers frequently used alphabetic writing as a yardstick for human development, consigning to backwardness New World peoples who appeared to fail Western standards of literacy.[34] Such ideas paved the way for Jean-Jacques Rousseau's landmark *Essay on the Origin of Languages* (1781), a treatise that influenced virtually every nineteenth-century American writer interested in the study of language and written script. For Rousseau, famously, "the depicting of objects" was "appropriate to a savage people; signs of words and of propositions, to a barbaric people; and the alphabet to civilized peoples."[35] Later on, Morgan himself would likewise claim that "the use of writing"—more than any other technological achievement, from the compass and the steam engine to the locomotive and the telegraph—"affords a fair test of the commencement of civilization. . . . Without literary records neither history nor civilization can properly be said to exist."[36]

Given the historical importance of thinking about technology to thinking about modernity, this line of influence is relatively unsurprising.[37] What is important to underscore here, however, is that Powell was first in the American context to place writing technology at the absolute center of the evolutionary model of cultural development, over and against a number of possible indicators of human progress. In the early stages of savagery, Powell argued, human language was "very imperfectly organized," and words were "very crude tools for the communication of thought."[38] Because they remained unwritten, "savage languages have the parts of speech very imperfectly differentiated . . . the grammatic processes and methods are heterogeneous and inconsistent, and . . . the body of thought which they are competent to express is greatly limited."[39] The movement out of this culturally stagnant state—the movement toward barbarism, the next major stage of human history—depended on the invention of what Powell termed "hieroglyphic symbols," which provisionally create the rudiments of a permanent historical record.[40]

By the advanced stages of civilization, in Powell's model, language and thought attain depth and complexity only as a consequence of history's most important recording technology: the phonetic alphabet. The invention of written alphabets allegedly enabled humans to communicate abstract ideas across space and time; they also gave cultural groups a reliable way to remember the past and accumulate knowledge about the world around them. As Powell summarized the historical progression in the "Human Evolution" trilogy's final essay, "the age of savagery is the age of sentence words; the age of barbarism the age of phrase words; the age of civilization the age of idea words. . . . In savagery, picture-writings are used; in barbarism, hieroglyphs; in civilization, alphabets."[41] In short, the course of history hinged on mankind's relative ability to store and communicate cultural data.

The ethnocentrism of Powell's account of human development almost goes without saying. To be sure, his thesis in the "Human Evolution" trilogy turns a blind eye toward the alternative forms of writing, record keeping, and communication that had flourished among indigenous populations across North and South America for centuries. We need only look as far as the history of wampum in New England, or the existence of the *quipu* in the Peruvian Andes, to see that the New World was full of its own forms and practices of media.[42] Moreover, as Phillip H. Round has demonstrated, even traditional Western technologies of collective memory and communication, such as the book, played a "constitutive role" in everyday Native American affairs from the seventeenth century onward.[43] Yet despite these obvious shortcomings (and despite the critiques of the orality–literacy divide that scores of twentieth-century thinkers have mounted in the name of poststructuralism), Powell's argument reveals the powerful set of ideas about racial capacity and technological progress that underwrote the late-nineteenth-century Indian language preservation project.[44] At bottom, Native Americans were mired in the lowest levels of savagery because they seemed constitutionally incapable of mediating their own culture in written form. This also provided an explanation for why their languages were disappearing. Hearkening back to Jefferson's elegy for Native American languages in *Notes on the State of Virginia,* Powell later warned that "opportunities for collecting [Native American] linguistic material are growing fewer day by day, as tribes are consolidated upon reservations, as they become civilized, and as the older Indians, who alone are skilled in their language, die, leaving, it may be, only a few imperfect vocabularies as a basis for future study."[45] Morgan, as we have already seen, sounded a similar alarm in his introductory remarks to *Ancient Society*: "While the fossil remains buried in the earth will keep for the future student, the remains of Indian arts, languages, and institutions will not. They are perishing daily, and have been perishing for upwards of three centuries. The ethnic life of the Indian tribes is declining under the influence of American civilization, their arts and languages are disappearing, and their institutions are dissolving. . . . These circumstances appeal strongly to Americans to enter this great field and gather its abundant harvest."[46]

Both of these accounts blame the extinction of American Indian language and culture on the usual historical suspects: racial inferiority, demographic change, and the disruptive "influence" of a vaguely defined "American civilization." But read against Powell's essays on cultural evolution during the 1880s, both accounts also implicitly suggest that indigenous "arts," "languages," and "institutions" were "dissolving" because native peoples lacked the capacity to immortalize them in writing. In the absence of modern technologies of cultural memory—in the absence of the media function—Indian culture allegedly eroded with the passage of each generation.

In the late 1870s and early 1880s, what seemed immediately necessary at the newly instituted Bureau of Ethnology was thus a permanent way to preserve Native American language and culture, a new system of writing and storage. What seemed necessary, in short, was an alphabet—and this was the first project that Powell's *Introduction to the Study of Indian Languages* (1877) undertook. It is to this landmark text, and its technological context, that I now turn.

Technologies of the Indian Word; or, "Fonĕtĭk Rĕprĭsĕnteshön"

The effort to invent a standardized alphabetic writing system for the sounds of Native American speech dates back to the 1600s. In the 1650s, for instance, the Puritan missionary John Eliot began recruiting Christianized Indians to help create a special orthography for the Massachusett language, a project that culminated in the publication of *Mamusse wunneetupanatamwe up-biblum God* (1663), the influential "Indian Bible" cited earlier.[47] By all accounts, however, the period between 1815 and 1825 represents the crucial turning point in the endeavor, with Peter Stephen Duponceau's "English Phonology; or, An Essay towards an Analysis and Description of the Component Sounds of the English Language" (1818) and John Pickering's *Essay*

on a Uniform Orthography for the Indian Languages of North America (1820)
serving as the primary touchstones in the tradition.[48]

Duponceau and Pickering represent the first of three possible sources
for Powell's evolutionary experiments with alphabetic writing in the BAE's
1877 *Introduction to the Study of Indian Languages.* While Duponceau worked
to establish the foundation for the modern science of "phonology" (the
study of the phonetic sounds produced by the human voice and their written equivalents), Pickering extended the project into the realm of indigenous languages, which, in his words, invariably caused "inconvenience and
confusion" for any individual hoping to reduce them to written characters.[49] "As naturalists are now investigating the structure and history of the
globe itself, by collecting fragments of the component parts, from the sum-
mits of its mountains to the depths of its seas," Pickering wrote in his 1820
Essay on a Uniform Orthography, "so we must study the constitution and
history of its possessor, man, by collecting specimens of him, especially of
his distinguishing characteristick [*sic*], language, from the most remote
and barbarous, as well as the most refined portions of the race. . . . Nothing, then, is more clearly necessary . . . than some *common and systematic
method of writing* [for the languages of the Indians]."[50] For both Duponceau and Pickering, who corresponded extensively throughout the 1810s
and 1820s, meeting this need merely entailed tweaking the standard Roman
alphabet, adding diacritical marks above and below each letter to account
for the seemingly unfamiliar "accents," "fluctuations," and "nasalisations"
that seemed to be common in Native American languages. Pickering's essay
concluded with telling confidence: "In the languages of the American
Indians, we have only to ascertain . . . every elementary sound, and then
arrange the letters, by which we may choose to represent those sounds, in
the order of our own alphabet."[51]

Others did not find the matter so simple. In 1821, a Cherokee silversmith
named George Guess—better known as Sequoyah—independently unveiled
a comprehensive script system for the Cherokee language based not on
any traditional phonetic alphabet but on eighty-six syllabic characters invented for the sole purpose of teaching Native Americans to read and write
(see Figure 1).[52] Scholars agree that the invention of the Sequoyah syllabary
(as the writing system came to be known in the 1820s and 1830s) constitutes
a momentous achievement in the history of Indian self-determination,

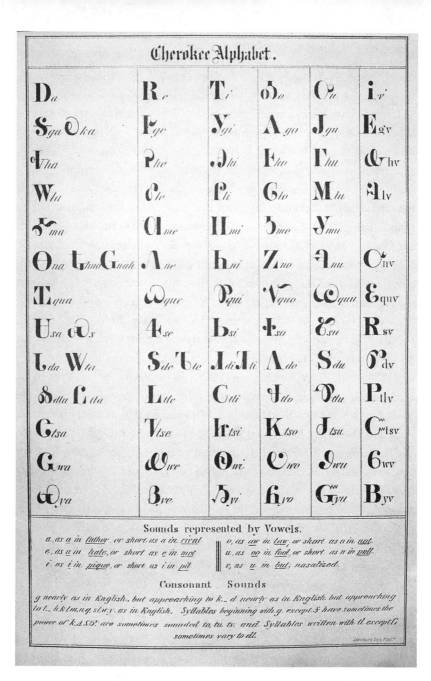

FIGURE 1 "The Cherokee Alphabet Invented by Sequoyah." Lithograph negative of *The Nineteenth Annual Report of the Bureau of American Ethnology, 1897–1898* (1900), Plate 5. Negative 999, National Anthropological Archives, Smithsonian Institution.

even if a handful of native communities across North America had been using independent writing systems for more than a century when it was invented.[53] The Cherokee Nation officially adopted the syllabary in 1825, rendering obsolete the standard phonetic alphabet that the American Board of Commissioners for Foreign Missions had attempted to impose on the community in the decades prior. [54] In 1828, as well, the General Council of the Cherokee Nation released the first issue of the *Cherokee Phoenix,* a Cherokee-language newspaper produced using a special printing press that could faithfully typeset Sequoyah's intricate syllabic writing system. Cherokee literacy rates increased dramatically in years that followed. By 1830, according to the *Phoenix's* first editor, Elias Boudinot, more than half of adult Cherokee men were literate in their own language.[55] By 1835, the U.S. Census found that 43 percent of Cherokee households contained men, women, or children who could read and write in Sequoyah's syllabic shorthand.[56]

As word of Sequoyah's invention spread, his ingenious method for representing the sounds of the Cherokee language by turns fascinated and outraged white writers and policy makers. The unlettered savage, it seemed, had suddenly commandeered civilization's most important communications technology. The success of the *Cherokee Phoenix* also seemed to augur the rise of an alternative Native American print republic that potentially challenged dominant channels of communication in nineteenth-century America. "Never has a tribe of the aborigines made such advances in civilisations," the American author John Howard Payne marveled in 1835. "They have even produced from among themselves an alphabet and letters of a fashion entirely original and they have books among them printed with their own language; and with this alphabet they daily communicate from one end of the nation to the other."[57] The syllabary thus represented a threshold onto a new Indian modernity—one based on the promise of communication and advancement through writing and print technologies. This is a detail in the story of the "American Cadmus," as Sequoyah's contemporaries often referred to him, that will become significant later on when we examine the biases that shaped Powell's own efforts in *Introduction to the Study of Indian Languages.*[58]

Whatever the Cherokee syllabary might have meant for the Cherokee community, nineteenth-century ethnologists—who were by nature concerned more with the supposedly authentic Indians of history than with

those actively reshaping the present—generally regarded Sequoyah's invention with disdain. This is because writing systems were themselves accorded
a strict hierarchy throughout the nineteenth century; alphabets and syllabaries existed on highly contested terrain. What linguists now call *semasio-
graphic* forms of writing—those that use visual signs to represent abstract
ideas, as in Egyptian hieroglyphs or Chinese logograms—were typically
viewed as primitive and backward during this period, forerunners to the
script systems used in so-called civilized societies.[59] *Glottographic,* or *phonographic,* forms of writing—those that use graphic marks to represent the
sounds of spoken language, as in the Roman alphabet—were viewed more
favorably. By definition, syllabic systems like Sequoyah's fall into the latter
category because they represent the syllables of a given language, rather
than the individual phonemic units that comprise its foundation. Yet during the nineteenth century, in a conceptual sleight of hand that underscores
just how desperately American anthropologists needed to fit living and
changing cultures into a static, hierarchical worldview, syllabaries were
nonetheless viewed as "grossly inadequate, even savage forms of writing"
because they seemed to use an excessive number of symbols to represent
the sounds of human speech.[60] Pickering dismissed the Cherokee syllabary
as "very unphilosophical" and "quite contrary to our notion of a useful
alphabetic system" on just these grounds.[61] "[Sequoyah's syllabary] consists
of eighty-three [actually eighty-six] arbitrary characters, instead of sixteen
or eighteen Roman letters," Pickering wrote in an 1827 missive. "He has . . .
taken the Roman letters as the basis, and has added to them some little
mark, or has distorted their shapes, in order to suit his purpose. This is
much to be regretted as respects the facility of communication between
these Indians and the white people."[62] What made alphabets more civilized
than syllabaries, in other words, was that they were more efficient, eco-
nomical, and technologically advanced. Despite its obvious success in the
Cherokee community, Sequoyah's syllabary seemed too ungainly, and thus
too primitive, for the everyday demands of communication and memory.

American ethnology's rejection of the Sequoyah syllabary as a viable
medium for Indian speech also stems from a more general uncertainty about
the relationship between hearing and writing in cross-cultural contexts, a
matter I take up in more detail in chapter 3. Well into the 1860s, missionaries and Native Americans scattered across "Indian country" continued to

invent phonetic alphabets to disseminate sermons and religious texts.[63] But by 1870, the American ethnologist George Gibbs, who had also tried his hand at standardizing Indian script while working for the Smithsonian Institution, would pessimistically resign himself to the position that writing systems for Native American languages were more often than not "beyond the comprehension of any but their inventors" and that "the explanation, in writing, of unusual sounds" was a "hazardous experiment" at best.[64] According to Gibbs, the problem was that the peculiar sounds of Native American languages were naturally resistant to all forms of written notation, whether alphabetic or syllabic. "There are . . . in every language, sounds peculiar to itself," he explained, "and the different Indian tongues abound in them, many being almost beyond our capacity to imitate and certainly to write." Despite the merits of the various script systems invented for the task, "the great difficulty, never fully overcome, has been to represent intelligibly such unfamiliar sounds without confusing the inquirer with new characters or numerous marks, or, again, by employing several letters to adopt a single sound."[65]

At least to white ears, then, Native American languages seemed inalterably foreign, and their failure to map onto conventional forms of written notation reconfirmed that Indians were prealphabetic and preliterate, hopelessly trapped in the earliest phases of mankind's evolutionary development.[66] In this way, as Lisa Gitelman has pointed out, documentary encounters with indigenous languages generally served as a "ground upon which literate English speakers negotiated their own identity and the identity of others, while at the same time experiencing writing as artificial, glimpsing everywhere the potential failure of textual representation to recuperate aural experience."[67] The writing of speech sound proved to be a way to reinforce which races were civilized and which races were savage, which groups had the capacity for the media function and which groups would surely languish in its absence.

Philologists and philosophers across Europe and America had long argued that the only way out of the problem of indigenous phonetic diversity that troubled men like Gibbs was to devise a "universal" writing system—and after the Sequoyah syllabary, their efforts constitute a third, and final, structuring context for understanding Powell's alphabetic experiments in the 1870s and 1880s. In the late eighteenth century, prominent American intellectuals such as Benjamin Franklin, Noah Webster, and William Thornton began trying their hand at inventing a "perfect alphabet": a phonetic system containing a distinct character for every sound in every language, one symbol for every sound conceivably produced by the human voice.[68] For philologists, the object of universal alphabetic notation was to facilitate the comparison of different languages and help discover their common points of origin. For philosophers, universal alphabets promised to dissolve communicative barriers between nations and cultures around the world. Either way, the search appeared to culminate in 1867 with the publication of Alexander Melville Bell's *Visible Speech: The Science of Universal Alphabetics; or, Self-Interpreting Physiological Letters, for the Writing of All Languages in One Alphabet*, which claimed to have solved the universal writing problem once and for all (see Figure 2).

Like Sequoyah before him, Bell believed that the standard Roman alphabet was wholly inadequate for capturing the sounds of the human voice. "The adoption of letters from existing alphabets [is] . . . irreconcilable with the desired conformity of symbol to sound," he wrote in the text of *Visible Speech*.[69] Accordingly, Bell felt that the logic behind Western forms of written script needed to be abandoned altogether, and he designed his universal Visible Speech method as a unique series of graphic marks based not on the sounds of individual phonemes or syllables (as in almost all glottographic writing systems) but on the anatomical location of their origin in the human mouth. In other words, Bell's alphabet attempted to represent the physiological sources for linguistic sounds, instead of linguistic sounds in and of themselves. Once mastered, the system purportedly allowed the average listener to pronounce or write any sound in any language, and throughout the 1860s and 1870s Bell promoted the universal alphabet's effectiveness across America and Europe in spectacular public demonstrations of elocution that featured his three sons.[70] (One of them, Alexander Graham, would of course go on to pioneer a much more celebrated sound technology a few years later.)

As Jill Lepore has pointed out, Bell took special care to promote Visible Speech as a state-of-the-art writing technology.[71] "Universal Alphabetics" was a "Science," Bell broadcasted on the title page of the 1867 edition *Visible Speech*, above a lengthy list of his academic credentials. He also self-consciously referred to his alphabet as a technological "invention" throughout the text,

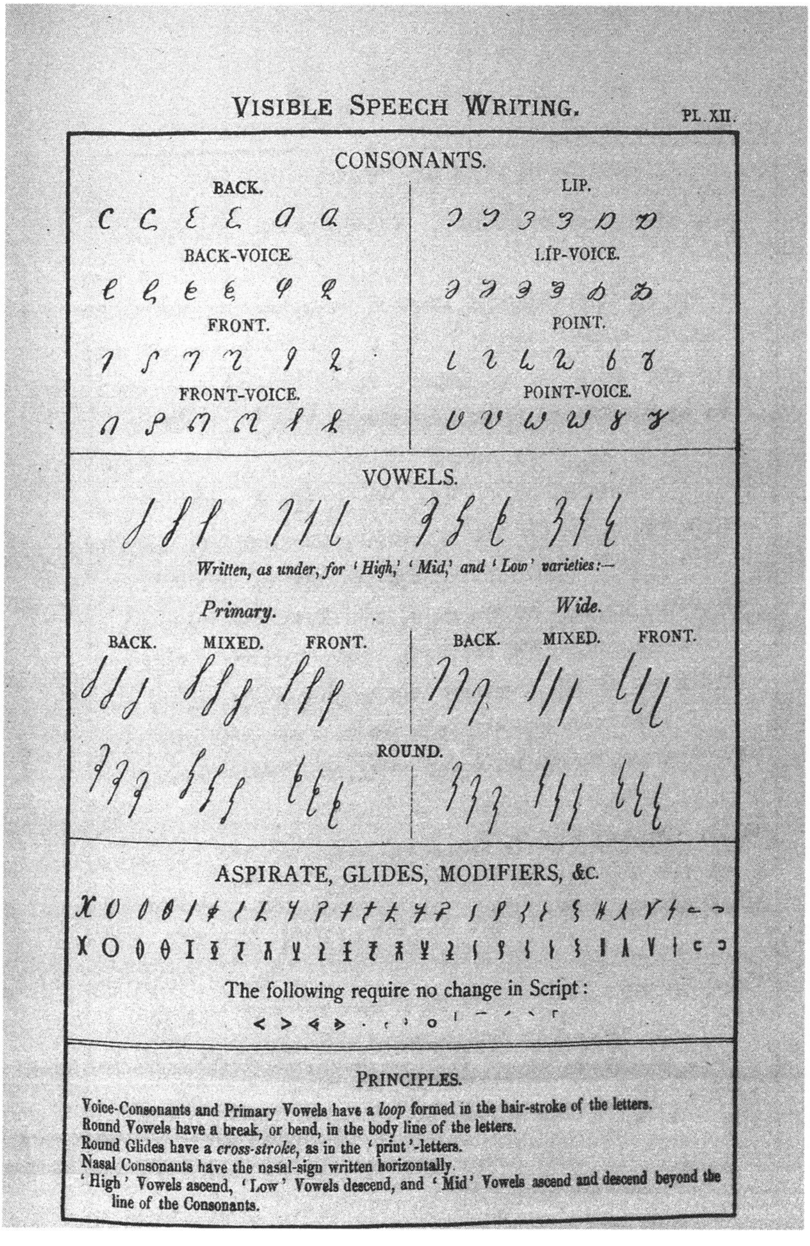

FIGURE 2 Alexander Melville Bell's Visible Speech system. *Visible Speech: The Science of Universal Alphabetics* (London: Simpkin, Marshall, 1867). Widener Library, Harvard College Library, 1241.5.

even going so far as to explain his decision to protect its use under copy-right.[72] According to Bell, the primary aim of the universal alphabet was to "macadamiz[e] the linguistic highways between nations."[73] But in the text of *Visible Speech,* he would mention "the study, comparison, and preserva-tion of fast-disappearing DIALECTS, and the universal tracing of the AFFINI-TIES OF WORDS" in an exhaustive list of potential uses for the system, along-side "the teaching of the ILLITERATE in all countries to read their Vernacular tongue," "the communication of the exact sounds of FOREIGN LANGUAGES to learners in all countries," and "the world-wide communication of any specific sounds with absolute uniformity; and, consequently, the possible construction and establishment of a UNIVERSAL LANGUAGE."[74] Bell would conclude his account by adding that "languages . . . which have never been reduced to writing may now be alphabetized by missionaries and travelers with such uniformity as—whatever the nationality of the writers—to con-vey a faithful copy of the native pronunciation which readers in all coun-tries will vocalize alike."[75] The implications for the nineteenth-century salvage ethnography could not have been more clear. Visible Speech was a technology that promised to transform even the most intricate and unfamil-iar of cultural speech sounds into permanent marks and symbols. The uni-versal alphabet, touted as a far more "advanced" system of writing than the primitive scrawl of the Sequoyah syllabary, finally appeared to solve the problem of mediation that had pushed Native American culture to the brink of evolutionary extinction.

In the end, the 1877 *Introduction to the Study of Indian Languages,* which Powell compiled as a first step toward standardizing the study of Native American life throughout the U.S. territories, would take a far more con-servative route in developing an Indian alphabet, effectively rebuffing the opposing technological solutions that Sequoyah and Bell offered. Yet Pow-ell's decision reflects the ascendancy of a modern media concept rooted in a similar set of evolutionary distinctions. "The study of an unwritten lan-guage should begin with committing it to writing," Powell asserted in the opening pages of the 1877 edition of the text.[76] For Powell, achieving the elusive goal of an Indian alphabet boiled down to following a rigid set of orthographical rules, which he honed in correspondence with William Dwight Whitney and first outlined in a manuscript draft of the text com-posed sometime in 1876 or 1877.[77] The method went something like this: first, separate the syllables of an Indian word with hyphens. Second, represent the "nasal sounds" typical in Native American languages through the use of superscript characters (a^n, e^n, i^n, o^n, u^n, etc.). Third, denote what Powell termed "interrupted" or "arrested" sounds with apostrophes. Fourth, use diacritical marks—macrons and accents—to represent "unusual prolongations" or "distortions" of ordinary speech sound. And finally, Powell offered one fundamental rule to be followed above all else: "When new sounds are to be provided for, *every effort must be made to produce them in common type*" (see Figure 3).[78] The 1877 *Introduction* emphasizes this last provision more explicitly:

1. The Roman alphabet must be used without additions, and with only such diacritical marks as are found in ordinary fonts of type.
2. Each sound must have a letter of its own.
3. Each character must be used to represent but one sound.
4. The Roman alphabet must be used for sounds in the Indian tongue the same or analogous to the sounds for which they are used in English and other civilized tongues.[79]

For Powell, then, the starting point for the new Indian writing system was the old phonetic alphabet, seemingly erasing decades of technological "innovation" in the field.

At first glance, Powell's return to standard alphabetic script may seem paradoxical, even overly simplistic. To be sure, when he finalized his system in an 1877 letter to Whitney, composed entirely in his invented form of Indian phonetic representation (or "fonĕtĭk rĕprĭsĕnteshön," as Powell lightheartedly rendered it on the page), his exclusive reliance on the Roman characters of "civilized tongues" and "common type" resembled John Pickering's initial approach to the Indian alphabetic project, first outlined in the 1820s.[80] The crucial difference here is that Powell's logic pivots on an evolutionary hierarchy of culture and media—one that firmly aligns the Roman alphabet with the future of human communication. For Powell, savagery and civilization were incompatible social states. More than any other form of writing, the "common" phonetic alphabet best ensured the preservation of primitive languages long after their speakers had vanished in the wake of human progress.

		I Set.	II Set.	III Set	IV Set	V Set.	Whitney.
1	Far	a				a	a
2	German hat		ă			â	ă
3	They	e				e	e
4	Then		ĕ			ê	ĕ
5	Figure	i				i	i
6	Pick		ĭ			î	ĭ
7	Note	o				o	o
8	French mol.		ŏ			ô	ŏ
9	Rule	u				u	u
10	Pull		ŭ			û	ŭ
11	Care, there,	ā	ā	â	ā	ā	ā̄
12	Cat		â	ä	ä	a̜	ă	ä
13	Stühle	ē	ē	ê	ē	ē	ū̄
14	Küssen		ê	ë	ê̤	e̜	ě	ǖ
15	Awe or, born	ō	ō	ô	ō	ō	â̄
16	Not, what		ô	ö	ö	o̜	ŏ	
17	Hurt	ū̄	ū̄	û̄	ū̄	ū̄	ō̄
18	But, hut		û	ü	ü	u̜	ŭ	ŏ
19	Aisle	ai				ai	ai
20	Out	au				au	au
21	Boil	oi				oi	âi
22	Pure	yu				yu	iu or yu

FIGURE 3 John Wesley Powell, "Table of Indian Vowel Sounds" (1877). Records of the Bureau of American Ethnology, "Materials connected with the establishment and revision of Powell's alphabet for recording Indian languages, ca. 1877; & 1903–1911," MS 3898, Folder 1, National Anthropological Archives, Smithsonian Institution.

The key to understanding this shift lies in Powell's "A Discourse on the Philosophy of the North American Indians" (1876), a curiously iconoclastic essay drafted alongside the *Introduction*. Addressing what he saw as the necessity of abandoning self-evident universal doctrines to understand the primitive state of American Indian life, Powell argues in this essay that

> we must, if we would fully understand Indian philosophy, leave behind that realm of thought where the sun is a great orb swinging in circles through the heavens, where the winds drift in obedience to cosmic laws, where falling stars reveal the constitution of the heavens, and go to that lower realm where the sun is but a little beast cowed by the heroic mien of a rabbit, and, in very fear, compelled to travel along in an appointed trail through the firmament, like an ass in a treadmill; where the wind is but breath, foul or fair, ejected from the belly of a monster; and where the falling star is but dung.[81]

One detects a rudimentary brand of cultural particularism here. At bottom, what Powell is saying is that savage and civilized viewpoints (or "philosophies," in his terminology) are basically irreconcilable. The American ethnologist must abandon universally accepted truths and "cosmic laws" to understand and preserve Native American language and culture—an entirely foreign "lower realm" in which "the sun is but a little beast cowed by the heroic mien of a rabbit . . . the wind is but breath . . . [and] the falling star is but dung." With much less in the way of literary flair, Powell effectively made the same point about the development of alphabetic scripts for Indian languages in the opening pages of the 1877 *Introduction*. "A language cannot be written until its sounds are mastered, and this is no easy task," he warned. "The number of distinct qualitative sounds that can be uttered by the human voice is very great, and without long training the ear cannot properly discern and discriminate them all. In the English language there are more than forty simple or elementary sounds. . . . In the study of the sounds of a savage or barbaric language the simplest elements into which each can be resolved are oftentimes even more complex than the elementary sounds of the English language."[82] Despite the clear divergence in subject matter here, what remains constant in both accounts is a kind of anti-universalism. For Powell, just as Indian "philosophies" exposed the limitations of supposedly universal ways of understanding the world, so, too, did Indian languages expose the limitations of supposedly universal forms of writing. So when it came to standardizing the project of Indian language preservation, the first step was inventing an alphabet that was attuned specifically to the local peculiarities of Native American speech, not to some imaginary global ideal.

Bell's universal Visible Speech alphabet was Powell's primary target here, even if the two men ended up amicably exchanging ideas on the subject of phonetic script in correspondence later on.[83] But Powell would also reject the viability of the Cherokee syllabic model, even as much as his ideas in "A Discourse on the Philosophy of the North American Indians" would seem to endorse the adoption of just such a system. In *Introduction to the Study of Indian Languages,* Powell went on to explain his avoidance of Indian-invented scripts like Sequoyah's using evolutionist rhetoric that implicitly figures the Roman alphabet as the primary agent of human progress. "There are other reasons than that of mere convenience why the Roman alphabet should be used," he wrote. The most important of which was that

> it is the alphabet with which the greater part of the civilized people of the world are acquainted, and if consistently used all such people can more easily study a tongue recorded with it than if unfamiliar characters are employed. Again, the Roman alphabet is used in all printing rooms where the English tongue is spoken, and in very many others; and if a new tongue is written in these characters it can be reproduced without difficulty in almost any printing office of the civilized world. If new characters are used or the Roman characters modified so that types for their printing cannot be found in ordinary printing offices, the literature relating to such a language will, to a large extent, be excluded from the scientific and popular publications of the world.[84]

Powell's interest in the logistics of both preservation and dissemination ("if a new tongue is written in these characters it can be reproduced without difficulty in almost any printing office of the civilized world") suggests that the aim of the *Introduction*'s Indian alphabet wasn't merely to record the sounds of Native American speech accurately. The aim was to render them technologically reproducible, assuring their persistence in civilization long after primitive languages vanish. To be sure, the repeated stress Powell places on "civilized people" and the "civilized world" is a symptom of this assumption, not to mention his failure to cite the Sequoyah syllabary as a viable technological alternative at any point in the text. The alphabet and the printing press are here figured as tools of a standardized communications society already in the process of leaving Indian languages and writing systems behind. As Powell later argued, "in all linguistic inventions through the coining of words and devising of grammatic methods and the invention of alphabets and of printing and of telegraphs and of telephones, invention has struggled with invention for existence. . . . The many have been sacrificed so that the few—the best—might remain."[85] For Powell in the *Introduction,* the Roman alphabet is presumably what will "remain" as the civilized technological standard in the wake of the ongoing evolutionary struggle. While Native Americans seemed fated to die out, the sounds of their languages were to survive only in the possibility of their alphabetic reproduction, on the surface of the printed page itself.

The Return of Primitive Man

Powell's account of writing and print in *Introduction to the Study of Indian Languages* offers a prediction about the future of human communication, in addition to a story about its past. While the phonetic alphabet and the printing press are viewed as having the potential to carry remnants of dying Indian languages forward in time, Indians themselves are implicitly absent as speaking subjects throughout the text, trapped in the earliest stages of mankind's social development, gradually receding from historical view. Powell never uses the word *medium* in his work to describe the significance of the phonetic alphabet in this transition. Yet it is difficult to overstate the importance of his ideas to the development of media and communications theory in the twentieth century. In the 1950s and 1960s, just as media studies and communications studies began to emerge as organized fields of academic inquiry in the United States, Powell's image of the unlettered–unmediated primitive man would return. Despite the fact that Boasian cultural relativism had by this time wholly discredited the evolutionist narrative in the fields of ethnology and anthropology, media and communications theorists would increasingly turn to native peoples to understand what life was like before the dawn of media technology.

Consider, for instance, Marshall McLuhan's pioneering studies of media and cognition *The Gutenberg Galaxy* (1962), *Understanding Media* (1964), and

The Medium Is the Massage (1967), all of which attempt to popularize ideas about media-technological change that are remarkably similar to the theories of the evolutionists. "It can be argued," McLuhan writes in *Understanding Media,* seemingly channeling Powell, "that the phonetic alphabet, alone, is the technology that has been the means of creating 'civilized man.' . . . The achievements of the Western world, it is obvious, are testimony to the tremendous values of literacy."[86] His argument continues along familiar lines, echoing the distinctive primitive-ear, modern-eye argument from Powell's "Human Evolution" trilogy almost verbatim:

> Civilization is built on literacy because literacy is a uniform processing of a culture by a visual sense extended in space and time by the alphabet. In tribal cultures, experience is arranged by a dominant auditory sense-life that represses visual values. The auditory sense, unlike the cool and neutral eye, is hyper-esthetic and delicate and all-inclusive. Oral cultures act and react at the same time. Phonetic [literate] culture endows men with the means of repressing their feelings and emotions when engaged in action. To act without reacting, without involvement, is the peculiar advantage of Western literate man.[87]

For McLuhan, the inventions of the phonetic alphabet and the printing press had forced modern man into an increasingly detached and individualized state. Yet at the dawn of the electric age, humanity once again seemed to be returning to its primitive roots. In a cultural shift that McLuhan famously termed "retribalization," radios and televisions increasingly appeared to plug the human mind back into the "hyper-esthetic" and "all-inclusive" communal closeness of oral culture.

If we look between the lines of *Understanding Media*'s notoriously deterministic narrative, however, it becomes clear that recurrent catchphrases like *tribal culture* and *retribalization* allow McLuhan to imagine how humans think and behave in the absence of the media function. Indeed, this constitutes one of his signature rhetorical moves. By my count, McLuhan deploys the image of the primitive man–tribal native as a foil for the modern mediated mind in at least thirty-seven separate instances in the text of *Understanding Media* alone. "Submerging natives with floods of concepts for which nothing has prepared them is the normal action of all our technology,"

McLuhan writes in a typical passage early on. "With electric media Western man himself experiences exactly the same inundation as the remote native. We are no more prepared to encounter radio and TV in our literate milieu than the native of Ghana is able to cope with the literacy that takes him out of his collective tribal world and beaches him in individual isolation."[88] Throughout *Understanding Media,* the phonetic alphabet is similarly said to "translate" primitive cultures "out of the closed tribal echo-chamber into the neutral visual world of lineal organization," propelling the human mind out of "the magical resonance of . . . the tribal trap" and into the detached world of civilized literacy.[89] "Natives," who by definition possess "very little contact with phonetic literacy and lineal print," allegedly exhibit confusion when first encountering photographs and motion pictures: "Non-literate people simply don't get perspective or distancing effects of light and shade that we assume are innate human equipment. . . . [They] do not know how to fix their eyes, as Westerners do, a few feet in front of the movie screen, or some distance in front of a photo. The result is that they move their eyes over photo or screen as they might their hands."[90] By the end of *Understanding Media,* the only role that communications technologies such as newspapers and magazines can possibly play in the lives of the Inuit Eskimo are as reinforcements for leaky igloo ceilings.[91]

Ultimately, McLuhan's references to a primitive time before the invention of media technology, to primitive people wholly ignorant of the media function's cultural magic, seem to reflect the persistence of Powell's evolutionary worldview. Furthermore, McLuhan's insistence on defining human history as a successive series of developmental stages—"tribal," "literate," "print," and "electronic," each according to a dominant system of communications technology—clearly mirrors the hallmark savagery-to-civilization model of cultural evolutionism.[92] Developmental accounts of media and communications history in fact remained in play for much of the twentieth century. For Harold Innis, McLuhan's immediate forerunner in media theory, the "subject of communications" was crucial to understanding the rise and fall of empires, and Innis's work in *Empire and Communications* (1950) and *The Bias of Communications* (1951) revolves around the recognizably evolutionist idea that "we can conveniently divide the history of the West into the writing and the printing periods."[93] Likewise, Walter Ong's pathbreaking 1982 study *Orality and Literacy,* mentioned earlier, advances a similar argument about the phonetic alphabet's historical significance. "More than any other single invention, writing has transformed human consciousness," Ong claims, echoing both McLuhan and Powell.[94] Yet for Ong, hearkening back to the theories of evolutionary disappearance that structure *Introduction to the Study of Indian Languages,* it is only when the technology of standardized, moveable type renders language globally reproducible that human groups can abandon the ear-centered world of "primary orality" and move up the evolutionary ladder: "Print replaced the lingering hearing-dominance in the world of thought and expression with the sight-dominance, which had its beginnings with writing but could not flourish with the support of writing alone. Print situates words in space more relentlessly than writing ever did. Writing moves words from the sound world into a world of visual space, but print locks words into position in this space."[95] Such variations on evolutionist themes suggest that Powell's ideas might actually represent an unheralded point of origin for classic North American media theory. Well into the twentieth century, primitive human groups were regarded as imaginary starting points for the history of human communication, living vestiges of a collective cultural past that lettered, wired, and digitized societies had time and again rendered obsolete.

Historians and critics have only just begun to unseat this narrative, and not simply on the grounds that it obscures a range of alternative media forms and practices that indigenous peoples actively maintained both outside of and in response to external technological influences.[96] As I demonstrate in chapters 2 and 3, moreover, the living presence of so-called primitive languages and cultures in the United States in fact powerfully shaped the emergent modern media of photography, phonography, and cinema during the late nineteenth and early twentieth centuries. To take one example of many, nineteenth-century phonetic writing systems like Powell's—oriented simultaneously toward preservation and reproduction, storage and dissemination—were instrumental in the cultural reception of Thomas Edison's phonograph, which was in part invented for the purpose of mechanizing the process of phonetic writing. There is good reason to make this historical connection here, even beyond the coincidental fact that *Introduction to the Study of Indian Languages* first appeared in 1877, the same year Edison publicly unveiled his celebrated talking machine. As Lisa Gitelman has pointed out, the terms *orthography* and *phonography* were actually interchangeable for the majority of the nineteenth century.[97] Moreover, some of the earliest public demonstrations of the phonograph's mechanical capabilities involved staging the very same kind of cultural work that Powell intended his Indian alphabet to perform. The *New York Times* and the *Washington Star,* for instance, enthusiastically reported on an April 1878 demonstration in which Edison attempted to market the machine's ability to "preserve the accents of the Onondagas and Tuscaroras [*sic*], who are dying out." As Edison assured a crowd of onlookers, "one old man speaks the language fluently and correctly, and he is afraid that he will die. You see, one man goes among the Indians and represents the pronunciation of their words by English syllables. Another represents the same words differently. There is nothing definite. The phonograph will preserve the exact pronunciation."[98] Implicit in Edison's rhetoric—and implicit in Powell's pragmatic adoption of the Roman alphabet in the *Introduction* at the exact same time—is an underlying admission of documentary failure, a sense that Native American languages appeared to resist all forms of written mediation. The phonograph, designed to preserve primitive linguistic material that otherwise seemed ephemeral, was thus the latest in a long line of writing technologies that claimed to solve the problems of phonetic reproduction that had dogged writers and ethnologists for centuries.

As we will see, debates about the reproducibility of Native American speech sound remained open in the decades that followed, dramatically influencing how American writers and anthropologists understood the newly invented phonograph's technological significance: its auditory fidelity, its mechanical objectivity, and its purported ability to record forms of cultural sound that earlier writing systems could not. But Powell's emphasis on phonetic reproducibility in *Introduction to the Study of Indian Languages* clearly encouraged his successors in the field to experiment with phonetic writing and phonographic technologies. Consider, in closing, the work of John P. Harrington, an American ethnologist who in many ways dedicated the majority of his career to finding a perfect medium to counter the evolutionary disappearance of Indian languages. When Harrington joined the BAE staff in 1915, after years of independent fieldwork throughout California, the American Southwest, and South America, his first charge was to develop a special oversized typewriter for the transcription of native speech sound, complete with extra phonetic characters of his own design.[99]

In addition to his experiments with the typewriter—doubtless derived from Powell's interest in reconciling the sounds of Native American speech with standardized technologies of writing and printing—Harrington also made hundreds of phonograph recordings during the 1910s, 1920s, and 1930s. "The phonograph provides us . . . with an ideal method for taking down texts," he asserted in an unpublished essay drafted around 1910.[100] Because phonetic scripts were typically "cumbersome" to reproduce, the phonograph provided Harrington with a mechanical supplement to the linguistic records he had already left behind in an invented form of phonetic notation he called "sonoscript," a "universal alphabet, the result of much work and endless experimentation . . . [the] best form invented up to this date."[101]

Formally, Harrington's sonoscript technique combined Powell's phonetic system with extra characters drawn from Sequoyah's syllabary and Bell's Visible Speech alphabet, two subjects he in fact wrote on intermittently well into the 1950s.[102] So in this sense, Harrington's work represents a fitting summation to the intercultural genealogy of script media experimentation I have outlined in this chapter. Whether alphabetic or syllabic, universal or particular, handwritten or mechanical, Harrington nonetheless expressed the same interest in evolutionary preservation through technological reproducibility that Powell articulated in *Introduction to the Study of Indian Languages*. "The writer has worked for a number of years on a revision of the [Powell] Smithsonian alphabet bringing [it] up to meet the requirements and refinements of modern phonetics writable on the ordinary typewriter and settable in the ordinary printing office," Harrington later wrote, fueled by the argument that Native American languages were on the verge of disappearing. "Without opposing any system supposed to be based on universal usage, the present [sonoscript] system gives for the writing of several sounds orthographies which are more scientific, and at the same time can be universally typed, printed, and quoted."[103]

Reading Harrington's manuscripts today, one gets the sense of Native American language preservation as a perpetually unfinished project. His paper trail at the Smithsonian Institution's National Anthropological Archives, the primary repository of his life's work, measures an astounding 683 linear feet. Pages and pages of written notes on native languages sit beside scores of photographs, phonograph recordings, and unpublished essays with titles like "The Sequoyah Syllabary," "Printing," "Shorthand

and Typewriting," and "The Phonograph."[104] Like Powell before him, Harrington's encounter with primitive Indian languages directly provoked an ongoing concern with the promises, and the limits, of modern technologies of writing and reproduction—a concern that would clearly continue to animate the work of McLuhan, Ong, and others. Moreover, a similar relationship between primitive races and modern media becomes apparent if we turn our attention to one of Powell's forgotten contemporaries, the anthropologist and amateur photographer Garrick Mallery. At the exact same time Powell and Harrington were wrestling with syllabaries, alphabets, and other evolutionary technologies of the Indian word, Mallery found himself captivated by a far more mysterious form of cultural communication—an indigenous language rooted not in the sounds of speech but in the movements of the human body.

2

Representing Plains Indian
Sign Language

F or Garrick Mallery, one of the most prolific researchers in the burgeoning field of anthropology in the late 1800s, the story of human
evolution could only be told as a tale of communications technologies. "Anthropology tells the march of mankind out of savagery," wrote
Mallery in 1881, using metaphors drawn from his early career in military
service.

> Some peoples have led with the fleet course of videttes or the sturdy stride
> of pioneers, some have only plodded on the roads opened by the vanguard,
> while others still lag in the unordered rear, mere dragweights to the col-
> umn. All commenced their progress toward civilization from a point of
> departure lower than the stage reached by the lowest of the tribes now
> found on earth, and all, even the most advanced, have retained marks of
> their rude origin.... Perhaps the most notable criterion of difference
> [among them] is in the copiousness and precision of oral language, and in
> the unequal survival of the communication by gesture signs which, it is
> believed, once universally prevailed.[1]

To Mallery, variations in communications—in this case, the "copiousness
and precision of oral language" and the "unequal survival of . . . communication by gesture signs"—explained basic variations among the world's
peoples. The history of communications media provided an easy way to

35

identify discrete "stages" in mankind's evolutionary march from savagery to civilization.

Garrick Mallery is no longer a household name, but his logic should sound familiar. As we saw in chapter 1, the idea that new media innovations signpost various phases of human history was one that a number of American intellectuals embraced at the end of the nineteenth century, John Wesley Powell chief among them. It was also an idea that media theorists such as Harold Innis, Marshall McLuhan, and Walter Ong popularized, both wittingly and unwittingly, well into the twentieth century. Our certainty that we live in a "digital age," categorically distinct from previous periods of time variously characterized by the dominance of "print" and "electronics," suggests that this way of thinking is still with us today.

Yet unlike contemporaneous thinkers like Powell—and unlike later thinkers like McLuhan—Mallery's understanding of media evolution emerged in reference to a highly localized cultural phenomenon: Plains Indian Sign Language (PISL), an elaborate system of sign language communication that had for centuries flourished among Native American tribes who spoke in different tongues (see Figure 4). Among anthropologists in the nineteenth-century United States, no medium of communication was more hotly debated, and no medium of communication was more widely misunderstood. In the interest of understanding the course of human evolution, Mallery organized a national project to document PISL in the 1880s and 1890s. When social transformations threatened to render the language obsolete, his efforts hastened a crisis of documentary representation that pushed the boundaries of established media forms and ethnographic practices at the end of the nineteenth century. This chapter examines that crisis, moving from the origin of language to the invention of cinema to establish PISL as one of modern media's crucial shadow archives. The story of PISL, and of Mallery's attempt to preserve it, not only places the evolutionary account of human difference at the center of late-nineteenth- and early-twentieth-century cultures of media and modernity, but also helps us to understand why modern media technologies seemed to hold enduring promise as agents of cultural preservation in this period.

In the first half of this chapter, I trace the arc of Mallery's early ethnographic career to reveal the basic ideas about PISL that took hold during the nineteenth century. For Mallery, as for many anthropologists in the

FIGURE 4 "Man (Lean Wolf?) in Partial Native Dress Making Sign Language Gesture, c. 1880." SPC Misc. Sign Language 01309500, National Anthropological Archives, Smithsonian Institution.

United States, PISL embodied a living relic of mankind's first and most primitive medium of communication—evidence of the earliest linguistic developments that had separated humans from animals, a phenomenon fated to vanish on the evolutionary march toward the civilized social state. In the second half of this chapter, I examine the landmark studies of PISL that Mallery produced in the early 1880s, many of which overtly experiment with forms of visual representation that are consistent with the period's innovations in serial photography. Here I discuss Mallery's formal interest in the photographer Eadweard J. Muybridge, whose famed experiments with capturing objects in motion suggested new ways to study and preserve PISL, a language rooted in the movements of the body rather than in speech or writing. In closing, I examine two figures who picked up the PISL project where Mallery left off: the U.S. Army general Hugh Lenox Scott and the Blackfeet interpreter Richard Sanderville (Chief Bull). Their efforts show how early-twentieth-century intellectuals engaged with Mallery's ideas through the medium of motion pictures and how Plains Indian signers actively represented themselves at a moment when their lives and languages were mistakenly consigned to extinction.

Plains Indian Sign Language: History and Prehistory

Born in 1831, in Wilkes-Barre, Pennsylvania, Garrick Mallery led a life that bears a striking resemblance to that of his mentor, John Wesley Powell.[2] After graduating from Yale College and attending law school at the University of Pennsylvania, Mallery, like Powell, interrupted an established professional career to serve in the Union Army. Like Powell, Mallery ascended the military chain of command after sustaining life-threatening wounds during the Civil War. And like Powell, Mallery came to the salvage ethnographic project while following the westward course of American empire.

In 1870, after a short stint supervising a branch of the Freedman's Bureau in Richmond, Virginia, Mallery accepted a position conducting meteorological research for the Signal Corps, a special division of the U.S. Army that worked to maintain military communications systems across the far reaches of the American continent. The job put him in frequent contact with a number of Native American tribes living in the western territories, and by 1876, when Mallery moved to the Dakotas and took command of the U.S. Army base at Fort Rice, he had already established himself as a national authority on Plains Indian culture and custom.[3]

Mallery's earliest published ethnographic article, "A Calendar of the Dakota Nation," appeared in 1877, quickly attracting Powell's attention in Washington.[4] That same year, he delivered a landmark address on "The Former and Present Number of Our Indians" at the twenty-sixth meeting of the American Association for the Advancement of Science in Nashville, Tennessee. A culmination of nearly six years' worth of travel and field-work across the American West, the paper is as significant for the light it sheds on Mallery's early theories of Indian culture as for the controversy it stirred at the time among American ethnologists and policy makers. Work-ing against the "lately-unquestioned law dooming all our native race to speedy death"—a position first codified in evolutionist cultural theory and subsequently carried out in genocidal legislative practice—the "Former and Present Number" address marshaled an extraordinary range of demo-graphic statistics to challenge the popular belief that American Indians were dying out from innate cultural deficiencies.[5] "At any points where the race is now degraded and diminishing," Mallery suggested, "it is not from an irrepressible conflict with civilization, but with civilization's unworthy local and Washington representatives."[6] Demographic change among native peoples was thus the product of "criminal misgovernment" on the part of American Indian policy, not of inborn "retrogradation" on the part of American Indians themselves.[7] Just one year removed from the bloodshed at Little Bighorn, the closing lines of Mallery's address must have seemed especially scathing: "Neither from views of their physiological, religious or sociological characteristics should [Native Americans] be regarded as an exceptional or abnormal part of the human race, or so treated in our national policy. Only those legislators and officials who are prepared to encourage downright murder can neglect their duty under the Satanic consolation of the convenient extinction doctrine. With continued injus-tice, more Sitting Bulls and Chief Josephs, driven into the last refuge of despair, will require expenditure of blood and treasure which simple truth and honesty would not only prevent, but would preserve, reclaim and ele-vate a race entrusted to our national honor, which may readily and with no long delay, become a valuable element in our motley community."[8]

To be sure, Mallery's position in the vanishing race debate was far more enlightened than that of his contemporaries, who regarded the disappearance of the Indian as a natural by-product of civilization's progress. Yet he was not without his own evolutionary biases. The extinction of a population may have been an ethnographic fiction, but the extinction of its culture was another thing entirely. And this was where Mallery's nascent ethnographic interest in what he variously called "gesture speech," "hand language," and "sign talk" among the Plains Indian nations first came into play.

Mallery first encountered PISL while working for the Signal Corps in the early 1870s. His relationship with the group's founder, Albert J. Myer, may have prompted his interest in the phenomenon. A retired army officer, Myer had used his knowledge of Native American signaling techniques to help invent wigwag aerial telegraphy, a powerful system of long-distance information transmission made famous on the battlefields of the Civil War.[9] But matters of communication were also of immediate importance to Mallery's own position. Aside from conducting meteorological research, his duties with the Signal Corps also included regular maintenance of the telegraph wires that stretched across the Great Plains.[10] In this context, Mallery's fascination with sign talk—one of many communications technologies linking the disparate communities of the nineteenth-century American West—seems almost inevitable.

Yet Mallery was by no means the first to study the phenomenon. Ethnographic descriptions of Indians "talking" with their hands, both to each other and to Western outsiders, begin cropping up in New World travel narratives as early as the sixteenth century. Accounts written by the early Spanish explorers Álvar Núñez Cabeza de Vaca (*La relación*, 1542) and Bernal Díaz del Castillo (*Historia verdadera de la conquista de la Nueva España*, circa 1568), for instance, contain extensive commentaries on the puzzling signs and gestures that native peoples used in their everyday interactions.[11] Well into the eighteenth century, as Robert Gunn has shown, travel accounts and colonial reports discussed sign talk as a peculiar form of "cryptolanguage": as a random, untranslatable supplement to spoken discourse rather than as an independent linguistic system in its own right.[12] Historians have used evidence derived from these sources to suggest that organized forms of indigenous sign language developed in the Americas long before European contact.[13]

In the early decades of the nineteenth century, the sign language systems of the Plains Indian nations, in particular, captured the attention of scientists and policy makers interested in westward expansion. Thomas Jefferson's January 1801 address to the American Philosophical Society, one of the last public appearances he would make before swearing in as the third president of the United States, was in fact titled "On the Language of Signs among Certain North American Indians." Derived from the travelogues of the Scottish explorer William Dunbar, Jefferson's presentation argued for the importance of studying PISL and attempted to compare the language with other nonwritten forms of communication around the globe: "Language by signs has been artfully and systematically framed. . . . Western Indians are so habituated to their signs that they never make use of their oral language, without instinctively at the same time tracing in the air all the corresponding signs, which they perform with the rapidity of ordinary conversation."[14] Two decades later, U.S. Army major Stephen H. Long answered Jefferson's call by including a descriptive index of more than one hundred Indian signs in his *Account of an Expedition from Pittsburgh to the Rocky Mountains* (1823), which he assembled while completing an early government-sponsored tour of the Great Plains region.[15] Thomas H. Gallaudet, cofounder of the first school for the deaf in the United States, later used Dunbar's fieldwork and Long's index to identify a "natural language of signs" that could aid in the development of American Sign Language.[16] This was the first of many scholarly attempts to discover lexical connections between PISL and its Anglo-American counterparts. More broadly, these kinds of sources indirectly helped shape the archetype of the "silent Indian" that emerged in American literature and popular culture during the first half of the nineteenth century.[17] At the time, only three options seemed available for representing Indians and their ability to communicate: native peoples either spoke unintelligibly, they spoke in signs, or they did not speak at all.

In Mallery's own day, the social, philological, and philosophical import of Native American sign language preoccupied a wide variety of thinkers. Aside from Gallaudet, who continued to use PISL as a point of reference for his research until his death in 1851, ethnologists such as E. B. Tylor and experimental psychologists such as Wilhelm Wundt wrote influential articles on Native American sign talk.[18] The rise of cultural evolutionism in the field of anthropology shed crucial new light on the phenomenon. As Tylor explained in his seminal evolutionist study *Researches into the Early History of Mankind and the Development of Civilization* (1865)—an important methodological precursor to Lewis Henry Morgan's *Ancient Society* (1877), discussed in the previous chapter—sign languages represented living fossils of mankind's collective past, cultural holdovers that could be traced back to the absolute origin of human communication:

> The Gesture-Language and Picture-Writing . . . insignificant as they are in practice in comparison with Speech and Phonetic Writing, have this great claim to consideration, that we can really understand them as thoroughly as perhaps we can understand anything, and by studying them we can realize to ourselves in some measure a condition of the human mind which underlies anything which has as yet been traced in even the lowest dialect of Language, if taken as a whole. . . . The idea that the Gesture-Language represents a distinct separate stage of human utterance, through which man passed before he came to speak, has no support from facts. But it may be plausibly maintained, that in the early stages of the development of language, while as yet the vocabulary was very rude and scanty, gesture had an importance as an element of expression, which in conditions of highly organized language it has lost.[19]

For Tylor, Indian gestures seemed to belong to the earliest phase of mankind's communicative development. In Mallery's opinion, similarly, they represented an "instructive vestige of the prehistoric epoch."[20]

Moreover, as Tylor and Mallery both suggested, the emergence of gestural signs may have even predated the emergence of spoken language in evolutionary time.[21] So studying communications systems like PISL appeared to have the potential not just to explain the development of the human linguistic faculty but to reveal the basic mental processes that had also separated humans from animals along the way. "The most interesting light in which the Indians of North America can be regarded is in their present representation of a stage of evolution once passed through by our own ancestors," Mallery concluded, building directly on Tylor's account. "Their signs . . . form a part of the paleontology of humanity to be studied in the history of the latter, as the geologist, with similar object, studies all the strata of the physical world."[22] The evolutionary connections between savagery and sign language were so strong in this period that educators actually suppressed the use of American Sign Language in deaf and dumb schools across the United States during the 1860s and 1870s. Speech, no matter how inaccessible, was simply seen as a more advanced way of communicating knowledge.[23] As Tylor summarized the dominant view, "the Indian pantomime and the gesture-language of the deaf-and-dumb are but different dialects of the same language of nature."[24]

Mallery's efforts are best understood in this intellectual context. Although his 1877 "Former and Present Number" address had rejected the nineteenth-century doctrine of extinction, cultural evolution nonetheless provided the primary ideological framework for his hypotheses about Indian sign talk—at once offering an explanation for its emergence in the earliest days of man, for its long history on the North American continent, and for its dim future in the territories of an expansionist nation. Why had Indians retained their gesture languages over time, when other racial groups had abandoned them for more civilized forms of communication such as speech and writing? The vast majority of nineteenth-century ethnologists (Powell chief among them) claimed that the absence of a codified alphabet for Indian languages represented one possible answer—a rationale consistent with the idea that Native Americans were technologically backward and thus relegated to the lowest rungs of the evolutionary ladder. Yet Mallery's pathbreaking theory, contra Powell and many others, was that PISL was in fact a vital cultural response to linguistic diversity. In the wide open spaces of the Great Plains region, where intertribal networks of migration and trade frequently put mutually unintelligible Indian groups into contact with one another, gesture effectively served as an expedient substitute for spoken language. As Mallery wrote in 1880, primarily in reference to the Plains Indian context, "where people speaking precisely the same dialect are not numerous, and are thrown into constant contact on equal terms with others of differing dialects and languages, gesture is necessarily resorted to for converse with the latter, and remains as a habit or accomplishment among themselves."[25] Sign talk, in other words, had evolved as a bridge language, an indigenous lingua franca. Far from a vestige of primitivism, PISL was an advanced technology of communication that helped eliminate cultural barriers among the Plains Indian nations.

It is a testament to the originality of Mallery's vision, and to the continued importance of his work, that the lingua franca theory remains the dominant interpretation of PISL in the fields of anthropology and linguistics today.[26] Yet during the late nineteenth century, Mallery's ideas about linguistic contact also had an unfortunate corollary, with special significance for the United States and the realization of its westward destiny. "While large bodies enjoying a common speech, and either isolated from foreigners, or, when in contact with them, are so dominant as to compel the learning and adoption of their own tongue, [sign language becomes] impassive in its delivery," he continued. "As the number of dialects in any district decreases so will the gestures, though doubtless there is also influence from the fact, not merely that a language has been reduced to and modified by writing, but that people who are accustomed generally to read and write . . . will after a time think and talk as they write."[27] So as the nineteenth century drew to a close, PISL was also at risk of disappearing altogether. The more American social "progress" (i.e., Indian assimilation, Indian removal) rendered the North American continent monolingual and monocultural, the more sign talk threatened to fade into obsolescence and disuse.

It was this final recognition that led Mallery to embark on his salvage ethnographic project. Conceding that PISL would "surely and speedily decay" in the wake of expansionist U.S. Indian policy, he moved to Washington in 1877 to spearhead the creation of an encyclopedic database for Native American sign languages at the Bureau of Ethnology.[28] By 1880, he had produced the first official scholarly effort in the field, *Introduction to the Study of Sign Language among the North American Indians as Illustrating the Gesture Speech of Mankind*. The title intentionally echoed Powell's earlier *Introduction to the Study of Indian Languages* (1877), and as a whole, Mallery's earliest work on sign language drew extensively on the systematizing impulses of his field-defining predecessor, seeking "to indicate the scope of a future publication [of a comprehensive sign language dictionary]; to excite interest and invite correspondence on the subject; to submit suggestions as to desirable points and modes of observation; and to give notice of some facilities provided for description and illustration. The material now collected and collated is sufficient to show that the importance of the subject deserves exhaustive research and presentation by scientific methods."[29] Later that same year, Mallery privately circulated *A Collection of Gesture-Signs and Signals of the North American Indians with Some Comparisons* (1880), which assembled well over one thousand Indian sign descriptions and triumphantly announced that "arrangements have been made . . . to procure all the gesture-signs of the aboriginal tribes of this country, which can still be rescued from oblivion."[30] The initial phase of Mallery's research culminated soon thereafter with "Sign Language among North American Indians Compared with That among Other Peoples and Deaf-Mutes" (1881), a lavishly illustrated three-hundred-page research survey, initially published in Powell's *First Annual Report of the Bureau of Ethnology*, containing sign language vocabularies from Native American tribes ranging from Abanaki and Arapaho to Wichita and Zuni.

Above all else, the encyclopedic ambitions of Mallery's early publications suggest that he maintained a steadfast belief in the preservative power of written texts. *Introduction to the Study of Sign Language, Collection of Gesture-Signs and Signals,* "Sign Language among North American Indians": the very existence of such works rests on the basic premise that the modern apparatus of writing—pen, print, and page—can viably serve as a permanent record of Indian sign talk, the "evanescent air-pictures" of Native America, as Mallery often called them.[31] Yet by the end of his life, after fifteen years of "brilliant investigation" into the nature and history of PISL (in Powell's view), Mallery would privately express doubts about such a state of affairs.[32] "It is probable that before any intelligible publication of any magnitude . . . can be issued that [Indian sign] language will be virtually disused," he wrote to a colleague at the Smithsonian in 1891, commenting not just on the scope of the PISL documentary project but on the printed page's inherent inability to sustain it.[33] When Mallery died in October 1894, his monumental efforts to collect, interpret, and preserve the silent aboriginal language of movement were left largely unfinished. His story is still relegated to the footnotes of American cultural history.

Why did Mallery eventually come to doubt the value of his life's work? Answering this question entails grappling with PISL not as a linguistic atavism but as a living communications technology—one that speaks at once to the possibilities, and the limits, of ethnographic representation itself.

Frozen Evanescence

To demonstrate PISL's importance to turn-of-the-century U.S. media culture, there is perhaps no better starting point than Mallery's belief in the fundamental *evanescence* of Native American sign languages, mentioned earlier. The term carries at least three connotations in his writings.

First, and most broadly, *evanescence* refers to something historical and political. In Mallery's view, as we have already seen, PISL was gradually fading away because of the diffusion of English throughout the western territories. To be sure, this was the result of a discrete set of social and political factors: improved transportation and trade; the growth of assimilation-oriented reservation schooling; and, especially for Mallery, the cultural violence of nineteenth-century U.S. Indian policy, culminating in the Dawes General Allotment Act of 1887. But we should take care not to discount the actions and choices Native Americans made in the context of these large-scale historical transformations. Though sign talk persisted well into the twentieth century through traditional forms of native storytelling (a fact that Mallery had neither the data nor the historical perspective to distinguish), it was nonetheless evanescent or vanishing in everyday usage because many Plains Indian nations found it increasingly advantageous to cast off the "old" ways.[34] For instance, the Lakota Sioux writer Zitkala-Ša's well-known "Letter to the Chiefs and Headmen of the Tribes" (1919) advocated for intertribal solidarity and native land rights through the adoption of a universal form of communication. But it was the English tongue, not sign talk, that was to break down long-standing barriers of language and custom among native peoples. "Very often I have wished that you [Indian chiefs] could write to me in a language we both would understand perfectly," she opined, strategically ignoring the fact that a lingua franca had flourished among the Plains Indians for centuries. "No doubt there have been occasions when you wished you could have expressed your thought in English. Remembering this experience, will you now encourage other Indians to make the effort to learn this language?"[35]

Cultural politics aside, Mallery's notion of evanescence also has a more specific ethnographic resonance—a second connotation that refers to some of the problems of native diversity that Powell and his predecessors had encountered in their effort to document a monolithic culture of the "American Indian." It wasn't just that sign talk was gradually falling into disuse as a result of external sociolinguistic pressures. The gesture systems that remained active across the Great Plains region also varied widely. Contrary to what was then the consensus among leading ethnologists in the United States and Europe, works like *Introduction to Sign Language* and "Sign Language among North American Indians" demonstrated that Indian sign talk was not, in fact, a "universal" language. Although "the attempt to convey meaning by signs" was clearly "universal among the Indians of the Plains, and those still comparatively unchanged by civilization," Mallery explained—and though Indians using different dialects of PISL could very often communicate with each other—Native American sign language systems showed absolutely "no uniformity" among different tribal nations.[36] He put the matter more succinctly elsewhere: "The result of the collation and analysis thus far made is that the alleged existence of one universal and absolute sign-language is . . . one of the many popular errors prevailing about our aborigines. In many instances there is an entire discrepancy between the signs made by different bodies of Indians."[37]

Native American sign languages were thus just as varied as the spoken languages they were meant to bridge. But by dispelling the myth of linguistic universality, Mallery had also revealed a fundamental flaw in his salvage project. If dialects of sign talk were fluid and infinitely diverse, the existing linguistic data necessarily exceeded man's capacity to salvage them. "No dictionary of signs will be exhaustive," he wrote in 1880, "for the simple reason that the signs are exhaustless, nor will it be exact because there cannot be a correspondence between signs and words taken individually."[38] Powell euphemistically made the same point in his preface to the original edition of Mallery's *Introduction to the Study of Sign Language,* noting that a "comprehensive treatment of [the] subject can only be obtained by the combined labor of many men," and Mallery's fieldworkers often admitted as much in their field correspondence with the bureau's Washington office.[39] "A compendium of the sign-languages of the Indians would long since have been satisfied," one of the Bureau of Ethnology's frustrated sign collectors observed. "I frankly admit that I cannot give the signs in a satisfactory manner, either by language or by drawing. . . . You [Mallery] have stated the literal fact in your address before the Anthropological Society that 'there is often a discrepancy between the signs made by different bodies of Indians to express the same idea.' You may go a great deal further and say that 'the sign language of each Indian differs from others, as differs the hand writing of white men.' . . . There are a thousand shades of gradation, which make a verbal or pictured description almost impossible."[40] In other words, Indian sign languages were evanescent because ethnographic coverage was forever incomplete.

Finally—and most importantly, because it bears directly on the theory of media Mallery's writings offer—the evanescence of PISL refers to something about the limits of written representation, something about the nature of archives and media themselves. As Mallery noted time and again in his published works, gesture languages are, by definition, languages of motion. Documenting them therefore required a form of writing that could capture both duration and succession, a new medium that could represent time and record movement. "The signs of the Indians appear to consist of *motions* rather than *positions*," Mallery wrote in 1880,

a fact enhancing the difficulty both of their description and illustration—and the motions are generally large and free, seldom minute. It seems also to be the general rule among Indians as deaf-mutes that the point of the finger is used to trace outlines and the palm of the hand to describe surfaces. From an examination of the identical signs made for the same object by Indians of the same tribe and band to each other, they appear to make most gestures with little regard to the position of the fingers and to vary in such arrangement from individual taste. Some of the elaborate descriptions, giving with great detail the attitude of the fingers of any particular gesturer and the inches traced by his motions, are of as little necessity as would be a careful reproduction of the flourishes of tailed letters and the thickness of downstrokes in individual chirography when quoting a written word. The fingers must be in some position, but that is frequently accidental, not contributing to the general and essential effect, and there is a custom or "fashion" in which not only different tribes but different persons in the same tribe gesture the same sign with different degrees of beauty, for there is calligraphy in sign-language, though no recognized orthography.[41]

For Mallery, then, Indian sign talk is ultimately evanescent because it resists written representation. Because PISL consists of active bodily movements rather than static manual positions, no "recognized orthography" exists for documenting it. Written "description" and printed "illustration" can thus only hope to approximate the embodied gestural event. In "Sign Language among North American Indians," Mallery addressed this problem even more directly: "Regarding the difficulties met with in the task proposed, the same motto might be adopted as was prefixed to [Gilbert] Austin's *Chironomia*: '*Non sum nescius, quantum susceperim negotii, qui motus corporis exprimere verbis, imitari scriptura conatus sim voces*' [I am not unaware, as much as I have undertaken the task, that expressing the movement of the body in words is like attempting to imitate the voice in writing]."[42]

These kinds of qualifications and complaints were actually quite common in published accounts of American and European sign languages during the nineteenth century.[43] For instance, the deaf author John Burnet wrote in 1835 that "to attempt to describe a language of signs by words, or to learn such a language from books, is alike to attempt impossibilities."[44] Likewise, E. B. Tylor, Mallery's primary intellectual model, made similar remarks in his *Researches into the Early History of Mankind and the Development of Civilization*, notably suffusing his account of print's inability to represent motion with gloomy images of linguistic death and decay: "When I write down descriptions in words of the deaf-and-dumb signs, they seem bald and weak, but it must be remembered that I can only write down the skeletons of them. To see them is something very different, for these dry bones have to be covered with flesh. Not the face only, but the whole body joins in giving expression to the sign."[45] For Mallery, working in the context of the Plains Indians, Tylor's tacit fantasy of an adequate archive for sign language—one that could reanimate the "dry bones" of gestural expression into a living language "covered with flesh"—betrayed the evolutionary distance between primitive and modern forms of communication and memory. Writing seemed to have evolved as a storage mechanism for spoken language alone, long after gestures and signs had been abandoned. The act of writing sign language thus constituted an evolutionary anachronism; imagining a system for recording PISL's "evanescence" was tantamount to bridging a vast gulf in human history.

Yet it was this same antagonism between (savage–primitive) signs and (civilized–modern) words that drove Mallery's unique experiments with ethnographic form in his published work. This becomes clear if we turn our attention not just to the curiously multimediated nature of texts like

Introduction to the Study of Sign Language and "Sign Language among North American Indians," but also to the late-nineteenth-century visual innovations that undoubtedly influenced Mallery's scientific practice.

Motion Writing

Both prior to and during the nineteenth century, thick description was the most common way to represent the world's sign languages. Whereas scholars working throughout Europe and the Americas had made numerous attempts at devising notation systems for dances and other forms of stylized bodily movement (according to the anthropologist Brenda M. Farnell, these kinds of efforts in fact date back to the 1400s), they generally settled for written prose instruction when it came to the problem of PISL.[46] To take a representative example, Jefferson and Dunbar's 1801 account of the native sign for *fear* consists of little more than a brief explanatory summary: "The two hands with the fingers turned inwards opposite to the lower ribs, then brought upwards with a tremulous movement as if to represent the common idea of the heart rising up to the throat."[47] At first glance, aside from taking care to include slight variations among different national sign language traditions, Mallery's *Introduction to the Study of Sign Language,* written almost eighty years later, does very little to improve on the descriptive method:

Fear:

1. Both hands, with fingers turned inward opposite the lower ribs, then brought upward with a tremulous motion, as if to represent the common idea of the heart rising up to the throat.

2. Head stooped down, and arm thrown up quickly as if to protect it.

3. Fingers and thumb of right hand, which droops downward, closed to a point to represent a heart, violently and repeatedly beaten against the left breast just over the heart to imitate palpitation. The Sioux use the same sign without closing the fingers to represent a heart. The French deaf-mutes, besides beating the heart, add a nervous backward shrinking with both hands. Our deaf-mutes omit the beating of the heart, except for excessive terror.

4. Point forward several times with the index, followed by the remaining fingers, each time drawing the index back, as if impossible to keep the man to the front.

5. May be signified by making the sign for a squaw, if the one in fear be a man or boy.

6. Cross the arms over the breast, fists closed, bow the head over the crossed arms, but turn it a little to the left.[48]

Mallery would consciously work to refine this representational practice in the coming years, modifying explanatory descriptions where necessary and adding dialectal variations when he encountered them. (For instance, the 1880 *Collection of Gesture-Signs and Signals* occasionally attempts to give an intelligible sense of bodily scale, as in a new variation on the sign for "fear" that includes approximate measurements and proportions: "Crook the index, close the other fingers, and with its back upward, draw the right hand backward about a foot, from eighteen inches in front of the right breast.")[49] But what is striking about the written entries in the initial *Introduction to the Study of Sign Language,* both here and throughout, is their constant recourse to as-if descriptive constructions ("as if to represent the common idea of the heart rising up to the throat"; "as if to protect it"; "as if impossible to keep the man to the front"; etc.). Such casual turns toward literary abstraction betray hidden recognitions of the text's own ethnographic shortcomings. For Mallery, perhaps, describing familiar bodily actions helped evoke in the mind of the reader the unfamiliar Indian movements that necessarily escaped written recitation.

The most obvious corrective to this problem was of course printed illustration, and Mallery's published sign language studies were novel in their extensive use of supplementary diagrams and visual aids. As Mallery admitted later on, "if the descriptive recital of the signs collected had been absolutely restricted to written or printed words the work would have been still more difficult and the result less intelligible."[50] The first factor that made Mallery's extravagant recourse to illustration possible was the largesse of Powell's Bureau of Ethnology, which spared no expense to avail Mallery of the latest technologies for mass-reproducing his sign language images in print form. The second was the artistic talent of Walter J. Hoffman, an ethnologist and amateur illustrator who worked under Mallery for nearly fifteen years, mostly specializing in the region populated by the Dakota, Blackfeet, and Ojibwe nations. It was Hoffman who created the visual templates that collectors around the country used to record the basics of

Indian sign talk, and it was Hoffman who provided the vast majority of the images that accompanied Mallery's published sign descriptions. "He has the eye and the pencil of an artist," Mallery boasted somewhat wishfully in the *Introduction,* "so that he seizes readily, describes with physiological accuracy, and reproduces in action and in permanent illustration all shades of gesture exhibited."[51]

Reproduced in different forms and contexts throughout *Introduction to the Study of Sign Language* and "Sign Languages among North American Indians," Hoffman's illustrations suggest some of the formal obstacles that Mallery faced in attempting to write and record an embodied language of motion. They also suggest just how conscious he was of the problem. For instance, Mallery and Hoffman's widely circulated "Outlines of Arm Positions in Gesture-Language" template—which features an anonymous body outline unnecessarily adorned with a stereotypical Indian headdress—encourages field collectors to make use of a standardized system of dia-critical marks to help evoke gestural movement on the printed page: dot-ted lines, to "indicate movements to place the hand and arm in position to commence the sign"; check marks, to "indicate commencement of move-ment in representing [the] sign, or part of [the] sign"; dashes, to "indicate the course of hand employed in the sign"; crossed "x" marks, to "represent the termination of movements"; and arrows, "used in connection with dashes, [to show] the course of the latter when not otherwise clearly intel-ligible" (see Figure 5).[52] Hoffman would resort to similarly baroque tech-niques for representing gestural motion in his own sign language sketches. Particularly in the images reproduced in Mallery's published texts, one en-counters elaborate arrangements of lines and dots that strain to indicate the courses of moving hands and arms (see Plate 1). In other illustrations—unpublished but nonetheless central to Mallery's armchair efforts to per-fect his written sign descriptions—faded, almost ghostly outlines of Indian body parts attempt to imply sequences of gestural motion over fixed pas-sages of time (see Figure 6).

Mallery later claimed that he encouraged such graphic practices to help minimize discrepancies between fieldworkers who worked with different dialects of sign talk. As he explained it, the main object of the templates was "to eliminate the source of confusion produced by attempts of differ-ent persons at the difficult description of positions and motions. . . . With

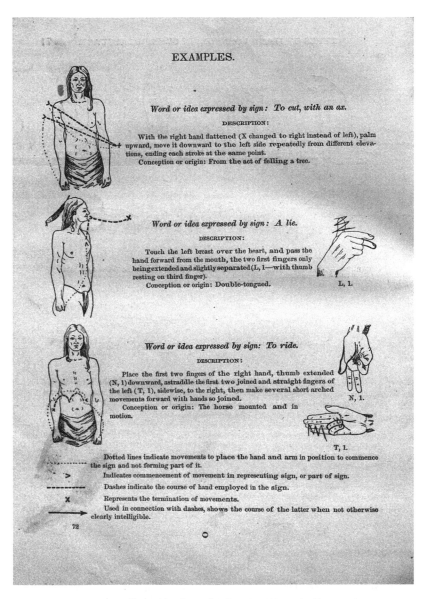

EXAMPLES.

Word or idea expressed by sign: To cut, with an ax.

DESCRIPTION:

With the right hand flattened (X changed to right instead of left), palm upward, move it downward to the left side repeatedly from different elevations, ending each stroke at the same point.

Conception or origin: From the act of felling a tree.

Word or idea expressed by sign: A lie.

DESCRIPTION:

Touch the left breast over the heart, and pass the hand forward from the mouth, the two first fingers only being extended and slightly separated (L, 1—with thumb resting on third finger).

Conception or origin: Double-tongued.

L, 1.

Word or idea expressed by sign: To ride.

DESCRIPTION:

Place the first two fingers of the right hand, thumb extended (N, 1) downward, astraddle the first two joined and straight fingers of the left (T, 1), sidewise, to the right, then make several short arched movements forward with hands so joined.

Conception or origin: The horse mounted and in motion.

N, 1.

T, 1.

Dotted lines indicate movements to place the hand and arm in position to commence the sign and not forming part of it.

Indicates commencement of movement in representing sign, or part of sign.

Dashes indicate the course of hand employed in the sign.

Represents the termination of movements.

Used in connection with dashes, shows the course of the latter when not otherwise clearly intelligible.

72

FIGURE 5 Garrick Mallery, "Outlines for Arm Positions in Gesture Language: Examples." *Introduction to the Study of Sign Language among the North American Indians as Illustrating the Gesture Speech of Mankind* (Washington, D.C.: U.S. Government Printing Office, 1880). Sci 3120.25.2, Widener Library, Harvard College Library.

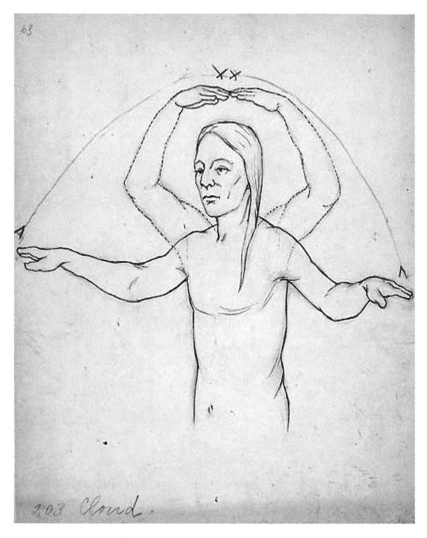

FIGURE 6 W. J. Hoffman's sketch of the PISL sign for *cloud* (tribal dialect unidentified). Garrick Mallery Collection on Sign Language and Pictography, Numbered Manuscripts 1850s–1980s, MS 2372, Box 8, National Anthropological Archives, Smithsonian Institution.

a set form of expressions for the typical positions, and skeleton outlines to be filled up and, when necessary, altered in a uniform style, this source of confusion is greatly reduced."[53] But clearly the problem of writing motion persists here. Dotted lines and check marks also serve as a necessary ethnographic supplement to an insufficiently static and two-dimensional medium. "The graphic lines drawn to represent the positions and motions on the same diagrams will vary but little in comparison with the similar attempt of explanation in writing," Mallery concluded. "Both modes of description were, however, requested, each tending to supplement and correct the other."[54]

From this perspective, the illustrations throughout Mallery's published work on PISL seem to signal the documentary inadequacy of the traditional descriptive method, while the graphic "supplements" (Mallery's term) to the illustrations seem to signal the documentary inadequacy of the printed page itself. Like Powell before him, Mallery understood the relationship between all of these competing media—signs, words, and images—in evolutionary terms. On one hand, as he explained at the outset of *Introduction to the Study of Sign Language*, PISL resisted writing because its origins seemed to predate, in evolutionary time, the successive inventions of pictographic writing and alphabetic script: "Apart from their practical value for use with living members of the tribes, our native semiotics will surely help the archaeologist in his study of native picture-writing, the sole form of aboriginal records, for it was but one more step to fasten upon bark, skins, or rocks the evanescent air-pictures that still in pigments or carvings preserve their skeleton outline, and in their ideography approach the rudiments of a phonetic alphabet."[55] On the other hand, he continued, writing itself resisted PISL because it failed to capture bodily motion in an adequate way:

> Gesture-language is, in fact, not only a picture-language, but is actual writing, though dissolving and sympathetic, and neither alphabetic nor phonetic. Though written characters are in our minds associated with speech, they are shown, by successful employment in hieroglyphs and by educated deaf-mutes, to be representative of ideas without the intervention of sounds, and so also are the outlines of signs. This will be more apparent if the [sign language] motions expressing the most prominent feature, attribute, or

function of an object are made, or supposed to be made, *so as to leave a luminous track impressible to the eye, separate from the members producing it.*[56]

Amid Mallery's densely theoretical claims about PISL's relationship to the evolutionary development of writing technology, what stands out in this passage is the impulse to see sign language reproduced in a way that leaves "a luminous track impressible to the eye, separate from the members producing it." This is a curiously prescient formulation: one that suggests that Mallery was familiar with a set of visual innovations that had captured the attention of scientists across Europe and America during the 1870s and 1880s—innovations that would fundamentally transform the project of cultural preservation in the decades that followed. What Mallery is describing here, in other words, is the process of chronophotography, which the French scientist Étienne-Jules Marey and the American photographer Eadweard J. Muybridge had pioneered to capture the "luminous tracks" of moving objects over fixed periods of time. Muybridge is of particular importance here. His experimental work in the field of chronophotography directly intersected with Mallery's work with PISL.

Sign Language and Chronophotography

Muybridge, the so-called father of cinema, is well known to historians of visual media.[57] As the story goes, sometime in 1872, the railroad tycoon Leland Stanford commissioned Muybridge, then working as a professional photographer in San Francisco, to take pictures of racehorses in motion. The stated object was to settle once and for all the long-standing popular debate surrounding the issue of "unsupported transit": whether, as Stanford and many others believed, all four legs of a trotting or running animal are at some imperceptible moment in time off the ground simultaneously.

After several years of technical experimentation (and after brutally murdering his wife's lover and temporarily fleeing the country, a series of events that only served to enhance his public notoriety), Muybridge devised an elaborate photographic apparatus able to capture instantaneous frames of objects moving at high speeds. By 1877, Muybridge had accumulated enough visual evidence to confirm the unsupported transit hypothesis, proving Stanford right. But viewing his animal locomotion images now, as many did in the decades that followed, it is almost impossible not to see a nascent form of "cinema before cinema," to borrow Virgilio Tosi's useful turn of phrase (see Figure 7).[58] Taken individually, Muybridge's photographs seem to arrest the flow of time, capturing physical movements far too rapid for the human eye to see. Combined and arranged in sequential order—as they were in Muybridge's famous locomotion studies, collected throughout the 1880s and 1890s—the frames appear to set the world in motion once again. Muybridge continued experimenting with instantaneous photography for the remainder of his life, shooting thousands of serial frames of animals, male athletes, nude women, and human body parts at various rates of motion. At the same time, he also popularized a line of novelty items that projected these images, both "still" and "moving," to mass audiences on both sides of the Atlantic. Modern motion pictures, it seemed, were born.

As Charles Musser, Marta Braun, and Tom Gunning have all suggested, Muybridge's eventual influence on the development of the cinematic apparatus lies as much in his desire to tap into a mass cultural marketplace as in his anticipation of the visual logic of the celluloid film strip.[59] Yet when

FIGURE 7 Eadweard J. Muybridge, "*Animal Locomotion*, Plate 626" (circa 1887). Eadweard Muybridge Collection, University of Pennsylvania Archives.

considered from the perspective of the late nineteenth century—and when considered alongside Étienne-Jules Marey's visual breakthroughs around the same time—Muybridge's ingenious photographic method at the very least provided a novel solution to the age-old problem of recording movement.[60] "With this apparatus," he claimed in an 1893 pamphlet on the chronophotographic process, "horse-races are reproduced with such fidelity that the individual characteristics of the motion of every animal can readily be seen; flocks of birds fly across the screen with every movement of their wings clearly perceptible; two gladiators contend for victory with an energy which would cause the arena to resound with wild applause, athletes turn somersaults, and other actions by men, women, and children, horses, dogs, cats and wild animals, such as running, dancing, jumping, trotting, and kicking, are illustrated in the same manner."[61] He continued, noting that the technique's primary contribution was to the science of kinesthesis, "It is also probable that these photographic investigations—which were executed with wet collodion plates, with exposures not exceeding in some instances the one five-thousandth part of a second—will dispel many popular illusions as to the gaits of a horse, and future and more exhaustive experiments, with the advantages of recent chemical discoveries, will completely unveil all the visible muscular action of men and animals even during their most rapid movements."[62] Promotional rhetoric aside, the public that viewed Muybridge's work during the 1870s, 1880s, and 1890s generally agreed with such grandiose assessments. The chronophotographic process appeared to redefine what science and technology could see and record— at once introducing the modern world to visual realities that otherwise eluded the naked eye, and creating the illusion of movement in a medium that otherwise seemed frozen in time.[63]

Eadweard Muybridge and Garrick Mallery were contemporaries, deeply engaged with the problem of recording motion at exactly the same time. While Muybridge garnered international acclaim for photographing the movements of animals, Mallery made his name on a much smaller scale, documenting the movements of the human race that seemed one small evolutionary link on the Great Chain of Being above them. But the connection between these two figures in fact goes well beyond the mere accident of historical simultaneity. Before embarking on the chronophotographic studies that secured his place in modern media history, Muybridge had made his living as a photographer of the American West. During the Modoc War of 1872–73, one of the last anti-Indian campaigns waged west of the Colorado River, he took pictures of Native Americans in northern California and Oregon under the auspices of the federal government.[64] Reproduced in the *San Francisco Chronicle* and *Harper's Weekly,* many of Muybridge's Indian photographs prefigure the visual styles popularized in early-twentieth-century ethnographic photography. The iconic images accompanying Edward S. Curtis's landmark twenty-volume study *The North American Indian* (1907–30) resonate particularly well with Muybridge's Modoc photographs: both Muybridge and Curtis staged the majority of their pictures of Indians to heighten a sense of primitive cultural authenticity.[65]

More importantly, Muybridge maintained contact with the Bureau of Ethnology throughout the 1880s and 1890s. In May 1887, John Wesley Powell sent Muybridge a letter inquiring about *Animal Locomotion: An Electrophotographic Investigation of Consecutive Phases of Animal Movements* (1887), Muybridge's first book of serial photographic studies.[66] The photographer responded a few months later, sending along a copy of the book and a separate series of chronophotographic plates in which the Bureau had a special interest.[67] Later on, in preparation for a never-published "larger work . . . devoted to primitive and aboriginal art," Muybridge actually wrote Powell to gain access to images of Indians and Indian pictography that Mallery and his fieldworkers had collected throughout the western territories while working on the PISL project.[68] Although the extant Muybridge correspondence never mentions sign language directly, there is good reason to believe that he was familiar with Mallery's ongoing efforts in the field. During the 1880s, while working at the University of Pennsylvania (Mallery's alma mater), Muybridge also spent an extended period of time photographing human hands at various rates of gestural motion (see Figure 8).[69]

In this context, Mallery's attempt to salvage sign talk seems best understood as a forgotten episode in the history of visual media. Indeed, Muybridge's experiments appear to have provided Mallery with a potential solution to the problem of PISL's evanescence. Consider, for instance, Mallery's attempts to reproduce the manual rudiments of PISL in his "Types of Hand Positions in Gesture-Language" guide, reproduced at the end of *Introduction to the Study of Sign Language* (see Figure 9). If the *Introduction*'s "Outlines of Arm Positions" template sought to represent the

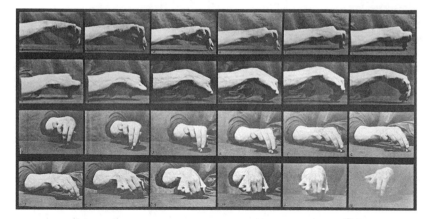

FIGURE 8   Eadweard J. Muybridge, "*Animal Locomotion*, Plate 532" (circa 1887). Eadweard Muybridge Collection, University of Pennsylvania Archives.

movement of Indian hands in relation to the gestures of the Indian body, its "Types of Hand Positions in Gesture-Language" index goes one step further, indicating the position of Indian fingers in relation to the movements of the Indian hand: "In order to provide for such cases of minute representation a sheet of 'Types of Hand Positions' has been prepared, and if none of them exactly correspond to a sign observed, the one most nearly corresponding can be readily altered by a few strokes of pen or pencil."[70] Here twenty-five different hands, stripped of their corporeal referents, are frozen in twenty-five separate gestural positions, with fingers either splayed out, closed, or pointed in a set direction. Together, they comprise a kind of iconographic alphabet for Native American sign talk. (The fact that Mallery uses standard Roman letters—"A," "B," "C," "D," and so on— to index each individual sign position further reinforces the alphabetic reasoning at work here.) Yet these units were also meant to create the illusion of diachronic movement in time. The point of isolating hand positions wasn't merely to break down Indian sign language into its synchronic component parts; it was to represent the rudimentary building blocks of more advanced "syntactical" sequences. Mallery even proposed "cutting and pasting them in the proper order" to "exhibit the semiotic syntax" and represent the language in implied serial motion.[71] So while disembodied and stationary on the page, Mallery's illustrated hand positions—like Muybridge's instantaneous photographs—are clearly conceived as individual frames that can be combined and arranged in sequential order, depicting a given course of a signed gesture over a fixed period of time.

Mallery also based these illustrations on a series of documentary photographs of Plains Indian signers taken in Washington around 1880. On the surface, he intended the images to function as mechanically reproduced checks on the cultural biases of the ethnographic observer, a matter that will occupy much of my interest in chapter 3. As Mallery assured his readers, "attention was specially directed to the importance of ascertaining the intrinsic idea or conception of all signs, which it was urged should be obtained directly from the persons using them and not by inference."[72] Photography, in this context, promised both cultural immediacy and representational accuracy. But as with the illustrated hand positions in the *Introduction,* one also senses a durational impulse here, a desire to overcome the synchronic nature of the photographic medium. To be sure, the images themselves are hauntingly silent and still: the out-of-date native garment clearly visible in each frame—yet another unnecessary staging of Indian authenticity—even seems to fossilize both the gesturing hand and the dying language it carries in a distant cultural past. But assembled as individual frames in a longer chronological series (see Figure 10), as Mallery no doubt encouraged given the stated intention of the "Types of Hand Positions" guide, the photographs appear to reenter the stream of time: hands move, temporarily bringing the signing body back to life; language reanimates, temporarily resuscitating the culture that has seemingly vanished along with it; and the photograph—the media artifact itself—temporarily evolves from stasis to motion, primitive sign to modern moving picture.

Indians, Signs, Cinemas

Garrick Mallery died in 1894. His unofficial successor at the Bureau of Ethnology, a decorated U.S. Army general named Hugh Lenox Scott, spent the next four decades intermittently working to complete the PISL preservation project. Scott's early writings on the subject clearly give evidence of Mallery's influence, often warning against the global diffusion of English and its role in the disappearance of Native American languages. "When another generation or so of Indians will have passed away," Scott predicted in a paper delivered at the 1893 World's Columbian Exposition, "their languages, vocal and gesture, will have disappeared with them. . . . The sole

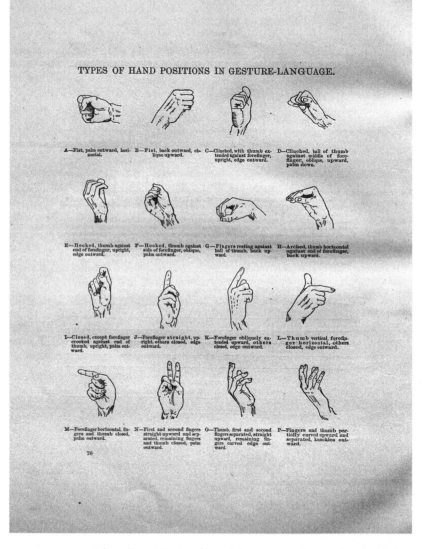

FIGURE 9 Garrick Mallery, "Types of Hand Positions in Gesture-Language." *Introduction to the Study of Sign Language among the North American Indians as Illustrating the Gesture Speech of Mankind* (Washington, D.C.: U.S. Government Printing Office, 1880). Sci 3120.25.2, Widener Library, Harvard College Library.

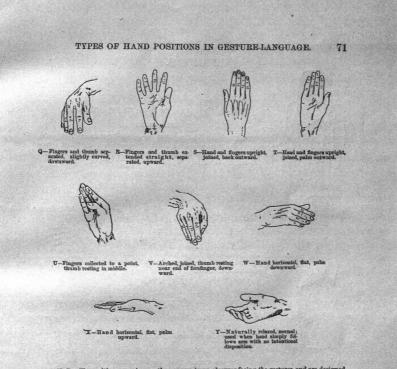

Q—Fingers and thumb sep-
arated, slightly curved,
downward.

R—Fingers and thumb ex-
tended straight, sepa-
rated, upward.

S—Hand and fingers upright,
joined, back outward.

T—Hand and fingers upright,
joined, palm outward.

U—Fingers collected to a point,
thumb resting in middle.

V—Arched, joined, thumb resting
near end of forefinger, downward.

W—Hand horizontal, flat, palm
downward.

X—Hand horizontal, flat, palm
upward.

Y—Naturally relaxed, normal;
used when hand simply follows arm with no intentional
disposition.

N. B.—The positions are given as they appear to an observer facing the gesturer, and are designed to show the relations of the fingers to the hand rather than the positions of the hand relative to the body, which must be shown by the outlines (see sheet of "OUTLINES OF ARM POSITIONS") or description. The right and left hands are figured above without discrimination, but in description or reference the right hand will be understood when the left is not specified. The hands as figured can also with proper intimation be applied with changes either upward, downward, or inclined to either side, so long as the relative positions of the fingers are retained, and when in that respect no one of the types exactly corresponds with a sign observed, modifications will be made by pen or pencil on that one of the types found most convenient, as indicated in the sheet of "EXAMPLES," and referred to by the letter of the alphabet under the type changed, with the addition of a numeral—e. g., A 1, and if that type, i. e. A, were changed a second time by the observer (which change would necessarily be drawn on another sheet of types), it should be referred to as A 2.

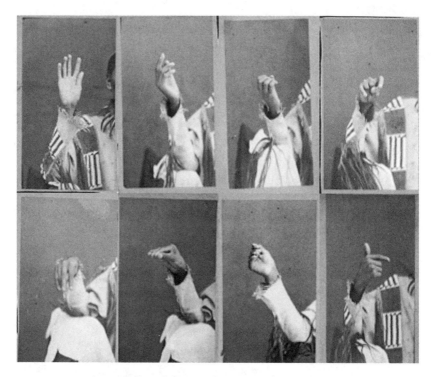

FIGURE 10 Photographs of Plains Indian Sign Language hand positions (circa 1880), arranged sequentially according to Garrick Mallery's instructions. Garrick Mallery Collection on Sign Language and Pictography, Numbered Manuscripts 1850s–1980s, MS 2372, Box 8, Images 001–008, National Anthropological Archives, Smithsonian Institution.

remainder of these will be their mummies, embalmed among our records in the characters of the language which has displaced them."[73]

More important, on the subject of PISL's "mummified" historical remains—a metaphor that tellingly anticipates André Bazin's "mummy complex" theory of media preservation, discussed earlier—Scott's writings also echo Mallery's basic concern with the problem of recording motion:

But you ask if the sign language cannot be acquired from the study of the elaborate works written with such care upon this subject. It has not been the experience of many persons coming from the East, struck with the picturesque novelty of the Indians as a people, who endeavored to learn from books to speak the sign language in order to converse with them, for we have seen that it is primarily a language of motions and not of positions, and the rates of these motions often vary in the different parts of the same sign, and cannot be accurately recorded by a description or by a stationary picture; and while many other signs can be properly described, no book can give an idea of the graceful and flowing sequence with which signs are used by a master of the art, and the books have soon been laid aside, to be taken up later as a means of comparison.[74]

Familiar enough: here Scott sounds a lot like Mallery describing the crisis of ethnographic representation surrounding PISL a decade prior. But note the crucial shift toward the cinematic that comes next in his account:

If you could have witnessed the scenes enacted in many of their lodges during the long nights of the winter, in some isolated village upon the buffalo range, or sheltered from the wind in a mountain park, when some one of their older and more skillful men, fired with enthusiasm for the memories of his youth, was relating his stories of the warpath and adventure, the ancient customs of his people, or the ceremonies of their religion, to a silent band of dusky warriors—then only could you realize the great force, the intense meaning, and the exceeding gracefulness and beauty of the sign language of the Plains Indian.[75]

Perhaps unsurprisingly, given his stubborn frustrations with the printed page ("no book can give an idea of the graceful and flowing sequence with which signs are used by a master of the art"), and given his romantic attachment to ideals of cultural authenticity, immediacy, and live motion ("If you could have witnessed the scenes . . . then only could you realize the great force, the intense meaning, and the exceeding gracefulness and beauty of the sign language of the Plains Indian"), Scott quickly turned to film in an effort to stave off PISL's extinction. According to one anthropologist at the Bureau of Ethnology, in the mid-1890s, Scott explicitly proposed adopting Muybridge's "succession photography" apparatus as a way to continue Mallery's work and "rescue from ultimate oblivion the American Indian sign language."[76] The idea never got off the ground. But in the 1920s, Scott began planning the production of a feature-length movie about

PISL, and in September 1930, after receiving a five thousand dollar appropriation from Congress, he convened elder representatives from twelve different Plains Indian nations in Browning, Montana, to film their dialects of sign talk, which had by then all but fallen into total disuse (see Figure 11).[77]

The thirty-three-minute motion picture that resulted, *The Indian Sign Language* (1930), remains a landmark document in the history of PISL, particularly because it appears to capture the language as Plains Indian signers themselves wanted it recorded.[78] Produced by the U.S. Department of Agriculture using new synchronized sound recording techniques, the movie documents the central proceedings of the 1930 Browning PISL conference—signed introductions of the participants, followed by performances of traditional "sagas in sign" staged for the camera—all framed by Scott's introductory remarks on the history and significance of the language.

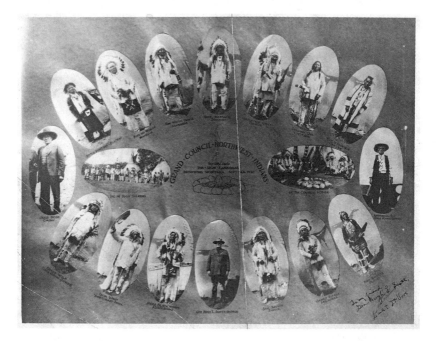

FIGURE 11   "Members of the Grand Council of Northwest Indians Meeting, Including General Hugh L. Scott, to Record Sign Language" (September 1930). Scott is pictured in the middle of the bottom row. SPC Miscellaneous Sign Language, BAE 4720-01310300, National Anthropological Archives, Smithsonian Institution.

At first glance, *The Indian Sign Language* clearly builds on the evolutionary theories of PISL that Mallery first proposed in the 1870s and 1880s. The film opens with a nattily dressed General Scott standing in front of a dark curtain, as if on stage addressing a listening audience. "The Indian sign language," he proclaims, backed by the plaintive sounds of a clarinet on the film's sound track, "is the most peculiar and interesting of all the languages of all the earth because . . . it has changed little, if at all, since [the development of] civilization, sometime before the dawn of American history." The choice to record the movie in synchronized sound becomes significant in light of Scott's next prefatory claim: that PISL "obeys all the general laws of linguistic science, save those of sound. . . . It appeals to the same human brain, to the same human thoughts, as do vocal tongues, the difference being that this appeal is made through the eye, rather than through the ear." The inclusion of the sound track—a new cinematic technology in 1930—thus performs the very same evolutionary divide between the modern and the primitive, the ear and the eye, that Scott's introductory remarks seek to address. Throughout *The Indian Sign Language,* we are able to hear both the voice and the technology of "civilization," yet the Plains Indian sign talkers who represent the film's ethnographic object are forced to make their "appeal" to history in total silence.

Despite its evolutionary underpinnings, *The Indian Sign Language* also documents an equally powerful Native American impulse toward linguistic survival and cultural self-determination. At the conclusion of Scott's explanatory lecture, the film immediately cuts to the Browning conference, with Scott seated among a group of Plains Indian signers dressed in elaborate ceremonial attire. "Young men are not learning your sign language, and soon it will disappear from this country," Scott signs to the conference participants, his gestures translated for the viewer in voice-over. "It is for us to make a record of it for those who come after us, before it becomes lost forever. . . . Talk to me with your hands."[79] In the ensuing scenes, shot inside of a traditional Piegan council lodge specially constructed for the film, each delegate offers a signed response to Scott's plea, introducing himself to the camera and noting the importance of gathering far-flung tribal "brothers" to converse in sign talk. Several "sagas in signs" follow. Mountain Chief (Piegan) stoically recites a "buffalo story of long ago." Strange Owl (Cheyenne) responds with a similar tale. Bitter Root

Jim (Flathead) tells a "classic and renowned" story of a dangerous bear hunt. And perhaps to underscore both the inherent modernity of Native American life and its importance to the development of American media culture, Tom White Horse (Arapaho) wittily signs comparisons between "the red man's medicine" and "the white man's medicine," shamanism and radio: "The red men used to communicate with their medicine in sleep, thus hearing things that they could not see. Now comes the white man with another kind of medicine [radio]. . . . The white man, with his mechanical medicine, is also now able to hear things that he cannot see." Instead of signing their stories to each other, the PISL conference participants notably choose to address Scott's camera head-on throughout the film. The effect is that the delegates appear to talk directly to future generations, underscoring that they may have regarded their encounter with the cinematic apparatus as a deliberate act of cultural survival.

Similar strategies of self-representation are also present in the film work of Richard Sanderville (Chief Bull), a Blackfeet Indian sign talker who had long served as Scott's primary informant in the field.[80] Born in Browning sometime in the early 1870s, Sanderville was the first member of his tribe to attend the Carlisle Indian Industrial School in Carlisle, Pennsylvania. After graduating in 1895, he returned home to serve as a tribal interpreter, mediating between the political interests of the Blackfeet Nations and those of the federal policy makers who had official jurisdiction over Blackfeet territory. At this point, Sanderville disappears from the historical record, but he resurfaces more than three decades later as an unseen inspiration for Scott's PISL film experiments. Although Sanderville's name is absent from the credits of *The Indian Sign Language*, his face never pictured, documents surrounding the production of the film suggest that he translated signs offscreen during the recording of the Browning conference.[81] Immediately following Scott's death in 1934, Sanderville also traveled to the Bureau of Ethnology's headquarters in Washington to record himself signing words, idioms, and stories for Scott's unfinished *Dictionary of Indian Sign Language* (1934), an experimental "cinematic dictionary" project that had been under way since 1930.[82] Sanderville's arrival in the nation's capital actually received considerable media attention. *The Literary Digest* for July 7, 1934, reported on his trip, hailing him as "the greatest living authority on the vanishing and almost forgotten universal sign language used by the American Indians,"

PLATE 1 W. J. Hoffman's illustration of the Dakota sign for *no, not,* later reproduced in Garrick Mallery's "Sign Language among North American Indians Compared with That among Other Peoples and Deaf-Mutes" (1881). Garrick Mallery Collection on Sign Language and Pictography, Numbered Manuscripts 1850s–1980s, MS 2372, Box 8, National Anthropological Archives, Smithsonian Institution.

PLATE 2 Untitled photograph by Frances Hubbard
Flaherty (circa 1923), later reproduced in the August 1925
issue of *Asia* magazine. The Robert and Frances Flaherty
Study Center, Claremont School of Theology, Claremont,
California, MO 0343b.

PLATE 3 Moana and Fa'angase perform a traditional
Samoan *siva* dance in Robert and Frances Flaherty's *Moana*
(1926). Untitled photograph by Frances Hubbard Flaherty
(circa 1923). The Robert and Frances Flaherty Study Center,
Claremont School of Theology, Claremont, California,
MO 1059.

PLATE 4 The beginning of the Samoan tattooing ritual reconstructed for Robert and Frances Flaherty's *Moana* (1926). Untitled photograph by Frances Hubbard Flaherty (circa 1923). The Robert and Frances Flaherty Study Center, Claremont School of Theology, Claremont, California, MO 1211.

PLATE 5 The tattooing scene in *Moana* (1926) captured in detail. Untitled photograph by Frances Hubbard Flaherty (circa 1923). The Robert and Frances Flaherty Study Center, Claremont School of Theology, Claremont, California, MO 1240.

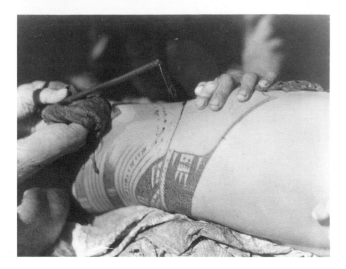

PLATE 6 The tattooing needle as phonograph needle.
Untitled photograph by Frances Hubbard Flaherty (circa
1923). The Robert and Frances Flaherty Study Center,
Claremont School of Theology, Claremont, California, MO 1242.

PLATE 7
Fred Payne Clatworthy,
"The Tom-Tom of the
Navajo Echoes through
the Grand Canyon"
(autochrome, circa
1923), later reproduced
in the April 1923 issue
of *National Geographic
Magazine.* Collection of
Mark Jacobs.

PLATE 8 Franklin Price Knott, "The Chief Priest of the Snake Clan: Hopi Tribe" (autochrome, circa 1916). Franklin Price Knott/National Geographic Stock.

PLATE 9 Franklin Price Knott, "The Hopi Basket Maker" (autochrome, circa 1916). Franklin Price Knott/National Geographic Stock.

PLATE 10 Franklin Price Knott, "A Hopi Indian and His Home" (autochrome, circa 1916). Franklin Price Knott/National Geographic Stock.

PLATE 11 Fred Payne Clatworthy, "The Sioux Were Once Lords of the West" (autochrome, circa 1927). Collection of Mark Jacobs.

PLATE 12 Fred Payne Clatworthy, untitled photograph of Māori women and meetinghouse in Rotorua, New Zealand (autochrome, 1928). Collection of Mark Jacobs.

and a week later, the *Science News Letter* prematurely announced that "the dictionary of the Indian Sign Language is at last finished."[83]

Although the vast majority of Sanderville's film contributions to Scott's *Dictionary of Indian Sign Language* have failed to survive the test of time, the extant footage, currently held in the Smithsonian Institution's Motion Picture Accession, suggests that sign talkers may have all along viewed the development of the cinema—a modern technology often touted for its ability to bridge linguistic and cultural barriers—as wholly consistent with their language's living legacy.[84] The Bureau of Ethnology's film begins with a three-quarter shot of Sanderville sitting in a chair on the lawn in front of the Smithsonian Museum. As with Tom White Horse in *The Indian Sign Language,* one immediately gets the sense that Sanderville is deliberately responding to evolutionary orthodoxy and staging his own modernity for the sake of the film. He sits in front of a row of cars parked alongside the National Mall rather than inside a "traditional" Indian lodge. He dresses in a tie and shirtsleeves rather than in any sort of "authentic" Indian attire. He gazes straight into eyes of an imagined filmgoing audience.

In the sequences that follow, Sanderville appears wholly at ease in front of the camera, exhibiting an extraordinary fluency in both the primitive language of signs and the modern language of cinema. After demonstrating three extended stories accompanied by written translations—"The Chief's Daughter," "The Buffalo Lodge Exchange," and "Buffalo Hunt"—he inserts a shot of a chalkboard that serves as a makeshift title card at the conclusion of the film. "JULY 11, 1934. SMITHSONIAN INSTITUTION. RICHARD SANDERVILLE, OR CHIEF BULL, SIGN TALKER," it reads, scrawled in what appears to be Sanderville's own hand, accompanied by a hand-drawn pictograph of a bull, his Blackfeet namesake. This last shot, a visual signature of sorts, seems intentionally provocative. From sign talk to alphabetic writing to pictography to cinema—Sanderville's film essentially records a comprehensive genealogy of human communications technologies. But rather than recapitulating the conventional narrative of media evolution, the chalkboard insert suggests that these technologies are contemporaneous analogues, systems of cultural communication that coexist and overlap while captured onscreen. From Sanderville's vantage point, then, sign talk hardly embodies a vestige of the primitive past. Responding to a tradition of ethnological thought that had long figured Native Americans as a perpetual past to audiovisual media's ongoing present, his films for the Bureau of Ethnology assert sign talk as a living language. Although that language remains "endangered" today, it hasn't completely disappeared. Eighty years later, contra Mallery, Scott, and an entire generation of anthropological thinkers, PISL lives on in the face of the media advances that have time and again appeared to mark its demise.

What, finally, are we to make of this tangled lineage—from Mallery's adoption of Muybridge's chronophotographic aesthetic, to Scott's seemingly instinctive recourse to film, to Sanderville's forays into cinematic self-preservation? What, ultimately, are we to make of the continued historical attraction between Indian sign talk, this most "primitive" of cultural languages, and the period's most "modern" media technologies? The field of deaf studies offers preliminary answers to this set of questions. Scholars have long championed the importance of moving images to the history of American Sign Language.[85] According to Christopher Krentz, because American Sign Language is rooted in a shared tradition of embodied performance—rather than in a fixed set of written texts, like standard English—the cinematic revolution of the early twentieth century did for the deaf what the print revolution of the early fifteenth century did for the West. Film codified and standardized formerly variable sign language practices; it fostered a common sense of identity among deaf signers scattered across the country; and, at least for a time, it helped move deaf culture in America from the social margins into the social mainstream.[86]

Yet the exact opposite is true for Native Americans and PISL during this same period. The birth of modern film technology in fact coincided with a nadir in the story of U.S.–Indian relations, the moment when the western frontier and the people who lived there were allegedly "closed" to the American nation for good.[87] For Mallery and Scott, at least, the cinematic impulse clearly stemmed from a basic certainty about sign talk's eventual disappearance, from an implicit acquiescence to the broader social forces that were allegedly rendering the language useless. So as much as Mallery's chronophotographic images seem to preserve faint traces of sign talk in motion—and as much the Bureau of Ethnology's films appear to bring PISL back to life—these preservationist documents also tacitly mark the passage of Indian culture into history. More to the point, although serial photography and cinema may well create the illusion of a Native American sign language moving and communicating in real time, that time is, almost by definition, wholly consigned to the past tense.[88]

For these reasons, the relationship between PISL and cinema appears far more fraught. Widespread certainty about sign talk's obsolescence—indeed, widespread certainty about the disappearance of Native Americans themselves—forced the language's confrontation with what were perceived to be more modern forms of media, decades before the earliest documentary films of American Sign Language and its European counterparts even appeared. Yet at the same time, the collision between these two communications technologies seems historically overdetermined, almost inevitable. Both PISL and the cinema were initially (and also incorrectly) regarded as "universal" languages.[89] Even more importantly, both PISL and the cinema support two of the West's foundational narratives of evolution: one cultural, the other media-technological. During the nineteenth century, Indian sign talk represented a primitive historical starting point for all linguistic and cultural communication. During the twentieth century, the cinema seemed to emerge as a modern historical end point for an era of extraordinary technological and communicative innovation. Each narrative reinforces the other: cultural evolution reinforces media evolution, and vice versa—primitive forms of communication were integral to the authority of the media technologies that outwardly seemed to signal their obsolescence. As I demonstrate in the chapters that follow, this dialectical relationship proved central to the anthropological project of racial documentation.

3

Originals and Aboriginals

Race and Writing in the Age of the Phonograph

ore than a third of the way through *The Grandissimes* (1880),
his classic novel of racial politics in nineteenth-century New
Orleans, George Washington Cable interrupts his narrative to
address his readers directly, lamenting his inability to reproduce the sounds
of the Louisiana Creole dialect in writing. "Alas," he exclaims at the beginning of chapter 25,

> the phonograph was invented three-quarters of a century too late. If type
> could entrap one-half the pretty oddities of Aurora's speech,—the arch, the
> pathetic, the grave, the earnest, the matter-of-fact, the ecstatic tones of her
> voice,—nay, could it but reproduce the movement of her hands, the elo-
> quence of her eyes, or the shapings of her mouth,—ah! but type—even the
> phonograph—is such an inadequate thing![1]

Even if Cable's final aside about the phonograph's insufficiency was more
of an editorial afterthought than a statement of conviction, the sequence
is arresting, almost shocking, buried as it is in a novel that goes to inordi-
nate lengths to "entrap" and "reproduce" the sounds of the human voice.[2]

In fact, what nineteenth-century readers found compelling about Cable
wasn't his vivid dramatization of the history of New Orleans in *The
Grandissimes* or his controversial view on racial inequality in the post-
Reconstruction South, but his apparent facility with the strange sounds of

French Creole and African American speech. According to contemporaneous reviews, the precision of Cable's dialect orthography was unmatched.
Contrary to his claims about the shortcomings of the written word, commentators regularly asserted that *The Grandissimes*—not unlike Thomas Edison's "fabulous phonograph," invented only three years prior—reproduced
vernacular sound with nothing less than perfect fidelity. The *Atlantic Monthly*
praised Cable's early fiction for the way "French and Spanish creoles, negroes,
half-breed Indians, and *Americains* of every grade circulate gaily through
the pages . . . and 'we hear them speak each in his own tongue,' for the
author's mastery over mongrel dialects is something marvelous. Surely
never before were such novel and varied vocal effects represented by the
twenty-six letters of the English alphabet and a few italics and apostrophes."[3] An anonymous writer for the *Literary World* testified that "a close
enunciation of [Cable's] words as spelled will be found to bring out the
dialect with wonderful precision, and to set the mongrel-blooded speakers
before the imagination with the reality of life. In this, it seems to us, is
Mr. Cable's strong point, though we should be sorry to be understood as
limiting his powers to a mere repetition of strange talk."[4] When reviewers
dissented, they did so on the grounds that novels like *The Grandissimes*
invested in dialect at the expense of easy reading.[5] It wasn't that Cable's
fictional voices were unrealistic. Rather, his approximations were so true
to life that they taxed the patience of the casual reader and bordered on
the unintelligible. Cable's white Creole audience was especially sensitive to
this last charge, defensively criticizing *The Grandissimes* for rendering their
voices with such intricate and vivid realism that they appeared to speak
in a nonsensical "lingo"—one that they were only accustomed to hearing
from the mouths of immigrants and former slaves.[6]

In short, nineteenth-century readers found little cause to differentiate
Cable's talking book from Edison's talking machine, and given such a narrow range of critical responses, it seems surprising that a writer of Cable's
reputation would take pains to underscore the insufficiency of his attempts
to reproduce the sounds of the human voice. Why, then, does *The Grandissimes* turn to the phonograph, a new technology with an uncertain social
future, in the way that it does? When, and on what basis, did judgments of
vernacular "precision" and auditory "fidelity" begin to matter to the U.S.
literary public? More generally, how and why did we come to recognize

the phonograph as a reliable medium for capturing the evanescent sounds of culture, whereas the dialect novel—a representational technology that clearly existed in a contiguous cultural field in Cable's day—now seems to embody something far less trustworthy?

My contention in this chapter is that our ongoing faith in the phonograph's cultural authority stems from sound technology's apparent ability to mediate racial differences, an idea that has origins in the salvage ethnographic project. Cable's seemingly digressive aside in *The Grandissimes* echoes a common late-nineteenth-century refrain about the inherently unfaithful relationship between the written word and its cultural sound sources—what we might call ethnographic *hearing loss*.[7] A diverse group of American writers and anthropologists discussed this problem with increasing urgency in this period. Their attempts to solve it, I argue, played a pivotal role in establishing qualitative documentary differences between culture preserved on wax and culture preserved on paper.

According to media theorists like Friedrich Kittler, the print medium's auditory failings would have only seemed pressing to a writer like Cable because the reproduction of empirical "sense data" was rapidly becoming the province of new media technologies.[8] To be sure, Edison's talking machine alerted a number of late-nineteenth-century writers to the limitations of the printed page. Cable, for his part, began making arrangements for the serialization of the manuscript that became *The Grandissimes* in summer 1878, just months after Edison unveiled the "acoustical marvel of the century."[9] His recognition of type as an "inadequate thing," unable to capture the sounds of a vanishing people, would seem to suggest that the invention of the phonograph, per Kittler, marked the precise moment at which "the dream of a real . . . audible world arising from words has come to an end."[10] Yet Cable's turn away from writing and print in *The Grandissimes* may also register a crisis of representation of a different sort, for the "pretty oddities" of the Creole vernacular voice, their resistance to standard approaches to phonetic listening and written documentation, are presumably what motivate the novel's interest in the possibilities of the phonograph in the first place. One finds similar ideas about cultural difference and sound reproduction dormant in Cable's dialect fiction and ethnographic writings well into the late 1880s, and he wasn't alone in this line of thinking. Amplified by a widespread sense that many of the world's cultures were on the brink of extinction, the sounds of their languages and musical traditions never to be heard again, Cable's doubts about the written word resonated across a wide range of salvage ethnographic discourses: from anthropology to linguistics, ethnomusicology to folklore studies.

In this chapter, I demonstrate that nineteenth-century reservations about the print medium's relationship to the sound of culture weren't merely the product of the phonograph's arrival, as more deterministic models of media history would seem to suggest. Ideas about hearing loss, even the documentary promise of phonographic sound fidelity itself, in fact developed in tandem with the ethnographic practice of documenting difference.[11] It was only after early dialect writers, anthropologists, and ethnomusicologists began attempting to preserve the sounds of vanishing cultures that the phonograph began to emerge as an authentic reproducer of the real. More to the point, it was only after nineteenth-century intellectuals recognized that the acts of listening and writing are culturally situated, even racially determined, that the new technology of mechanical sound reproduction made the old medium of the written word appear, in Cable's phrase, "an inadequate thing."

With this end in mind, the first half of this chapter addresses Cable's writing and its immediate historical context, situating *The Grandissimes* alongside an array of late-nineteenth-century literary and ethnographic writings that explicitly call attention to the challenge of documenting the sounds of speech and music cross-culturally. For Cable, as for a number of American ethnologists working in the field at the time, the auditory limitations of the print medium represented a symptom of a far more basic problem: humanity's inability to comprehend objectively, on their own terms, the particularities of racial and cultural difference. The writings of the anthropologist Franz Boas will become pivotal in my account here—particularly his landmark 1889 essay "On Alternating Sounds," which posited that ethnographic observers are unable to hear the sounds of cultural groups outside of their own without filtering them through preconditioned perceptual biases. What Boas had discovered, and Cable had seemingly intuited, was that cultures are effectively deaf to each other. The ethnographic documentation of language and music thus appeared to be compromised from the very start, for how can one salvage the sounds of a vanishing race without the ability to hear them accurately in the first place? This question would eventually become central to debates about the merits of cultural relativism in the first half of the twentieth century, as writers and anthropologists began attempting to rid the modern project of "writing culture" from subjective preconceptions and ethnocentric prejudices.[12] But in earlier Gilded Age narratives like Cable's *The Grandissimes,* as we will see, the cultural politics of listening surfaced in more subtle ways, both formal and thematic.

It was primarily in response to new relativist theories of listening that writers and ethnologists across the United States began to turn their attention to the phonograph, a new technology that seemed to offer a degree of cultural detachment that the written word could not. In the second half of this chapter, I consider the late-nineteenth-century practice of audio ethnography, which sought to harness the phonograph's documentary possibilities and capture the "fugitive sounds" of difference—an intellectual mission that both Cable and Boas prefigured.[13] Within the parameters of audio ethnography, cultural sounds that had long been regarded as resistant to written notation (African American dialects, for instance, or American Indian languages and musical forms) were instead preserved mechanically, by a new technology of listening and writing that appeared to be uncontaminated by the biases of the ear and the pen. The work of Jesse Walter Fewkes and Benjamin Ives Gilman, two audio ethnographers not ordinarily examined in dialogue with more canonical figures like Cable and Boas, will become important for us here as well. Along with a number of their interlocutors in nineteenth-century ethnology, philology, and ethnomusicology, both Fewkes and Gilman were instrumental in framing the phonograph as an ideal cultural listener: as an unmediated medium that could objectively record the auditory data of difference, even as much as its mechanically reproduced product remained severed from the presence of human sources.[14] When compared to the limitations of the dialect novel and the ethnographic field note—limitations that were as much cultural as technological, as much a pitfall of the message as of the medium— the phonograph appeared to embody a more universal form of cultural preservation.

In the end, Cable's turn to the phonograph in *The Grandissimes* was by no means a foregone conclusion at the end of the nineteenth century. The ethnographic value of early sound technology only emerged out of considerable debate, amid widespread controversy over the auditory fidelity of phonograph recordings and the material instability of the phonographic medium. For late-nineteenth-century writers and anthropologists, the "lower frequencies" of race and culture, to borrow Ralph Ellison's famous turn of phrase, exposed the ethnographic limits of the ear and the pen: this forced writing to give way to writing technology; art to give way to science; the human, ultimately, to give way to the machine.[15] The intellectual affinities between Cable and Boas allow us to begin to chart this series of transformations.

Hearing Lost

Though set in New Orleans at the time of the Louisiana Purchase, George Washington Cable's *The Grandissimes* (1880) was largely conceived as an artistic response to the rise of the Jim Crow South. As Cable stressed throughout his career, the novel represented an attempt to dramatize the realities of the color line after radical Reconstruction. "It was impossible that a novel written by me then [the late 1870s] should escape being a study of the fierce struggle going on around me," he later wrote in an unpublished autobiographical essay. "I meant to make *The Grandissimes* as truly a political work as it had ever been called. . . . I wrote as near to truth and justice as I knew how, upon questions that I saw must be settled by calm debate and cannot be settled by force or silence; questions that will have to be settled thus by the Southern white man in his own conscience before ever the North and South can finally settle it between them. This was part of my politics and as a citizen I wrote."[16] By 1882, according to one contemporary observer, *The Grandissimes* had firmly established Cable as "the most cordially hated little man" in Louisiana.[17]

Cable's antiracist politics were somewhat extraordinary given his personal background. Born to a slaveholding family in 1844, Cable grew up in New Orleans and went on to fight for the Confederacy during the Civil War. "Slow to learn," as he later put it, "what boundless ability men and communities everywhere have for deceiving themselves," his political change of heart came during the early 1870s while reporting on Louisiana's public school system for the New Orleans *Picayune*.[18] The experience led him to adopt a forward-looking stance against segregation that would find its most coherent and lasting form a decade later in essays like "The

Freedman's Case in Equity" (1885), "The Silent South" (1885), and "The Negro Question" (1888), all of which were written for mainstream periodicals that catered to Northern audiences.[19] The Southern backlash against his work may have hastened his decision to move his family to Northampton, Massachusetts, in 1886.

Both by necessity and by design, however, Cable cautiously shrouded the ideological subtext of *The Grandissimes* in what the novel's narrator calls "an atmosphere of hints, allusions, faint unspoken admissions, ill-concealed antipathies, unfinished speeches, mistaken identities and whisperings of hidden strife" (96). Displacing the novel's temporal backdrop was one way of submerging the inflammatory critique of the Southern order it contained. And aside from the inclusion of a few statements of overt social protest voiced through the mouth of his German immigrant protagonist, Joseph Frowenfeld, Cable's progressive racial viewpoint mostly operates on the level of political allegory, which surfaces in the novel's two main plot lines.[20] The first, the novel's "white" plot line, revolves around Frowenfeld's relationship with Honoré Grandissime, the favored son of a powerful French Creole family whose social and economic standing begins to crumble with the coming of American rule to the Louisiana territory. The second narrative trajectory, the novel's "black" plot line, centers on Frowenfeld's relationship with Honoré's estranged half brother—also named Honoré—a free man of color whose mixed ancestry further threatens the sanctity of the Grandissime lineage. At bottom, the brothers Honoré function as symbolic testaments to Louisiana's violent multiracial past and present. The "twinning" of their names and stories—a narrative strategy that anticipates the plot structure of Mark Twain's more celebrated *Pudd'nhead Wilson* (1894)—reflects Cable's earliest convictions about the injustices of slavery, the failed promises of Reconstruction, and the mutual interdependence of African Americans and whites living in the postbellum South.

Ultimately, *The Grandissimes* brings together this constellation of ideological concerns in the "dark story" of Bras-Coupé, an interpolated tale about a West African–born slave who is violently executed after assaulting his master and living as a fugitive on the outskirts of New Orleans (168). Cable often referred to Bras-Coupé's fictional rebellion, which takes place eight years before the novel's main frame of action begins, as the novel's moral and political "foundation."[21] Based on a local Louisiana folk legend, the story is recounted at several key points in the text, further grounding *The Grandissimes* in a New World "tradition of marronage and insurrection," as Barbara Ladd has argued.[22]

The political significance of the *Grandissimes* project has generally tended to overshadow the novel's ethnographic ambitions. Cable conceived of the book's basic architecture around 1877, just as he began making formal research forays into the local culture of southeastern Louisiana alongside the folk historian Lafcadio Hearn.[23] Above all, Cable's curiosity centered on the region's racially mixed vernacular folkways, particularly as they were expressed in French and African Creole languages and musical forms. As Hearn colorfully put it several years later, the strange sounds that visitors heard in the streets and parlors of New Orleans were the product of a vital history of "linguistic miscegenation" that seemed to be dissipating as the nineteenth century drew to a close.[24] Cable, for his part, attempted to capture this state of affairs in *The Grandissimes* by having his characters speak in a startling array of local dialects and hybrid linguistic deformities— ranging from standard English and French to French Creole appropriations of English, African Creole patois (a mix of French and West African tongues popularly referred to as "Gumbo"), and a version of "black English" derived from philological renderings of slave dialect in the low country of Virginia.[25] The final product embodies a form of what we might call *literary polydialectalism*, at times switching back and forth between several different speech codes in the span of mere sentences.

Of equal ethnographic import are the novel's varied attempts to incorporate traditional Afro-Creole slave songs and spirituals, which Cable began collecting with Hearn while working on a collaborative history of New Orleans's Congo Square during this same period.[26] Cable pursued venues for publishing his Creole music transcriptions as early as February 1878. While in the final stages of drafting his first collection of short stories, *Old Creole Days* (1879), he wrote to his editors at Scribner, Armstrong, and Company that he possessed "a lot of old Creole songs gathered with great difficulty . . . strangers to printer's ink" and wanted to "quote from these at the head of each story."[27] The musical headnotes idea, which presages W. E. B. Du Bois's oft-discussed introductory technique in *The Souls of Black Folk* (1903), never materialized. But the melodies would find their way

into the final manuscript of *The Grandissimes* two years later, both as fragments of italicized lyrics in Cable's prose and as staff-notated musical transcriptions spilling out into the margins of the page (see Figure 12).

The Congo Square research later formed the foundation for two landmark essays that Cable wrote for the *Century* magazine in 1886, "The Dance
in Place Congo" and "Creole Slave Songs," both of which would furnish
crucial material for twentieth-century historians of jazz and modern American music.[28] Yet it was primarily in reference to Cable's earlier use of the
Creole slave transcriptions that Hearn would deem *The Grandissimes* "the
most remarkable work of fiction ever created in the South . . . a genre
study of inimitable verisimilitude," even with the knowledge that Cable's
final manuscript hadn't actually lived up to its full ethnographic promise.[29]
(Cable had apparently planned on scattering as many as fifty of the Congo
Square transcriptions throughout the text, yet the published version contains only nine.)[30] "We must specially call the attention of our readers
to the Creole songs and refrains, published with the music, throughout
the work," Hearn remarked. "They are very curious, and possess a special
philologic value. One, in particular, an African chant, sung by the negroes
in cutting down the cane, deserves special notice."[31] The anthropologist
Melville Herskovits echoed Hearn's sentiments in 1941 when he hailed *The
Grandissimes* as "one of the richest stores of data pertaining to Negro custom . . . hold[ing] special significance for research into the ethnography of
United States Negroes. Based on intimate knowledge of the locality and its
history, [the novel] must be accepted as a valid document if only on the
basis of comparative findings. It is thus a real contribution to our knowledge of life in this area during the time of slavery, and a book which investigations into present-day custom should take into careful account."[32]

Perhaps more so than any of his contemporaries, then, Cable's engagement with cultural sound had fundamentally ethnographic aspirations. As
many scholars of nineteenth-century U.S. literary history have pointed out,
the regional realist dialect movement was "politically various."[33] Not all of
its practitioners made use of the sound of vernacular culture in the same
way, or for the same underlying purposes. Whereas Plantation School writers like Thomas Nelson Page employed dialect out of nostalgia for the ante-
bellum racial order, segregating minority culture from the white mainstream on the level of language—and whereas African American writers

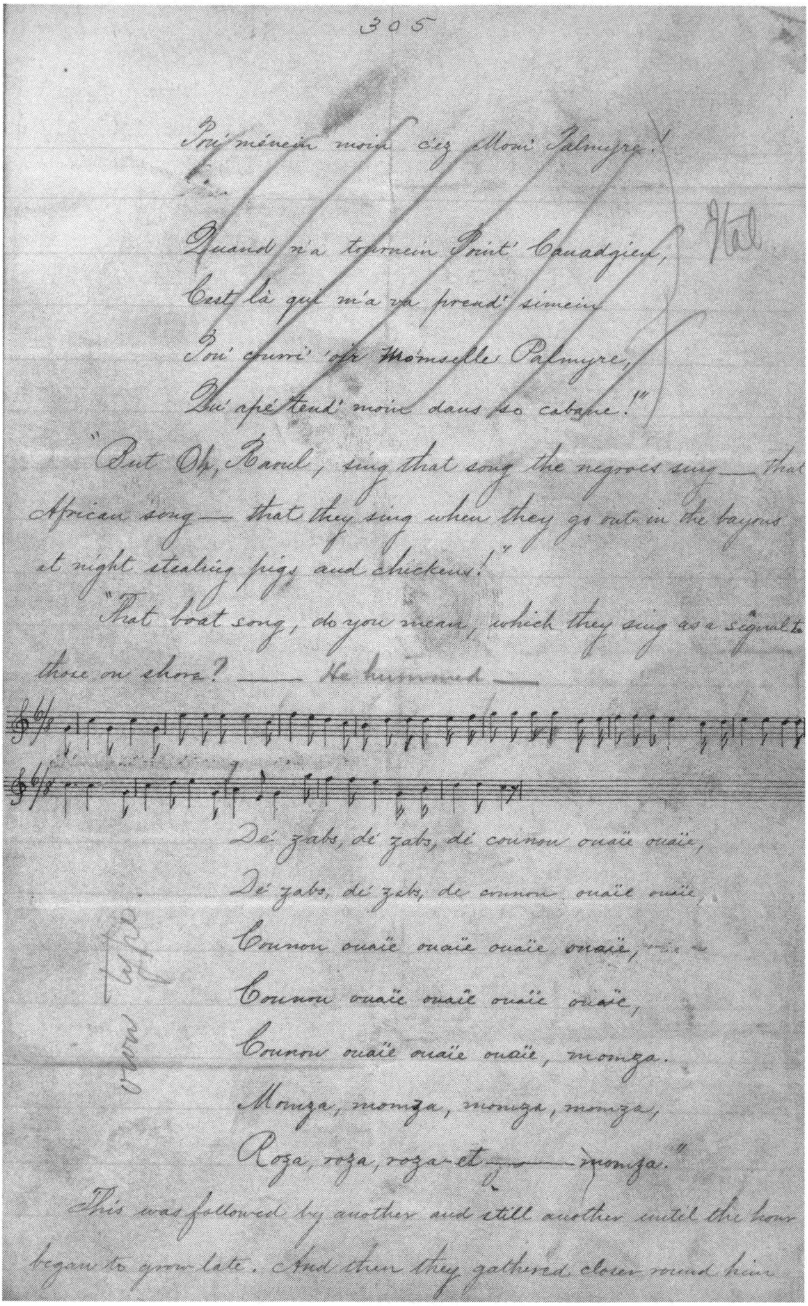

FIGURE 12 Printer's copy of George Washington Cable's *The Grandissimes* (circa 1879). George Washington Cable Papers (MS Am 1288.4), Houghton Library, Harvard University.

such as Charles Chesnutt and Paul Laurence Dunbar wrote in dialect to gain access to, and subtly critique, a popular literary marketplace from which their work was otherwise severed—Cable's "mongrel-blooded speakers" straddled both sides of the color line and were much more in keeping with anthropological investigations of language and music that were ongoing during the second half of the nineteenth century. As we will see, Cable's work had more in common with the newly emerging enterprise of audio ethnography than with the regional realist tradition as such.

Unquestionably, novels like *The Grandissimes* displayed much more than the customary regional realist "obsession with linguistic exactness," as Michael Elliott has described it.[34] Recent philological studies of Cable's orthography have found that his written approximations of French-Creole English and African-Creole patois in *The Grandissimes* were surprisingly accurate given his lack of training in phonetic shorthand.[35] Despite publicly taking up the position that "it is probably best that dialect should be sketched rather than photographed" (perhaps more to deflect questions about the readability of his fiction than to discount its true-to-life fidelity), Cable also made a point of writing a series of editorial letters to *The Critic* railing against a host of orthographical inconsistencies in Thomas Nelson Page's 1884 plantation story "Marse Chan."[36] "It does not appear to me to require much skill or art to string a lot of outlandish words and phrases together—or togedder—often as destitute of sense as of orthography, and call it a dialect," Cable wrote.[37] Crucially, for Cable, the issue was as much about racial politics as it was about phonetic accuracy. The problem with Page's dialect writing wasn't simply that it misrepresented the sounds of black American speech. Page had also committed the cardinal documentary sin of having his black characters speak in a stereotyped dialect, while his white characters somehow managed to stay in perfect tune with the King's English: "Why is it that they [dialect writers like Page] spell phonetically words which a Negro pronounces exactly the same as a white man does? For instance, the Caucasian will be made to say 'enough said'; the African, ''nuff sed.' Why shouldn't they both be written alike, at least as far as they go? They are pronounced so. . . . This is one evidence of how much nonsense there is in the whole system of dialect (?) writing."[38] As Gavin Jones has pointed out, perhaps Cable's most subversive literary practice—one consistent with his ethnographic interests, to be sure—was his tendency to approximate the "real" speech sounds of his fictional characters regardless of their racial origins or social status.[39]

On the whole, however, Cable left behind few clues as to how he conceptualized his orthographic practice. One of the glaring exceptions to this rule is the extended account of French-Creole English included at the end of Cable's 1884 historical study *The Creoles of Louisiana,* one of the many published products of his early work with Lafcadio Hearn:

> [New Orleans's] languid airs have induced in the Creole's speech great softness of utterance. The relaxed energies of a luxurious climate find publication, as it were, when he turns final *k* into *g;* changes *th,* and *t* when not initial, to *d;* final *p* to *b,* drops initial *h,* final *le,* and *t* after *k;* often, also the final *d* of past tenses; omits or distorts his *r,* and makes a languorous *z* of all *s*'s and soft *c*'s except initials. On the other hand, the old Gallic alertness and wire-edge still asserts itself in the confusing and interchanging of long *e* and short *i*—sheep for ship, and ship for sheep—in the flattening of long *i,* as if it were coming through cane-crushers, in the prolonging of long *a,* the intrusion of uncalled-for initial *h*'s, and the shortening and narrowing of nearly all long and broad vowels.[40]

Outside of the opening pages of "Creole Slave Songs," which appeared two years later, this is as close as one gets in Cable's work to a statement of method. More representative, perhaps, is the paragraph that immediately follows in *The Creoles of Louisiana.* Here Cable shifts his account to the Afro-Creole patois of the region's black population, and with it comes a noticeable shift in the text's mode of ethnographic address:

> The African slave in Louisiana—or, it may be more correct to say, in St. Domingo, before coming to Louisiana—corrupted the French tongue as grossly, or even more so, than he did the English in the rice plantations of South Carolina. No knowledge of scholarly French is a guarantee that the stranger will understand the "Creole" negro's *gombo.* To the Creole *sang pur* this dialect is an inexhaustible fountain of amusement. In the rural parishes the harsh archaisms of the Acadian perform the same office and divide the Creole's attention. But in "the City" the Acadian dialect is hardly known, and for a century or more the melodious drollery and grotesqueness of the

negro *patois* has made it the favorite vehicle of humorous song and satirical prose and verse. It would make a long chapter to untangle its confused mass of abbreviations, suppressions of inflections, *liasons,* nasalizations, omissions, inversions, startling redundancies, and original idioms.[41]

Although both of these passages from *The Creoles of Louisiana* are clearly grounded in close listening, Cable strangely makes no attempt to codify or transcribe the Afro-Creole sounds he is addressing here. The modifying descriptors that animate the first passage—"languorous," "soft," "hard," "long," "short," all of which attempt to supplement Cable's phonetic approximations and lift the printed text off the page toward the realm of spoken sound—are entirely absent in the second passage, and the final implication is that Cable's "long chapter" for documenting the distinctive sounds of Afro-Creole New Orleans remains unwritten. Black vernacular "*gombo*" is thus subtly placed outside the book's orthographical scheme, a move that may reflect an understanding of the idea—widely held at the time and also present in *The Grandissimes,* as we will see—that certain cultural sounds resist notation because outside listeners cannot hear them accurately. Here we arrive at the basic formal paradox that animates much of Cable's work for *The Grandissimes* and the *Century* (and *The Creoles of Louisiana,* for that matter): at the same time that the complexities of Cable's dialect writing seem to call attention to its ethnographic fidelity, subtle textual details suggest that dimensions of the vernacular voice necessarily fall beyond the reach of the observer's ear, beyond the reach of the print medium itself.

This, in any event, is the very same predicament with which Joseph Frowenfeld, the protagonist-hero of *The Grandissimes,* is faced at the beginning of Cable's narrative. We first meet Frowenfeld as he travels with his family down the Mississippi River into southeastern Louisiana, "a land hung in mourning, darkened by gigantic cypresses, submerged; a land of reptiles, silence, shadow, decay" (9). The novel's omniscient third-person narrator—to whom Cable twice refers as a "Recording Angel" in the opening pages, perhaps to underscore the book's documentary ambitions—initially lets us in on a conversation between Frowenfeld's father and a Creole boatman about the figure we later come to know as Bras-Coupé: "Yes, sir! Didn' I had to run from Bras Coupe in de haidge of de swamp be'ine de 'abitation of my cousin. . . . You can hask 'oo you like" (4–5, 10). The inclusion of the Creole dialect here is significant, if for no other reason than that it presents the reader with a phonetic transcription of speech sounds, rendered in "a *patois* difficult, but not impossible, to understand," that Frowenfeld cannot himself access (10). As the exchange continues, we also learn that Frowenfeld fails to hear these lines; the conversation remains just beyond the range of his ear. A similar play between hearing and not hearing surfaces later on in the chapter, when Frowenfeld struggles to follow the Afro-Creole patois of a nurse who helps him recover from yellow fever: "He was too weak to speak again, but asked with his eyes so persistently, and so pleadingly, that by and by she gave him an audible answer. He tried hard to understand it, but could not, it being in these words: '*Li pa' oulé vini 'ci—li pas capabe*'" (12).

These are seemingly minor details in the scope of the narrative, yet they are the first of several instances in *The Grandissimes* that would seem to connect the inability to hear culture with the inability to understand it, both within and against the more obvious issue of translation. Frowenfeld in fact remains in this precarious position throughout the first third of the novel. A few chapters later, as he listens to his primary local contact narrate the history of the Creole people in Louisiana, he finds himself similarly shut out: "To Frowenfeld—as it would have been to anyone, except a Creole or the most thoroughly Creoleized Américain—[the] narrative, when it was done, was little more than a thick mist of strange names, places and events. . . . Frowenfeld's interest rose—was allured into this mist—and was there left befogged" (15). Later on he is told that he must learn the language of the Creoles, both black and white, to close this cultural gap— he must listen to the unfamiliar rhythms of their speech and uncover the hidden psychology behind their failing social order: "You must get acclimated . . . not in body only, that you have done; but in mind—in taste—in conversation. . . . They all do it—all who come" (37). But despite his best efforts, certain aspects of the local culture—usually those that raise the specter of the color line—forever seem to elude his comprehension. When he first encounters the "weird, drowsy throb of the African song and dance" (96) ongoing in Congo Square, for instance, his train of thought is disrupted and he is forced to close his ears. At this point in the text, Frowenfeld can hear only "discord, faint but persistent" (96), which ultimately prevents him from discovering what Cable would later famously call the "affluence of bitter meaning" hidden beneath the music.[42]

In part, Cable includes these details to signal Frowenfeld's status as a participant–observer in the drama that unfolds, an archetype of the cultural outsider that was just then beginning to take shape as the fledgling discipline of ethnology struggled to leave behind its "armchair phase" and institutionalize the practice of fieldwork.[43] Crucially, this position also mirrors that of Cable himself as he worked with Hearn to find ways to preserve the sounds of New Orleans and Congo Square. And just as the fictional Frowenfeld eventually gives up his attempts to capture the community's daily life in an all-encompassing historical almanac—the "newly found book, the Community of New Orleans . . . [written] in a strange tongue," an "unwriteable volume" (103, 137)—Cable's narration, too, often openly founders when attempting to transcribe vernacular sounds he deems too unfamiliar for the ordinary ear: "Who could hope to catch and reproduce . . . the sweet broken English with which she now and then interrupted him; also the inward, hidden sparkle of her dancing Gallic blood; her low, merry laugh; the roguish mental reservation that lurked behind her graver speeches; the droll bravados she uttered against the powers that be," the narrating "Recording Angel" asks as Frowenfeld converses with Aurora, a Creole woman who later emerges as the white Honoré's secret love interest. "These things, we say, we let go,—as we let butterflies go rather than pin them to paper" (91–92). Both here and elsewhere, Cable's doubling of author and protagonist seems to suggest that writing the sound of culture is not merely a matter of language and translation, a matter of signifiers and signifieds. It is, at times, a more elemental matter of hearing and perception—a matter as fragile and fleeting as a butterfly in flight.

Alternating Sounds

Cable was hardly alone in his sense that print media were unable to "catch and reproduce" vernacular sound at the end of the 1800s. Nor was he alone in his sense that problems of cross-cultural listening were intimately linked to problems of cross-cultural understanding. Frowenfeld's outsider status throughout *The Grandissimes* anticipates important ideas about auditory perception and racial difference that would begin to take root in American

anthropological circles as the nineteenth century drew to a close. The closest point of intellectual contact here is Franz Boas's landmark 1889 essay
"On Alternating Sounds," which examines a phenomenon that real-life
Joseph Frowenfelds encountered with puzzling frequency while attempting to advance the salvage project: the tendency for indigenous languages
and dialects to contain variable—or "alternating"—pronunciations of simple words and phrases.[44]

Boas first noted the phenomenon of the alternating sound during his
initial efforts to document Indian languages in British Columbia and the
Pacific Northwest during the mid-1880s. As Boas recounts in the text of the
1889 "Alternating Sounds" essay, his phonetic rendering of the Tsimshian
word for "fear" inexplicably tended to fluctuate between two discrepant
pronunciations: *päc* and *bas*.[45] Similarly, his field notes on Inuit Eskimo dialects contained an inventory of common words that his native informants
appeared to enunciate with little regularity: *operníving, upernívik, uperdnívik;
kikertákdjua, kekertákdjuak, kekertáktuak; nertsédluk, neqtsédluk,* and so on.[46]
American ethnologists found themselves baffled by these sorts of phonetic
"alternations" throughout the 1870s and 1880s. Boas's longtime correspondent at the Bureau of Ethnology, John Wesley Powell, had warned fieldworkers of the problem as early as 1877. "Much difficulty is sometimes
occasioned by the indefinite character of some of the sounds of a language,"
Powell remarked in the opening pages of the *Introduction to the Study of
Indian Languages*. "In the Hidatsa there is a sound of such a character that
the English student cannot decide to which of the sounds represented by
b, w, or *m* it is most nearly allied; and there is another which the student
cannot distinguish from *l, n, r,* or *d* . . . . Such sounds are very common in
Indian tongues and occasion no little difficulty to collectors."[47]

Somewhat predictably, Powell and his contemporaries interpreted the
phenomenon of the "synthetic" or "alternating" sound through the lens of
cultural evolution. At the time, the consensus among American ethnologists was that variations in phonetic pronunciation were survivals from a
more rudimentary phase in the history of human communication.[48] Much
like the indigenous sign languages we encountered in chapter 2, alternating sounds appeared to represent primitive vestiges of civilized society's
collective past, holdovers from an earlier stage of linguistic and cultural
development. The more consistent the phonetics of a language, the logic

went, the higher the stage of its evolutionary maturity—the more advanced
its place in the historical continuum from orality to literacy, savagery to
civilization. "The primitive speech of man was far more rudimentary than
any language known to us," wrote the ethnologist Daniel Garrison Brinton in 1888, summarizing the viewpoint of the evolutionists. "So fluctuating were its phonetics . . . that its words could not have been reduced to
writing, nor arranged in alphabetic sequence."[49]

Boas's essay was in part conceived as an attempt to refute this ethnocentric stance, marshaling an impressive range of evidence to suggest that
evolutionist interpretations of the alternating sounds phenomenon were
actually the product of a faulty ethnographic methodology. The thesis was
based on two related observations. First, after a thorough examination
of his field notes and published writings, Boas came to realize that there
were actually clear patterns in the variable pronunciations that seemed
to frustrate his documentary efforts—patterns that depended not on the
primitive speech system under consideration but on the native language
and nationality of the ethnographic observer who had attempted to com-
mit it to paper. "It is found that the [transcribed] vocabularies of collectors,
although they may apply diacritical marks or special alphabets, bear evidence of the phonetics of their own language," Boas posited. "This can be
explained only by the fact that each apperceives the unknown sounds by
the means of the sounds of his own language."[50] This pivotal finding suggested, second, that inbuilt cultural biases may in fact influence the act of
listening. Speech sounds are not always heard in the same manner in which
they are spoken—they are mediated, and at times distorted, by the languages
and sounds that we already know.[51] *Päc* and *bas*; *operniving, upernívik,* and
uperdnívik; *kikertákdjua, kekertákdjuak,* and *kekertáktuak*: in the end, what
at first seem like variable pronunciations are, in reality, culturally conditioned "mishearings," impositions of familiar phonetic combinations onto
unfamiliar speech sounds that fall wholly outside of orthographic convention. "There is no such phenomenon as synthetic or alternating sounds,"
Boas went on to conclude. "Their occurrence is in no way a sign of the
primitiveness of the speech in which they are said to occur. . . . Alternating
sounds are in reality *alternating apperceptions* of one and the same sound."[52]
In short, the alternating sound represented a problem of transcription rather
than a problem of expression, a defective manner of listening and writing

rather than an inconsistent manner of speaking. For Boas, it was a mere illusion—a fault in perception brought about by an ethnographer's inability to avoid filtering sensory information through his or her own culturally conditioned patterns of thought.

Boas termed this perceptual impasse *sound-blindness*: the inability to hear and write, as he described it, "the essential peculiarities of certain sounds" situated in certain contexts.[53] He would elaborate on the idea more fully in his 1911 preface to *The Handbook of American Indian Languages*, reverting to a mode of address that resembles Powell's account of the Hidatsa tongue in *Introduction to the Study of Indian Languages* and Cable's account of Afro-Creole patois in *The Creoles of Louisiana*:

> Certain sounds that occur in American languages are interpreted by observers sometimes as one European sound, sometimes as another. Thus the Pawnee language contains a sound which may be heard more or less distinctly sometimes as an *l*, sometimes an *r*, sometimes as *n*, and again as *d*, which, however, without any doubt, is throughout the same sound, although modified to a certain extent by its position in the word and by surrounding sounds. It is actually an exceedingly weak *r*, made by trilling with the tip of the tongue at a point a little behind the roots of the incisors, and in which the tongue hardly leaves the palate, the trill being produced by the lateral part of the tongue adjoining the tip. As soon as the trill is heard more strongly, we receive the impression of an *r*. When the lateral movement prevails and the tip of the tongue does not seem to leave the palate, the impression of an *l* is strongest, while when the trill is almost suppressed and a sudden release of the tongue from the palate takes place, the impression of the *d* is given. The impression of an *n* is produced because the sound is often accompanied by an audible breathing through the nose. This peculiar sound is, of course, entirely foreign to our phonetic system. . . . The different impression is brought about by the fact that the sound, according to its prevailing character, associates itself either with our *l*, or our *r*, *n*, or *d*.[54]

For Boas, then, the problem of the alternating sound is one of enculturation. Ethnographic observers are unable to hear the speech sounds of cultural groups outside of their own without mapping them onto the speech sounds to which they are already accustomed. The net result is a form of phonetic and cultural interference, a form of hearing loss. Boas's explanation even seems to bear witness to this idea on the level of form, as well. Despite his microscopic attention to physiological and phonetic detail in *The Handbook of American Indian Languages,* one gets the sense that the Pawnee *r/l/n/d* eludes his descriptive capacities altogether. Without the ability to strip the ethnographic observer of his mental habits and predispositions, efforts to preserve the disappearing sound of culture seemed flawed from the very start.

The importance of the alternating sounds thesis to the development of salvage ethnography during the late nineteenth century, from the dialect novel to the phonograph, cannot easily be overstated. If dialect writers like Cable and ethnologists like Boas had anything in common, it was that they seem to have had very little faith in the accuracy of the cultural sounds they were hearing, and even less faith in their ability to transpose them onto the page.[55] Mediated through human perception—and thus the unstable domain of culture—to the extent that written texts were, the real sounds of human difference seemed impossibly "fugitive."[56] This was the position that the philologist J. A. Harrison would take up in 1884 while working on a comprehensive phonetic glossary of what he termed "Negro English," a genre of salvage documentation that was common at the time. Harrison complained, "It has been impossible to register scientifically the varied phenomena of Negro phonetics or to re-produce the quite indescribable intonation with which [Negro] sounds are uttered; but an effort has been made to approximate a correct re-production of the pronunciation by an imitative orthography and by key-words serving to show the dialectal variations of various localities."[57] Anticipating Boas's idea of sound-blindness, Harrison eventually termed this phenomenon of documentary failure *otosis*—literally, "mishearing," or chronic "error of the ear."[58] He had also made similar claims in "The Creole Patois of Louisiana" (1882), a study of local New Orleans dialects that Cable in fact read in preparation for his research on Congo Square.[59] Earlier still, in an influential 1867 essay on "Negro Spirituals," Thomas Wentworth Higginson explained that his orthographical system for transcribing song lyrics necessarily settled for approximation rather than accuracy: "The words [of the songs] will be here given, as nearly as possible in the original dialect; and if the spelling seems sometimes inconsistent, or the misspelling insufficient, it is because I could get no nearer."[60]

The folklorist John Mason Brown simply capitulated that "to convey a correct idea of Negro pronunciation by ordinary rules of orthography is almost impossible."[61]

That both Higginson and Brown articulate their reservations about hearing and writing dialect in the context of essays on slave songs and spirituals is no accident: during the nineteenth century, interest in documenting the sound of speech was inseparable from interest in documenting the sound of music.[62] As early as 1862, Lucy McKim Garrison famously conceded that the medium of the written text was an inadequate tool for dealing with the unfamiliar complexities of the black American spiritual. "It is difficult to express the entire character of these negro ballads by mere musical notes and signs," she admitted. "The odd turns made in the throat; and the curious rhythmic effect produced by single voices chiming in at different irregular intervals, seem almost as impossible to place on score, as the singing of birds, or the tones of an Aeolian Harp."[63] In *Slave Songs of the United States* (1867)—a landmark anthology of musical transcriptions that also contains an extended, and often overlooked, philological account of the black "Port Royal" dialects of the Carolina Sea Islands—William Allen made a similar series of claims: "The best we can do . . . with paper and types, or even with voices, will convey but a faint shadow of the original. The voices of the colored people have a peculiar quality that nothing can imitate; and the intonations and delicate variations of even one singer cannot be reproduced on paper."[64]

Recognitions of the print medium's inability to evoke vernacular sound—what Ronald Radano has called "partiality"—were hardly limited to Euro-American encounters with African American music, however.[65] Nineteenth-century commentators echoed these kinds of sentiments in attempts to document all manner of exotic sounds, and the rhetoric generally worked to codify ideas about the familiar and the foreign in an age of increasing interracial contact. In the United States, for instance, the issue of sound-blindness also pervaded ongoing anthropological debates about the character of Native American languages and musical practices. The ethnologist Alice Cunningham Fletcher, for instance, wrote candidly of her struggles to hear the music of the Omaha tribe, which seemed more like chaotic noise than an organized system of expression: "Although from habit as a student I had endeavored to divest myself of preconceived ideas and to rise above prejudice and distaste, I found it difficult to penetrate beneath the noise and hear what the people were trying to express. I think I may safely say that I heard little or nothing of Indian music the first three or four times that I attended dances or festivals, beyond a screaming downward movement that was gashed and torn by the vehemently beaten drum."[66] Crucially, rather than attribute her difficulties to Indian backwardness, as many before her had, Fletcher would consciously place the blame on her inability to process the sounds of Native American music outside her own Eurocentric point of view: "The sound was distressing, and my interest in this music was not aroused until I perceived that this distress was peculiarly my own, everyone else was so enjoying himself (I was the only one of my race present) that I felt sure something was eluding my ears."[67] Boas himself expressed similar sentiments in an October 1886 diary entry, written while collecting songs and folktales among the Indian tribes of the Northwest Coast: "So far I have transcribed only one [Indian] melody. The melody is so foreign to me that I find it difficult to record, and I am very much out of practice."[68] The alternating sounds thesis, which on the surface dealt only with indigenous languages, likely evolved out of these sorts of musical encounters as well.

The observation that human hearing and written notation are inadequate for capturing "exotic" sounds was of course age-old. Radano has shown that isolated examples of this kind of thinking date back to the middle 1700s, perhaps even earlier, and in some ways terms like *sound-blindness* and *otosis* merely put technical labels on what may have seemed like common sense by the 1880s and 1890s.[69] Yet the crucial point here is that by the turn of the twentieth century, following Boas's methodological intervention, hearing loss had been formally diagnosed as a problem of the observer rather than a problem of the observed—a pivotal theoretical shift not only in the intellectual emergence of cultural relativism but also, as we will see, in the formation of new modern techniques for preserving sound itself. When Cable complained of the written word's auditory failures, even when he made the seemingly minor choice to supplement the written manuscript of *The Grandissimes* with musical staff notation, he was thus tapping into a much more complicated set of debates about the "audio–racial" limits of human perception and written representation, a set of debates that transcended any simple black–white binary.[70] Perhaps nowhere in Cable's novel are these issues more apparent than in his rendering of the "dark story" of Bras-Coupé (168).

"The Story of Bras-Coupé," the point in *The Grandissimes* at which all of Cable's divergent narrative strands seem to converge, appears in chapters 28 and 29 of the novel, interrupting what is otherwise a linear plot structure. Preceded by a chapter that contains no less than three of the book's nine Creole slave song transcriptions—the last, "Dé Zabs," is accompanied by extensive musical notation (see Figure 12)—Bras-Coupé's tale enters, somewhat surprisingly, in total silence. Instead of "hearing" the story firsthand, we are only afforded an account in indirect discourse, which effectively distances us from the sound of its original speech sources:

> "A very little more than eight years ago," began Honoré—but not only Honoré, but Raoul also; and not only they, but another, earlier on the same day,—Honoré, the f.m.c. [free man of color]. But we shall not exactly follow the words of any one of these. Bras-Coupé, they said, had been, in Africa and under another name, a prince among his people. In a certain war of conquest, to which he had been driven by *ennui,* he was captured, stripped of his royalty, marched down upon the beach of the Atlantic, and, attired as a true son of Adam, with two goodly arms intact, became a commodity. (169)

At first glance, this rather unwieldy narrative device merely seems to be the product of artistic convenience. By "not exactly follow[ing] the words," Cable of course saves himself the work of having to write the entire tale in Creole dialect, which would have seriously jeopardized its readability. Moreover, because "The Story of Bras-Coupé" was in fact written as a stand-alone narrative as early as 1873, framing the tale in this way also helped Cable incorporate what was already a fully formed piece of fiction into the novel's overall plot structure. (A number of prominent publishers rejected the original manuscript, titled "Bibi," on account of its "unmitigatedly distressful effect," as one horror-struck editor at the *Atlantic Monthly* put it.)[71] But the fact that the tale is told multiple times—once by Honoré, once by Raoul, and once by Honoré's mixed-race half brother—is itself curious, and a closer look suggests that the entire story is in fact structured as a large-scale episode of ethnographic hearing loss. More to the point, we do not "follow the words" here because Cable cannot reproduce and preserve them in full.

This deficiency becomes more and more evident as the Bras-Coupé legend progresses throughout *The Grandissimes*. Recall that we first hear of Bras-Coupé in a brief conversation between Frowenfeld's father and a Creole boatman at the beginning of the novel. His name appears at several other early points in the text, always in passing, and when he finally appears "in the flesh" at the outset of chapter 28, Cable suddenly switches to a distant free indirect discourse, even going so far as to inscribe the sound of his name as a graphic absence in the body of the text: "His name, he replied to an inquiry touching that subject, was ——, something in the Jaloff [Wolof] tongue, which he by and by condescended to render into Congo: Mioko-Koanga, in French Bras-Coupé, the Arm Cut Off. . . . He made himself a type of all Slavery, turning into flesh and blood the truth that all Slavery is maiming" (171–72). As Bryan Wagner has argued, it is at this moment in the novel that Cable reveals both the speech sound of Bras-Coupé's name and the racial violence for which it stands as wholly "unavailable to representation."[72] Yet the fragment of song that Bras-Coupé sings to his bride, Palmyre Philosophe, later in the same chapter reads just as suggestively when compared with a similar transcription that Cable published five years later in "Creole Slave Songs":

"Ah! Suzette" in *The Grandissimes* (178)	"Ah! Suzette" in "Creole Slave Songs"[73]
En haut la montagne, zami,	M'al-lé haut montagne, zamie
Mo pé coupé canne, zami,	M'al-lé coupé canne, zamie
Pou' fé i'a'zen' zami,	M'al-lé fé l'a'-zent chére amie,
Pou' mo baille Palmyre.	Pou' po' té donne toi.
Ah! Palmyre, Palmyre mo c'ere,	Ah! Suzette, chère amie,
Mo l'aimé'ou'—mo l'aimé ou'.	To pas lai-mein moin.

Obviously these versions of "Ah! Suzette" differ in content and address, which accounts for some of the more obvious lyrical variations between them. But the subtle phonetic discrepancies in what appear to be the same Afro-Creole patois constructions in lines 3 and 6—*i'a'zen'/l'a'-zent* and *l'aimé/lai-mein*—directly bear witness to Boas's sound-blindness hypothesis, suggesting that the fugitive "partials" in Bras-Coupé's voice fail to map onto the orthographical techniques that Cable has at his disposal. Hearn would reproduce this same song in an 1885 essay for *Harper's Weekly* and offer yet another phonetic variation on the penultimate word in line 6: *l'aimin*.[74] Thus, just as the terrible realities of race and slavery in "The Story of Bras-Coupé" remain, even in multiple tellings, unavailable to us on the level of form, so, too, do the sounds of Bras-Coupé's language escape Cable's (and Hearn's) pen on the level of content. Bras-Coupé's story turns out to be the ethnographic truth that cannot be told. To tell it, ultimately, a more pure form of cultural listening, and a new form of cross-cultural writing, were necessary.

Hearing Found

Intellectual historians and literary critics have made passing note of the similarities between Cable's work and Boas's early ethnographic theories.[75] Yet they have generally failed to consider the wider network of "media relations" in which their shared interest in cross-cultural listening took shape.[76] Working in the wake of the alternating sounds thesis, American ethnologists proposed a variety of solutions to the problem of sound-blindness. Nearly all of them revolved around the assumption that ethnographic listeners needed to be liberated from their perceptual "shackles," as Boas referred to them, to capture and preserve the auditory dimensions of language and culture in full.[77] In the case of linguistic documentation, acquiring language fluency and teaching native speakers to write phoneti-cally were two possible options, but these seemed comparatively unrealis-tic given constraints on time and resources. In the context of musical study, the road was much less clear.[78]

The solution that eventually emerged on both fronts—and not with-out controversy—was the use of new sound reproduction technologies as culturally neutral substitutes for the ears of the human observer: the use of *phono*graphs as *ethno*graphs, so to speak. By the turn of the twentieth century, the practice had taken off within the anthropological subfield of audio ethnography, led by figures such as Jesse Walter Fewkes, Washing-ton Matthews, Benjamin Ives Gilman, Alice Cunningham Fletcher, James Mooney, Frances Densmore, and even Boas himself, who turned to the talking machine in 1893 to document Kwakwaka'wakw and Thompson River Indian dialects (see Figure 13).[79] As Fewkes, the pioneering figure in the field, claimed in an 1890 essay for the journal *Science*, "what specimens are to the naturalist in describing genera and species, or what sections are

FIGURE 13 "Mountain Chief, Chief of Montana Blackfeet, in Native Dress with Bow, Arrows, and Lance, Listening to Song Being Played on Phonograph and Interpreting It in Sign Language to Frances Densmore, Ethnologist" (1916). SPC Plains Blackfoot BAE (4720-00327300), National Anthropological Archives, Smithsonian Institution.

to the histologist in the study of cellular structure, the cylinders made on the phonograph are to the student of language. . . . The phonograph renders it practicable for us to indelibly fix [American] languages, and preserve them for future time after they become extinct or their idiom is greatly modified."[80] As a permanent record of the sounds of vanishing races the world over, the phonograph was "destined to play an important part in future researches," Fewkes predicted.[81]

On the subject of the phonograph's documentary promise, as we have already seen, *The Grandissimes* adopts a slightly more guarded stance. To be sure, Cable's text holds up the talking machine as a solution to the sound-blindness problem, nostalgically mourning forms of cultural sound (Louisiana Creole French–English, Creole patois, the Afro-Creole slave song) that seem to have "passed on" in the absence of mechanical reproduction: "Alas, the phonograph was invented three-quarters of a century too late" (145). Yet Cable also fleetingly mentions the possibility that the phonograph is itself unable to reproduce the complexities of vernacular culture: "ah! but type: even the phonograph—is such an inadequate thing" (145). He is suggesting that the new device may also have had inherent limitations of its own. This is an important detail to consider.

If the idea of the phonograph as a more perfect (or, more likely, less compromised) form of sound preservation seems somewhat self-evident by today's standards, it bears emphasizing that the talking machine's ability to "talk" remained in question throughout the 1880s and 1890s, even amid widespread fascination with the technology's uses and possibilities.[82] As Jonathan Sterne has shown, popular understandings of phonographic sound quality in fact varied widely during the initial phases of the device's social life.[83] Despite Edison's repeated claims about the phonograph's ability to reproduce "all manner of sound-waves heretofore designated as 'fugitive' . . . with all their original characteristics," many early listeners felt that it was almost impossible to decipher the sources of the unintelligible "scratches" and faint "noises" that the apparatus tended to bring forth.[84] Moreover, archival permanence was no guarantee. Well into the 1890s, commentators in the United States and Europe complained about the fragility of phonograph cylinders themselves, which occasionally failed to withstand more than a few uses.[85]

The parameters of perfect fidelity—an aesthetic judgment about documentary sound preservation that remains a source of debate in our present age of digital reproduction—thus needed to be socially constructed over time, and the matter was especially difficult to define when it came to the early phonograph's ability to record the phonetic textures of human speech.[86] Edison had initially envisioned the talking machine to work as a stenographic aid in American business offices, but, as we saw in chapter 1, he also touted the "preservation of languages" among a host of potential uses for the device in an 1878 publicity article for the *North American Review*.[87] When Edison finally hailed the commercial availability of a "Perfected Phonograph" a decade later, language reproduction was in fact his first point of reference: "We are now able to register all sorts of sound and all articulate utterance—even to the lightest shades and variations of the voice—in lines or dots which are an absolute equivalent for the emission of sound by the lips; so that, through this contrivance, we can cause these lines and dots to give forth again the sound of the voice, of music, and all other sounds recorded by them, whether audible or inaudible."[88]

All the while, however, listeners on both sides of the Atlantic were much less certain about the technology's capabilities. Many questioned the "absolute equivalence" between the "lines and dots" on Edison's phonograph cylinders and the embodied speech sounds that they supposedly preserved.[89] For instance, when in 1878 the British engineers William Henry Preece and Augustus Stroh began conducting a series of experiments comparing phonographic reproductions of vowel sounds with traditional written techniques of phonetic inscription, they were disappointed to find that "the phonograph is in reality a very imperfect speaker, and it requires the aid of much imagination and considerable guessing to follow its reproductions. It produces music with wonderful perfection, but it fails to reproduce most of the 'noises' of which speech is so largely made up."[90] Preece carried out similar tests on telephonic sound around the same time (with similar results, notably), and he would later criticize the phonograph's tendency to distort the "finest shades" of consonant phonemes as well. "The instrument has not quite reached that perfection when the tones of a Patti can be faithfully repeated; in fact, to some extent it is a burlesque or parody of the human voice," he noted. "There are some consonants that are wanting altogether. The s at the beginning and end of a word is entirely lost, although it is heard slightly in the middle of a word. The d and the t are exactly the same; and the same in m and n. Hence, it is extremely difficult to read what is said upon the instrument; if a person is put out of the room and you speak into it, he can only with difficulty translate what it says."[91] As late as 1891, articles in *Phonogram: A Monthly Magazine Devoted to the Science of Sound and Recording of Speech* noted obvious "inaccuracies of tone" in wax cylinder recordings.[92] Clearly the phonograph's ability to listen and write with documentary accuracy was on the surface no better than the ethnographer's.

When ethnologists and dialect writers began to look to the talking machine as a potential solution to the speech–writing (and music–writing) divide at the end of the nineteenth century, it wasn't simply because the device appeared to offer a more "accurate" or "faithful" form of sound reproduction in and of itself. The shift actually had far more to do with the device's apparent mechanical neutrality: the fact that the phonograph wasn't human and therefore, more importantly, wasn't *cultural*—the fact that it seemed to be able to short-circuit the linguistic and perceptual biases of listening and writing, objectively reproducing cultural sounds on their own terms. We can see these assumptions at work more clearly if we turn to figures such as Jesse Walter Fewkes and the ethnomusicologist Benjamin Ives Gilman, who implicitly framed their earliest audioethnographic efforts as responses to Boas's ideas about cultural sound-blindness.

Born in Newton, Massachusetts, and originally trained in the discipline of comparative zoology, J. W. Fewkes first came to the phonograph while heading Harvard University's Hemenway Ethnological Expedition, which began conducting systematic ethnographic research on Indian lifeways in the American Southwest in the early 1880s.[93] The project's financial patron, Mary Hemenway, was a minority shareholder in the Edison Company at the time, which partially explains her decision to support initial efforts to outfit Fewkes's expedition team with phonograph cylinders.[94] Threatened by foreign competitors (especially Emile Berliner's more durable gramophone, patented in 1887), the phonograph was still struggling to find an economic foothold in the late 1880s and early 1890s. Scientific research would have seemed as likely a potential market as any. Yet Hemenway's initial group of researchers had also reported back to Harvard that initial efforts to document southwestern Native American dialects had been slowed, once again, by the absence of "stenographic characters" that could fully "represent and reproduce the sounds of [languages] so remote from ours."[95] So the phonograph may well have appeared to offer a new methodological solution to a more long-standing documentary problem.

Accordingly, early experiments with the device's archival capabilities had motivations that were in equal parts economic and ethnographic. After assuming direction of the Hemenway Expedition's research agenda, Fewkes began working with the talking machine almost immediately: first in a trial run documenting Passamaquoddy tribal music and folklore in Calais, Maine, in March 1890 (almost exactly a year after the publication of Boas's "Alternating Sounds" essay), and later in the recording of Zuni and Hopi music and language in the American territories that would eventually become New Mexico and Arizona. "These remnants of the language of the old people we are fast getting on the little magic wax tablets to preserve after the tribe has lost what little of its old language it now has," Fewkes wrote to Hemenway in an 1890 letter from the field. "The same story is true here as in Zuni. . . . The older men still remember the old habits, but with them will die much of value in the story of their race. There is need for immediate action. . . . I shall be able to fill about three dozen cylinders with songs, stories, &c, &c."[96] Given the foundational theory of phonographic objectivity that evolved out of Fewkes's findings, his reference to the phonograph cylinder as a "little magic wax tablet" was much more than a metaphor.

There is some debate whether Fewkes was in fact the first ethnographer to use the phonograph for fieldwork purposes.[97] His predecessor Frank Hamilton Cushing may have actually beat him to the punch just before relinquishing his post with the Hemenway Expedition. What is certain is that between May and November 1890, Fewkes produced a flurry of publications that would redefine the phonograph's cultural potential and establish the theoretical foundation for anthropological, ethnomusicological, and even literary engagements with sound reproduction technology that would hold sway well into the late twentieth century. Fewkes's main argument, articulated in a series of research updates written for the *Journal of American Folklore, Science,* and the *American Naturalist,* was that the phonograph offered ethnography "a most valuable auxiliary in linguistic researches."[98] Crucially, this was more a result of the machine's check on the vagaries of human hearing than its ability to reproduce sound faithfully—or rather, more precisely, the latter because of the former. "Even with the assistance of the admirable system of letters and conventional signs which have been proposed for the purpose," Fewkes noted, conjuring Boas's alternating sounds theory directly,

> there are many difficulties besetting the path of one who would accurately record the aboriginal languages, which are but imperfectly met by [the written] method. There are inflections, gutturals, accents, and sounds in aboriginal dialects which elude the possibilities of phonetic expression. . . . The study of folk-lore can never stand on a scientific basis as far as Indian tales are concerned until we reduce to a minimum the errors of interpretation which may creep in through the translator. . . . As long as there is a possibility that the hearer adds to or detracts from the story as he hears it, by so much is the value of a story for scientific comparison diminished. The phonograph records the story exactly as the Indian tells it; and although free translation

of it may, and probably must, be made, to render the story comprehensible, we can always preserve the phonograph record as a check on exaggeration, or as a reference in critical discussions of the subject matter of the story. In this way the phonograph imparts to the study of folk-lore, as far as the aborigines are concerned, a scientific basis which it has not previously had.[99]

Here Fewkes makes use of a common rhetorical trope in the discourse of early audio ethnography: the personification of the phonograph ("the phonograph records the story exactly as the Indian tells it") as a disinterested third party in the relationship between observer and observed—a third party uncontaminated by language, culture, and perception.[100] (One sees similar rhetoric at work in Cable's aside about the phonograph in *The Grandissimes*, as well.) Because the machine is inherently able to "do away with the errors of the translator," as Fewkes repeatedly emphasizes, it can "record any language with precision" and bring forth the "exact words of the speaker" indefinitely.[101] Whereas phonetic transcription seemed to introduce the unavoidable possibility of sensory misrecognition and cultural misinterpretation, phonography thus seemed to isolate the ethnographic encounter with language and music from the unstable realm of human subjectivity.

The larger methodological point here, echoed throughout Fewkes's essays in the 1890s, is that the phonograph is a phonograph, nothing more. As a hearing and writing machine, its workings appeared to abolish residual traces of human influence on the collection of auditory data, intrinsically divorcing the documentation process from the racial and cultural differences that cause sound-blindness to occur in the first place. In other words, Fewkes's idea was that the phonograph offered methodological assurance of what Lorraine Daston and Peter Galison have termed *mechanical objectivity*: the ability to reproduce the world with as little human intervention as possible, avoiding the "subjective distortions" of an "observer's personal tastes, commitments, or ambitions."[102] Boas himself turned to the phonograph for these same reasons, positing that the new sound technology was a more transparent and universal version of the ethnographic observer: "The writing of single individuals cannot replace the dictated [phonograph] record because the individual characteristics of the writer become too prominent, and may give a false impression in regard to syntactic and stylistic traits."[103] Fewkes described the phonograph's utility in similar terms. "Phonetic methods of recording Indian languages are not wholly satisfactory," he lamented. "It is very unlikely that two persons will adopt the same spelling of a word never heard before. . . . Conventional signs and additional letters have been employed for this purpose, the use of which is open to objection. . . . The difficulties besetting the path of the linguist can be in a measure obviated by the employment of the phonograph, by the aid of which the languages of our aborigines can be permanently perpetuated."[104] Ultimately, these sorts of claims about the phonograph as an unmediated medium—one that could transform cultural sounds into permanent ethnographic texts without the intervening biases of the human listener—begin to suggest that reproduced sound was accurate only insofar as it was objective. If turn-of-the-century audio ethnographers regarded phonetic writing as an unpredictable art, phonographic inscription promised, at least in theory, the precision of an exact science.

In practice, however, Fewkes's ideas about a disinterested phonographic methodology were slightly more difficult to carry out. Without a viable apparatus for the reproduction and distribution of cylinder recordings, and without a central archive that assured some semblance of material permanence, audio ethnographers still had to revert back to the written word to process and preserve their documentary material.[105] For instance, Fewkes's seminal 1890 essay "A Contribution to Passamaquoddy Folk-Lore"—the first to adhere to what he termed the *phonographic method* for collecting and analyzing linguistic field data—follows repeated claims about the phonograph's ethnographic utility with extended written summaries of the contents of each cylinder recording. For Fewkes, these kinds of "derived" transcriptions were no less objective than the phonograph recordings themselves, because they were the product of an analytical method that included repeated listening and undistracted auditory attention.[106] Sound is by definition evanescent, the argument went, but the phonograph makes it both repeatable and portable. This appeared to enable the listening observer to check against individual mishearings and block out the sensory distractions of fieldwork.[107]

It was Benjamin Ives Gilman, another member of the Hemenway research team, who took Fewkes's early ideas about audioethnographic listening to their logical conclusion. Widely considered one of the foundational figures in the history of ethnomusicology, Gilman was in charge of

cataloging and analyzing the musical material that Fewkes collected in
the field. In so doing, he became the first to use the phonograph as an
aid to cross-cultural musical study. (Fewkes, for his part, seems to have
worked with the linguistic material on his own.) In "Zuñi Melodies" (1891),
Gilman's chief object of inquiry was Fewkes's recordings of southwestern
Native American music, which, like Cable's Afro-Creole songs before it,
seemed to frustrate conventional methods of hearing and writing.[108] But
the phonograph's potential as a safeguard against subjective distortion
nonetheless persisted as an animating issue:

> The apparatus proves to be a means by which the actual sound itself of
> which a music consists may, even in many of its more delicate characteris-
> tics, be stored up by the traveler in a form permanently accessible to obser-
> vation. . . . By the aid of the phonograph what would appear to be a very
> accurate reproduction of the music to which it has been exposed can be
> brought to the ears of any observer to be examined at his leisure. It can
> be interrupted at any point, repeated indefinitely, and even within certain
> limits magnified, as it were, for more accurate appreciation of changes in
> pitch, by increasing the duration of the notes. A collection of phonograph
> cylinders like that obtained by Dr. Fewkes forms a permanent museum
> of primitive music, of which the specimens are comparable, in fidelity of
> reproduction and convenience for study, to casts or photographs of sculp-
> ture or painting.[109]

As with Fewkes's account in "A Contribution to Passamaquoddy Folk-
Lore," Gilman's understanding of phonographic fidelity is rooted not just
in a mechanization of the ethnographic encounter (the use of the phonograph) but also in a new mechanical technique for analyzing its recorded
product (the practice of phonographic listening). He underscores that
the reproduced record can be "interrupted," "repeated," and "magnified,"
which allegedly makes the obstinate "habitudes of melodic invention" in
Zuni music—the product of a tonal system that fails to map onto the
Western diatonic scale—less fugitive to the outside ear and more reducible to written transcription.[110] Here the apparatus of sound recording
merely represents a means to a documentary end rather than a documentary end in and of itself. For Gilman, the phonograph seems to act as a

kind of culturally sealed container that preserves musical "specimens" for further study. Through repeated listenings, isolated from the distractions of the field encounter, a more accurate and scientific reproduction of cultural sound is rendered possible.

Gilman's early theories sparked controversy among intellectuals who remained skeptical of the talking machine and its attendant listening practices.[111] Yet Gilman responded almost fifteen years later in *Hopi Songs* (1908), the final public report on the Hemenway Expedition's cultural sound studies. Gilman's title was in many ways misleading: more than an analysis of the music that Fewkes and others collected, the true subject of *Hopi Songs* is phonographic ethnography itself. Gilman devotes well over three-quarters of the report's sixty-eight-page introductory section to theorizing his use of the phonograph and explaining his elaborate methodological steps to ensure its objective accuracy. The most important of these—an improvement, seemingly, on Fewkes's written summary technique in "A Contribution to Passamaquoddy Folk-Lore"—was that his final transcriptions of Hopi music paired examples of conventional Western musical notation with new experiments in what Gilman called "phonographic notation" (see Figure 14), structured not only to capture the subtle departures from the European diatonic norm that had frustrated outside listeners for so long, but also to yield a more "impartial record" of the songs themselves.[112] Comparing these two forms of sound-writing, Western and phonographic, Gilman concluded that

the diatonic form of the present [Western] notations by ear is in part the invention of the observer. The accurate observation of a [Hopi] musical performance of any length is beyond the power of the unaided ear. . . . The invention of the phonograph has given to science a new field of observation, that of music in the making. Fixed on a wax cylinder in reproducible form, the sequence of tone concerned in a performance of music can now be observed and recorded to within minute intervals. This has been attempted in the present phonographic notations, and during the process and later the melodies were written down currently by ear in the customary musical notation. On comparing the two records, the actual (carefully estimated) notes proved in many cases far from the pitch which the unaided ear assigned to them and which in general brought them within the bounds of the scale.[113]

a

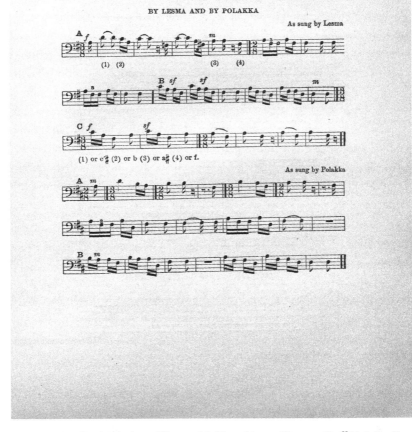

FIGURE 14 Benjamin Ives Gilman, (*a*) "Anoshkaey: Western Staff Notation" and (*b*) "Anoshkaey: Phonographic Notation." *Hopi Songs* (Houghton Mifflin, 1908). Widener Library, Harvard College Library, Sci 3120.100, vol. 5.

b

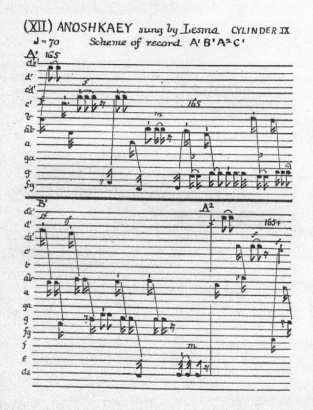

Again, here, accuracy and objectivity go hand in hand. Gilman contends that phonographic staff notation is more faithful than Western staff notation both because it takes into account the "minute intervals" of Hopi song and because it remains, like the talking machine itself, uncontaminated by cultural expectations. The phonograph; the phonographic listening method; phonographic notation—figures like Gilman considered this methodological trajectory as sound-sight to the problem of sound-blindness. "The widest lesson of the whole inquiry is the discovery of how great a part is played by the mind in apprehending a work of art; and how little of the veritable creation can often be grasped by an alien," he later wrote in conclusion. "It is our own ears that are oftenest at fault when we hear in exotic music only a strident monotony or a dismal uproar to be avoided and forgotten."[114]

More broadly, Gilman's invention of phonographic notation in *Hopi Songs*—indecipherable to the average reader but, as he repeatedly emphasizes, an "undistorted copy" of the original sound source nonetheless—underscores just how far the salvage ethnographic project seems to have gone in the search for auditory neutrality, the incredible pains it took to abstract ethnographic encounters from human influence and perceptual bias.[115] In certain respects, Gilman's interest in objective fidelity borders on the obsessive; the intricacies of his new phonographic notation system essentially make Hopi music unreadable. Yet, in important ways, *Hopi Songs* embodies both the realization and the failure of a fantasy about perfect auditory preservation that was clearly common during the turn-of-the-century era—a fantasy in which Cable's *The Grandissimes* also seems to indulge, despite its divergence in genre and subject matter. Both texts attempt to re-create sound in "standard" practices of transcription (Cable's, in phonetic orthography; Gilman's, in Western staff notation), yet both find their respective media inadequate for the documentary task at hand. Cable, for his part, supplements *The Grandissimes* with the elaborate orthographical flourishes and snatches of melody that would become central to his work for "Creole Slave Songs" and "The Dance in Place Congo." Yet, as we have seen, he often further marks their phonographic insufficiency by including musical staff notation throughout the text. Gilman seemingly takes the matter one step further. In *Hopi Songs,* hearing loss becomes the occasion for a new form of sound notation itself—one that attempts to match the phonograph's objective accuracy but perhaps devolves into unintelligibility. Both texts—Cable's *The Grandissimes* and Gilman's *Hopi Songs*—should thus be read as failed phonographs. At bottom, the project of salvaging cultural sound seems to have demanded an unwriteable writing. At the turn of the twentieth century, at least, it demanded the workings of a machine.

Originals and Aboriginals

"One does not want to accord it any form other than the one it itself exhibits," Theodor Adorno wrote in 1934, looking closely into the hieroglyphic grooves inscribed on the surface of the phonograph record, just as Cable, Fewkes, and Gilman had more than fifty years beforehand. "It is covered with curves," Adorno continues,

> a delicately scribbled, utterly illegible writing, which here and there forms more plastic figures for reasons that remain obscure to the layman upon listening; structured like a spiral, it ends somewhere in the vicinity of the title label, to which it is sometimes connected by a lead-out groove so that the needle can comfortably finish its trajectory. In terms of its "form," this is all it will reveal.[116]

Yet the "writing" on the face of the phonograph record—the spiraling "groove of history" etched into its surface, to borrow again from Ralph Ellison—of course signifies much more than this.[117] Even as mass-media technologies like radio and sound cinema were rapidly transforming into mouthpieces for totalitarian propaganda (a future eerily foreshadowed in Fritz Lang's 1933 film *Das Testament des Dr. Mabuse*), Adorno would continue to hold out hope for the phonograph—not only that its seemingly indelible grooves might represent "the last remaining universal language since the construction of the tower [of Babel]" but that its opaque acetate surface might also prove to be "the black seals on the missives that are rushing towards us from all sides in the traffic with technology; missives whose formulations capture the sounds of creation, the first and the last sounds, judgment upon life and a message about that which may come thereafter."[118]

In many ways, we still share Adorno's hope. The myth of the phonograph as a "universal language" technology—the myth of the mechanically reproduced record as a form of writing immune to the influences of culture and contingency—remains remarkably resilient. To claim that the phonograph possesses something like a culturally situated "gaze" makes little sense. By now it goes without saying that cameras contain the unspoken ideological biases of the photographers who use them.[119] Yet arguing that the phonograph's mechanical ear might be similarly constructed in terms of race, language, or history—arguing that the phonographic record might itself bear the cultural imprint of the human subjects who are inevitably behind Adorno's "curve of the needle"—still seems somewhat counterintuitive. The phonograph's authority is only just now beginning to receive the sustained critical attention it deserves.

In effect, this chapter has demonstrated that Adorno's utopian fantasies about the "universal language" of phonography have a long and complicated history, a history rooted in a varied set of modern texts and technologies that made powerful claims on the promise of ethnographic sound preservation. Cable's dialect orthography; Fewkes's wax cylinders; Gilman's phonographic sound notation: during the late nineteenth and early twentieth centuries, all of these representational inventions were part of a contested auditory–cultural field that took shape as media technologies like the phonograph began to find new social uses and as the modern enterprise of cultural preservation struggled to come to terms with the global realities of human diversity. The origins of the phonograph's privileged ethnographic status ultimately seem to lie in this historical moment.

Perhaps unsurprisingly, these kinds of relationships were often rehearsed in the Edison Company's efforts to market the talking machine during the turn-of-the-century period. Consider, in closing, an advertisement printed in 1909, one year after the publication of Gilman's *Hopi Songs*. The image is somehow familiar enough: a group of American Indians in ceremonial dress congregates around an Edison brand phonograph (see Figure 15).[120] Perched on the stump of a tree in the middle of an imaginary tribal village—an archetypal American past disappearing in the wake of capitalist expansion, institutional disfranchisement, and forced assimilation—the presence of the phonograph seems oddly necessary here: as much a romanticized stereotype of technological civilization as headdresses, arrows, and teepees are of premodern savagery.[121] It is unclear whether the "native" figures depicted in the image are listening or being listened to—an ambivalence,

FIGURE 15 Edison Company "Original and Aboriginal" advertisement (*Profitable Advertising*, April 1909). Courtesy of the University of Wisconsin Libraries.

an irony, captured in the unforgettable slogan that frames this strange scene of the machine in the garden: "The Edison Phonograph: Original and Aboriginal."[122]

To be sure, the Edison Company's "Original and Aboriginal" advertisement tells a story about mechanical sound reproduction that complicates any simplistic understanding of the relationship between phonographic copies and cultural originals. At first glance, two interpretive readings seem possible here. On one hand, the advertisement's talking machine clearly extends the audioethnographic tradition that Cable, Fewkes, and Gilman helped to inaugurate, presumably operating as a transparent mediator between the middle-class American home and the primitive mise-en-scène that it re-creates with objective accuracy. This is *the* Edison phonograph, the advertisement insists, the "original." This is the brand whose ability to reproduce the sounds of difference cannot be imitated or surpassed by other market competitors. Tellingly, in this reading, the culturally conditioned ear of the ethnographic observer—the standard human broker between the worlds of savagery and civilization, Cable's Joseph Frowenfeld figure—is missing from the frame.

On the other hand, the advertisement also posits Native Americans (or, at least, a romantic idea about Native American cultural difference) as a necessary ideological middle ground in the construction of phonographic sound fidelity. In this case, the Edison phonograph requires the presence of an "aboriginal" listening subject to corroborate its particular brand of technological alchemy—a reading consistent with the long-standing Western tradition of representing primitive peoples as all at once fascinated, seduced, and mastered by the magical workings of modern technology.[123] In the early decades of the twentieth century, as the business of recorded sound began to consolidate its global reach, such images became standard fare. The phonograph industry's longest-running trade journal, *Talking Machine World,* published similar illustrations of technological "first contact" throughout the 1910s and 1920s, depicting exotic foreigners from rural China, Chile, and central Africa in childlike wonder at civilization's audiovisual triumphs.[124] As Michael Taussig has pointed out, bringing sound technology abroad, into the world's most remote corners, was a symptom of its growing banality at home: "To take the talking machine to the jungle is to emphasize and embellish the genuine mystery and accomplishment of mechanical reproduction in an age when technology itself, after the flurry of excitement at a new breakthrough, is seen not as mystique or poetry but as routine."[125] This is sound media as second nature, right down to the garland of flowers that encircles the bell of the Edison phonograph's horn.

Perhaps the most notorious parallel in this context is Robert J. Flaherty's 1922 film *Nanook of the North* (widely cited as one of the most influential examples of early ethnographic filmmaking and a text to which I return at length in chapter 4), which stages a memorable encounter between the film's Inuit Eskimo protagonist, Nanook, and a phonograph owned by a trader at a trading post. Here, in the words of Flaherty's prefatory title card, we see the iconic figure of the backward "aboriginal" confronted with the "principle of the gramophone—how the white man 'cans' his voice" (see Figure 16). And as with the Native American figures depicted in the Edison Company advertisement, Nanook's cocked ear, his bewildered smile,

FIGURE 16 "In deference to Nanook, the great hunter, the trader entertains and explains the principle of the gramophone—how the white man 'cans' his voice." Still from *Nanook of the North* (1922), directed by Robert J. Flaherty.

his almost carnal attachment to the artifact of the acetate record itself—these stereotypically primitive gestures seem to confirm that mechanical sound reproduction technologies can, in fact, mechanically reproduce sound in the first place. No small feat, of course, in a film recorded during the silent era.

In the end, neither side of the "original and aboriginal" equation can be teased apart from the other. What matters about the Edison image here is how clearly it illustrates the reciprocal logic of ethnography and phonography, race and media, in this period. The "original" authenticates and constructs the "aboriginal": the phonograph inscribes preexisting ideas about race and cultural difference into the groove of history. It stores them; it renders them audible; it transforms them into commodities and circulates them in global flows of culture and capital. At the same time, the "aboriginal" authenticates and constructs the "original": ideas about race and cultural difference themselves encode the myth of the phonograph's objectivity, its ability to reproduce the real over and against contiguous representational media like dialect writing and phonetic shorthand. In both cases, the "unexpected" native use of modern technology—the possibility that the Indians in the advertisement own and operate the phonograph in question, the possibility that Nanook is actually acting out Western ideas about native backwardness rather than encountering modern technology for the first time—is written out altogether.[126] The phonograph's status as a reliable documentary medium, its claim on disinterested ethnographic objectivity, thus hinges on a racialized encounter that implicitly silences native autonomy and modernity.

Part and parcel of this dialectic, the ethnographic turn to sound technology at the end of the nineteenth century was not a turn toward auditory fidelity. It was, instead, an attempted turn away from culture, a turn away from what many American writers and anthropologists recognized as the human ear's inbuilt cultural biases. Rather than connecting America, as so many accounts of mass media and mass culture have suggested, the modern logic of the phonograph in fact depended on—even upheld—the racial and cultural boundaries that it was supposedly dissolving into the grooves of the wax cylinder.

4

Race, Empire, and the Skin
of the Ethnographic Image

In August 1925, a twenty-four-year-old Columbia University student named Margaret Mead set sail for a small chain of islands off the eastern coast of American Samoa. Inspired by the theories of Franz Boas, her academic mentor, Mead was primarily interested in traveling to the South Seas to discover whether the emotional turmoil of human adolescence was the product of nature or nurture, biology or culture. Seventy-five hundred miles from her Philadelphia home, moreover, the Samoan Islands also promised solutions to a far more urgent problem. "Even in remote parts of the world, ways of life about which nothing was known were vanishing before the onslaught of modern civilization," Mead wrote in her 1972 autobiography, recalling the genesis of the project that catapulted into the national spotlight both her career and the tiny island territory on which it rested. "The work of recording these unknown ways of life had to be done now— *now*—or they would be lost forever."[1] In her preface to the forty-fifth anniversary edition of *Coming of Age in Samoa* (1928), the controversial ethnographic study that elaborated her findings in the South Seas, Mead explained the rationale behind her early fieldwork in similar terms: "I feared [in 1925] that the grace and zest and gaiety of the Samoans, carried only by them as a people, without the kind of art and literature and architecture which has left us something of Greece and Egypt after their civilizations were gone, would disappear altogether, transmuted beyond recognition by the diffusion of Euro-American culture around the world. I did not know then, could not know then, how extraordinarily persistent Samoan culture would prove, and how fifty years later the grace that I had attempted to record as something that was surely going to vanish would still be there."[2]

As we have seen, Mead's fascination with the disappearance of primitive peoples amid the "onslaught of modern civilization" would have been unexceptional in the specialized science of anthropology during the late nineteenth and early twentieth centuries. Yet the myth of lost cultural innocence behind her Samoan research—a time-honored storyline that quietly haunts *Coming of Age's* account of the transition from youth to adulthood among native Samoan women—also prevailed in the popular domain. After arriving at her destination in the Manu'an Islands, Mead set up shop on the back porch of a medical dispensary. Friends and informants who visited her makeshift home would have been welcomed by scores of photographs hanging on her walls. Alongside a likeness of "Papa Franz," whimsically adorned with a garland of red hibiscus flowers, Mead affixed a series of images clipped from the pages of *Asia,* a widely circulated American magazine.[3] A Samoan woman demonstrates the art of basket making to a young girl. A Samoan man carefully examines a knife in preparation for a ritual dance. Two elder Samoan tribesmen, dressed in elaborate ceremonial attire, sit together to discuss the affairs of their village (see Plate 2).[4] Taken with the intention of preserving representative Samoan types and authentic South Seas settings, the images on Mead's walls would have looked like the snapshots of a photographer well schooled in the ethnographic conventions of the period. Yet these images weren't captured by a trained anthropologist. They were, instead, the photographic records of two popular filmmakers, Robert and Frances Flaherty, who had traveled to the Samoan Islands only two years prior to shoot a big-budget Hollywood movie, *Moana: A Romance of the Golden Age* (1926). Today, their film is remembered less for its painstaking attempts to reconstruct vanishing Samoan traditions than for its status as the first motion picture to be labeled "documentary" in the modern sense of the term.[5]

The appearance of the Flahertys' photographs on the walls of Margaret Mead's Samoan home underscores the porousness of the divide between anthropological science and popular mass media during the early decades of the twentieth century. To be sure, no two figures did more to disseminate anthropology's myths about "primitive, little-known people whose cultures were fast fading" in this period than Robert and Frances Flaherty, yet no two figures have occupied a more embattled position in the canons of documentary and ethnographic cinema.[6] When we encounter them on the walls of Mead's Samoan home, alongside a portrait of the father of modern anthropology, the Flahertys' images suddenly seem to possess an ethnographic value that critical "demystifications" of their influential film practice have stubbornly dismissed.[7]

Like Mead and many others in this period, the Flahertys came to the anthropological project of cultural preservation through circuitous channels. Born in 1884, in Iron Mountain, Michigan, Robert Flaherty grew up hoping to follow in the footsteps of his father, who worked as a mining prospector across the upper Midwest and Canada.[8] In 1910, under the auspices of the Canadian railroad entrepreneur Sir William Mackenzie, the young Flaherty embarked on a series of treacherous commercial prospecting expeditions to the Hudson Bay area of northern Quebec, eventually working to explore and map the Belcher Islands. Along the way, he passed the time by developing thousands of photographic portraits of the native Inuit Eskimo who served as his local guides.[9]

It wasn't until 1912 or 1913—shortly before he married Frances, a well-traveled graduate of Bryn Mawr College—that Flaherty's employer convinced him to try his luck with "one of those newfangled things called a motion-picture camera," hoping that he might someday make a movie that would help defray the cost of the Hudson Bay expeditions.[10] The result, after almost a decade of trial and error, was *Nanook of the North* (1922), a film that garnered international acclaim for its stark and sympathetic portrayal of Inuit life in the Nunavik region off Hudson Bay. As a whole, *Nanook* captures little more than a fragmentary series of staged reenactments and cultural simulations. At Flaherty's own suggestion, cast members donned traditional clothing that would only have been worn in the time of their grandparents, hunted with spears and harpoons that firearms had long since rendered obsolete, and feigned childlike unfamiliarity with modern media technologies like the phonograph, as we have already seen. Yet audiences in the 1920s widely accepted the film as ethnographic fact, occasionally even reverting to the word "document" to describe the truth-value of the images they encountered onscreen.[11] "One often has to distort a thing to catch its true spirit," Flaherty later conceded.[12]

In light of the charges of inauthenticity that have dogged the Flahertys since at least the 1930s, it is crucial to remember that reconstructions of authentic cultural customs and simulations of traditional indigenous lifeways were commonly accepted practices in ethnographic film and photography during the early decades of the twentieth century.[13] Flaherty's allegiance to the nascent discipline of anthropology in the years leading up to *Nanook's* release provides an important case in point here. Throughout the 1910s the Flahertys (both Robert and Frances) insisted that the "real intrinsic value" of their collective labor was "scientific, ethnological and geographical," and in 1915, they even went so far as to screen early footage of the Inuit movie for the American ethnologist Edward S. Curtis, whose feature film *In the Land of the Headhunters* (1914) had also made dramatic use of reconstructed ethnographic material.[14] The Flahertys would eventually attempt to court the box office as much as the anthropological society. But on the heels of *Nanook's* success, both Robert and Frances disputed the validity of such distinctions. "It seems to me possible to record the life of primitive people in such a way as to preserve scientific accuracy and yet make a picture which ha[s] vivid and dramatic interest for the average man or woman," Robert Flaherty told a *New York Globe* reporter in 1922. "Plenty of pictures have been made of the life of savages in various parts of the world, especially in the tropics. The difficulty is that such pictures are usually episodic, showing unrelated scenes, with little to hold the wandering attention of one who has not a scientific interest in the lives of primitive people. In 'Nanook of the North' . . . we secure a dramatic value which is both legitimate and absorbing."[15] For Flaherty, as for more established anthropological luminaries like Boas and Curtis, what separated documentary from fiction, ethnography from artifice, was far less defined than what we would accept today.

By the time that the Flahertys (then working as a husband-and-wife team) traveled to Samoa to shoot the film that would inspire Margaret Mead, their commitment to the popular ethnographic approach had only intensified. This chapter charts their trajectory during this period, revealing along the way the dynamic interplay of race and technology in the making of early ethnographic cinema. As I demonstrate, the Flahertys' most significant contributions to the anthropological project of cultural preservation surfaced in ways that aren't immediately visible onscreen. Faced with the reality that their "fast fading" Samoan subjects were living real, modern lives on the other side of the camera, Robert and Frances Flaherty essentially made *Moana* a film not about a disappearing culture but about a new technology that promised to preserve it. *Moana*'s most lasting cinematic achievement wasn't its inauguration of the so-called documentary tradition but its pioneering use of color-sensitive panchromatic film stock—a choice that emerged out of the Flahertys' compulsive attempts to reproduce Samoan skin color in accordance with modern anthropological understandings of human variety.[16] Hidden behind the exotic images of "primitive, little-known people" that the Flahertys projected to the world in *Moana*, as we will see, were state-of-the-art motion picture technologies explicitly adopted in the service of the salvage ethnographic imperative, in direct response to ongoing scientific debates about racial difference.

Looking back on their careers in documentary and ethnographic cinema, the Flahertys would insist that all of their films were produced with one underlying principle in mind: "non-preconception," the discovery of the unknown. "To discover and to reveal—that is the way every artist sets about his business," Robert explained in a late essay, hearkening back to his early work as a commercial prospector. "All art is, I suppose, a kind of exploring. Whether or not it's true of art, that's the way I started filmmaking. I was an explorer first and a filmmaker a long way after."[17] Frances would adopt a similar stance on the importance of cinematic "non-preconception" in subsequent years: "The first hard lesson of what it takes to make a *true* film . . . [is] that you cannot preconceive. If you preconceive you are lost, off to a false start before you begin. What you have to do is to let go, let go every thought of your own, wipe your mind clean, fresh, innocent, newborn, sensitive as unexposed film to take up the impressions about you, and let what will come in. This is the pregnant void, the fertile state of no-mind. This is non-preconception, the beginning of discovery."[18] Ultimately, this chapter argues that the Flahertys' contributions to the traditions of salvage ethnography were nothing if not "preconceived." Yet unlike the conventional account of their work, and unlike the conventional account of the cinematic techniques and technologies that they helped to popularize in the 1920s and 1930s, this is a story that cannot be told in neutral terms, free from global entanglements of race and empire. To tell it, we must begin, like Mead and the Flahertys before us, in the Samoan Islands.

America's Samoa

Contrary to popular myths about the South Seas as an unspoiled natural paradise, the Samoan Islands hardly existed in cultural isolation when Robert and Frances Flaherty first arrived to shoot *Moana* in spring 1923.[19] Indigenous Samoan encounters with seafaring explorers and Christian missionaries date back to the 1700s. In the middle decades of the nineteenth century, the Samoan Islands gained strategic geopolitical importance when European powers like Germany and Great Britain began vying for global control of the commercial production of copra, a valuable commodity derived from the meat of dried coconuts. A protracted struggle for land holdings in Oceania and the Pacific Rim ensued, lasting well into the twentieth century. Remarkably, by the end of World War I, the Samoan Islands had witnessed the rise and fall of four different colonial regimes in fewer than five decades.[20]

America's involvement in Samoa, often omitted in historical accounts of Open Door–era U.S. imperialism, begins in the 1870s.[21] While Germany and Great Britain sought to secure treaties for copra-rich territories in the western portion of the Samoan archipelago, the United States set its sights on Tutuila, a tiny eastern island that provided an accessible stopover for American steamships traveling to strategic ports in the Pacific Rim. Coupled with an unstable network of colonial alliances with native factions across the islands, the subsequent struggle for dominance in the region almost set off one of the earliest armed conflicts over overseas territory in American history. (Almost, because a massive tropical storm in March 1889 destroyed the naval warships sent to defend each country's political interests.) A decade later, the Tripartite Convention of 1899 officially settled what came to be known as the "Samoan tangle," annexing the entire archipelago to Western control.[22] Whereas the British colonial administration formally renounced its claims on the region in exchange for German holdings in Tonga and West Africa, the United States incorporated the southeastern Samoan islands as an overseas protectorate, now commonly known as "American Samoa," leaving the remaining territory to Germany. After World War I, a series of League of Nations mandates surrendered Germany's portion of colonial Samoa to New Zealand, which in essence acted as a diplomatic proxy for Great Britain until the western islands gained independence in the early 1960s.

As Fatimah Tobing Rony has pointed out, the Flahertys' decision to base *Moana* on such unstable terrain is symptomatic of salvage ethnography's "taxidermic" representational predisposition: its tendency to make the dead appear as if it were the living, the cultural past as if it were the cultural present.[23] This impulse shaped much of the film's production history, and in Samoa it emerged out of a complicated set of local circumstances and necessities. Scrambling to capitalize on the unexpected commercial success of *Nanook of the North* (the filmmaker Asen Balikci has aptly characterized the crazed popular response to Flaherty's first film as "Nanookmania"), Paramount Pictures/Famous Players-Lasky effectively wrote a blank check for the venture that eventually became *Moana*.[24] "I want you to go off somewhere and make me another *Nanook*," Jesse Lasky, Paramount's studio production president, reputedly told Flaherty in 1922, despite having passed on the distribution of the Inuit film only two years prior. "Go where you will, do what you like—I'll foot the bills. The world's your oyster."[25] The Samoan Islands only emerged as a potential setting for *Nanook*'s Hollywood sequel at the suggestion of the American travel writer Frederick O'Brien, a close friend of the Flaherty family whose best-selling account of "fatal contact" between Polynesian culture and white society in the Marquesas, *White Shadows in the South Seas* (1919), had ignited a short-lived popular vogue in the United States for all things Oceanic.[26] O'Brien advised Flaherty at a meeting in New York shortly after Paramount announced its intention to back the new film expedition, "I know what appeals to you more than anything else is the racial differences. . . . [In Samoa] the white man has had the least influence."[27] O'Brien continued, offering the words that would sell Flaherty on the location and explicitly link his cinematic mission there to the salvage ethnographic imperatives of early-twentieth-century anthropology: "You may still be in time to catch some of that beautiful old culture before it passes entirely away."[28]

True to form, the Flahertys believed that the medium of film was uniquely suited for such an undertaking. But they soon discovered that the reality on the ground in Samoa, America's "foster-child" territory in the Pacific, wasn't exactly as O'Brien had led them to believe.[29] By 1923, much of the "beautiful old culture"—or *fa'a Samoa*, in the local parlance—had evolved to meet modern Samoan needs after generations of native islanders had struggled to adopt, reshape, and even resist the Western norms that were

forcibly imposed on them. By 1923, as well, an organized anticolonial movement had begun to make its presence felt on the western islands.[30] Even
in the region's most remote enclaves (a geographical misconception to
begin with, both because the Samoan population was extremely mobile,
and because the Samoan Islands were situated at the crossroads of several
different indigenous migration routes across the Pacific), traditional customs had been rooted out by the influence of Christian missionaries, while
local systems of governance and exchange had eroded under the interna-
tionalizing pressures of the copra trade.[31] In short, the Flahertys arrived
only to find what the anthropologist Claude Levi-Strauss would later
famously call the "impossibility of escapism": the authentic, pure "old
culture," if it ever existed in such terms, had essentially disappeared.[32]
Twentieth-century Samoans were carving their own path into an uncertain global future rather than nostalgically holding on to an isolated pre-
colonial past.

Reality to the contrary, the *Moana* project pressed on with the age-old
archetype of the unspoiled South Seas in mind. The Flahertys' initial vision
for the film, like Mead's motivation for *Coming of Age in Samoa,* involved a
romantic fixation with vanishing racial purities and endangered cultural
authenticities: a Samoa completely free from the contaminating effects of
Euro-American society, an Edenic Samoan paradise outside of modern history altogether. "We were going to the glamorous South Seas to film the
life of the Polynesian as he had lived it in his islands before the white man
came with his strange God, his strange manners, his strange and wonderful commodities," Frances later recalled, channeling O'Brien's initial travel
advice. "We should go to Samoa, for of all the Polynesians the Samoans
remained the finest, the most firmly rooted in their own racial traditions,
the least blemished by an alien civilization. We should go to the island of
Savai'i, in western Samoa, for of all the Samoans those on Savai'i retained
their old ways to the highest degree. And we should go to the village of
Safune on the island of Savai'i, for here we would find the first essential of
our business—fresh cold water for the development of our motion picture
film."[33] Perhaps unsurprisingly, when Frances arrived in Safune in spring
1923, she immediately described the people she intended to film as "creatures from another time," willfully turning a blind eye to the obvious signs
of cultural change that surrounded her.[34]

These kinds of inconsistencies reveal as much about the pressures of the commercial marketplace as about the biases and shortcomings of the Flahertys' cinematic vision. Cultural transformation and political unrest weren't the only complications that Robert and Frances encountered in Safune. Commercial expectations also dictated an approach to Samoan culture that heavily favored the romantic over the real. Paramount first backed the expedition with the understanding that Robert and Frances were planning to hew closely to *Nanook*'s original narrative formula. The idea was so deep-seated that early correspondence from Paramount explicitly referred to *Moana* as "Nanook of the South."[35] On the occasion of the Flahertys' departure from the United States, moreover, Paramount released a flurry of promotional materials for the movie that announced a "new epoch" in the history of filmmaking, all while emphasizing continuities with the foundational premises of the *Nanook* experiment: "Just as [Flaherty] brought the Eskimo as a living, human being to the screens of America and the world, so he will bring the South Sea people. Of course, he will stress the human element just as he did in 'Nanook,' a picture which is entertainment, yes, but also education in the sense that it breaks down artificial barriers between peoples by showing one people to another, telling a story in the universal language of the motion picture."[36]

For the Flahertys, living up to Paramount's endorsement meant making a movie that universalized cultural particulars by dramatizing basic human struggles for food and shelter, kinship and community. As Frances explained in a series of articles for *Asia* and *Magazine World,* written in 1925 while *Moana* was still in the cutting room, the "big idea . . . was that we should make a film after the pattern of 'Nanook of the North.' We should find a man just like Nanook, the Eskimo, a sturdy, dignified chief and head of a family, and then build our picture around him, substituting the dangers of the sea here in the South Pacific for those of snow and ice in the North. We would present the drama of Samoan life as it unrolled itself naturally before us."[37] But this plan quickly ran aground. As the Flahertys came to understand, the realities of "North" and "South" were wholly incompatible. Unlike the Inuit of Hudson Bay, the native islanders of Samoa found food in abundance and lived a life of comparative ease. And though early shooting schedules for the film went so far as to outline scenes that pitted heroic Samoans against man-eating sharks and giant octopi—clearly in an

effort to replicate the drama of *Nanook*'s man-against-nature storyline—
no such creatures could be found in the vicinity.[38] As a result, much of the
Flahertys' original plan for the film had to be scrapped.

This brief sketch of *Moana*'s troubled production history should underscore just how deeply early-twentieth-century cinematic encounters with
allegedly vanishing foreign peoples were informed, and even constrained,
by cultural and commercial expectations. Samoa's climate of social transformation and anticolonial resistance; the Flahertys' ethnocentric preconceptions about life in the South Seas; Paramount's interest in tapping into
a preexisting market niche—all of these factors help to explain why *Moana*
took the shape that it did, abolishing traces of Western influence from the
island mise-en-scène and misleadingly depicting the Samoan present as a
changeless past. All of this, as well, is made clear from the outset of the
film, which opens with Moana and Fa'angase, the Flahertys' male and female
leads, gathering palm fronds amid lush greenery. The sequence is book-
ended by a low-angle shot of a towering, twisted tree—clearly intended as
a symbol of stability and timelessness, a signpost marking our passage into
an Edenic world that exists in civilization's distant prehistory.

At the beginning of the film, we find ourselves "on the trail of the jungle's one dangerous animal," the wild boar, as Moana constructs a snare
out of branches and vines. We witness a procession of native villagers into
a valley, interspersed with 180-degree panoramic shots of clear skies and
seaside vistas. After several extended scenes of boating, fishing, and swimming (the Flahertys had a peculiar affinity for shots of their Samoan actors
gliding just beneath the ocean's surface, more on which in a moment), the
film abruptly cuts to a woman kneeling indoors, carefully coiling and un-
coiling tree bark to make fabric for a dress. The scene is regularly punctu-
ated by explanatory title cards that attempt to adopt a more objective and
authoritative mode of ethnographic narration: "Mother Tu'ungaita has a
dress to make. . . . She strips the bark of the mulberry tree. . . . Red seeds
of sandalwood, for dye. . . . The costume of the country—the *lavalava*."
Disembodied close-up shots of her hands concentrate our attention on the
intricacies of her labor and craft. The camera focuses on similar details
later as Moana's younger brother, Pe'a, makes a fire out of coconut husks
and as the community prepares for a celebratory feast.

The second half of *Moana* adopts a more self-consciously anthropological stance, often staging events for the camera to heighten the imagined authenticity of what is recorded onscreen. In one of the film's most celebrated sequences, the Flahertys' camera gradually tilts higher and higher to follow Pe'a as he climbs an immense coconut tree that extends well beyond the upper reaches of the cinematic frame. The scene is carefully structured to create the illusion of real continuous space, reinforcing the sense that Samoan islanders possess an inborn resourcefulness that allows them to overcome a natural environment that appears to render them small and powerless. By contrast, later on in the film, we see more intimately constructed shots of Moana and Fa'angase lathering themselves in oil and performing a traditional Samoan *siva* dance, once again capturing the exotic body in controlled and detailed motion (see Plate 3). The film finally culminates with an extended sequence in which Moana endures a painful tattooing ritual (more on this later, as well). Filmed over the course of six excruciating weeks, eventually composing almost one-third of *Moana*'s seventy-seven-minute run time, the Samoan tattooing ritual seemed to embody a central metaphor for the struggle of authentic Samoan culture against outside Western influences. "Through this pattern of the flesh," one of the film's concluding intertitles reads, "to you perhaps no more than cruel, useless ornament, the Samoan wins the dignity, the character and fibre which keep his race alive." A similar sense of cultural life, rather than cultural death, pervades the final scenes of *Moana* as well. In contrast to *Nanook*—which ends, as several critics have noted, with the film's heroic protagonist asleep in a corpselike position, suggesting the imminent disappearance of authentic Inuit culture—the Flahertys' South Seas picture concludes with a fully tattooed Moana taking part in a ritual dance, suggesting the persistence of *fa'a Samoa* through the preservative medium of motion pictures.[39]

Despite *Moana*'s fragmentary narrative construction, the film clearly revolves around two central themes. The first theme is the strength and beauty of *fa'a Samoa,* the traditional "Samoan way," broadly defined. *Moana* thus unfolds not as a "true picture romance of life and love in the South Seas," as advertisements for the film's February 1926 opening misleadingly billed it, but as an ethnographic progression toward community and tradition, culminating in the ritual that supposedly gives structure to all indigenous life on the islands.[40] This first narrative arc runs from ocean and wilderness to village and home, from picturesque nature to ethnographic culture. (This represents a major departure from *Nanook,* ending as it does with the film's protagonist lost in an arctic snowstorm, isolated both from his community and from the influence of modern society.) Flaherty perhaps best articulated this emphasis in a 1925 letter: "Our task [was] capturing the spirit of the true Polynesian in all its pure, living beauty, on a strip of film . . . the Samoan's own story, the story of his life as he lived it before his Eden was invaded by the ever-encroaching, ever-despoiling white. These golden-bronze people of Samoa, they alone, were to provide our drama."[41]

Flaherty's seemingly offhand recourse to stock visual language here ("golden-bronze people of Samoa") also bears witness to the film's second structuring principle: the exotic spectacle of the Samoan body. Throughout *Moana* the Flahertys' camera lingers, at times in lush and tactile detail, on bare Samoan skin: on hands at work; on arms and legs swimming and dancing; ultimately, as we will see, on the tattooed body as a canvas for cultural expression and racial projection. Jeffrey Geiger has pointed out that such an aesthetic emphasis suggests that Robert and Frances had absorbed the idea that culture's deep structures are discernible through the body's visible physiognomic surfaces, a sentiment popular among American and European anthropologists throughout the second half of the nineteenth century.[42] "Simply in the beautiful movement of a hand," Frances later wrote, evoking what was then a bygone era in the history of anthropological thought, "the whole story of [a] race can be revealed."[43]

Yet the Samoan body was much more to the Flahertys than a mere synecdoche for the total texture of Samoan culture. Skin, in particular, also testified to the ethnographic authenticity of the cinematic image itself, effectively functioning as a physical site—a living screen, of sorts—on which visual realism could be projected and technical experimentation could be showcased. Here it is crucial to consider the Flahertys' pioneering use of color-sensitive panchromatic film stock throughout the production process. This seemingly neutral technological choice, the Flahertys' stopgap solution to the problem of Samoan cultural change, reveals just how indelibly emergent anthropological debates about racial difference shaped *Moana*'s visual style.

Color Correction

First undertaken sometime late in 1923, after shooting several months' worth of tepid preliminary footage, the Flahertys' experiments with panchromatic film unquestionably represent the most novel aspect of their South Seas salvage project.[44] During the silent era, Hollywood industry cinematographers primarily relied on what is known as *orthochromatic* film stock, a standard type of nitrate emulsion that captures an image of sharply defined blacks and whites, but with little of the color spectrum accurately implied in the gray scale between. The visual limitations of the orthochromatic process tended to distort color relations that fall outside of the blue-green range—in the study of optics, the technical term for this phenomenon is *spectral insensitivity.* In the 1900s and 1910s, orthochromatic film's spectral insensitivity to certain colors significantly constrained efforts to shoot outdoor footage. Without the ability to control the color palate of the space in front of the camera, as directors and cinematographers of course could while shooting on closed sets, certain areas of the image incorrectly developed as dark black when working on location. In the absence of special lens filters and elaborate lighting schemes, filmmakers working with orthochromatic emulsion were often forced to avoid shooting shades of yellow, red, blue, and brown altogether.[45]

In the early 1910s, hoping to solve this massive logistical problem, the Eastman Kodak Company began experimenting with the application of new *panchromatic* film negatives that reproduced all visible wavelengths of color in realistic relation to each other, even within the narrow confines of a black-and-white palette.[46] Yet despite its apparent utility, the format initially failed to catch on. Kodak's original color-sensitive emulsion was physically unstable and prone to quick deterioration, not to mention far more expensive to use.[47] Industry researchers unveiled an improved black-and-white panchromatic negative shortly after World War I, and as early as 1921, articles in the *American Cinematographer* were endorsing "panchromatic film and filters" as essential materials for shooting exterior location scenes.[48] By 1925 Kodak's promotional pamphlets were touting additional cinematographic benefits, as well: "[Panchromatic film] is of great advantage in close-ups; the flesh tones are much more accurately rendered and the whole appearance is more natural when panchromatic film is used. It is also valuable for outdoor sets, the general tones of the landscape being better rendered, and clouds being photographed as they appear in a blue sky."[49]

Despite the Flahertys' frequent claims to the contrary, *Moana* was not the first film to experiment with "panchro" cinematography.[50] The color-balancing panchromatic process was used sparingly as early as 1920, starting with selected exterior scenes in Maurice Tourneur's feature-length adaptation of James Fenimore Cooper's *The Last of the Mohicans* (1826), a novel that has an important ideological kinship to the Flahertys' work in that it draws extensively on the vanishing race storyline. Edward Venturini's *The Headless Horseman* (1922), a short movie financed by Kodak to promote the capabilities of the process, is ordinarily identified as the earliest motion picture photographed entirely on panchromatic stock.[51] But certainly no other feature-length film of the period, much less a feature-length film with ethnographic aspirations, showcased corrective color sensitivity as extensively as *Moana*. As Frances Flaherty repeatedly emphasized, the panchromatic process necessarily functioned as the primary organizing principle for the images recorded in *Moana*, essentially providing the movie's entire raison d'être. In the absence of the universal drama of human survival that made *Nanook of the North* an international success, she later admitted, "the drama of our picture [w]ould lie in its sheer beauty, the beauty of *fa'a Samoa*, rendered by panchromatic film."[52] By the late 1920s and early 1930s, Eastman Kodak panchro was the most commonly used photographic negative in Hollywood, by and large rendering standard orthochromatic emulsion completely obsolete.[53] The Flahertys' experimental efforts in Samoa, which exposed panchro's visual effects to a much wider commercial audience than short promotional films like *The Headless Horseman* ever could, did much to bring about this shift.

Film historians have long discounted the significance of the ortho-chromatic–panchromatic switch during the 1920s. Kristin Thompson, for instance, has claimed that the technical and visual gains of panchromatic film were marginal at best, and most scholars of motion picture technology tend to consider the emergence of color-sensitive photography, if at all, as a minor development in the larger course of cinematic history.[54] But during the 1930s, 1940s, and 1950s, filmmakers and critics across the United States and Europe actually championed panchro—and the Flahertys' experimental use of it in *Moana*, in particular—as though the color-sensitive process had marked a decisive turning point in the evolution of cinematographic realism, as though the technology had altogether revolutionized the cinema's visual capabilities. The documentary filmmaker and critic Paul Rotha, whose *The Film till Now* (1930) represents one of the earliest attempts at a retrospective survey of international film history, enthusiastically praised *Moana*'s "pictorial value," arguing that the Flahertys' experiments with panchromatic color sensitivity represented a pathbreaking first step toward the realization of a "pure visual cinema."[55] The Flahertys' images even seemed realistic enough for Rotha to dispute the need for further research and development in the field of full-color cinematography. "All the colour that the cinema may need is obtainable by the use of panchromatic stock," he boldly predicted in his next book.[56]

History, needless to say, turned out otherwise. Advances in full-color processes such as Technicolor, Agfacolor, and Kodachrome, which eventually supplanted the industry's uses of black-and-white Eastman panchromatic, were already well under way in Rotha's day. But other prominent voices still made claims for color-sensitive black-and-white photography as a crucial vanishing mediator in the history of cinematic realism. Not only did the technology seem to allow for a more "natural" and "flexible" cinematographic product, it also gave the camera a greater degree of freedom when shooting unstaged location footage, an essential technological precondition for later iterations of the documentary and ethnographic style. For example, the Hollywood cinematographer Joseph Valentine argued in 1939 that "the most important single factor in . . . cinematography is the relation between the colour-sensitivity of an emulsion and the reproduction of pleasing flesh tones," an aesthetic achievement directly related to the emergence of panchromatic processes during the silent era.[57] In "The Evolution of the Language of Cinema," written during the 1950s, André Bazin famously advanced a different theory, arguing for the importance of deep focus cinematography and its ability to draw passive film spectators into more active perceptual relationships with the moving image. Yet Bazin still proclaimed in the same landmark essay that the international transition to panchro during the late 1920s and early 1930s had the effect of turning "visual values upside down" for filmmakers and audiences alike.[58]

Whatever their ultimate historical influence, industrial uses of panchromatic film stock both evolved and gained traction during the 1920s out of American ethnographic encounters with racial difference. Simply put, racial thinking motivated early experiments with the technology.[59] In the case of *Moana,* the Flahertys turned to panchro—then largely unused, except in special cases—only after they discovered that the industry's standard photographic schemes invariably failed to depict the exotic image of the Samoan body in accordance with modern anthropological understandings of racial variety. As Robert and Frances discovered in Safune, the optical imbalances of the orthochromatic process grossly misrepresented the "golden" and "reddish-brown" skin of the Samoans that they hoped to project onscreen. Distorted early rushes of the film set off a frantic search for a combination of lighting and emulsion that would capture Samoan "flesh tones" with suitable fidelity. "The difficulty began with the first film tests of native characters whom we proposed to use," Robert Flaherty recalled in a 1926 article on emergent cinematographic techniques for the Society of Motion Picture Engineers:

> The complexion of the Samoans is a light reddish-brown. In our tests made with the ordinary orthochromatic film they stood out on the screen as dark as Negroes, a lifeless black, so much so that we realized the hopelessness of keeping on unless a color correction could be made. But the problem went even further; for in the greens of the jungle and the water, the deep blue of the sea and the sky, and in the cloud forms, so much a part of Polynesia, this too must be captured. This Polynesian scene, unlike *Nanook* which was a study in black and white and was in all its essentials a dramatic fight for the food wherewith to live, was an idyllic thing, a painter's picture, and all that we had for drama was the inherent beauty of the country and its almost Grecian people. Obviously, there was only one film medium to use and that was panchromatic film. . . . To us, the method was a revelation not only in the balance of reds and blues and greens, but in the way it brought out through this balance the sculpturesque values of arms and hands and figures, and the forms of trees and leaves as uncorrected orthochromatic film could never hope to do.[60]

At first glance, Flaherty's account of *Moana*'s production is consistent with a wider set of early Hollywood practices that implicitly figured nonwhite skin as a technical obstacle to be overcome in the film production process. Note, for instance, how the "difficulty" of native Samoan "complexion" necessitates what Flaherty here calls "color correction," a euphemistic formulation that appears to corroborate Richard Dyer's influential work on the development of classical motion picture photography. As Dyer points out, when filmmakers and engineers began to codify technological standards for the cinema in the 1920s, they proceeded with whiteness as a default visual norm. "The [film] apparatus was developed with white people in mind and habitual use and instruction continue in the same vein, so much so that photographing non-white people is typically construed as a problem," Dyer writes. "Stocks, cameras, and lighting were developed taking the white face as the touchstone."[61] To be sure, Flaherty's difficulties with orthochromatic film—which, according to the preceding account, photographs red and yellow color values as a flat "lifeless black"—are a symptom of this issue. Calibrated to an ideal of whiteness, the existing motion picture technology made reproducing lifelike images of nonwhite skin a logistical nuisance, if not an outright impossibility.

Yet Frances also later explained the "happy technical discovery" of panchro in terms that help to refine Dyer's thesis, which revolves around a monolithic black–white model of racial difference:

> When we projected our first experiments on the screen, the [Samoan] people came out black like Negroes, and there was nothing pleasant about them at all. The orthochromatic film we were using did not give the proper color-value to their beautiful, light-brown skin. An orthochromatic film takes red as black, and wherever red enters into a color, it is seriously distorted. We had brought with us a color-camera, however, with the idea of making some experiments in motion-picture color-work. In color-photography panchromatic film is used—a color-corrected film, sensitive to red. It was an experimental use of this film with our ordinary camera that threw the first gleam of light on our difficulty. We found that the panchromatic film, used in direct sunlight, gave an extraordinary, stereoscopic effect. The figures jumped right out of the screen. They had roundness and modeling and looked alive and, because of the color correction, retained their full beauty of texture. The setting immediately acquired a new significance. . . . At last we had the solution to our problem.[62]

Aside from Frances's comments about the "unpleasant" appearance of black American skin (a troubling aside to which we return momentarily), one notes in this account much of the rhetoric about *Moana* that we encountered earlier on. According to Frances, the film's value lies primarily in the visual spectacle of the Samoan body, made possible by the technological advances of panchromatic color sensitivity and color correction. But the key idea here is the panchro gray scale's alleged "stereoscopic effect," a descriptive turn of phrase that often reappears in the Flahertys' later writings. (Frances, for instance, wrote of *Moana*'s "stereoscopic" ability to "bring out . . . every shade of reality and its roundness . . . the illusion of the actual" in an undated missive composed just as the film neared completion; Robert similarly recalled the South Seas images as having a "stereoscopic quality" in a 1934 essay suggestively titled "Filming Real People.")[63] The term was a deliberate misappropriation, more marketing flourish than visual reality. By no means should we regard the film as literally achieving three-dimensionality. But the Flahertys' frequent references to "stereoscopic effects" and "illusions of the actual" do give a sense of the breadth of their investment in panchro's ability to create the illusion of mediated "liveness" in the images onscreen, to borrow the terminology of the performance theorist Philip Auslander.[64] In direct opposition to the "lifeless" look of orthochromatic emulsion, panchro, according to Frances, gives life back to—literally, it *reanimates*—a culture supposedly on the brink of extinction: "The figures jumped right out of the screen. They had roundness and modeling and looked alive and, because of the color correction, retained their full beauty of texture." The film's frequent returns to high-angle shots that peer down at Samoan bodies gliding beneath the ocean's surface were in fact an effort to enhance this same set of effects. As Robert later explained, in the right light, the waters off Safune essentially "acted as a reading glass before the camera," at once magnifying the racial spectacle of Samoan skin and showcasing the realistic visual values of new color-sensitive panchromatic technology.[65] The film's recurring "underwater" sequences were thus one of many techniques that the Flahertys used to stage the illusion of life in a culture that seemed to have passed away.

Sameness, with a Difference

Taken together, the Flahertys' accounts of panchromatic color correction reveal a number of problematic assumptions about race lying behind *Moana*'s cinematographic experiments. On one hand, the Flahertys' use of panchro is symptomatic of the film's broader narrative effort to affirm the cultural sameness of its Samoan subjects—hardly an uncommon move to make in this period. As Thomas Cripps has pointed out, Hollywood filmmakers often turned to the South Seas as a comparatively "safe" staging ground for racial representation during the 1920s.[66] Whether fiction or nonfiction, films set in exotic colonial locales like Samoa—an ocean away from the color line at home—served as an important mass-cultural site for testing the boundaries of permissible public discourse about race in the United States. According to Cripps, one way filmmakers steered clear of the political controversies that black-and-white race films usually provoked was to distance Oceanic and Polynesian subjects from African Americans.[67] In this sense, the Flahertys' ongoing preoccupation with maintaining "proper color value," to borrow Frances's antiseptic language, masked a broader effort to whiten the people of Samoa for permissible public consumption. In private correspondence, the Flahertys actually discussed *Moana*'s racial agenda in similar terms. "With orthochromatic film it was impossible to secure a good rendering of the flesh tones of the Samoans," Robert wrote to a friend in 1926. "They appeared on the screen as dark and uninteresting as Negroes—a fatal defect if we hope to secure the sympathy of audiences (and upon this depends the success of any film) toward the characters we were to use to typify on the screen the Samoan race of people."[68]

On the other hand, evidence also suggests that the Flahertys saw Samoans as nearly white to begin with. "In some ways the Samoans are curiously like us," Frances admitted in the series of articles in *Asia* that went on to inspire Margaret Mead. "Physically I have no sense of difference, color notwithstanding. There was not a facial type among them that I could not recognize as familiar—but for the expression of the eyes. There was the difference, the gulf, the chasm."[69] Here it is difficult to disentangle what Frances actually felt while working in Samoa—sameness, with a difference—from what she wanted her American audience to feel while watching Samoa projected onscreen. Yet it is certainly clear that this kind of thinking also implicitly carries the weight of late-nineteenth- and early-twentieth-century anthropological taxonomies of race, which constitute a second major ideological influence on the film's experiments with panchromatic color sensitivity. The intellectual backstory is worth sketching here briefly.

Modern ethnological subdivisions among Pacific Island populations date back to the writings of the French explorer Jules-Sébastien-César Dumont

D'Urville, who, in the early 1830s, popularized a fourfold scientific distinction between "Polynesians," "Melanesians," "Micronesians," and "Malay-
sians," later assigning each group a discrete place on the evolutionary continuum from savagery to civilization.[70] (This arrangement was streamlined
into a tripartite system as the nineteenth century wore on, with the "Malay-
sian" classification gradually fading from common scientific usage.) Among
these groups, Melanesians—identified by their dark skins and "Negroid"
physical features—were thought to exist on the lowest rungs of the evolutionary ladder. Polynesians, by contrast, were typically considered white
once removed. Groups like Samoans, who had long appeared to Western
explorers to possess physical features "in the European range," were generally thought to share the same Caucasian genealogical origins and hereditary material as white Americans: they seemed to represent lost racial
ancestors, separated from the civilized present by a vast gulf of evolutionary time.[71] In many ways, the roots of the Edenic South Seas archetype lie
here. In the faces and bodies of Samoans and other Polynesian peoples,
Europeans and white Americans basically saw an image of themselves
before the Fall, uncorrupted by social institutions and unfettered by the
pressures of modern life. Clearly this set of assumptions also played an
important role in the unique form of Euro-American colonialism that
took shape in the Samoan Islands as the nineteenth century drew to a
close.[72]

As Jeffrey Geiger has pointed out, however, the Polynesians-as-ancestrally-
white formulation wholly failed to guarantee that Samoans would occupy
a normative position in the global racial alchemy.[73] From Bougainville and
Stevenson to Melville and Gauguin, representations of Polynesia in literature, visual art, and popular culture had almost always stressed the foreign,
the exotic, and the primitive amid the racially familiar. More important, in
the early decades of the twentieth century—just as established American
definitions of whiteness (legal and otherwise) began to erode in the face of
immigration at home and imperialism abroad, and just as the Flahertys
began to shoot film footage in the South Seas—the Polynesian–Caucasian
link began to come under ideological scrutiny.[74] In 1923, the U.S. Supreme
Court's landmark ruling in *United States v. Bhagat Singh Thind* argued that
the Caucasian racial category was itself a bankrupt invention, explicitly
mentioning Samoans (along with "Hindus," the primary racial group then

under legislative consideration for U.S. citizenship) as a population spe-ciously deemed white by "scientific manipulation."[75] At the time, the place of Polynesia in American anthropological discourse was no less contested. In 1925, an article in *National Geographic Magazine* quoted Louis R. Sullivan, a former curator of anthropology at the American Museum of Natural History, as reporting that "rapidly accumulating data on the biology of the inhabitants of the Pacific islands [is] beginning to indicate clearly that the 'Polynesians' are in no sense to be considered a uniform racial type. The 'Polynesian type' is, in fact, an abstract concept, into the make-up of which have entered the characteristics of several varying physical types."[76] By 1941, J. A. Rogers's influential multivolume study *Sex and Race: Negro–Caucasian Mixing in All Ages and All Lands* would similarly insist that Poly-nesian groups actually constituted "a vast jumble of 'races' shot through with a Negro strain in which the Mongolian and the Caucasian sometimes appear."[77] Rogers was of the opinion that Pacific Islanders only became white, if at all, after several centuries' worth of racial intermixture. "It is difficult to say how much, if any of [the Caucasian hereditary strain], existed prior to the coming of the white man," he wrote, reflecting what had become the dominant view in U.S. anthropological circles. "Europeans have been coming to the Pacific for more than four centuries and have been mixing their blood with the islanders. . . . Some writers who insist that certain Pacific Islanders"—that is, Samoans, among others—"are a Caucasian race, and were originally so, forget that they have had nearly four centuries of amalgamation with whites."[78] Thus, for Rogers and many others, Polynesian origins were not white but "decidedly Negroid." Native islanders, he concluded, were actually "divided into three groups: Melane-sian, Micronesian, and Polynesian. The first are unmixed Negroes; the sec-ond are a mixture largely of Negro and Mongolian; the third, among whom are some pure blacks, are a mixture of Negro, Caucasian, and Mongolian, with sometimes the last named predominant."[79]

Debates about Pacific racial origins continued well into the second half of the twentieth century. What is important for our purposes here, how-ever, is that at the time of *Moana*'s release, Samoans and other Polynesian groups would have existed somewhere in an ambivalent space between whiteness and otherness in the American ethnographic imagination, a matter that explains Frances's seemingly paradoxical formulation that she noticed "no sense of difference" from her Samoan subjects, "color not-withstanding." In *Moana*, nowhere are all of these strands of ambivalence more visible than in the film's climactic tattooing sequence, which captures a ritual practice that Western outsiders had long considered emblematic of racial inferiority and, in the process, deliberately draws attention to the culturally contested surface of Samoan skin.[80]

As *Moana* draws to a close, the Flahertys' explanatory intertitles reveal that all of the events recorded onscreen—hunting and fishing, climbing and swimming, cooking and dancing—have been performed in preparation for a ritual tattoo ceremony, a "great event" in Moana's young life. Bowls are washed. Mats are laid down. Special tools are blessed and arranged. The tattooing rite then begins: Moana's skin is pulled taught as a needle of bone hammers into his bare back (see Plates 4 and 5). Blood, darkened with dye, is wiped away, gradually revealing the pattern of an immense body tattoo: an unreadable cultural message, stretching from back to knee, written on color-corrected skin. The film captures the entire process in painstaking detail, interspersed with intimate close-up shots of Moana's face as he winces in pain. Outside, the men of the community perform a ritual dance to offer him courage throughout the excruciating ordeal.

Both in *Moana* and in later writings, the Flahertys explicitly figure tattooing as *the* central ritual of Samoan cultural persistence. As one of the film's title cards tells us, "Through this [tattooed] pattern of the flesh, to you perhaps no more than cruel, useless ornament, the Samoan wins the dignity, the character and fibre which keep his race alive"—as if to suggest that enduring the painful rite gives native islanders the spiritual strength to preserve their traditional ways and survive in the face of global change. In promotional articles on *Moana* published in advance of the film's 1926 release, Frances wrote about tattooing in similarly romantic terms:

> Tattooing is the beautification of the body by a race who, without metals, without clay, without cotton or silk, with practically no tools, express their feeling for beauty in the perfection of their own glorious bodies. Deeper than that, however, is its spring in a common human need, the need for struggle, for some test of endurance, some supreme mark of individual

worth and proof of the quality of the man. . . . And so it is that tattooing stands for valor and courage and all those qualities in which a man takes pride. . . .

There [Moana] lay one day, flat on his stomach on the floor, surrounded by his gentle and sympathetic and admiring friends—all the members of our "movie" family. The *tufunga* [tattoo artist] plied his hammer, and the needles bit sharp into the flesh. There was pain in the clenched hands stretched out on the matting. [Moana's] face, when he looked up, was twisted and pale, but in it was no thought of flinching. It was not only his own pride that was at stake but the honor of all Samoa. And faithfully the camera made its record of a ceremonial that, like so much else in the South Seas, seems destined soon to pass before an inrushing tide of alien civilization.[81]

The irony (and, perhaps, the cruelty) here is that the tattooing "ceremonial" was carefully negotiated and prearranged for the film. The ritual had long since waned as a consequential event in the everyday lives of indigenous Samoans. By the 1920s, tattooing was in fact legally prohibited in many regions of the islands.[82] Generations of Christian missionaries, and generations of native Samoans themselves, had disavowed the ritual. What the Flahertys depicted as most indicative of Samoan authenticity was thus a symptom of cultural adaptation and change. Tattooing was, in other words, a thing of the past.

The resurrection of the tattooing ritual allows us to read *Moana* as the product of a complicated set of negotiations and exchanges between the Flahertys and their Samoan subjects—the product, ultimately, of the early-twentieth-century encounter between cinematic technologies and racial bodies, stock and skin. On one hand, as several critics have noted, it is unlikely that Ta'avale (the real-life actor who played the film's fictional Moana) would have agreed to undergo the disfiguring process if the Flahertys hadn't first offered him generous compensation.[83] For *Moana's* Samoans, then, the tattooing ritual provided not just a platform for recording a heritage that they deemed worthy of memorialization but an opportunity for financial gain. In this there is little to distinguish them from many early-twentieth-century subjects of ethnographic film and photography, who often willingly performed outmoded cultural practices for the camera for communal benefit and individual profit.[84]

On the other hand, for the Flahertys, the tattooing ritual was less about the "struggle" and "endurance" of Samoan culture, as stated in *Moana's* intertitles, than about the film's ability to preserve it with absolute fidelity, its ability to grant eternal life—form, motion, panchromatic color balance—to "a ceremonial that, like so much else in the South Seas, seems destined soon to pass before an inrushing tide of alien civilization." As the camera slowly pans over Moana's bare torso at the end of the film, surveying the elaborate design inscribed on his back and chest, it becomes clear that the Flahertys' interest here is in the surface of the skin itself: as a visual spectacle to be appreciated for its aesthetic beauty; as a contested signifier of Samoan sameness and difference; as a second screen for projecting the preservative possibilities of panchromatic film technology. One is even tempted to read the entire tattooing sequence as a performance of the legal and anthropological debates about Polynesian origins that surrounded the production of the film. By the end of *Moana,* the archetypal Samoan has literally become nonwhite. Scarred, darkened, and disfigured by the tap of the tattooing needle, Moana's skin passes back into the domain of the racial other.

More broadly, the tattooing ritual in *Moana* functions as a metaphor both for the totality of Samoan culture and for the ethnographic process of preserving it—a metaphor for the same evolutionary genealogy of writing and media that we encountered in earlier chapters. Skin becomes the primary racial text on which *fa'a Samoa,* "authentic" Samoan culture, is written. The tattooing needle becomes a kind of premodern inscriptive technology, a distant technological cousin to the needle we witnessed spiraling hieroglyphic grooves into the surface of Adorno's phonograph record at the conclusion of chapter 3 (see Plate 6). But within the overall logic of the film, neither technology, neither skin nor needle, can function and endure in the absence of the motion picture camera: the new form of writing for the contemporary moment—in Flaherty's words, the "great pencil of the modern world."[85] In short, *Moana's* epidermal fascination was as much about media as it was about culture.

Skin, Color, Texture

Moana premiered at New York's Rialto Theater in February 1926. Financially speaking, the results were lukewarm.[86] Yet critics and commentators uniformly declared the Flahertys' efforts an aesthetic and ethnographic achievement, praising *Moana* for its "poetic" feel and "naturalistic" look, even if the film in fact bore remarkably little resemblance to life in Samoa as it was lived in the early 1920s. As Alison Griffiths has argued, "oppositions between real and faked, authentic and fabricated, and genuine and imitation were . . . subject to flexible interpretation in the early cinema period." In the case of early ethnographic cinema, especially, the ability to distinguish between cultural reality and romantic artifice was largely "determined by [spectators'] previous exposure to native cultures. . . . Audiences judged cinematic depictions to be more or less real based on exhibition practices associated with precinematic forms of ethnographic representation and the framing discourses of verisimilitude."[87] Put differently, cultural expectations configured what was, and what was not, "documentary" for early-twentieth-century audiences. (And one could certainly add here that this has remained the case for generations of filmgoers ever since.) According to Griffiths's argument, *Moana*'s ethnographic reality effect derives from the simple fact that the film's content seems to confirm long-standing myths about Samoa in the Western mind: its exotic and picturesque natural landscapes; its rapidly disappearing indigenous customs; its distance, in evolutionary time, from modern civilization. American audiences would have *anticipated* witnessing a film about real Samoan lives "unspoiled by the sham of civilization, laid in nature's richest and most glamorous setting," as promotional advertisements printed in the *New York Times* repeatedly put it.[88] When they did, *Moana* became something more than a mere feature-length motion picture romance. It became an ethnographic document.

But the historical record suggests that Griffiths's argument about cultural expectations doesn't tell the entire story, especially when considering the number of spectators in the 1920s who addressed the matter of *Moana*'s ethnographic authenticity with reference to color, texture, smell, and sound—sensory effects not immediately represented onscreen. In many ways, the film's realism seems to have rested not on its adherence to time-honored South Seas stereotypes but on its ability to provoke sensuous responses outside of the realm of the eye, a phenomenon that Laura U. Marks has called "haptic visuality."[89] For example, John Grierson's oft-cited 1926 *New York Sun* review of *Moana*—which effectively inaugurated modern uses of the term *documentary,* as we have already seen—repeatedly praises the authenticity of the Samoan rituals seemingly "imprisoned" in the Flahertys' film. Yet, despite responding to images shot solely in black and white, Grierson ultimately attributes *Moana*'s cultural value to the "golden beauty of primitive beings," most likely a reference to the effect of Samoan skin projected on color-sensitive film stock.[90] Writing for the *Toronto Star,* Arthur Heming displayed a similarly synaesthetic fascination with the visual spectacle of the Samoan form in motion: "What wholesome-looking natives! For days one is haunted with a charming memory of those godlike people of whom it has been said, 'They do not walk, they dance; they do not talk, they sing.'"[91] Where Grierson saw color, Heming heard sound—in a silent film, no less.

Most egregious, perhaps, in a long line of such responses is an anonymous 1926 review that describes the Flahertys' vision of the South Seas as a "heaven of voluptuousness," breathlessly extolling the tactile liveness of the film's imagery in terms that seem to verge on pornography: "That there is abundant sex interest in the dance of Moana and Fa'angase cannot be denied. Moana is the epitome of masculine appeal; and all the ripplings of his arms, his hands, every movement of his faun-like body, every inclination of his hibiscus-crowned head, and the wild in his eyes—all are for the delectable Fa'angase of fresh joy and virginal beauty, who dances tantalizingly beside him. Now he is at her feet, his dancing arms encircling but never touching her smooth body. One feels the magic rhythm of this primitive dance without hearing a note of music."[92] Other commentators, like the noted architect C. Grant La Farge, made more tempered links between the film's authenticity and its visual representation of the textures of the Samoan body. "Those pictures of yours are so beautiful that they give a new value to the camera," La Farge wrote to Flaherty after seeing photographic rushes from the film. "They tell, in black and white, the story of color and texture—of leaves and sky and clear water and human skin."[93] The artist Rockwell Kent also wrote to Flaherty that same month to praise his panchromatic stills: "I find it difficult to recall myself to praise of your photography, for it is as a participation in the life of the Paradise of the Samoan islands that the experience of seeing your picture is remembered. . . . It is, of course, by the perfection of your photography that the illusion of reality has been achieved, and I suspect that in seeing your picture one is more privileged than the casual traveler who may visit Samoa, for you have recalled a life whose virgin beauty has been lost and vested it with a glamour which only your own close association with these people could have revealed to you. I *know*, now, through you, a new part of the world, another civilization, and one of the most beautiful."[94]

At first glance, it is tempting to interpret the contemporary response to *Moana* through the tried-and-true lens of psychoanalytic film theory. Certainly the experience of viewing the film has a great deal to do with "scopic pleasure."[95] In a sensational bit of Hollywood film lore, one Paramount publicity executive is reputed to have lobbied against *Moana*'s distribution on account of the Flahertys' failure to "fill the screen with tits," an unsubtle nod to the notorious appeal of indigenous nudity in periodicals like *National Geographic*, a magazine that we examine in detail in chapter 5.[96] Yet, as Jacqueline Najuma Stewart has argued, "collapsing differences between racial and gender oppression, and then equating the cinematic objectification of women and people of color, does not acknowledge the unique questions race raises regarding spectatorial identification and mastery."[97] In the context of *Moana*, the psychoanalytic reading potentially obscures both the racial significance of the Flahertys' corporeal fascination and the mechanisms, technological and otherwise, through which many early-twentieth-century ethnographic films managed to create their reality effect. From Grierson to Kent, all of these reviews and responses on some level link cultural authenticity to technological novelty and aesthetic appearance. The racial body, reproduced in sensuous, "golden beauty" and lifelike tactility, is what seems to have given *Moana* its "documentary value" in the 1920s. The panchromatic "story of color and texture," scrubbed clean of the corrupting influence of the modern world, was what staged and constituted the "real" for the film's contemporary audience.

It would be wholly inaccurate, however, to suggest that the Flahertys were unique in exploiting these kinds of relationships. As we will see, part of what gives *Moana* its ethnographic authority is its legibility in a much wider culture of preservation that embraced a variety of media forms and technological practices, both visual and nonvisual. To approach this issue in further detail, we must return to the modern media forms that alerted Margaret Mead to the Flahertys in the first place: the photograph and the magazine.

5

Local Colors

The Work of the Autochrome

In May 1923, just as Robert and Frances Flaherty arrived in Samoa to begin shooting *Moana,* the American author and landscape painter Frederick S. Dellenbaugh sent an angry letter to the editors of *National Geographic Magazine,* already one of the most widely read periodicals in the United States. After thumbing through his copy of the journal's April issue, Dellenbaugh wanted to express his concerns about "Western Views in the Land of the Best," an insert of sixteen photographs depicting the scenery of the American West in brilliant natural color.[1] Amid the magazine's customary assortment of the spectacular and the exotic, it wasn't the novelty of color photography that had captured his attention. The problem, for Dellenbaugh, was the use of two of the images in the article as statements of scientific fact.

In the first photograph, breathlessly titled "Where Nature's Colors and Shadows Collaborate to Form a Wonderland," the bluish gray waters of the Virgin River wend their way through the cliffs of Utah's famed Zion Canyon.[2] To Dellenbaugh's eye, the image in the magazine was "absolutely different in color" from the Zion Canyon of real life. "The picture is all blue," he remarked, "whereas Zion Canyon is always red and white— very red and creamy white. This picture gives not the slightest idea of the coloration."[3] Even more disquieting was the color plate on the next page, an ethnographic portrait of a Navajo man holding a ceremonial drum, accompanied by a explanatory caption that reads, "The Tom-Tom of the

Navajo Echoes through the Grand Canyon. . . . It is not the tocsin of war, however, but one of the picturesque trappings of a people who have been led into the paths of peace" (see Plate 7).[4] This, too, seemed questionable. Judging by the color of his garments, the drummer in the photograph was not a genuine Navajo Indian. "The Navajos are nowhere near the Grand Canyon except the two or three ridiculous showmen at Tovar," Dellenbaugh insisted, clearly expecting a more authentic representation of the American West's vanishing races in the magazine's pages. "This plate is all wrong, including the title."[5]

National Geographic took Dellenbaugh's accusations seriously, for he knew something of what he spoke. At the age of seventeen, Dellenbaugh had accompanied John Wesley Powell on the 1871 Colorado River Expedition (see chapter 1), helping to conduct the first geographical survey of the Zion and Grand Canyon regions. He had also assisted in Powell's initial attempts to document the Native Americans who lived there.[6] Later on, Dellenbaugh authored a book-length account of his experience on the journey, as well as *The North-Americans of Yesterday* (1900), a lavishly illustrated ethnographic study of Native American culture with a title that reflected his belief that "while there are still some Amerinds extant . . . they are merely remnants of a people whose sun has set, and who therefore properly belong to yesterday."[7] In response to charges of inaccuracy coming from a reader with such impressive qualifications, the head of the *Geographic*'s Illustrations Division, Franklin L. Fisher, sent an urgent query to the photographer who took the pictures in the April 1923 issue, a color specialist named Fred Payne Clatworthy: were the photographs of Zion Canyon and the Navajo drummer real?

In the case of the former, Fisher let Clatworthy off the hook. After all, he reasoned, commercial color photography was still in its infancy—exposure times varied, negatives deteriorated, and mass-market reproduction techniques seldom did justice to the hues of an original image. Even in the best of circumstances, the changing light conditions at Zion were likely to account for the differences between the muted blues of the published picture and the "very red and creamy white" of Dellenbaugh's memory. But a misidentified Navajo drummer was a much more serious matter. "In the case of the Indian subject," Fisher informed Clatworthy, "we have referred this picture to the Bureau of American Ethnology,

Smithsonian Institution, which advises us that the picture is a fake throughout, and that the supposed Indian is in reality not an Indian at all."[8] Given
National Geographic's commitment to recording the world's cultures in the
popular idiom of the mass-market magazine, the implications of such a
mistake were especially grave. "We are of course at fault for not having
submitted this picture to the Bureau of Ethnology before we printed it,"
Fisher continued,

> but I assumed that you [Clatworthy] knew what you were talking about and
> that the information you gave was accurate. We of course feel that you have
> been imposed upon and your error may be excused on the ground that you
> were looking at this subject strictly from a pictorial point of view, it having
> had no ethnologic interest for you. I am sure, however, that you will appre-
> ciate what a serious matter it is to have such criticism leveled at one of our
> illustrations. It would not matter so much in an ordinary popular magazine
> but The Geographic is supposed to be scientifically precise even though its
> information is presented in popular style.[9]

Fisher closed the letter by imploring Clatworthy to adhere to the magazine's lofty standards of scientific accuracy. "I am writing this letter," he
warned, "to impress upon you the necessity for *exact data,* even in the case
of purely pictorial subjects."[10]

The exchange among Dellenbaugh, Fisher, and Clatworthy in the wake
of *National Geographic's* April 1923 issue reflects many of the challenges
that the new technology of color photography posed to the salvage ethnographic project. From the standpoint of photographic production, early
color processes were notoriously unreliable. Whether dealing with dramatic natural landscapes or exotic ethnographic subjects, securing a faithful image depended on a photographer's ability to overcome a host of
technical obstacles, not to mention the difficulty of managing the realities
of life on the other side of the camera. To Fisher, the trouble that Clatworthy had in capturing the color of Zion Canyon was excusable because
the existing photographic technology wasn't entirely suited for the documentary task at hand.

From the standpoint of cultural reception, moreover, color photography
posed even thornier problems. The photographic medium has been called

the "salvage tool *par excellence,*" and we often think of color as a crucial aspect of a photograph's indexical relationship to prior events in time and space.[11] But to many early-twentieth-century observers, the revolution in color images only seemed to compromise photography's evidentiary status. Dellenbaugh's concern with the Navajo drummer is symptomatic of color photography's peculiar position between realism and pictorialism, scientific data and artistic adornment, during the 1910s and 1920s. It wasn't a foregone conclusion that color photographs could actually record and preserve culture in any lasting or meaningful way. In the pages of *National Geographic,* the new technology seemed to obscure as much as it revealed.

This chapter traces the contested history of ethnographic color photography in the early decades of the twentieth century, a subject that has received curiously scant attention given its visibility in American print culture during this period.[12] Elizabeth Edwards has noted that ethnographic photographs were rarely shot in color before the 1930s, when the breakthrough inventions of Kodachrome and Agfacolor made color work easier for anthropologists who sought to document the world's disappearing cultures.[13] Yet the project of salvage ethnography had a foothold in the mass marketplace long beforehand, as Fisher's insistence on marrying "ethnologic interest" with "popular style" clearly suggests, and if we look beyond the institutional confines of professional anthropology, a vastly different story comes into view. Despite early color's technical drawbacks— and despite the frequent complaints of specialist readers like Dellenbaugh, who were skeptical of its scientific utility—color photographs emerged as *National Geographic*'s most recognizable feature during the 1910s and 1920s. Moreover, the magazine's experiments with color photography weren't simply a way to appease the nation's limitless appetite for the spectacular and the exotic.[14] As I argue in this chapter, the *Geographic*'s color fetish was the product of a conscious attempt to stem the global tide of cultural disappearance. For *National Geographic* photographers like Clatworthy, an ethnographic photograph in black and white provided merely "half a picture."[15] If primitive races were vanishing with the passage of time, the most visible and vibrant artifacts of their lives could only survive in the promise of color images—in the grains of a fragile and short-lived photographic technology known as the *autochrome,* the twentieth century's first commercially viable color process.

In what follows, I bring together three narrative threads in the story of the ethnographic autochrome before 1930. The first thread, which focuses on the mid-1900s, considers the invention of the autochrome process, its possibilities and limitations, and its initial patterns of use. The second narrative thread, which focuses on the mid-1910s, considers *National Geographic*'s earliest investments in color photography, which paradoxically drew on the autochrome's distinctive "pictorial point of view" (Fisher's phrase) to record the colors of primitive material culture for science and posterity. The final thread, which focuses on the 1920s, examines how color photographers like Clatworthy attempted to reconcile the unreliability of the autochrome process with the broader expectations of the salvage ethnographic project.

Taken together, these three narrative threads—three case studies, in miniature—demonstrate the importance of popular racial thinking to the culture of color photography in the early decades of the twentieth century. The autochrome required work, as we will see, and in the United States that work was increasingly motivated by ethnographic imperatives. My account concludes with a return to Clatworthy's April 1923 photograph of the Navajo drummer, whose performance of cultural authenticity suggests alternative readings of the color photography processes that *National Geographic* popularized in this period.

"Color-Mad"

A surprising number of scientists successfully experimented with color image-making processes prior to the twentieth century.[16] To be sure, the dream of color photography is as old as the medium of the photograph itself. In the 1850s, for instance, the New York minister Levi Hill developed a makeshift technique that yielded color daguerreotypes, an effect that the French inventor Claude Félix Abel Niépce de Saint-Victor fleetingly attained through different means around the same time. In 1861, aided by new research in the field of optics, the Scottish physicist James Clerk Maxwell pioneered an indirect "three-color" photographic process, and inventors such as Louis Ducos du Hauron and Charles Cros independently experimented with similar methods in the decade that followed. In the 1890s, Frederick Eugene Ives and Gabriel Lippmann discovered sophisticated color development techniques that captured the public's attention on both sides of the Atlantic. Lippmann's work even earned him a Nobel Prize. Yet among the litany of innovations, few were deemed reliably faithful to nature, much less suitable for commercial use. Alleged breakthroughs in color photography were so frequent, new processes fizzled so often, that by the early twentieth century, the photographer Edward J. Steichen charged the industry of "cry[ing] wolf" when it came to the latest developments in the field. "During the last twenty years we have been periodically informed by the daily press that color photography was an accomplished fact," Steichen wrote in the pages of *Camera Work*, the period's leading journal of fine art photography. "Every time some excitable individual got a little chemical discoloration on his photographic plate or paper, the news was sent sizzling over the globe and color photography was announced in big type, corporations were formed, and good friends were given another chance to invest in a sure thing. As usual, the public soon yawned."[17]

It wasn't until Auguste and Louis Lumière introduced the Lumière Autochrome to the French Academy of Sciences in May 1904 that the prospect of a viable color process appeared within reach.[18] (The Lumière brothers actually began tinkering with color photography in the early 1890s, but a certain novelty side project ended up overshadowing their initial successes in the field.) Ingeniously employing a photosensitive plate covered with thousands of grains of dyed potato starch, the autochrome process created stunningly vivid full-color images. Upon exposure, each individual grain absorbed a complementary pixel of colored light; in the darkroom, the refracted field of pixels could be reversed to mirror the colors of nature. In the intensity of their hues, and in the scientific principles behind their creation, autochromes are often compared to impressionist or pointillist paintings. The resemblance is no accident. As Anne Hammond has pointed out, the Lumières shared with the Monets and Seurats of the art world an abiding interest in the fundamentals of modern color theory, which suggested that the human eye perceives different colors by mixing together individual points of light.[19] Because the colors of the image were an internal creation of the mind rather than an external product of the medium, autochromes were thought to provoke heightened emotional states in the viewer and achieve deeper chromatic effects.

Unlike its photographic predecessors, the Lumière autochrome didn't require the use of multiple exposure plates, a cumbersome necessity that ended up limiting the nineteenth-century innovations based on Maxwell's three-color technique. And unlike their photographic competitors—Ives's Kromogram process and Lippmann's interference method—autochromes were unburdened by expensive viewing equipment and capable of reproducing the entire range of the color spectrum. Yet the disparities between the popular response to the autochrome and its subsequent patterns of use are an object lesson in the unpredictable social lives of new technologies, which often present users with possibilities that are unattainable in material practice.[20] As we will see, the autochrome's incompatibility with twentieth-century economies of photographic production and circulation appeared to doom the process to premature obsolescence. If not for the editors at *National Geographic*—and if not for the time-honored myth of vanishing races that encouraged their efforts—autochromes might have gone the way of the color technologies that preceded them.

Perhaps predictably, the invention of the autochrome was met with widespread public acclaim. Ignoring the lessons of previous advances in the field, Alfred Stieglitz, editor of *Camera Work*, pronounced the Lumières' results "uncommonly realistic," joining a chorus of European and American commentators who hailed the process as the inaugural step in an impending color revolution. "The seemingly everlasting question whether color would ever be within the reach of the photographer has been definitely answered," Stieglitz claimed in 1907, shortly after the Lumière Company made autochromes commercially available to photographers around the world. "Thanks to their science, perseverance, and patience, practical application and unlimited means, these men [the Lumières] have finally achieved what many of us had looked upon practically as unachievable. . . . We venture to predict that in all likelihood what the Daguerreotype has been to modern monochrome photography, the Autochromotype will be to the future of color photography. . . . Soon the world will be color-mad, and Lumière will be responsible."[21] Stieglitz's *Camera Work* quickly adopted the autochrome as one of its signature aesthetic projects, promoting the technology as a groundbreaking new vehicle for artistic expression. The journal printed some of the first reproductions of color photographs in the United States, taken by pictorialists associated with the American Photo-Secession movement.[22]

Outside of the rarified world of fine art photography, observers matched Stieglitz's enthusiasm. Three aspects of the autochrome were initially singled out for praise: its photographic realism, its chromatic brilliance, and (above all else) its apparent technical simplicity. A February 1908 article in the *Los Angeles Times*, for instance, recounted the story of J. Edward Greene, an aptly named amateur photographer in Pasadena, California, who began experimenting with color images soon after the autochrome became available in the United States: "Not only has he [Greene] demonstrated the fact that reds, greens, yellows, and blues can be faithfully reproduced, but he has succeeded in making some portrait studies in which the flesh coloring more closely approaches the original than has heretofore been possible for any painter to accomplish. . . . There appears to be no end to the color scope of the Lumière process."[23] After viewing an exhibit of autochrome reproductions of famous works of art, a reporter for the *New York Times* announced that it was at last "possible to reproduce the most wonderful things with perfect accuracy."[24] The *Chicago Tribune* praised the autochrome's "remarkable exactness" on similar grounds: "The autochrome plate of the Lumières has made the taking of photographs in colors not only a possibility for professionals, but it has given to the hands of even the amateur photographer the power to reproduce even the most delicate shades of color found in still life and in nature. . . . It is not merely a scientific experiment, as the other color processes in photography have been. It does not involve the long and intricate processes, the tedious hours of work in the dark room, the expert knowledge, the keen eye for color, [or] the extravagant use of chemicals that other inventions for photographing colors have demanded."[25]

In truth, however, the autochrome demanded all of these things: the tedious hours, the expert knowledge, the keen eye—even the use of harsh chemicals, which more often than not failed to reward photographers with passable results. Put simply, the autochrome wasn't all it was made out to be. The historical record is in fact littered with on-the-ground accounts that belie the idealistic rhetoric surrounding the Lumières' invention. "In candor I must also say that the results are not always lovely," wrote one of the format's disenchanted adopters in 1909. "The ways of the Autochrome are vain at times, and the woes and words of the autochromer would fill a book, if they were fit to print. Simple enough in its theory, and simple enough in its successful practice, there are yet perplexities galore always, even for the most skilled worker."[26] The Lumière Company suggested as much in the promotional pamphlet that it distributed to stateside photographers, euphemistically warning that the process of producing a successful color image was "excessively delicate."[27] Helen Messenger Murdoch, one of *National Geographic*'s early color experimentalists, later admitted that the oft-cited visual "delights" of the autochrome "were mainly due to the high number of failures that made the occasional successes all the more thrilling."[28] While many observers rushed to declare the world "color-mad" (Stieglitz's phrase) in the years following the Lumières' invention, photographers themselves discovered that the autochrome was a technology riddled with material limitations.

Early-twentieth-century photographers encountered three main problems with the autochrome, and they are worth outlining to underscore just how unlikely it was for the process to have ushered in the twentieth century's "chromatic revolution," to borrow Stephen Eskilson's terminology.[29] In the first place, autochromes were materially unstable; by no means was the technology reliable, permanent, or even easy to use. Unlike standard monochrome photographs, which by 1900 employed user-friendly photographic film, autochromes were exposed and developed on transparent glass plates. The plates were fragile; they cracked with the slightest mishandling. They also deteriorated rapidly, both before and after the developing process. Color photographers who were careful enough to avoid damaging the surface of the autochrome transparency plate had to contend with its exceedingly brief shelf life. As the Lumières warned in American promotional pamphlets,

> Autochrome plates will not keep in good condition indefinitely; they may, after several months, show traces of deterioration, which appear more rapidly if the plates are not preserved from the influence of *heat and damp*. The wrapping in which Autochrome plates are packed bears a date indicating the period within which they should be used. This date is a *minimum limit* only, and is not intended to imply that after such date, the plates will inevitably show traces of deterioration, as they may remain in good condition for

a much longer period, up to several months in fact, according to their having been more or less protected against heat and damp. We have however,
wished to indicate a date within the limits of which the plates may be relied
upon to retain their qualities unimpaired.[30]

Even according to the Lumières themselves, then, the autochrome was a
perishable commodity. This made life especially difficult for photographers
who hoped to take pictures in remote locations. A 1920 article on color
photography in Africa, for instance, cautioned readers about transparency
plates spoiling prior to development. "Between latitudes 10 and 20 the difficulties in the way of the colour photographer are like locusts—you cannot
see them for the multitude of them," the author noted. "With the ther-
mometer at 102 in the shade at eight o'clock in the morning, the prospect of
getting successful autochromes might very well seem to be remote. . . . The
climatic conditions with which we have to contend out here are such that
when once a box of autochrome plates has been opened, they must be used
within forty-eight hours, or they are done for."[31] Autochrome plates that
didn't shatter in transit thus ran the risk of "going bad," like milk or meat.

Early autochromists who managed to keep the transparency intact still
had to deal with the technology's second major photographic constraint:
exposure time. Depending on the light source, autochromes took anywhere
from twenty to one hundred times longer to shoot than standard monochrome photographs—a matter of seconds, to be sure, but long enough to
negate the possibility of instantaneous work and require the use of unwieldy
camera supports.[32] The lengthy exposure time of the Lumière process helps
to explain why so many early autochromists chose to limit their attention
to still lifes and landscapes.[33] Moving objects blurred color images, and
human subjects were forced to pose unnaturally before the camera—two
problems of photographic composition to which we return later on. As
Paula Amad has pointed out, the slowness and immobility of the Lumière
process rendered early-twentieth-century color images curiously out of joint
with a modern world defined by speed, shock, and change.[34] Long exposure times meant that the autochrome was a throwback to early photographic processes such as the time-consuming daguerreotype, which had
fallen into obscurity over half a century earlier. Autochromes were thus
anachronistic in every sense of the word.

The autochrome's third major drawback was that it was virtually un-reproducible. Photographers who attempted to duplicate autochrome trans-parencies typically did so at great financial expense, and even the most exacting reproduction techniques compromised the color values of the original image. This problem was by far the most significant in terms of the technology's practical application, and many users in fact took issue with it from the outset. In 1907, for instance, an anonymous article in the monthly color supplement to the *British Journal of Photography* (then a new feature of the magazine) noted that "very little attention has been given by workers of the Autochrome process to the duplication of the results"—this, despite the fact that "the desire for more than one copy is bound to arise in the case of many employing the method in a serious way." The author went on to list a number of common difficulties in the search for faithful autochrome reproductions (most important, image degradation and chromatic irregularity), ultimately dismissing the possibility of quality color copies as an impractical and expensive "matter of chance."[35] Repro-duction problems likewise surfaced in the pages of Alfred Stieglitz's *Cam-era Work* around the same time, a complication seldom noted in discussions of the Photo-Secession's celebrated artistic experiments with color photog-raphy in the late 1900s and early 1910s.[36] In his earliest writings on the auto-chrome, Stieglitz worried that "no print on paper will ever present the colors as brilliantly as those seen in the transparencies."[37] His fears were quickly realized when faulty color reproductions marred the initial print run of *Camera Work*'s first "Color Number," delaying its official release by several months.[38] As soon as color images began appearing in the journal, reproduced using a costly four-color printing method developed by a pub-lishing firm in Munich, the photographer who shot them—none other than Edward Steichen, cited earlier—made a point of highlighting the visual discrepancies between the images on the page and the color of the original transparency plates: "One thing we must not lose sight of: it is futile . . . to give an exact reproduction of a color transparency, any more than a paint-ing on canvas can represent the effects of a painting on glass. In this way the screen plate will always possess value and beauty that are not to be copied—and color that cannot exist on paper."[39]

Steichen closed his apologetic remarks in *Camera Work* with a caveat that captures much of the autochrome's technical instability in the early years of its commercial use: "As I write these notes prints of the color plates from the edition of those appearing with these pages in *Camera Work* are before me. . . . The engravings are remarkable; they are technically by far the best reproductions that have been made from Autochromes up to the present; but their relationship to the originals, as regards color, vitality, and harmony, as I remember them, is as—well, comparison fails completely! There is no relationship. They are a thing apart. . . . They are neither representative of Autochrome photography, nor of color photography: they are a compromise—an experiment."[40] Steichen's flawed color "experiments" reveal what the Lumières' early promoters had failed to see. Autochromes were literally "a thing apart." Affixed to fragile glass plates, severed from the burgeoning global economy of image circulation, every autochrome was by necessity an original.

Taken together, the problems of fragility, exposure time, and nonreproducibility underscore the technical precariousness of early color photography in the years following its invention. Promotional rhetoric to the contrary, the autochrome was a technology that was perilously out of step with the times; its future would only be written with great difficulty. Yet the process ended up enduring, against what now seem like insurmountable odds. By 1914, the Lumière Company was producing more than six thousand color transparency plates per day, a rate that wouldn't decrease until the early 1930s.[41] What, then, accounts for the autochrome's cultural staying power? In the United States, at least, it was *National Geographic* magazine, a once-obscure scientific journal with a massive popular following, that helped rescue the technology from speedy obsolescence. In the Lumière process, the *Geographic*'s editors saw a way to combine the dazzling appeal of color with the magazine's long-standing goal of recording cultures that were threatening to disappear—"the world and all that is in it," as the slogan famously went. In the popular domain, the ethnographic myth of vanishing races literally helped to keep early color photography alive.

Vanishing Red: The Autochrome and the *Geographic*

When *National Geographic* began its print run in the late 1880s, there was little in the magazine's pages to foreshadow the massive investments in color technology that its editorial staff would make twenty years later. Founded as the promotional arm of the National Geographic Society

(NGS), an organization of scientists, explorers, and Washington elites who made it their mission to "increase and diffuse geographical knowledge" at the end of the nineteenth century, the *Geographic* had ties to several figures whom we have already encountered in these chapters, counting among its early cosigners Alexander Graham Bell, John Wesley Powell, and a number of researchers associated with the Smithsonian Institution's Bureau of American Ethnology.[42]

In keeping with the scientific leanings of the NGS and its constituents, much of the *Geographic*'s content during the late 1880s and early 1890s remained narrowly specialized and torturously dry, at times bordering on academic incomprehensibility. Articles in the earliest issues of the journal reproduced the minutes of the latest NGS meetings, reported on federal land surveys, and summarized recent findings in the fields of geology, archaeology, and meteorology—nothing that was likely to appeal to the average American reader. By the early 1920s, however, *National Geographic* boasted a circulation of more than one million, exceeding the combined distribution of six prominent periodicals that had put the medium of the magazine at the center of American mass culture in the early decades of the twentieth century: the *Atlantic Monthly*, the *Century, Harper's, Outlook, Scribner's*, and *World's Work*.[43] The only American magazine with a wider domestic circulation in this period was the *Saturday Evening Post*, which had the distinct advantage of arriving on a weekly basis.[44]

The *Geographic*'s reversal of fortunes was mostly the result of the canny maneuvering of its young editor in chief, Gilbert H. Grosvenor, who modified the magazine's content in response to two major turn-of-the-century developments. The first was America's increasingly energetic role in world affairs. As Julie Tuason and Susan Schulten have shown, *National Geographic* saw its first major uptick in circulation in the wake of the controversial U.S. military conflicts of 1898, which provided the NGS with its first real market niche.[45] As soon as Grosvenor began replacing the *Geographic*'s bland technical articles with accessible accounts of the overseas territories that were at the center of America's new hemispheric design, readers started to take notice. The islands of Cuba, Samoa, Puerto Rico, and the Philippines, never before chronicled in the pages of *National Geographic*, were the subject of fifty-six informational articles between 1898 and 1905 alone.[46] "Half of world may not know how the other half lives," wrote assistant editor John Oliver La Gorce, looking back on the magazine's turn-of-the-century move toward popular ethnography. "But the experience of the *National Geographic* is proof positive that it is deeply interested in finding out, for its unparalleled growth is eloquent witness of the widespread interest of man in his fellow-man, his surroundings, his mode of living, his customs and his beliefs."[47] What La Gorce labeled as cordial ethnographic "interest" was intimately connected to the promise of an American empire whose destiny extended far beyond the nation's continental borders. His sly allusion to Jacob Riis's photographic touchstone *How the Other Half Lives* (1890) suggests that the *Geographic* was working to update the mission of documentary photography for a newly globalized age, preserving primitive peoples in distant lands.

If the first historical shift that structured the rise of *National Geographic* was geopolitical, the second was technological. In the late 1890s and early 1900s, Grosvenor also capitalized on sea changes in printing technology that made it cheap and easy to reproduce high-quality photographs on type-compatible paper. The most significant innovation in this period was the development of the halftone printing process, which came to prominence in the 1880s.[48] American magazines such as *McClure's* and *Munsey's* had long used visual images to enhance their mass-market appeal.[49] Even when employed sporadically, images attracted readers more than text. Yet the halftone process enabled popular journals to include visual illustrations with greater regularity, and during the 1890s and 1900s, Grosvenor distinguished *National Geographic* from the pack by making high-quality halftones the magazine's defining editorial feature. To read an article in the *Geographic* in this period is to read what amounts to an extended image caption: then, as now, the NGS privileged the content of its illustrations over the content of its written articles. By 1908, cheaply produced halftone photoreproductions—"realistic ones, replete with human interest," as Grosvenor characterized them—composed well over half of every issue.[50] According to La Gorce, writing just as the magazine began its meteoric rise to popularity, the lopsided ratio of images to text reflected the NGS's interest in speaking the "new universal language" of photography, a "language which takes precedence over Esperanto and one that is understood as well by the jungaleer as by the courtier; by the Eskimo as by the wild man in Borneo; by the child in the playroom as by the professor in the college; and by the woman of the household as well as by the hurried business man." Photographs, by this logic, allowed the average reader to absorb ethnographic information without expending excess mental energy. "Most magazines use illustrations for the elucidation of the text," La Gorce continued, "whereas the *Geographic* uses what might be termed 'talking pictures,' which tell their own story. So fascinating is the story they tell of the curious and characteristic customs in many corners of the world that the reader cannot help absorbing the authoritative articles, and the knowledge is planted without the reasoning process being unduly taxed or by subsequent disturbances of the mental digestive track in the assimilation of new facts. Human interest is as wide as the human race, and science, when translated into the every-day language [of photography], proves after all to be pure human interest."[51] The *Geographic* ideal of effortless global consumption through the universal language of the image, honed at the dawn of the twentieth century, remains one of the magazine's cornerstones today.

On the whole, Grosvenor's interest in the autochrome was the natural extension of these two structuring trends—the intensification of America's global mission, on one hand, and the rise of halftone print reproduction, on the other—which decisively shifted the *Geographic*'s content toward the ethnographic and the visual. The speed with which Grosvenor began experimenting with the autochrome process suggests such an interpretation. *National Geographic* adopted new color technologies at a rate, and with a production price tag, that no other American periodical came anywhere close to matching. In 1906, a year before the Lumières publicly unveiled the autochrome, the *Geographic* began using expensive color halftone techniques developed by a Philadelphia printer named Max Levy to enliven maps and illustrated sketches.[52] In 1910, the magazine's November issue included a twenty-four-page spread of hand-painted monochrome photographs—a common practice in the motion picture industry at the time and one that the magazine would employ intermittently well into the mid-1920s.[53] The *Geographic* took on the autochrome in 1914, limiting its experiments to small-scale still lifes of trees and flowers.[54] But by 1916, after toying with an extravagant four-color adaptation of Levy's color printing method, Grosvenor felt sufficiently comfortable with the autochrome to include an insert of thirty-two transparency reproductions in the magazine's April issue on U.S. national parks. In 1920, Grosvenor established an in-house color laboratory, which, in the subsequent decade alone, went on to publish more than eighteen hundred color photographs of scenes in Ceylon, India, China, Iraq, Spain, Puerto Rico, Tunisia, Bolivia, the Marquesas Islands, and the American West (among other locations).[55] The overwhelming majority of these images were autochromes.

A cursory glance at the autochromes printed in the pages of the *Geographic* during this period suggests that Grosvenor turned to the technology as a special visual strategy for documenting cultures in fatal contact with civilization. To take a representative instance, consider the early autochrome work of Franklin Price Knott, which Grosvenor featured in the magazine's first extended color photo series in April 1916.[56] A latecomer to professional photography, Knott started his career in the visual arts as a miniature and portrait painter; he only began experimenting with the autochrome process while traveling abroad in the early 1910s, abandoning his paintbrush and canvas soon thereafter. In a 1928 article for *National Geographic*, he would recall his professional jump from painting to photography as a relatively seamless transition:

> For years I was a painter of miniatures. Faces, beautiful and dull, ugly and interesting, passed before my brush. Then came the magic of autochromes. By color photography, millions who read this magazine may glimpse the glories of Nature—God's own great studio. Like an artist's brush, now the camera catches every tint and shade from the Arizona desert or Alpine sunset to the gorgeous panoply of Indian rajah courts and the bronze beauty of jungle maids asplash in lotus pools. So it came I laid down my brushes and took up the color plates. And from the Ganges to the Great Wall, from Pyramids to Buddhist temples, I have wandered. To catch their color and portray these dream places to the millions here at home who long to see them—that, now, is my avocation.[57]

Knott's account predictably indulges in the romantic vision of travel and exploration that the *Geographic* made famous in this period. It also elides the complications of the autochrome process in the service of representing color photography as flawless technological "magic." More important for our purposes, however, is the fact that Kott's rhetoric implies an understanding of the autochrome as an indeterminate middle ground between

popular art and ethnographic science, pictorial spectacle and cultural documentation. At the same time that he connects the process to the fine art
practices that influenced its invention (color photography is here explicitly
likened to an "artist's brush," one step removed from the "tint and shade"
of modern painting), he also takes care to note that the autochrome's primary social import lies in its ability to reproduce the vibrant color of disappearing peoples in distant places: the "gorgeous panoply of Indian rajah
courts," the "bronze beauty of jungle maids asplash in lotus pools," and
so on. By 1929, a year before his death, Knott wrote several letters to
the *Geographic's* staff expressing his desire to travel to the far corners of
the globe in search of soon-to-vanish primitive cultures. "My position is
this," he declared in private correspondence with Franklin L. Fisher. "I am
no longer interested in Society Life and my greatest pleasure should be in
searching for color pictures in the most primitive countries."[58] Knott may
have wanted to go where the maps were still blank, like Joseph Conrad's
Marlow before him, but he made certain to bring thousands of glass transparency plates along the way.

As we might expect from a color photographer with Knott's artistic
background, the autochromes in the April 1916 issue of *National Geographic*
mingle pictorial and ethnographic styles simultaneously—at times employing color to capture the aesthetic "glories of Nature—God's own great
studio," at other times employing color to document civilization's encroach-
ment on authentic primitive life. As Knott understood, these approaches
to color image making were by no means mutually exclusive. For instance,
Knott's April 1916 series scatters full-color photographs of Hopi, Blackfeet,
and Salish Indians amid spectacular color views of the national parks of
the American West. This was a common practice in the pages of the *Geographic* at the time—one intended to present Indians as natural curiosities
of the American landscape, local color that needed to be preserved in the
face of destructive historical change.[59] A similar mix of aesthetic spectacle
and ethnographic science is evident in Knott's autochrome "The Chief
Priest of the Snake Clan," which displays a low-angle shot of a Hopi priest
sitting atop a craggy rock formation, accompanied by a caption that neu-
trally translates what we see in the image: "His face and body are smeared
with black and white and yellow paint. His ornaments are many. A gray
fox skin dangles from his back. On his legs are bound shells of the desert

terrapin with points of antelope hoofs inside to serve as rattles. Eagle feathers are carried in one hand, with which the snakes are stroked and pacified. A prayer stick is also in his hand. Some claim that the priests drink an herb tea before the dance which renders them immune to the poison, but all agree that the snake's fangs are not extracted" (see Plate 8).[60] The autochrome seems to pull in two directions at once: while the sitter's classical pose suggests the image's pictorial appeal (as well as an iconography of the noble savage that calls to mind the work of the American painter George Catlin), the alternating reds, blacks, and grays of the picture highlight the cultural "ornaments" that are presumed to be authentically representative of an endangered Hopi tradition.

Knott employs the same techniques in "Medicine Men Compounding Their Potions," which shows two Blackfeet men seated in profile in a grassy meadow. On one hand, the autochrome clearly attempts to give off the impression of high visual art. The native sitters are represented as symmetrical mirror images: the first colorfully clad in red and blue garments, the second nearly nude. On the other hand, the autochrome also traffics in the standard ethnographic logic of typage, because its caption explicitly identifies the men in the picture as ideal specimens of Blackfeet customs: "'Big Springs' and 'Black Bull,' the medicine men of the Blackfeet Indians, are among the best examples of their race. 'Black Bull' wears his hair unbound as the badge of mourning for the death of a child."[61] One of the most arresting and peculiar images in the April 1916 series captures the statuesque profile of a Hopi man, clad only in a loincloth and standing on top of a rocky cliff. Here we see visual art meet ethnographic science head on: it's as though Knott has taken a nineteenth-century anthropometric photograph and substituted the spectacular expanse of the Grand Canyon for the standard Lamprey measuring grid.[62]

Knott's autochromes are representative of the brand of color photography that Grosvenor and the NGS pioneered in the decade following World War I. Though many of the magazine's color images are landscapes and still lifes, most adhere to the "pictorial" style of visual ethnography that *National Geographic* had already begun to popularize in black and white.[63] Individuals are consciously depicted as illustrative of broader cultural types, appreciated as much for their picturesque aesthetic appeal as for their endangered cultural authenticity. Subjects are usually pictured wearing colorful garments that help call attention to the visual powers of the auto-chrome. And the photographer himself (for most of the *Geographic*'s color photographers in this early period were men) is structured as a neutral witness to the exotic scene at hand, innocently divorced from the vanish-ing world of color that lies on the other side of the camera's lens.[64] In this way, the autochrome enlarged a more established *National Geographic* iconography that accorded to Grosvenor's scientific mission of represent-ing the world with "absolute accuracy" and "permanent value" through the photographic arts.[65] This was an iconography first honed in halftone reproductions of monochrome photographs and later extended into the domain of color. La Gorce recalled that Grosvenor used monochromes and autochromes for the same general purposes, turning to color when it was "impracticable to create the real atmosphere of a far-away country in black and white . . . so that readers, young and old, may readily under-stand the actual conditions without drawing unduly on their imagina-tions."[66] In this sense, color photography was a deliberate choice, in equal parts aesthetic and ethnographic, employed to offer readers an authentic view of cultural difference that monochrome photography could not.

Viewed from our contemporary vantage point, it may seem strange to categorize popular photographs that self-consciously aspire to the condi-tion of fine art as ethnographic documents. Yet this is only the case if we project our present-day assumptions about the popular and the ethno-graphic onto the early twentieth century, when the dividing lines between these two fields were far less rigid. Anthropologists of the period would have been wary of the *Geographic*'s approach to color, but for an entirely different set of reasons. For most of the nineteenth century, photographs were considered the sine qua non of ethnographic science. Visual images were put to a variety of anthropological uses in this period—as anthropo-metric data testifying to racial characteristics, as indexical records of tradi-tional artifacts and ritual behaviors encountered in the field, as illustrations in written publications, archival collections, and museum exhibitions—all of which hinged on the conviction that culture was something that an outside observer could *see*. At the time, surface appearances (human bod-ies, most especially) were regarded as reliable symptoms of underlying racial tendencies, evolutionary capacities, and patterns of affiliation; differ-ence was as visible as the paint on the face of the Hopi priest in Knott's

1916 autochrome. By this logic, photography constituted the last word in cultural evidence. Because culture was a visible phenomenon—itself a product of the rise of photography, to be sure—it stood to reason that a photographic image depicting a sign language gesture or a tattoo marking revealed something definitive about the people who produced it. The camera was an effective way to augment and externalize the scientist's own powers of visual apprehension and ethnographic understanding.[67]

By the time that the *Geographic* began printing color reproductions, however, the culture-as-visible-surface hypothesis had begun to fall out of favor. As a number of scholars have shown, institutionally connected anthropologists started to question the efficacy of visual data in the 1900s and 1910s.[68] More than anything else, this was the product of changing disciplinary norms. To many early-twentieth-century anthropologists, the rules governing social organization increasingly seemed implicit and hidden rather than explicit and visible. The goal of ethnography became the decoding of culture's deep internal structures (networks of kinship relations, for instance, or systems of belief) rather than the documentation of its external surfaces. This meant that vision was unreliable and photographic evidence was insufficient; in and of itself, of course, an image would be hard-pressed to capture the complexities of a kinship network or a belief system. In the twentieth century, then, photographic images seemed to capture little of ethnographic value. Alternatively, as Deborah Poole has pointed out, they also seemed to capture *too much*. Aside from their inability to penetrate the visible surface of things, photographs ran the risk of containing extraneous and distracting aesthetic information. Anthropologists who remained committed to visual methods, despite the field's growing skepticism, firmly believed that written analysis needed to accompany all ethnographic photographs. Explanatory text was the best way to cancel out the excess aesthetic "noise" that images tended to produce.[69]

Historians of visual media often single out anthropology's changing attitude toward the visual image as a case study in the flexibility of photographic meaning over time. (Even more to this point, photography came back into fashion in the human sciences during the second half of the twentieth century.) Yet the cultural career of the autochrome provides a valuable counterweight to the narrative about visual evidence that this canonical account entails. Even as the ethnographic value of the photographic image waned—and even as anthropologists began to repudiate visual indices of difference, such as skin tone or cranial size—color remained an important metonym for customs and practices that were allegedly succumbing to rapid historical change.[70]

The colors of material culture, for instance, were widely regarded as reliable markers of identity and difference in this period: whereas the colors and designs of garments and handcrafts helped to distinguish between native populations (as in Dellenbaugh's reading of the "fake" Navajo man at the beginning of this chapter), losses of color were thought to be symptomatic of a group's assimilation into the dominant order.[71] Against the rising tide of skepticism about photography's ethnographic utility, Grosvenor in fact rationalized the *Geographic*'s investments in color images along these same lines. Because primitive people seemed to be disappearing with the passage of time, he explained, the magazine's autochromes were a way to create records of the colors and materials that were fading along with them: "For historians, ethnologists, and scientists of future generations, the [National Geographic] Society's rich album of natural-color photographs . . . reproduced for us and posterity in the *National Geographic* . . . constitutes a priceless, not-to-be-duplicated record, authentic in proportion and tint, of the dress, scenery, architecture, and daily life of the civilized nations and isolated tribal communities of the present age. Thousands of costumes have been copied from these pages."[72] As Grosvenor understood, a color image could register meaningful ethnographic data that other forms of documentation could not: recording the design of a ceremonial garment, capturing the pattern of a hand-woven rug, or simply re-creating the general "atmosphere" of a remote region of the world. Even when shot with purely "aesthetic" or "pictorial" aspirations in mind, then, an autochrome could perform the work of cultural preservation.

Grosvenor's logic helps to explain the persistent emphasis on material detail in Franklin Price Knott's autochromes during the 1910s. What often seems visually significant in images like "The Chief Priest of the Snake Clan," for example, isn't so much the body of the photographic sitter in question but the colors and designs of his identifying cultural "ornaments": the black of his face paint, the red of his headdress, the gray of his ceremonial fox skin. This rule applies to many of the autochromes included in the April 1916 insert. Knott often sets brightly colored baskets, rugs, and garments against comparatively drab backgrounds to throw into more brilliant relief the "untutored" material arts of Native Americans, as he called them, with their "lively appreciation of color values and combinations, and of geometric designs" (see Plate 9).[73] Several of the photos in the series use this chromatic juxtaposition technique to foreground the color red. "Another Kind of Pale Horse and His Rider" depicts a Hopi man riding a mule while dressed in a red garment and a red headscarf.[74] "A Venerable Flathead Chief, Over Eighty Years of Age" depicts a three-quarter portrait of a Salish man wearing a large headdress streaked with red and white feathers.[75] "A Hopi Indian and His Home" depicts a Hopi man draped in vibrant red fabric in front of a colorless mesa dwelling, "the brilliant red of his blanket proclaim[ing] the success of the Southwestern Indian in producing fast colors" (see Plate 10).[76]

Knott's focus on red was more than simply a way to record the brightly colored materials that were thought to be the special province of primitive people like the Hopi and Salish, however. (As David Batchelor and Michael Taussig have demonstrated, writers and thinkers in Europe and America have long associated bright colors with the lives of the uncivilized.)[77] Red also happened to be the color that autochrome transparencies captured most vividly—the color that the *Geographic*'s rudimentary four-color printing process reproduced most consistently.[78] Red Hopi garments and red Salish headdresses thus also helped to showcase the visual possibilities of the autochrome format. By mixing pictorial and ethnographic elements in the service of recording Native American material cultures, Knott's pictures bear witness to the reciprocal logic of race and media that we have encountered throughout these chapters. While the powers of the autochrome preserve the material colors of the primitive, the material colors of the primitive corroborate the powers of the autochrome.

The Work of Color

Reproduced in the April 1916 issue of *National Geographic,* Knott's autochromes appear bright and glossy, almost polished. Yet the mass-market sheen of his published images obscures the experimental labor that went into producing them. Behind a color photograph like "The Chief Priest of the Snake Clan" lies hundreds of miles of travel with hundreds of pounds of equipment, dozens of shattered or expired transparency plates, and any number of versions that may have failed as a result of variable lighting conditions, incorrect exposure times, or other minor missteps in the long road from transparency development to print reproduction. Twenty years after taking on his father's duties as editor of *National Geographic,* Melville Bell Grosvenor captured the difficulty of the autochrome experiments of the 1910s and 1920s when he spoke of the magazine "pouring it in" with color research and development, despite the mounting expenses and the technological challenges. There were misgivings, certainly; many members of the NGS felt that color photography was "too extravagant, overdoing it." But the public "liked color," the younger Grosvenor recalled. Readers of the magazine, both lay and specialized, "wanted things to look natural, and we tried every method as soon as we could find them—adopted them, tried them out."[79] Afforded the benefit of hindsight, Grosvenor's account suggests that the twentieth-century revolution in color media was far from an inevitable or determined outcome of the autochrome's invention. To borrow Raymond Williams's terminology, the life of the autochrome was the product of *intention*—the images published in *National Geographic* were one of many cultural possibilities that the raw materials of early color technology were deliberately made to realize.[80]

The career of Fred Payne Clatworthy, the photographer who published the pictures that we encountered at the outset of this chapter, provides an excellent example of the intentional work required to transform new and unpredictable technologies like the autochrome into viable color media. His images also illustrate how *National Geographic* photographers attempted to overcome the limitations of early color photography to meet the demands of the magazine's popular ethnographic mission. Born in Dayton, Ohio, in 1875, Clatworthy began his career as a professional photographer after moving west and settling in a picturesque Colorado town in the middle of Rocky Mountain National Park. He initially made his name working in the venerable tradition of western landscape photography. (As a brief biographical sketch published in 1914 described his style, "Mr. Clatworthy is primarily a lover of nature, especially in her grandest and loneliest aspects. . . . His chosen work has required an open-air life far from the encroachments of man, tramps of literally thousands of miles, and inexhaustible enthusiasm for natural beauty wherever found.")[81] Gilbert Grosvenor wrote to inquire about Clatworthy's "excellent" black-and-white "photographs of the West" as early as 1914, but it was only after Clatworthy began experimenting with autochromes that the *Geographic* took his work into serious consideration.[82]

Clatworthy's first published color photograph, a hand-painted monochrome view of the Rocky Mountains, appeared in *National Geographic* in 1920.[83] In the intervening years, he began crisscrossing the nation on a series of lecture tours, displaying magnified slide projections of his autochrome transparencies to audiences across the United States.[84] By 1928, when Clatworthy began traveling further afield in search of more exotic photographic subjects, he estimated that more than two hundred thousand individuals had attended his lecture shows in the span of a decade.[85] One of the most prolific and accomplished early color photographers in the United States, Clatworthy claimed to have developed almost ten thousand autochromes over the course of his career, billing them as the "last word in adequate representation . . . untouched by the brush of the colorist . . . the nearest you can possibly get to the scenes portrayed, without actually going there."[86]

By his own admission, Clatworthy was interested solely in the "pictorial side" of the autochrome.[87] He made few pretentions to ethnographic science in his photographic work. But it's precisely for this reason that his images are instructive; in the pages of *National Geographic,* the "pictorial side" of the autochrome was inseparable from its ethnographic capabilities. Moreover, Clatworthy's color photographs adhere to a far more entrenched visual vocabulary for representing the disappearance of the American West and the Indians who lived there.[88] As Clatworthy explained in a 1948 interview, the West had long proved a fertile field for photographic experimentation, but in the wake of the autochrome's invention "everything in the [region], most colorful of all countries, had to be done over in colors."[89] Accordingly, many of Clatworthy's photographs look like retouched versions of iconic nineteenth-century survey views and ethnographic scenes, updating the visual conventions of photographers like William Henry Jackson, Timothy O'Sullivan, John K. Hillers, and even Edward S. Curtis (one of Clatworthy's most like-minded contemporaries) for the age of color.[90]

Clatworthy's chosen subject matter wasn't simply the product of his proximity to the West's most scenic attractions, however. The technical challenges of the autochrome process—the work of early color, spurred on by the *Geographic*'s cultural mission—directly shaped the course of his photographic practice. Consider the three major color features that Clatworthy published in *National Geographic* during the 1920s: "Western Views in the Land of the Best" (April 1923), "Photographing the Marvels of the West in Colors" (June 1928), and "Scenic Glories of Western United States" (August 1929). At first glance, most of the autochromes in these articles are indistinguishable from those of Franklin Price Knott: they regularly intersperse landscape views of the Grand Canyon, Pike's Peak, and other scenic destinations with stock images of Native Americans dressed in traditional attire; they deliberately combine pictorial and ethnographic elements; and they exhibit a keen interest in the colors of material culture. At bottom, the visual similarities between the autochromes of Clatworthy and Knott are the result of their general adherence to the *Geographic*'s house color photography style. Adding local flair to an otherwise colorless landscape, as we have already seen, helped showcase the autochrome's capabilities for the magazine's mass-market readership. ("I made another trip to the Grand Canyon of Arizona," Clatworthy wrote to the magazine's staff in September 1923, describing the autochromes that would provide the seeds for his features in the magazine in 1928 and 1929. "As you suggested, [I] secured some very fine color plates of the Grand Canyon, in which Indians, both Hopi and Navajo, appear in various poses. I am glad I followed your suggestion, as the Indians in their gay colored costumes add a needed variety of color.")[91] Making the autochrome as vibrant as possible also had scientific utility. The more colorful the native subjects were in the original transparency, the more likely the reproduced image was to capture something of ethnographic value. Many of the autochromes that Clatworthy submitted to the magazine in the mid-1920s were actually rejected because they lacked sufficient color to retain ethnographic intelligibility on the other side of the reproduction process.[92]

There are important differences between Knott and Clatworthy, however, and most of them have to do with how each photographer managed the limitations of early color technologies. Knott's Indian pictures, for instance, have the feeling of portrait paintings—an effect that stems from his background as a visual artist as well as from his interest in capturing color combinations that call attention to the powers of the autochrome process. His ethnographic subjects are thus "sitters" in both the photographic and the colloquial sense of the term: they are posed for the camera in limited visual settings, devoid of implied physical movement. By contrast, Clatworthy's ethnographic subjects seem to be naturally pictured in situ, interrupted amid quotidian events already taking place. In one of the 1928 images, a group of Lakota Sioux—men, women, and children together—gathers in front of the camera before performing a ritual ceremony that demonstrates how intrepidly they have staved off "the oncoming tide of the white man's civilization," in the words of the autochrome's explanatory caption (see Plate 11).[93] In another image published in 1929, titled "Bright Hues Delight the Indian Maiden's Heart," two women of the Santa Clara Pueblo pause in front of the camera to exhibit the multicolored blankets wrapped around their shoulders.[94] In the same series, a Pueblo Indian man is pictured sitting on a rock, pondering the "departed glory of his tribe, lords of the Southwest in Coronado's day," and taking in a vast tract of adobe dwellings that recedes into the background of the image.[95]

What is most striking about this set of color photographs is their overwhelming sense of stillness. It's as though Clatworthy has staged the autochromes to resemble museum displays or life-group dioramas, arresting a moment in time either before or after some naturally ongoing course of action. In this way, his color work gives new meaning to ethnographic photography's oft-noted "stasis effect"—its freezing of native subjects in a distant past tense, beyond the reach of historical change.[96] In Clatworthy's images, however, stasis was both a function of evolutionary ideology and a product of mechanical necessity. Because the autochrome's extended exposure times required the absence of movement to work properly, stasis was literally built into the photographic apparatus itself.

Pictorial stasis is perhaps the most visible sign of the deliberate labor of early color photography, a subject that in fact preoccupied Clatworthy over the course of his career. "Few readers of the many who now, as a matter of course, look for the natural-color pictures in the *National Geographic* magazine, realize the great difficulties experienced in securing the originals," he underscored in the article that accompanied "Photographing the Marvels of the West in Colors," his 1929 autochrome series for the magazine.[97] To be sure, part of the problem had to do with the geographical inaccessibility of Clatworthy's chosen subjects. Near the end of his life, he estimated that he had traveled the equivalent of twenty-five times around the world in search of suitable color images.[98] Yet it should come as no surprise that he would also directly attribute his "great difficulties . . . in securing the originals" to the autochrome's unreliability. Although Clatworthy ultimately claimed that the Lumière process marked "the greatest advance in photography in fifty years," he hastened to add that the autochrome was only a temporary solution to the unanswered question of the direct color photograph: "Not only does it [the autochrome] require from 60 to 100 times the length of exposure of an ordinary photographic plate, precluding all motion work, but the fact that the plate is sensitive to all colors . . . makes it extremely difficult to handle."[99] Clatworthy understood that the autochrome's viability as a medium of recording wasn't a technological given. With its delicate transparency plates and extended exposure times, early color photography took actual hard work.

As Clatworthy's career progressed—and as the novelty of *National Geographic*'s color images began to diminish—the ethnographic allure of the remote and the primitive encouraged that hard work. Starting in 1928, Clatworthy began making trips to Mexico, Hawaii, New Zealand, and Tahiti to augment his magazine submissions and lecture tours. The farther he traveled, however, the more trouble he had in getting the autochrome to meet his (and the *Geographic*'s) needs. Clatworthy's New Zealand trip proved particularly unsuccessful—his statements about the autochrome's difficulties in "Photographing the Marvels of the West in Colors" can in fact be read as a direct response to the technical problems he encountered while traveling in the Pacific earlier that same year. Intending to capture the color of "unique scenic beauties" and "typical natives," as his official letter of introduction to the local tourist bureau put it, Clatworthy spent the better part of his thirty-day trip to New Zealand struggling to photograph landscape scenes and ethnographic portraits of the Māori who lived in Rotorua, the hub of indigenous life on the country's North Island.[100] Upon returning to the United States, he sent thirty-five of his New Zealand transparencies to the *Geographic*. Roughly half of these were of Māori subjects, and all were rejected by the magazine's illustrations division.[101] The images never ended up seeing publication.

The explanation for *National Geographic*'s lack of interest in what would otherwise seem to be valuable photographic documents lies in a letter that Clatworthy wrote to his hosts in New Zealand shortly after returning to

Colorado.[102] Unable to secure the proper materials for developing autochromes on site, Clatworthy had been forced to transport hundreds of
exposed glass transparencies on the long trip home. Many ended up spoiling along the way. "My taking autochrome plates so far and back again
before developing them, as I told you, would be somewhat of an experiment," Clatworthy admitted. "The two months and a half, between the
making and developing a part of my New Zealand plates was evidently too
long a time, as I lost considerable [sic] in color and brilliancy . . . altho[ugh]
I took them in sealed tins. . . . They do not do New Zealand justice. I feel
very badly about it, but it cannot be helped."[103] The remainder of the letter
suggests that the surviving transparencies fell victim to the narrow range
of conditions that were conducive to successful color work at the time,
and more than eight decades later, the images bear subtle witness to the
challenges that Clatworthy describes.[104] Several of the landscape views of
New Zealand's South Island have a dull bluish grey tint to them, a telltale
sign of autochromes shot in difficult lighting conditions.[105] The color photographs of the Māori, clearly intended to document traditional culture in
National Geographic's pictorial ethnographic style, are also compromised.
Although many of the pictures dutifully attempt to capture the designs
of native dress and architecture, and a few even focus on Māori tattooing
patterns, the majority lack variety and look uncomfortably staged for the
camera (see Plate 12). Once again, this was the result of a tricky combination of technological factors and local circumstances: the autochrome's
exposure limitations hindered Clatworthy's ability to shoot in varied settings, and because the Māoris in Rotorua were a diverse group of communities long accustomed to balancing traditional ways with Western norms,
Clatworthy had to stage his ethnographic images to conform to a monolithic stereotype of native simplicity. Based on Clatworthy's experience in
Rotorua, an editor at National Geographic went so far as to advise Franklin
Price Knott, then searching for a suitably primitive location to "go native"
for the sake of the salvage project, against shooting color photographs in
New Zealand altogether.[106]

Back in the United States, in the meantime, Clatworthy's published
color images were once again coming under fire. (The year 1928, it seems,
wasn't the best of years for the photographer.) In response to his article
in Geographic's June issue, the magazine received a number of unsolicited

letters of complaint about Clatworthy's autochromes not being "true to color" or "true to life."[107] Echoing the concerns of Frederick Dellenbaugh five years earlier, readers questioned whether the "natural-color" landscapes and ethnographic scenes in the magazine in fact represented any preexisting visual reality, honing in on several color views of Bryce Canyon and the image of the Lakota Sioux discussed earlier. Franklin L. Fisher, the *Geographic's* illustrations editor, responded by defending Clatworthy's abilities as a photographer and the magazine's commitment to scientific accuracy. Yet he also admitted that after a decade's worth of trial and error, the color reproduction challenges of the late 1900s and early 1910s remained largely unresolved. "There is always something lost between the original [autochrome] and the reproduction which follows," Fisher lamented. "As you perhaps know, some detail cannot be reproduced by any known printing process. . . . We are constantly striving for improvement in reproduction and personally I think we are making progress. The processes available at present each leave something to be desired."[108] Twenty years after its invention, then, ethnographic color photography remained a risky bet and color reproduction an imperfect proposition. There was nothing natural about Clatworthy's natural-color autochromes.

By all accounts, Clatworthy was the autochrome's leading practitioner in the United States, largely responsible for exposing the technology of color photography to a wider national audience.[109] Why dwell on his photographic failures in the 1920s—autochromes lost and rejected, images that either never made it into print or reproduced poorly when they did? His experience in this period is important for what it reveals about the limitations, and the labors, of early color media. In Clatworthy's case, the autochrome wasn't the start of a "color revolution"; the technology didn't offer an open field of visual possibility. The ends to which he put the process—color landscapes that retouched iconic nineteenth-century views, ethnographic tableaux that staged visual encounters with material detail—were the product of a delicate balancing act between the preservative project of the magazine and the visual restrictions of the technology. At a time when color was expensive, unreliable, and otherwise difficult to use, Clatworthy and the *Geographic* continued to wrestle with the autochrome because it was the only remotely viable means of recording a world in which the colors of certain cultures seemed to be fading away. Their efforts were not always successful.

Holding Still

Autochrome use in the United States and Europe dropped sharply in the early 1930s, and the technology's fall into obsolescence is visible in the pages of *National Geographic*. By 1934, when Clatworthy published his last series for Grosvenor and the NGS, color photographs were appearing in the magazine more frequently, yet fewer of the images were autochromes.[110] Cheaper, faster, and more reliable color processes had come along. It didn't hurt that these processes also yielded images that were easier to reproduce on the page.

Clatworthy, for his part, spent the remainder of his life taking color pictures of landscape views and ethnographic scenes, using them as guides for hand-painted postcards that he sold to travelers and tourists who wanted keepsakes of the Rocky Mountains. But he never published another autochrome. Five years before his death in 1953, he wrote a brief retrospective of his own career for a local photography journal that treated the Lumière process as little more than a relic of a bygone era.[111] Much like the photographic technology on which he had built his career, Clatworthy had become outmoded.

Nevertheless, it would be a mistake to read his efforts during the 1920s solely as a testament to the autochrome's impending obsolescence. Behind Clatworthy's autochromes lie not just the labors of shattered plates and faulty exposures but the actions and interests of the native people who willingly posed in front of his color camera. The men and women who appeared in Clatworthy's ethnographic views, live and in brilliant color, had motivations that aren't wholly reducible to the logic of disappearance and preservation that shaped the autochrome's popular history in this period. Reading his color photographs against the grain reveals another story altogether—a story of performance, exchange, and survival.

Take the disputed 1923 photograph of the Navajo drummer with which we began this chapter (see Plate 7). Frederick Dellenbaugh, recall, doubted the drummer's Navajo identity based on the color of his garments, a judgment about cultural authenticity that would scarcely have been possible in the context of a black-and-white photograph. After contacting the Bureau of American Ethnology on behalf of *National Geographic*, Franklin Fisher even doubted whether the sitter was a "real Indian" at all. He was an imposter, Fisher claimed; the photographer had been "imposed upon" after failing to inquire into the "status of his subject."[112] But what about the man in the picture? Who was he, and why was his presence in front of the camera so vexing to Dellenbaugh, Fisher, and the experts at the Bureau of American Ethnology?

Clatworthy's response to the petty controversy begins to answer these questions—and his account is noteworthy for what it reveals about the cultural worldview that underwrote the autochrome's popular ethnographic application in the early decades of the twentieth century. For Clatworthy, the error of the 1923 image had to do with tribal identification, not cultural authenticity. It is worth quoting his animated rebuttal to Fisher's charges at length:

> In regard to plate 14, which was taken beside the Hopi House at the Grand Canyon, this Indian, whose English name is Joe Abbott and who I have known for three years, is not a Navajo but a Hopi. As you know, the Hopi, comparatively few in number, live on the Painted desert [sic], to the south and east of the Grand Canyon and their small reservation is surrounded by the larger reservation of the more numerous tribe of Navajos—the latter, are frequent visitors at the Grand Canyon. . . . With all due respect to the Bureau of American Ethnology, they are absolutely wrong in their diagnosis and I dare the man who said Joe was not an Indian, to go to the Canyon and tell him that to his face. . . . Joe Abbott was educated, I was told at the Indian School at or near Kayenta on the reservation near the Grand Canyon. He is the leader in the daily Indian dances given for the benefit of the tourists stopping at El Tovar. . . . So far as I can see, the only mistake I made was in calling a Hopi Indian a Navajo. As you say, I am more interested in the pictorial side of Indian life than the particular tribe they belong to. Of course to a man like Dellenbaugh, who has lived among the Indians, their nationality is of more importance. . . . However, I thoroughly agree with you that one should be accurate to the very best of their knowledge in making a statement for the Magazine.[113]

Notwithstanding Clatworthy's disclaimers about photographic "pictorialism," his response to Fisher is typical of the salvage ethnographic paradigm in several respects. It subscribes to static definitions of cultural authenticity (the Navajo drummer is "not a Navajo but a Hopi"). It validates its assertions by making claims to the authority of direct personal experience

(Clatworthy has known him "for three years"). And along the way, it implicitly denies that the man in the image, Joe Abbott, could have had any definitive stake in the photographic encounter other than as a disappearing object of visual curiosity ("The only mistake I made was in calling a Hopi Indian a Navajo. . . . I am more interested in the pictorial side of Indian life than the particular tribe they belong to").

Yet very little of Clatworthy's rationale—a rationale that was as widespread as it was flawed, as we have seen throughout this book—can account for the fact that Abbott sat for the autochrome with his own interests in mind. Whether Navajo or Hopi, Abbot's pose, dress, and demeanor had more to do with the exigencies of cultural performance than with any static idea of authentic Indian identity. After all, Clatworthy's letter positively identifies him as a "leader in the daily Indian dances given for the benefit of the tourists stopping at El Tovar"—in other words, he was a photographic sitter who was literally in the business of public self-representation. (The same goes for the Lakota Sioux pictured in Plate 11, it turns out. A later interview with Clatworthy's children revealed that the men and women pictured in the autochrome were regular visitors to the Clatworthy studio during the 1920s, in conjunction with their role as performers in the annual Cheyenne Frontier Days Festival.)[114] To be sure, the definitions of cultural authenticity to which men like Dellenbaugh, Fisher, and Clatworthy all held fast, tourists in a world they believed to be passing away, were wholly incommensurate with the fact that men like Abbot were actively carving their own path through history. Reading the April 1923 issue of *National Geographic* in terms of performance rather than preservation, fluidity rather than fixity, reveals Clatworthy's autochrome, not as a faulty ethnographic record or as a bad magazine photograph, but as a visual artifact of cultural exchange. The autochrome may have emerged out of a cooperative dialogue between photographer and subject; it may have resulted from a shared desire for monetary compensation; or it may represent the result of ephemeral motivations and moments of chance that aren't available to history. The image served Clatworthy's interests, and it served the interests of the *Geographic*—this much is known. But it also very likely served Joe Abbott's.

Here we arrive at the final limitation of the ethnographic autochrome—a limitation that we might also ascribe to the ideas behind the salvage paradigm itself. The technology, like the ideology, fails to capture the fact that cultures are always in process; they are flexible rather than fixed, mobile rather than static, contingent rather than absolute. Indeed, as James Clifford famously argued almost three decades ago, cultures seldom "hold still for their portraits"—regardless of a photograph's exposure time, we might add.[115]

Fictions of Permanence

This book began with the image of Jesse Walter Fewkes recording the dying sounds of the Passamaquoddy tribe in March 1890. Go forward in time 120 years, and Fewkes's recordings live on. So do the Passamaquoddy.

Consider Language Keepers, an ongoing digital media project that uses documentary film and descriptive linguistics to restore many of the Passamaquoddy traditions that interested Fewkes in the early years of the phonograph. Established by Ben Levine and Robert M. Leavitt, a filmmaker and a linguist, respectively, who have worked under the guidance of Passamaquoddy tribal representatives for well over a decade, Language Keepers aims to record the Passamaquoddy–Maliseet language as it sounds today. More broadly, the project works to create an online infrastructure for cultural revitalization in the contemporary Passamaquoddy community. According to Levine and Leavitt, the main idea behind Language Keepers is to create a "self-sustaining documentation resource" so that cultural groups whose heritage languages are at risk can eventually become "self-documenting."[1]

The cornerstone of the Language Keepers project is the Passamaquoddy–Maliseet Language Portal, an online database that allows Internet users to access an eighteen-thousand-word heritage dictionary and engage with a growing archive of documentary films featuring native speakers in conversation.[2] Since Levine, Leavitt, and their collaborators recognize Passamaquoddy–Maliseet as a living language—one of the oldest in North America, in fact—the portal also allows users to add content to the digital archive, providing a way for community members to document their own culture and stimulate heritage language use in everyday settings. Since its inception in 2006, Language Keepers has received funding from several high-profile government agencies, including the National Science Foundation and the National Endowment for the Humanities Documenting Endangered Languages Program. Along with Levine and Leavitt, the Passamaquoddy hope that their successes in the digital arena will spark similar initiatives among Native American communities across the United States.

At first glance, Language Keepers seems to embody a contemporary update of Fewkes's documentary project, a new brand of salvage ethnography for the digital age. On closer inspection, however, the initiative represents a comprehensive rejection of the salvage paradigm. For one thing, as Levine and Leavitt explain, what makes the Language Portal unique is that it encourages "speaker groups to use heritage language in traditional and contemporary activities while recording it for language learning, dictionary development, research, cultural transmission, and revival."[3] In other words, the online archive functions as a creative platform for the persistence of Passamaquoddy culture rather than as a technological memorial to its expected extinction. Moreover, the Language Portal is as much the product of the native community's efforts as it is the product of Levine's documentary filmmaking and Leavitt's linguistic research.[4] Where Fewkes's experiments in Calais sought to mask the collaborative nature of the ethnographic encounter, hiding behind the invented objectivity of wax cylinders and talking machines, Language Keepers recognizes ethnography as a shared cross-cultural endeavor, wholly conditional and perpetually unfinished.

And yet something of Fewkes's experiment remains here, not least of which is the fact that the architects of Language Keepers maintain an abiding interest in using new media technologies to capture the sounds of Passamaquoddy culture. The 1890 cylinder recordings even show up in some of the films that are currently posted online in the Language Portal. In one Language Keepers segment, recorded on video in 2010 and titled *Let's All Sing,* a group of Passamaquoddy men and women gathers for a healing ceremony, honoring members of the community who were physically abused for using their language at a local religious school during the 1950s and 1960s.[5] After capturing a short discussion of the benefits of speaking the native tongue today ("It makes you feel good," exclaims one voice off-camera), the footage begins with Maggie Paul, a heritage speaker who

appears in a number of Language Keepers videos, launching into a powerful version of "Esunomawotultine" (Let's trade), a traditional Passamaquoddy song that celebrates the vital role of commerce in the community's
long history. At first, the group is hesitant to join in. Several of the women
on camera protest that they can no longer recall the old songs. But soon
they add their voices to the chorus, matching the strength of Maggie
Paul's refrain and tapping along with the urgent beat of her drum. At the
completion of the performance, the men and women in the video smile
and laugh together, wondering where Maggie first learned her version of
the traditional Passamaquoddy trading song. Her reply, translated in sub-
titles, is as poignant as it is telling. "We got that song long ago. When they
first made those—what are they called?—wax tapes?" Here she falters,
momentarily forgetting the name of the sound technology in question,
searching for the correct term in both Passamaquoddy and English.

"Wax cylinders," a voice offscreen interjects.

"Yes, wax cylinders—that's where we got that song," she replies, language
and memory restored. Maggie Paul had learned her version of the Passamaquoddy trading melody from a copy of Fewkes's cylinder recordings.

This is an outcome that dramatically overturns many of the narratives
of culture and history that Fewkes and his nineteenth-century contemporaries regarded as fact. Put simply, the sounds, and the people who made
them, were supposed to have disappeared, gradually receding into the
shadows of history. This, at least, was the misguided assumption that had
brought Fewkes to Calais in 1890, phonograph in tow. His field notes from
the expedition describe the Passamaquoddy trading song as part of a "very
old" trading custom that few members of the community practiced at the
time. "A person singing a song goes to the wigwam and then knocks and
enters," he jotted in his diary. "Then, dancing around for some time and
singing, he asks for something which he seeks in trade. The occupant or
owner is obliged to close the [unintelligible] or to give something of equal
value in exchange. Each trader is clothed in the old fashion. . . . The song
is given on Cylinder 17."[6] According to Fewkes, the exchange ceremony
had begun to fall out of favor among the Passamaquoddy who lived in the
region surrounding Calais. Writing in the *Journal of American Folklore* a few
months later, he predicted that the trading dance and the song that accompanied it were soon to be "wholly lost or greatly modified."[7]

Yet, as Maggie Paul explains in Language Keepers, "Esunomawotul-tine" was in fact alive and well in the mid-1980s, when magnetic copies of cylinder 17 began circulating among members of the Passamaquoddy community. Beneath the pulsating hiss and crackle of Fewkes's record-ing, degraded over the course of a century, the Passamaquoddy knew exactly what they were hearing when they encountered the trading song on tape almost a century later. "We kept listening to it," Maggie tells the group in the film. "We kept listening to it for so long—we didn't know for how long—but finally we could make it out. It sounded so wonderful, didn't it?"

Maggie Paul and Language Keepers offer us two important lessons about the histories of race and media in the period between Fewkes's Passama-quoddy experiment and the present. As such, they serve as a fitting post-script to this book. First off, to underscore a point that is perhaps already self-evident, Maggie Paul's story of musical persistence disproves the pre-dictions about native cultural disappearance that American writers and anthropologists made at the end of the nineteenth century. In the pro-cess, it also reveals the contingency of the documentary records that they left behind, their vulnerability to reinterpretation and change over time. Today, the Passamaquoddy regard Fewkes's phonograph cylinders not as documents of social exploitation or as relics of technological experimenta-tion but as enduring evidence of cultural vitality—as a usable past that lives on in the present and helps guide the future. Salvage ethnography thus remains a "potent ideological force in our current moment," as Pauline Wakeham has argued, but not as its turn-of-the-century practitioners would have anticipated.[8] Over the last thirty years, the rediscovery of early ethnographic recordings, photographs, and films has enabled native com-munities across the United States to transmit valuable cultural knowledge from one generation to the next.[9] Ethnographic documents that were once languishing in obscurity have been reclaimed—salvaged, really—to fashion new meanings in the present.

Maggie Paul's story of the "wax tapes" is more common than we might at first think. During the late 1970s and early 1980s, in conjunction with the passage of the American Folklife Preservation Act of 1976 and the inaugura-tion of the Federal Cylinder Project (FCP), scores of Native Americans had the experience of recognizing the sounds of their ancestors on recordings that American ethnologists originally made at the turn of the twentieth century. Formally chartered in 1979, the FCP was given the formidable task of cataloging more than eight thousand salvage ethnographic recordings, copying them onto state-of-the-art preservation audio formats, and repatriating them to their individual tribes of origin. Over the years, the project has acquired a dual significance in native communities across the United States: at the same time that it serves as an ongoing reminder of a cultural past ripe for recovery in an uncertain present, it also serves as a material marker of persistence and change over time.[10] According to one of the FCP's fieldworkers, Native Americans who were "knowledgeable in the traditions of their communities" often found it possible to sing along when they first listened to the repatriated cylinders, suggesting that "despite all the acculturation pressures over the years, the traditions, the songs, *have* survived."[11] And although many of the songs and stories that audio ethnographers recorded remain recognizable in the present day, others have been altered in the intervening century, rearranged for new occasions and reimagined for new realities.

Wayne Newell and Blanche Sockabasin, two award-winning Passamaquoddy musicians who appear in several Language Keepers videos, know a great deal about the FCP and its legacy. At a recent concert at the American Folklife Center in Washington, D.C., Newell and Sockabasin sang an updated version of the "snake song" that Fewkes originally captured on wax in 1890.[12] As the musicians were quick to remind the audience, the song had "evolved into something that it wasn't previously" in the long interim between Fewkes's recording and their performance. "This is a snake dance song that we sing now," Newell remarked in between musical numbers. "It is now used to close a gathering, rather than open a gathering. But long ago, another song was used to gather people in the village for a celebration or ceremony, and over time it has changed its purpose." In other words, the tunes transform with the times, and so do the people who sing them. But this doesn't necessarily mean that the old traditions, captured on record and repatriated by the FCP, fail to have utility in the present. As Newell went on to explain, several members of the community were also studying copies of Fewkes's recordings to reincorporate the original version of the snake song into contemporary Passamaquoddy gatherings:

"The [old] song is being learned now to replace this [new version] as part of the snake dance. A year ago, a group of men in our community learned the song and danced in and surprised the children as part of the snake dance song. . . . These wax cylinders are being worked on at home by speakers of the language so that we can resurrect older songs that were recorded by our people more than a hundred years ago." Fewkes may have seen the music as dying in 1890, but Newell's account underscores that the songs are still alive over a century later, as much the result of creative cultural adaptation as of deliberate historical recovery.

The same could be said for Maggie Paul's performance in Language Keepers, a fact that I quickly discovered when I first listened to Fewkes's recording of the Passamaquoddy trading song. Along with the rest of the materials associated with the legendary phonograph experiments of 1890, a magnetic copy of cylinder 17 currently resides in the collections of the American Folklife Center at the Library of Congress, a short bus ride from my apartment in Washington, D.C. In August 2013, I decided to go and hear it for myself. After braving the late-summer humidity and navigating the lengthy corridors of the library's Thomas Jefferson Building, I arrived at the Folklife Center and introduced myself to a longtime archivist named Judith Gray, one of the original members of the FCP. When I told her I wanted to listen to a few of the Passamaquoddy recordings, she led me to a corner of the library outfitted with a reel-to-reel deck, and she rushed off to retrieve the relevant holdings. She returned a few minutes later to find me somewhat embarrassed. I had no idea how to use the audio equipment (I remember thinking that the device looked like something Gene Hackman's character in *The Conversation* might have used in his bleak warehouse office), and she spent the next few minutes patiently teaching me how to work the profusion of spools and dials on the machine. The other researchers at the center looked on in mild amusement.

It took me a while to locate the contents of cylinder 17 on the FCP's magnetic reel, but when I finally did, I found myself puzzled. On the 1890 recording, Fewkes's voice clearly identifies the trading song in question, but the singing that follows his introduction is barely audible. What little I could hear fading in and out of the staticky old recording sounded slow, low, and mournful—completely different from the dynamic rendition I knew from Language Keepers. Had Fewkes made a mistake in 1890?

Worse yet, had Maggie Paul misremembered where she first learned the Passamaquoddy trading song?

My questions were eventually answered after I fiddled with the dials on the deck and listened to the recording a few more times. The tune and the mood were different, the sound quality had suffered over the years, but suddenly I began to hear faint outlines of "Esunomawotultine" beneath all of the distortion—a ghostly ancestor from a different time. Only then did I realize that I'd been thinking like Fewkes. I came to the Folklife Center with the preconceived notion that Passamaquoddy music was something singular and fixed, naively assuming a perfect line of continuity between the two versions of the song. But the 1890 recording ended up frustrating these expectations, and not just because of its diminished sound quality. In retrospect, what I heard in the magnetic copy of Fewkes's cylinder 17 was an audible symptom of change over time. Like many Passamaquoddy singers before her, Maggie Paul had reinterpreted the "original" rendition of the trading song for her own purposes—for the occasion of the healing ceremony, for the interest of the Language Keepers footage, and for an unrecorded future to come. Her performance suggests that the Passamaquoddy haven't remained static in the century between Fewkes's experiment and today. Their culture is perpetually in process, forever remaking the remnants of the past for the exigencies of the present. For this reason, songs like "Esunomawotultine" have ended up outliving the cylinder recordings that were originally thought to serve as their final resting place.

This brings us to the second lesson of Language Keepers—a lesson about the realities of technological permanence in an age defined by accelerated cultural change and continuous media invention. In the 1890s, at a time when the phonograph's social future was largely uncertain, Fewkes listened to his experimental recordings and predicted that the songs of the Passamaquoddy tribe would live forever in the grooves of the wax cylinder. His assistant, Benjamin Ives Gilman, went even further, claiming that the phonograph preserved even the notoriously fleeting "minute intervals" of Native American music for all time.[13] Yet, when Maggie Paul first encountered the FCP's copy of cylinder 17 a century later, she had to fight through noise and distortion to recognize the trading song that members of her community had been singing for years ("We kept listening to it for so long—we didn't know for how long—but finally we could make it out").

Of course, I had the exact same experience when I first heard the Folklife Center's magnetic transfers of the Passamaquoddy cylinders. The recordings were riddled with unpredictable jumps and murky fades. At times—in the case of cylinder 17, in particular—the hiss and static in my headphones drowned out the songs that the ethnologists of the late 1800s considered to be salvaged for posterity. Where Fewkes and Gilman initially heard the embodied presence of a disappearing cultural source, Maggie Paul and I initially heard little more than an unintelligible muddle of noise. So what, exactly, has cylinder 17 preserved over the years?

This isn't an easy question to answer. Standards of sound fidelity have, of course, changed a great deal since the end of the nineteenth century, and many of the difficulties that contemporary researchers face when listening to copies of Fewkes's recordings have to do with the limitations of the device that he used in the field. However, as Christopher Ann Paton and Jonathan Sterne have both pointed out, the auditory imperfections that make some early recordings difficult to decipher are also a direct result of the deterioration of the audio formats on which they were made.[14] Wax cylinders were notorious for their material fragility. Excessive use caused them to fade over time, and improper storage techniques (exposure to heat and humidity, in particular) have only served to exacerbate the problem. Subsequent audio formats have proven no less susceptible to long-term decay. According to Paton, acetate records often suffer from a condition known as "delamination"; plastic, glass, and tinfoil formats are easily scratched and deformed; and many other sound technologies have ended up playing unsuspecting hosts to destructive colonies of mold and fungi. Magnetic tape, once the gold standard for long-term audio preservation, generally allows no more than twenty-five years of use before it begins to wear down, a shorter life-span than that of an ordinary sheet of paper.[15] "Virtually all sound recordings are degraded by playback," Paton notes, echoing what many preservation archivists have been saying for decades. "None of the instantaneous formats . . . can be shelved for 'permanent' storage as paper can; all require regular attention, and will still deteriorate fairly quickly to the point that re-recording is necessary."[16]

Like most early sound recordings, then, cylinder 17 began its slow march into inaudibility as soon as Fewkes began studying the results of his phonographic experiment in the 1890s. Although a number of audio ethnographers had the foresight to duplicate their cylinders in the 1920s and 1930s, the Passamaquoddy recordings had a less fortunate fate, spending the better part of a century gathering dust on the shelves of Harvard University's Peabody Museum of Archaeology and Ethnology.[17] When they finally made their way to the Library of Congress in the early 1970s, many of the cylinders in the collection were in jeopardy of catastrophic loss. Archivists could only hope to safeguard against further deterioration by migrating what was left of Fewkes's work onto magnetic reels. Such stories of duplication and reduplication are, of course, common in the lives of early sound recordings, with preservation transfers occurring about once every four decades. In the case of cylinder 17, it's a story that would have ended more happily if archivists had recognized the long-term instability of Fewkes's cylinders when they arrived at the Peabody Museum four decades after they were first made—and if open-reel magnetic tape had also lived up to its billing as a permanent storage format four decades after the Library of Congress made its last-ditch preservation transfer.[18] Today, the contents of Fewkes's cylinder 17—now known as reel 4260 in the American Folklife Center's collection—are barely intelligible. Digital innovations provide a great deal of hope for solving the age-old problem of format deterioration. For example, a group of American physicists has recently discovered a way to reconstruct sound recordings that were never even playable in the first place.[19] But given the crowded graveyard of audio technologies that lies behind us, it seems entirely likely that we'll end up facing many of the same challenges with digitally reconstructed files of the Passamaquoddy cylinders four decades hence—perhaps even sooner.[20]

Many of the technologies of cultural preservation that we encountered in this book ended up following a similar path over the course of the twentieth century. The published autochromes of Franklin Price Knott, for instance, have long been stored in the vaults of the National Geographic Image Collection. The majority of his early color photographs now retain little of their original chromatic brilliance, and the digital preservation copies that photo-archivists have produced in recent years clearly lack the luminous textures that viewers found so alluring at the turn of the twentieth century. Thus, although the Lumières' photographic breakthroughs may well have satisfied Knott's fantasies of permanent cultural preservation in the short term, time has gradually revealed a much less colorful reality. Attempts to study early motion pictures like *Moana* have similarly suffered from the physical instability of celluloid film, an obstacle that the Flahertys knew all too well in their lifetime.[21] (In 1918, Robert Flaherty almost lost his life when the ashes of a careless cigarette fell on a nitrate print of *Nanook of the North.*) Viable copies of *Moana* still exist, of course. In 1999, the U.S. National Film Preservation Foundation sponsored an archival restoration of an original 35mm print, currently housed at the Museum of Modern Art in New York City. Yet, until recently, when low-quality DVDs of *Moana* began turning up online, my only point of visual reference for the Flahertys' Samoan venture was a dim 16mm copy owned by the Harvard Film Archive, which preservation archivists appear to have transferred from a failing 35mm version sometime during the 1940s. It should come as no surprise that the visual effects of the Flahertys' experiment with panchromatic film stock got lost in the shuffle. When I first viewed *Moana* in the mid-2000s, the Samoan actors and actresses who were once thought to exhibit the "golden beauty of primitive beings" (as John Grierson famously put it in 1926) were occasionally overrun by harsh overexposures and inky black shadows; sporadic visual distortions even rendered a few moments of the film's climactic tattooing sequence difficult to follow.[22] Whether the 16mm copy that flickered across the screen actually preserved a relic of the Flahertys' cherished *fa'a Samoa* is difficult to say.

Above all else, such stories help to remind us of the *ephemerality of permanence,* a fundamental paradox of modern media history that has become increasingly conspicuous in the digital age.[23] By almost every conceivable measure, the technologies that appeared to fulfill the ethnographic fantasy of perfect cultural preservation at the turn of the twentieth century have failed to withstand the basic test of time. In all likelihood, the technologies that promise fidelity and longevity today will end up following suit.[24] There is no such thing as a permanent medium, in other words, and the ongoing problem of material shelf life is itself compounded by the speed at which technologies of all sorts now seem to rush toward obsolescence. While wax cylinders fall victim to mold and humidity, and while celluloid prints suffer the slow ravages of vinegar syndrome, technological loss of a higher order is allegedly taking place. If the analog hasn't disappeared yet, we are told, it will disappear soon. Print is now dying, cinema is suddenly filmless, and the age of mechanical sound reproduction is soon to become a distant memory.[25] In short, many of the twentieth century's most familiar forms of storage and communication appear to be teetering on the brink of extinction, destined to vanish into an invisible stream of ones and zeros. Or perhaps they are already gone, already forgotten? Witness Maggie Paul's inability to remember the words "wax cylinder" in her story of how she learned the Passamaquoddy trading song, or my own ignorance of the workings of a reel-to-reel deck, unwitting product of the cassette tape and the compact disc—and now the MP3—that I am.

The reality of history is, of course, far more complicated than the dominant narratives of media transformation would lead us to believe.[26] Whatever significance we end up ascribing to the rise of the digital—and there is no doubt that its implications are profound, and will remain so for the foreseeable future—sweeping pronouncements of the disappearance of the analog should by now have an eerie ring of familiarity about them: late-nineteenth- and early-twentieth-century anthropologists talked about race and culture in similarly elegiac terms. To be sure, what we now regard as "old" media have gradually emerged as the disappearing objects of the twenty-first century's version of the salvage imperative, and documentary initiatives like Language Keepers are actually doing valuable work in preserving them. Witness Maggie Paul, Wayne Newell, and Blanche Sockabasin, whose musical efforts have ensured that the dying sounds of Fewkes's cylinders will continue to reach audiences around the country. Witness, as well, the case of James Woodenlegs, a Northern Cheyenne sign talker who recently collaborated with sign language scholars Jeffrey E. Davis and Melanie McKay-Cody (Chickamauga Cherokee / Choctaw) to study the contemporary legacy of Plains Indian Sign Language (PISL), which has faded in and out of use since Garrick Mallery first began his sign collection efforts at the Bureau of Ethnology in the 1880s.[27] While working to understand the persistence of PISL in today's Plains Indian communities, their research led them to the forgotten films of Hugh Lenox Scott and Richard Sanderville, which had been wasting away on the shelves of the U.S. National Archives since the 1930s. In the interest of historical restoration and global access, the films have since been digitized, and the cycle of technological decay and preservation starts all over again. The "vanishing races" and "disappearing cultures" of the turn-of-the-century period thus haven't merely survived over the years. Instead, they have found innovative ways to salvage the media that were once used to salvage them.

At the dawn of the twenty-first century, then, we are left with a striking irony. In the 1890s, when Fewkes traveled to Calais with his cylinder phonograph, Americans firmly believed that if cultures around the world were disappearing, modern media technologies would live on to tell their tale. Now, 120 years later, the opposite is the case: cultures are said to survive, and media seem to disappear. The truth, of course, lies somewhere in between these two imagined extremes, but the reversal is itself a testament to powerful historical shifts, reminding us that cultures and technologies are never as permanent, never as absolute, as they might seem at any given moment in time. As we race headlong into the digital age, at once hopeful and uncertain of the future to come, we would do well to keep such lessons in mind.

ACKNOWLEDGMENTS

I've incurred substantial debts while writing this book, and thanks are in order—a whole lot of them.

The research for this project began in the History of American Civilization program at Harvard University (now American Studies), and I am grateful for the extraordinary community of scholars and friends I found there. I'd like to thank my advisers, in particular. Lawrence Buell provided wisdom and guidance at every turn. David Rodowick encouraged me in the classroom and, in the process, helped redefine the stakes of my work as a writer. Marc Shell asked the hardest questions and offered brilliant answers. And whether halfway around the world or just around the corner, Werner Sollors shared books, told jokes, and pushed me to think of my work as a part of something bigger. My debt to this incomparable group of teachers is ongoing, and the only way I can begin to think of repaying it is by passing on their generosity and warmth to my own students. It will take a lifetime, I'm sure. Further thanks go to Glenda Carpio, for her guidance and good humor; to Nancy Cott, for her generosity and patience; and to Brad Evans, for helping me start to turn the first draft of my dissertation into a real, live book. I also want to acknowledge the mentors who helped launch me on the academic road long before I started working on this project, especially Bruce Diehl, Jeff Ferguson, Farah Griffin, Marisa Parham, and Karen Sánchez-Eppler—I always look forward to seeing them and reminding myself of how far I still have to go. To Barry

O'Connell, whose voice and friendship were there at the very beginning: none of this would have happened without you.

More recent thanks go to the faculty and staff at Georgetown University. Over the past few years, I've benefited immensely from the wisdom of my faculty mentors, Gay Cima and Ricardo Ortiz, and from the steadfast support of our department chair, Kathryn Temple. The final shape of the book owes a great deal to two remarkable working groups on Georgetown's campus. The members of the English department's Junior Faculty Writing Group read countless drafts, offered advice and inspiration, and generally helped show me the ropes in my first few years on the job. To Caetlin Benson-Allott, Ashley Cohen, Nathan Hensley, Cóilín Parsons, Samantha Pinto, Nicole Rizzuto, Daniel Shore, and Mimi Yiu: the encouragement has meant so much, and it has made all the difference. The same goes for the members of the Georgetown University Americas Initiative—especially Katherine Benton-Cohen, Denise Brennan, Anna Celenza, Marcia Chatelain, Soyica Colbert, Derek Goldman, Gwen Kirkpatrick, Erick Langer, Adam Lifshey, Chandra Manning, Doug Reed, Miléna Santoro, and John Tutino—all of whom read chapters at various stages of the game and provided valuable food for thought along the way. Thanks also go to Bernie Cook, Pam Fox, Dana Luciano, Brian McCabe, Lori Merish, Angelyn Mitchell, Anne O'Neil-Henry, Robert Patterson, Henry Schwarz, and Noel Sugimura, fabulous friends and colleagues alike. And without the ongoing support of Donna Even-Kesef, Karen Lautman, Hannah Calkins, Bailey Yeager, and Jessica Williams, I'm sure I'd be very lost, indeed.

I'm grateful to the institutions that generously provided research and publication assistance over the years, especially the Charles Warren Center for American History at Harvard University, the Georgetown University Graduate School of Arts and Sciences, the Georgetown University Film and Media Studies Program, and the Georgetown College Office of the Dean. I'm also grateful to the librarians, archivists, and curators at the American Folklife Center, the Dibner Library of Science and Technology, History Colorado, the Library of Congress, the National Geographic Society Archives, the Peabody Museum of Archaeology and Ethnology, the Robert and Frances Flaherty Study Center, and the Smithsonian Motion Picture Collection, as well as at the manuscript libraries at Columbia University, Harvard University, and the University of Pennsylvania. All along,

I've said that the people who work at these places deserve to be listed as coauthors on the cover of this book. I'd like to extend a special thanks to the staff at the National Anthropological Archives, especially Rose Chou, Leanda Gahegan, and Daisy Njoku—their expertise helped shape this project in ways that I'm still discovering. Likewise for the historian of photography Mark Jacobs, who gave me free rein to work with his astonishing collection of early color photographs as I gathered the research for chapter 5. There isn't an adequate way to express how grateful I am for his notes, his feedback, and his kindness. Thanks also go to Ben Levine and Judith Grey; my conversations with them helped me finish this book.

I consider myself lucky to have had the opportunity to work with the University of Minnesota Press, especially Jason Weidemann and Danielle Kasprzak, who believed in this project from the beginning and helped shepherd me through all phases of the publication process. A number of anonymous readers offered insightful comments on the early drafts of this book. I appreciate their time, energy, and support—I know the final product is much, much better for their efforts. Special thanks go to Kim Hogeland, whose guidance helped get me started, and to Randolph Lewis, whose sympathetic comments ended up pushing me into new territory as I began working on revisions. Portions of chapter 3 were previously published in *American Literature,* and I thank the journal's editors for providing such targeted responses to my writing and ideas. I've had the good fortune to present material from this book to audiences at conferences and venues across the country, but I'll never forget my conversations with Alan Liu and Rita Raley at the University of California, Santa Barbara: their advice and enthusiasm helped give new life to what ended up becoming chapters 1 and 2.

Countless friends and fellow travelers sustained and inspired me as I wrote and rewrote over the years, especially Eli Cook, Erin Dwyer, Erica Fretwell, Nick Gaskill, Sara Gebhardt, David Kim, Erich Nunn, Scott Poulson-Bryant, Richard So, and Katherine Stevens. But I owe everything, probably more, to an amazing group of friends and readers who have been reviewing drafts, talking shop, devouring fries, raining threes, sustaining injuries, and making it all worthwhile for almost a decade now—their ideas and voices lurk behind every word, on every page. To George Blaustein, Nick Donofrio, Maggie Gram, Jack Hamilton, Hua Hsu, Pete L'Official,

Brian McCammack, and Tim McGrath: all of this has meant far more than I'm able to express here, so know for the time being that the next few rounds are on me. Thanks also go to the ACBL, whose members include many of the aforementioned and Derek Etkin. I stopped keeping score a long time ago, but the game never dies.

I'm grateful to the friends who have provided levity, encouragement, and really good reasons to travel, both very recently and for as long as I can remember: Brett Brehm, Peter and Katie Colarulli, Kevin Cole, Adeyemi Cole, Marc and Abby Glick, Caroline Howe, Jeff Jablow, Anthony Jones and Anna Lobonova, Patrick and Sarah Kennedy, Russell Lang and Erin Dittus, Rory and Mike Leraris, Jeff and Tara Malbasa, Scott and Mary Malbasa, Laura McCammack, Tom Miller, Spencer Paul, Eddie Pryce, Kevin Rosenberg and Meghan Bollinger, Jeff and Katie Sunderland, Jude Volek, and Matt and Molly Zeiger. I'm equally grateful to my aunts, uncles, and cousins; to Marcia and Paul Gaskill; and to Mark Rosse, Kaye McWane, and Jonathan McWane, for their patience and support.

My final words of thanks are for my family. My sister, Lisa Hochman, remains an inspiration, always there to make me laugh and remind me of what matters. My parents, Carol and Ken Hochman, remain my best advocates, best teachers, and best friends. I love you all so much. And finally, to Hillary: I've said it before, but I can never say it enough—all of this, and everything else, is for you.

NOTES

Introduction

1. Fewkes, "A Contribution to Passamaquoddy Folk-Lore," 258.

2. Fewkes, "On the Use of the Phonograph," 269.

3. Ibid.

4. On the origins and history of the vanishing race myth in the United States and Europe—a myth as old as the New World itself—see Mitchell, *Witnesses to a Vanishing America*, 93–188; Dippie, *Vanishing American*; Maddox, *Removals*, 15–50; and Brantlinger, *Dark Vanishings*, 1–16.

5. See Jesse Walter Fewkes, "Passamaquoddy Diary: A Trip to Calais, Maine, for the Purpose of Experimenting with the Phonograph as an Instrument to Preserve the Ancient Language of that Tribe, March 16–19, 1890," Jesse Walter Fewkes Collection, American Folklife Center, Library of Congress, Washington, D.C.

6. Fewkes, "A Contribution to Passamaquoddy Folk-Lore," 260. Laboring under the misapprehension that the Passamaquoddy were trapped outside of history, Fewkes was surprised to find that Josephs and Selmore spoke fluent English and already knew something about the recording apparatus that he had brought along with him. See Fewkes, "Passamaquoddy Diary." See also Fewkes, "A Contribution to Passamaquoddy Folk-Lore," 260: "Most of [the Passamaquoddy] speak English very well, and are ready to grant their assistance in preserving their old stories and customs. The younger members of the tribe are able to read and write, and are acquainted with the ordinary branches of knowledge as taught in our common schools."

7. Fewkes, "A Contribution to Passamaquoddy Folk-Lore," 258–59.

8. Ibid.

9. Jesse Walter Fewkes to Mary Hemenway, March 15, 1890, Hemenway Southwest Expedition Records (1886–1914), Box 9, Peabody Museum of Archaeology and Ethnology, Harvard University.

10. Fewkes, "Additional Studies of Zuni Songs and Rituals," 1097–98.

11. See Brady, *A Spiral Way*, 52–56; Sterne, *Audible Past*, 315–21; and Makagon and Neumann, *Recording Culture*, 3–4.

12. Fewkes, "A Few Summer Ceremonials at Zuñi Pueblo," 58.

13. Sterne, *Audible Past*, 298–99.

14. "The expense at the present time for the use of the instrument is possibly a practical difficulty, which it is hoped may be lightened for those using the instrument for scientific purposes," wrote Fewkes in an 1890 essay. "Certainly no idea could show a more disinterested personal interest than a wish to permanently preserve the fast vanishing languages of the American Indians. It belongs to the realm of pure science, and the scientific student will probably be met in a similar liberal spirit by those who control the patents of the phonograph." Fewkes, "On the Use of the Phonograph in the Study of the Languages of American Indians," 269.

15. Fewkes, "A Few Summer Ceremonials at Zuñi Pueblo," 55.

16. "Edison Phonograph," 748.

17. Fewkes, "Additional Studies of Zuni Songs and Rituals," 1098.

18. On the influence of salvage ethnography on literature, film, and the arts in the United States and Europe, see Gruber, "Ethnographic Salvage and the Shaping of Anthropology," 1289–99; Rony, *Third Eye*; Hegeman, *Patterns for America*; Edwards, *Raw Histories*; Elliott, *Culture Concept*; Griffiths, *Wondrous Difference*; Evans, *Before Cultures*; Wakeham, *Taxidermic Signs*; and Edwards, "Salvaging Our Past," 67–87.

19. Clifford, "On Ethnographic Allegory," 112–13. Clifford has also written on the subject of salvage ethnography and its relationship to changing definitions of culture in "Of Other Peoples," 120–30, 142–50; *Predicament of Culture*; and *Routes*.

20. On the origins of the culture concept in Europe and the United States, see, among many others, Kroeber and Kluckhohn, *Culture*, 9–38; Stocking, *Race, Culture, and Evolution*, 195–233; and Williams, *Keywords*, 87–93.

21. On the influence of French, Scottish, and German Enlightenment philosophy on evolutionary anthropology, see Stocking, *Victorian Anthropology*, 8–45.

22. See Stocking, *Race, Culture, and Evolution*, 110–32; Stocking, *Victorian Anthropology*, 144–273; and Brantlinger, *Dark Vanishings*, 1–67.

23. Darwin, *Descent of Man*, 212.

24. Morgan, *Ancient Society*, iv.

25. Boas, "Ethnological Problems in Canada," 331. Among scores of books and articles produced in this period, see also Draper, "Last of the Red Race," 244–46; Curtis, "Vanishing Indian Types," 657–71; Mooney, "Passing of the Indian," 174–79; Dixon and Wanamaker, *Vanishing Race*; and Hrdlička, "Vanishing Indian," 266–67. The wistful elegy for the vanishing Indian is perhaps the most notorious product of a peculiarly modern way of thinking about race and culture that the anthropologist Renato Rosaldo has diagnosed as "imperialist nostalgia." "Curiously enough," writes Rosaldo, "agents of colonialism . . . often display nostalgia for the colonized culture as it was 'traditionally' (that is, when they first encountered it). The peculiarity of their yearning, of course, is that agents of colonialism long for the very forms of life they intentionally altered or destroyed . . . mourn[ing] the passing of what they themselves have transformed." Rosaldo, *Culture and Truth*, 69.

26. Sapir, "An Anthropological Survey of Canada," 793.

27. Bazin, "Ontology of the Photographic Image," 9. Bazin's theories have exerted a massive influence on the course of cinema and media studies, far too large to enumerate in the space of an endnote. Often overlooked in the (at times, contentious) debates about Bazin's "mummy complex" thesis is its historical location. I read "Ontology of the Photographic Image" as a reflection on an age of media preservation dominated by photography, phonography, and film that was in fact waning at the time Bazin put pen to paper. Either way, several studies in the Bazinian tradition have influenced my thinking about time, media, and technological preservation throughout this project, particularly Rosen, *Change Mummified*; Doane, *Emergence of Cinematic Time*; and the essays collected in Andrew, *Opening Bazin*.

Bazin's ideas about the "mummy complex" also align with a body of scholarship that has theorized the work of salvage ethnography as a form of cultural *taxidermy*—the presentation of the past as if it were the present, the cultural "dead" as if it were the cultural "living." See Haraway, "Teddy Bear Patriarchy," 237–29; Rony, *Third Eye*, 99–128; and Wakeham, *Taxidermic Signs*.

28. Bazin, "Ontology of the Photographic Image," 9.

29. Jonathan Sterne brilliantly examines links between sound reproduction and embalming processes in *Audible Past*, 287–334. On the "storage revolution" of the late nineteenth and early twentieth centuries, more generally, see Kittler, *Discourse Networks*, 229; Kittler, *Gramophone, Film, Typewriter*, 1–19; Gitelman, *Scripts, Grooves, and Writing Machines*; and the essays collected in Gitelman and Pingree, *New Media*.

30. See Elliott, *Culture Concept*, 35–60; Evans, *Before Cultures*, 7–11.

31. For more on media archaeology and its methodological applications, see Parikka, *What Is Media Archaeology?*; Thorburn and Jenkins, *Rethinking Media Change*; and Huhtamo and Parikka, *Media Archaeology*.

32. Elsaesser, "New Film History as Media Archaeology," 96.

33. Ibid., 93.

34. Grierson, "Flaherty's Poetic *Moana*," 25. My account here is also informed by discussions of the documentary in Stott, *Documentary Expression and Thirties America*, 1–64; Barnouw, *Documentary*; Tagg, *Burden of Representation*, 1–33; and Nichols, *Representing Reality*, as well as by the essays collected in Renov, *Theorizing Documentary*, and Gaines and Renov, *Collecting Visible Evidence*.

35. See Corner, *Art of Record*, 2–15; Winston, *Claiming the Real*, 11–17.

36. For more on the "documentary" as the "creative treatment of actuality," see Grierson, "First Principles of Documentary," 145–56.

37. *Oxford English Dictionary Online*, s.v. "documentary." http://www.oed.com.

38. Rosen, *Change Mummified*, 234–40. As I demonstrate in chapter 1, the term *media* itself underwent a similar crisis in this same period.

39. Gilder, "Recording Tendency and What It Is Coming To," 634–35.

40. Mary Louise Pratt has defined the *contact zone* as a social space "where disparate cultures meet, clash, and grapple with each other, often in highly asymmetrical relations of domination and subordination—such as colonialism and slavery, or their aftermaths as they are lived out across the globe today." Pratt, *Imperial Eyes*, 7. With

Pratt's definition in mind, it is worth noting that the cases I present here are hardly unique to the United States. To be sure, most of the major early theorists and practitioners of salvage media ethnography did their work in the continental United States and its satellite territories. Yet the definitions of race and culture that helped to determine the course of their efforts were themselves global constructs, developed among a transnational network of writers and thinkers and established in response to cross-cultural encounters the world over.

41. Omi and Winant, *Racial Formation in the United States*, 55.

42. Ibid., 56.

43. Ibid.

44. Representative studies in several historical fields include hooks, *Black Looks*; Lott, *Love and Theft*; Smith, *American Archives*; Bernardi, *Birth of Whiteness*; Savage, *Broadcasting Freedom*; and Tawil, *Making of Racial Sentiment*. All of these studies in one way or another rely on the idea that forms of media representation—from novels to films to radio broadcasts—construct racial fictions for society at large. For alternatives to this model of analysis, see Wendy Hui Kyong Chun and Lynne Joyrich's special issue of *Camera Obscura* 24, no. 70 (2009), "Race and/as Technology," esp. Joyrich, "Bringing Race and Media Technology into Focus," 1–5; Chun, "Race and/as Technology," 6–35; and Coleman, "Race as Technology," 176–207.

45. Williams, *Television*, 14.

46. Williams, *Marxism and Literature*, 158–64. Here I am drawing on Williams's oft-cited distinction between technologies (raw "materials") and media ("material social practice").

47. Larkin, *Signal and Noise*, 3. See also Marvin, *When Old Technologies Were New*, 3–8, and Gitelman and Pingree, *New Media*, xi–xxii.

48. A number of incisive studies of native agency and media representation have influenced my approach in this book, such as Ginsburg, "Indigenous Media," 92–112; Ginsburg, "Culture/Media," 5–15; Vizenor, *Fugitive Poses*; Deloria, *Indians in Unexpected Places*; Prins, "Visual Media and the Primitivist Perplex," 58–74; Deger, *Shimmering Screens*; and Raheja, *Reservation Reelism*, 1–45.

49. Deloria, *Indians in Unexpected Places*, 52–108.

50. On the "parallel realities" contained in all ethnographic images, see Edwards, "Talking Visual Histories," 84. For excellent surveys of work in this vein, see Poole, "An Excess of Description," 159–79, and Edwards, "Tracing Photography," 173–77.

51. See Ortner, "Resistance and the Problem of Ethnographic Refusal," 173–93, and Johnson, "On Agency," 113–23. My own thinking about the problem of agency is probably closest to Ortner's. As she persuasively argues, "agency is not an entity that exists apart from cultural construction (nor is it a quality one has only when one is whole, or when one is an individual). Every culture, every subculture, every historical moment, constructs its own forms of agency, its own modes of enacting the process of reflecting on the self and the world and of acting simultaneously within and upon what one finds there." Ortner, "Resistance and the Problem of Ethnographic Refusal," 186.

52. Lynne Joyrich and Alice Maurice have recently offered similar analyses. According to Joyrich, "race . . . is not simply something on which technologies may

operate. Rather, the apparatus of race (in complex intersection with apparatuses of gender, generation, sexuality, class, nation, and so on) is configured and reconfigured by and through our material and signifying technologies: the very ways in which we think, experience, and enact race are tied to our media forms, just as race (and gender, generation, sexuality, class, nation) mediates our interpretations and uses of these forms in turn. . . . Our imaginaries of race have been technologized and our imaginings of technology have been racialized." Joyrich, "Bringing Race and Technology into Focus," 2. Maurice comes to similar conclusions in a study of early cinema, arguing that race was "fundamentally intertwined with the cinema's self-fashioning" in the early decades of the twentieth century, serving as a "significant rhetorical tool for the cinema's claims to presence, authenticity, and meaning." Maurice, *Cinema and Its Shadow*, 3–4. My argument here differs from theirs both in its source base and in its interest in examining nonvisual technologies of representation.

53. In following this timeline, this book contributes to the history of the period between the identification of the anthropological culture concept and its public adoption—what Alfred L. Kroeber and Clyde Kluckhohn famously termed the cultural "lag" in their 1952 study *Culture: A Critical Review of Concepts and Definitions*. See Kroeber and Kluckhohn, *Culture*, 34, and Evans, *Before Cultures*, 4–7.

54. On the ethnographies of Frank Hamilton Cushing, see Evans, *Before Cultures*, 24–50. On the Fletcher–Lomax tradition of "song collecting," see Filene, *Romancing the Folk*. On Edward S. Curtis's pioneering work in film and photography, see, among others, Gidley, *Edward S. Curtis and the North American Indian, Incorporated*; Trachtenberg, *Shades of Hiawatha*, 170–210; and Wakeham, *Taxidermic Signs*, 87–128.

55. See, among many others, the essays collected in Biolsi and Zimmerman, *Indians and Anthropologists*, as well as Lamothe, *Inventing the New Negro*.

56. Charles R. Acland uses the term *residual media* to describe technologies that have social and material lives beyond their effective obsolescence. See Acland, *Residual Media*, xx: "The residual can be artifacts that occupy space in storage houses, are shipped to other parts of the world, are converted for other uses, accumulate in landfills, and relate to increasingly arcane skills. How do some things—whether in archives or attics, minds or training manuals—become the background for the introduction of other forms? In what manner do the products of technological change reappear as environmental problems, as the 'new' elsewhere, as collectables, as memories, and as art? What are the qualities of our everyday engagement with the half-life of media forms and practices and with the formerly state of the art?" Acland's questions animate much of the rationale for this book.

57. Pynchon, *Crying of Lot 49*, 149.

1. Media Evolution

1. Powell, "From Savagery to Barbarism," 173.

2. Ibid., 173–74.

3. Ibid., 194.

4. Ibid., 193.

5. Powell, "From Barbarism to Civilization," 97, 101.

6. There is little consensus among linguistic historians as to how many Native American languages were actually in existence at the time of white–Indian contact. According to the linguist Lyle Campbell, estimates have ranged anywhere from four hundred to twenty-five hundred different languages. See Campbell, *American Indian Languages*, 3. On the history and politics of North American multilingualism more generally, see Simpson, *Politics of American English*; Kramer, *Imagining Language in America*; Shell, "Babel in America," 103–27; Sollors, *Multilingual America*; Gray, *New World Babel*; and Shell, *American Babel*.

7. Andresen, *Linguistics in America*, 14–15; Conn, *History's Shadow*, 82–83.

8. Jefferson, *Notes on the State of Virginia*, 143.

9. As Brian W. Dippie has shown, this basic idea remained a virtual constant among white intellectuals and policy makers during the eighteenth and nineteenth centuries. Dippie, *Vanishing American*, xi–xii. See also Berkhofer, *White Man's Indian*, 86–96.

10. Gray, *New World Babel*, 111.

11. Powell, "Human Evolution," 180.

12. Brinton, "American Languages, and Why We Should Study Them," 17–18.

13. For standard accounts of the history of Indian language studies, with a particular focus on nineteenth-century America, see Pedersen, *Discovery of Language*; Mitchell, *Witnesses to a Vanishing America*, 162–66; Bieder, *Science Encounters the Indian*; Andresen, *Linguistics in America*; Kramer, *Imagining Language in America*; Campbell, *American Indian Languages*, 1–89; Mithun, *Languages of Native North America*; Gray, *New World Babel*; Lepore, "Wigwam Words," 97–108; Duranti, "Language as Culture in U.S. Anthropology," 323–47; and Conn, *History's Shadow*, 79–115.

14. Guillory, "Genesis of the Media Concept," 321–62.

15. Ibid., 321. "The concept of a medium of communication was absent but *wanted* for the several centuries prior to its appearance," writes Guillory, and the "emergence of the media concept in the later nineteenth century was a response to the proliferation of new technical media . . . that could not be assimilated to the older system of the arts" (321).

16. Stegner, *Beyond the Hundredth Meridian*, 1–8.

17. Aside from Stegner, *Beyond the Hundredth Meridian*, see Worster, *A River Running West*.

18. Goetzmann, *Exploration and Empire*, 530–76.

19. See Powell, "Cañons of the Colorado," 293–310, 394–410, 523–38; Powell, "An Overland Trip to the Grand Canyon," 659–78; and Powell, "Physical Features of the Colorado Valley," 385–99, 531–92, 670–80.

20. Elliott, *Culture Concept*, 98–99. Curtis M. Hinsley Jr. also expertly chronicles the institutional rise of the U.S. Bureau of Ethnology in *Savages and Scientists*, 125–289, and Powell's role in the intellectual formation of the BAE was the subject of several articles in a 1999 special issue of the *Journal of the Southwest* dedicated to BAE anthropology: see Zedeño, "Preface: BAE Anthropology, Its Roots and Legacy," 273–81; Woodbury and Woodbury, "Rise and Fall of the Bureau of American Ethnology," 283–96; and Shaul, "Linguistic Natural History," 297–310.

21. Powell, *First Annual Report of the Bureau of Ethnology to the Secretary of the Smithsonian Institution,* xxviii: "The great boon to the savage tribes of this country, unrecognized by themselves, and, to a large extent, unrecognized by civilized men, has been the presence of civilization, which, under the laws of acculturation, has irresistibly improved their culture by substituting new and civilized for old and savage arts, new for old customs—in short, transforming savage into civilized life." The entry for "acculturation" in the *Oxford English Dictionary Online* (2nd ed., http://www.oed.com) attributes the first use of the term to the second edition of Powell's *Introduction to the Study of Indian Languages* (1880). But this text was likely written after *First Annual Report,* even if it appeared in print one year earlier.

22. Ibid., xi.

23. Elliott, *Culture Concept,* 99–101.

24. Powell, *First Annual Report of the Bureau of Ethnology to the Secretary of the Smithsonian Institution,* xv.

25. On Whitney's contribution to the history of linguistics, see Andresen, *Linguistics in America,* 135–68. On Enlightenment philosophies of language, see Gray, *New World Babel,* 85–111.

26. Whitney, *Language and the Study of Language,* 7–8.

27. George Stocking has argued that this idea eventually formed the foundation of the "comparative method" of ethnological analysis. Stocking, *Victorian Anthropology,* 144–85.

28. For a concise summary of the development of the evolutionist paradigm in American anthropology, see Haller, "Race and the Concept of Progress in Nineteenth-Century American Ethnology," 710–24. George Stocking has also offered a number of overviews of the development of evolutionary anthropology on both sides of the Atlantic, and his ideas have influenced my account here immensely. See Stocking, *Race, Culture, and Evolution,* 110–32, and Stocking, *Victorian Anthropology,* 144–273.

29. Morgan, *Ancient Society,* i–ii.

30. Ibid., ii.

31. Hinsley, *Savages and Scientists,* 133–40, 158–61.

32. Ong, *Orality and Literacy,* 79.

33. Powell, "Human Evolution," 197–98.

34. Mignolo, *Darker Side of the Renaissance,* 29–68. See also Pagden, *Fall of Natural Man,* 126–32, 179–86.

35. Rousseau, "Essay on the Origin of Languages," 17.

36. Morgan, *Ancient Society,* 31. For Morgan, writing was one technology among many that emerged in the civilized culture-stage: "The principal contributions of modern civilization are the electric telegraph; coal gas; the spinning-jenny; and the power loom; the steam-engine with its numerous dependent machines, including the locomotive, the railway, and the steam-ship; the telescope; the discovery of the ponderability of the atmosphere and of the solar system; the art of printing; the canal lock; the mariner's compass; and gunpowder" (29–30). See also Whitney, *Language and the Study of Language,* 436–74. Whitney made similar claims about the

development of writing technology, but he stopped short of applying them to the evolutionist narrative.

37. See Adas, *Machines as the Measure of Men*, 271–342.

38. Powell, "Human Evolution," 181.

39. Powell, "From Savagery to Barbarism," 180.

40. Ibid., 189.

41. Powell, "From Barbarism to Civilization," 121.

42. For more on "alternative" literacies and practices of writing, see the essays collected in Boone and Mignolo, *Writing without Words*.

43. Round, *Removable Type*, 223. See also Brooks, *Common Pot*, 219–45. In short, Powell's viewpoint explicitly denied the possibility of what Gerald Vizenor has famously termed "survivance"—the fact that native peoples were both negotiating with and actively shaping the very same technological forces that appeared to be sweeping them aside. See Vizenor, *Fugitive Poses*, 15, and Vizenor, "Aesthetics of Survivance," 1–24.

44. See Derrida, *Of Grammatology*, and Derrida, "Plato's Pharmacy," 61–84.

45. Powell, *Indian Linguistic Families of America North of Mexico*, 102.

46. Morgan, *Ancient Society*, iv.

47. Round, *Removable Type*, 26.

48. See Andreson, *Linguistics in America*, 97–110; Mithun, *Languages of Native North America*, 34–36; Shaul, "Linguistic Natural History," 300; and Lepore, *A Is for American*, 63–90. For a more general account of the alphabet's history in the United States, see Crain, *Story of A*.

49. Duponceau, "English Phonology," 228–64; Pickering, *An Essay on a Uniform Orthography for the Indian Languages of North America*, 2.

50. Pickering, *An Essay on a Uniform Orthography for the Indian Languages of North America*, 8–9; emphasis original.

51. Ibid., 2.

52. Lepore, *A Is for American*, 73–85.

53. Bender, *Signs of Cherokee Culture*, 35–36. For indigenous appropriations of writing prior to the Sequoyah syllabary, see Brooks, "Characters Cut in the Trees," 162.

54. Round, *Removable Type*, 125.

55. Boudinot, "Invention of a New Alphabet," 58.

56. Perdue, "Sequoyah Syllabary and Cultural Revitalization," 117.

57. Payne, "Cherokee Cause [1835]," 19. Quoted in Lepore, *A Is for American*, 82.

58. Knapp, *Lectures on American Literature*, 28.

59. Rasmussen, *Queequeg's Coffin*, 22.

60. Lepore, *A Is for American*, 75–76.

61. See John Pickering to Baron Wilhelm von Humboldt, December 27, 1827, in Pickering, *Life of John Pickering*, 352–53.

62. Ibid., 353.

63. Round, *Removable Type*, 81–96. See also Walker, "Native Writing Systems," 158–84.

64. Gibbs, "On the Language of the Aboriginal Indians of America," 367. Quoted in Hinsley, "Savages and Scientists," 54.

65. Gibbs, *Instructions for Research Relative to the Ethnology and Philology of America*, 14.

66. Gray, *New World Babel*, 4–6. See also Luciano, *Arranging Grief*, 69–117.

67. Gitelman, *Scripts, Grooves, and Writing Machines*, 52.

68. Lepore, *A Is for American*, 42–60.

69. Bell, *Visible Speech*, 18.

70. The 1867 text of *Visible Speech* includes a number of secondhand accounts of Bell's public demonstrations: "The mode of procedure was as follows: Mr. Bell sent his two Sons, who were to read the writing, out of the room . . . and I dictated slowly and succinctly the sounds which I wished to be written. These consisted of a few words in Latin, pronounced first as at Eton, then as in Italy, and then according to some theoretical notions of how the Latins might have uttered them. Then came some English provincialisms and affected pronunciations; the words 'how odd,' being given in several distinct ways. . . . The result was perfectly satisfactory—that is, Mr. Bell wrote down my queer and purposely-exaggerated pronunciations and mis-pronunciations, and delicate distinctions, in such a manner that his Sons, not having heard them, so uttered them as to surprise me by the extremely correct echo of my own voice. Accent, town drawl, brevity, indistinctness, were all reproduced with surprising accuracy" (22).

71. Lepore, *A Is for American*, 164.

72. Bell, *Visible Speech*, vii–ix.

73. Ibid., ix.

74. Ibid., 20–22; emphasis original.

75. Ibid., 91.

76. Powell, *Introduction to the Study of Indian Languages*, 1. My interest in Powell's *Introduction* builds on Laura J. Murray's argument that Indian vocabularies represent a pervasive yet underappreciated genre of writing in the literature of contact. See Murray, "Vocabularies of Native American Languages," 590–623.

77. See John Wesley Powell to William Dwight Whitney, July 17, 1877; William Dwight Whitney to John Wesley Powell, July 25, 1877; and John Wesley Powell to William Dwight Whitney, July 31, 1877, Records of the Bureau of American Ethnology, "Materials connected with the establishment and revision of Powell's alphabet for recording Indian languages, ca. 1877; & 1903–1911," MS 3898, Folder 1, National Anthropological Archives, Smithsonian Institution.

78. John Wesley Powell, "Alphabet for the Languages of the North American Indians" [1877], Records of the Bureau of American Ethnology, "Materials connected with the establishment and revision of Powell's alphabet for recording Indian languages, ca. 1877; & 1903–1911," Folder 3; emphasis added.

79. Powell, *Introduction to the Study of Indian Languages*, 3–4.

80. John Wesley Powell to William Dwight Whitney, May 7, 1877, Records of the Bureau of American Ethnology, "Materials connected with the establishment and revision of Powell's alphabet for recording Indian languages, ca. 1877; & 1903–1911," Folder 3.

81. Powell, "A Discourse on the Philosophy of the North American Indians," 253–54. The most cogent summary of Powell's position here can be found in G. K.

Gilbert's posthumous tribute to Powell's legacy, written shortly after Powell's death in 1902: "Work on American ethnology had previously been discursive, unorganized, and to a large extent diletanti [sic]. He gave to it definite purposes conformable to high scientific standards, and personally trained its corps of investigators. . . . He realized, as perhaps few had realized before him, that the point of view of the savage is essentially different from that of the civilized man, that just as his music cannot be recorded in the notation of civilized music, just as his words cannot be written with the English alphabet, so the structure of his language transcends the formulae of Aryan grammars, and his philosophy and social organization follow lines unknown to the European." Gilbert, "John Wesley Powell," 564.

Powell's line of thinking would seem to point the way toward Franz Boas's cultural relativism, although to my knowledge the connection between Powell and Boas has yet to be examined in these terms. On the emergence of Boasian relativism, see Stocking, *Shaping of American Anthropology*, and Stocking, "Boas Plan for the Study of American Indian Languages," 60–91. Connections between Powell and Boas may be found in Boas, *Introduction to the Handbook of American Indian Languages*, which attempted to update Powell's model and is often reprinted alongside Powell's earlier study *Indian Linguistic Families of America North of Mexico*. In addition, Boas was one of Powell's most trusted fieldworkers at the Bureau of Ethnology.

82. Powell, *Introduction to the Study of Indian Languages*, 1. In a written draft of the *Introduction,* Powell put a finer point on the matter: "No two languages are made up of precisely the same sounds. Every Indian tongue will be found to contain sounds which are unknown in English and it will be hard to understand and reproduce them. . . . The English alphabet is rather scanty, and very much confused in its usages, so that one is puzzled as to how he shall use it to represent the strange tongue to which it has to be applied." Records of the Bureau of American Ethnology, "Materials connected with the establishment and revision of Powell's alphabet for recording Indian languages, c. 1877; & 1903–1911," Folder 2.

83. Alexander Melville Bell to J. W. Powell, January 7, 1882, Records of the Bureau of American Ethnology, Series 1 (Letters Received, 1879–1887), Box 63: "I enclose two diagrams which I think you may find useful. The first shows the position in the Visible Speech Alphabet of all the elements in your phonetic Schema; and the second includes such additional sounds as may be incorporated with your Alphabet on the same basis of notation. Some of the latter are really necessary to anything like precision in writing. . . . There can be no doubt that the [easiest] way to master your alphabet will be to study it in relation to the General alphabet of Visible Speech. The latter is easily learned when orally explained, and the student has then at his command a perfectly unambiguous interpreter of any system of letters. It will give me real pleasure to put myself at your service in any way that can assist your most interesting work."

84. Powell, *Introduction to the Study of Indian Languages*, 2–3. See also John Wesley Powell to William Dwight Whitney, July 17, 1877, Records of the Bureau of American Ethnology, "Materials connected with the establishment and revision of Powell's alphabet for recording Indian languages, ca. 1877; & 1903–1911," Folder 1: "In the

preparation of an alphabet it seemed wise to be governed in part by the following considerations, and where they conflict, effect a compromise: I) The alphabet should be easily reproduced in any common printing office, for two reasons, viz: (a) all of my printing is done at the government office, and if new characters are to be cast, I must either pay for them out of my appropriation—a proceeding of doubtful legality—or I must obtain special legislation. (b) If strange characters are used the work is excluded from the general literature of the country, i.e., from the magazines and papers, or it is mutilated." Moreover, Powell continued, "experience shows that it is not wise to use diacritical marks at the bottom of the letter, for where the manuscript is crowded and the writing careless it often becomes difficult to determine whether such marks are intended for letters standing above or below," and "a systematic method for marking the letters should be observed, so that they may be easily learned and remembered."

85. Powell, "Competition as a Factor in Human Evolution," 311.

86. McLuhan, *Understanding Media*, 84. See also McLuhan, *Gutenberg Galaxy*, 18.

87. McLuhan, *Understanding Media*, 86. The linguistic anthropologist Edward Sapir's oft-cited essay "Communication" represents one possible link between Powell's evolutionary ethnology and McLuhan's media theory. For Sapir, whereas "fundamental techniques" of communication, such as speech and gesture, are common to all human groups, only "secondary techniques" of communication—writing, most importantly—ensure the capacity for social progress. Yet secondary techniques allegedly emerge "only at relatively sophisticated levels of civilization" (78). Clearly these ideas owe something to the evolutionist narrative of the media function, but Sapir's comments on the effects of writing and communications technology also seem to point the way toward McLuhan's famous arguments about the "global village" of the electronic age: "The multiplication of far-reaching techniques of communication has two important results. In the first place, it increases the sheer radius of communication, so that for certain purposes the whole civilized world is made the psychological equivalent of a primitive tribe. In the second place, it lessens the importance of mere geographical contiguity" (80).

88. McLuhan, *Understanding Media*, 16.

89. Ibid., 92, 155.

90. Ibid., 286.

91. Ibid., 215.

92. In addition to *Understanding Media*, variations on these four basic distinctions are present throughout McLuhan's *Gutenberg Galaxy*, as well as McLuhan and Fiore, *Medium Is the Massage*.

93. Innis, *Empire and Communications*, 23, 27. See also Innis, *Bias of Communication*.

94. Ong, *Orality and Literacy*, 76.

95. Ibid., 119.

96. See Cohen, *Networked Wilderness*, 19–28, and Rasmussen, *Queequeg's Coffin*, 17–43. See also Goody, *Domestication of the Savage Mind*, and Goody, *Interface between the Written and the Oral*, which attempt to disentangle the influence of theories of writing on cognition from narratives of evolutionary development.

97. Gitelman, *Scripts, Grooves, and Writing Machines*, 24–25. According to Gitelman, the term phonograph was in fact used in the 1850s and 1860s to describe invented writing systems like Bell's, denoting either "the graphic or written sign of a vocal element," as the nineteenth-century orthographer Andrew Jackson Graham put it, or any act of writing using those signs. See, for instance, Graham, *Exhibits of the State of the Phonographic Art*, iv.

98. "An Interesting Session Yesterday: Edison, the Modern Magician, Unfolds the Mysteries of the Phonograph," quoted in Gitelman, *Always Already New*, 32.

99. Stirling, "John Peabody Harrington," 373.

100. John P. Harrington, "Untitled Essay" [1910], Papers of John Peabody Harrington, Records Relating to Phonetics, Box 1104, Folder 2004-9, National Anthropological Archives, Smithsonian Institution.

101. John P. Harrington, "Untitled Note" (n.d.), Papers of John Peabody Harrington, Records Relating to Phonetics, Box 1104, Folder 2004-1.

102. Harrington drafted two essays on Sequoyah during the 1940s, "The Sequoyah Syllabary" (n.d.) and "The Sequoyah Syllabary Doubles Letters for Capitals" (n.d.), Papers of John Peabody Harrington, Miscellaneous Writings on Various Linguistic Topics, Box 1112, Folders 2012-23, 2012-24. In 1948, Harrington also wrote a review essay for the *International Journal of American Linguistics* that incorporated the history of the Visible Speech system. See Harrington, "Visible Speech," 134–35.

103. John P. Harrington, "Revised Smithsonian Alphabet" [1950], Papers of John Peabody Harrington, Miscellaneous Writings on Various Linguistic Topics, Box 1112, Folder 2012-16.

104. Harrington drafted several essays on the history of writing technologies, mostly during the 1940s. See, for instance, "Phonomatocycle" (November 1943), "The Stenotype" (September 1947), "Paper" (October 1947), "Phonograph" (October 1947), "The Typewriter" (October 1947), "Printing" (October 1947), "Shorthand and Typewriting" (October 1947), Papers of John Peabody Harrington, Miscellaneous Writings on Various Linguistic Topics, Box 1112, Folders 2012-2-2012-26 and Box 1113, Folders 2013-5-2013-17.

2. Representing Plains Indian Sign Language

1. Mallery, "Gesture Speech of Man," 407.

2. My account of Mallery's biography, both here and in the paragraphs that follow, draws on three main sources: Fletcher, *Brief Memoirs of Colonel Garrick Mallery*; Hinsley, *Savages and Scientists*, 167–71; and Davis, *Hand Talk*, 33–50.

3. Davis, *Hand Talk*, 36.

4. Hinsley, *Savages and Scientists*, 167. See Mallery, "A Calendar of the Dakota Nation," 4–25.

5. Mallery, "Former and Present Number of Our Indians," 353.

6. Ibid., 365.

7. Ibid., 365–66.

8. Ibid., 366.

9. Davis, *Hand Talk*, 36. According to Davis, Myer also wrote a doctoral thesis at Buffalo Medical College titled "A New Sign Language for Deaf-Mutes."

10. Fletcher, *Brief Memoirs of Colonel Garrick Mallery*, 6.

11. Bonvillian et al., "Observations on the Use of Manual Signs and Gestures," 132–65.

12. Robert Gunn, "On Plains Indian Sign Language," paper presented at the Prospects: A New Century conference of the Society of Nineteenth-Century Americanists, Berkeley, Calif., April 12–15, 2012.

13. Wurtzburg and Campbell, "North American Indian Sign Language," 153–67. Aside from Davis's recent work in *Hand Talk*, the most authoritative linguistic study of PISL is Farnell, *Do You See What I Mean?* On the semiotics of gesture more generally, see Kendon, *Gesture*.

14. Dunbar, "On the Language of Signs among Certain North American Indians," 1–2.

15. See James, *Account of an Expedition from Pittsburgh to the Rocky Mountains*, and Davis, *Hand Talk*, 23.

16. See Gallaudet, "On the Natural Language of Signs, Part I," 55–60, and Gallaudet, "On the Natural Language of Signs, Part II," 79–93. On Gallaudet's life and times, see Lepore, *A Is for American*, 91–110.

17. On the "silent Indian" and its paradoxical relationship to the study of Native American languages during the nineteenth century, see Simpson, *Politics of American English*, 205–16, and Conn, *History's Shadow*, 79–115.

18. Tylor's account of "gesture-language" in *Researches into the Early History of Mankind and the Development of Civilization* influenced Mallery's work immensely. Tylor and Mallery corresponded with each other later in life. Wilhelm Wundt, the founder of experimental psychology, also wrote intermittently on gesture languages throughout the turn-of-the-century period. His thoughts were later collected in a single volume titled *The Language of Gestures*. Davis, *Hand Talk*, 44.

19. Tylor, *Researches into the Early History of Mankind and the Development of Civilization*, 15. Lewis Henry Morgan made the exact same point in *Ancient Society*: "A sign language is easier to invent than one of sounds; and, since it is mastered with greater facility, a presumption arises that it preceded articulate speech. . . . Growing up and flourishing side by side through savagery, and far into the period of barbarism, they [sign language and speech] remain in modified forms, indissolubly united. Those who are curious to solve the problem of the origin of language would do well to look to the possible suggestions from gesture language" (36).

20. Mallery, "Gesture Speech of Man," 407.

21. Aside from Tylor's comments in note 19, see Morgan, *Ancient Society*, 5 ("Human speech seems to have been developed from the rudest and simplest forms of expression. Gesture or sign language . . . must have preceded articulate language, as thought preceded speech"), and Mallery, *Introduction to the Study of Sign Language among the North American Indians*, 8–9 ("The preponderance of authority is that man, when in the possession of all his faculties, did not choose between voice and gesture, both being originally instinctive, as they both are now, and never, with those faculties, was in a state where the one was used to the absolute exclusion of the other. . . . [But] oral speech remained rudimentary long after gesture had become an art").

22. Mallery, "Gesture Speech of Man," 421.

23. Baynton, "Savages and Deaf-Mutes," 39–74. See also Baynton, *Forbidden Signs*, and Baynton, "Out of Sight."

24. Tylor, *Researches into the Early History of Mankind and the Development of Civilization*, 35.

25. Mallery, "Sign-Language of the North American Indians," 2. Mallery was primarily building on Tylor's work here: "It is well known that the Indians of North America, whose nomadic habits and immense variety of languages must continually make it needful for them to communicate with tribes whose language they cannot speak, carry the gesture-language to a high degree of perfection, and the same signs serve as a medium of converse from Hudson's Bay to the Gulf of Mexico." Tylor, *Researches into the Early History of Mankind and the Development of Civilization*, 35. But the basic idea was implicit even in Jefferson and Dunbar's early account of PISL. To be sure, Jefferson's address, via Dunbar, never states the lingua franca thesis outright. Yet it does make implicit connections between sign talk and linguistic diversity: "Almost all the Indian nations living between the Mississippi, and the Western American ocean, understand and use the same language by signs, although their respective oral tongues are frequently unknown to one another." For Dunbar, this was the key to the "systematic order which has been observed in its [PISL's] formation." Dunbar, "On the Language of Signs among Certain North American Indians," 2. Powell, as well, had made similar comments in "A Discourse on the Philosophy of the North American Indians": "The conditions of Indian life train them in natural sign-language. Among the two hundred and fifty or three hundred thousand Indians in the United States, there are scores of languages, so that often a language is spoken by only a few hundred or a few score of people; and as a means of communication between tribes speaking different languages, a sign-language has sprung up, so that an Indian is able to talk all over—with the features of his face, his hands and feet, the muscles of his body" (265–66). Mallery was the first to bring all of these scattered ideas into a coherent theoretical framework.

26. See Davis, *Hand Talk*, 1–17.

27. Mallery, "Sign-Language of the North American Indians," 2–3.

28. Mallery, "Sign Language among North American Indians Compared with That among Other Peoples and Deaf-Mutes," 326.

29. Mallery, *Introduction to the Study of Sign Language among the North American Indians*, 1. Mallery also published a companion article in *American Annals of the Deaf and Dumb* at the same time.

30. Mallery, *A Collection of Gesture-Signs and Signals of the North American Indians*, 8, in Garrick Mallery Collection on Sign Language and Pictography, Numbered Manuscripts 1850s–1980s, MS 2372, Box 2, National Anthropological Archives, Smithsonian Institution.

31. Mallery, "Sign-Language of the North American Indians," 18.

32. See Powell's "Report of the Director" in *The Sixteenth Annual Report of the Bureau of Ethnology to the Secretary of the Smithsonian Institution, 1894–1895*, xxxii.

33. Garrick Mallery to A. G. Draper, February 25, 1891, Garrick Mallery Collection on Sign Language and Pictography, Numbered Manuscripts 1850s–1980s, MS 2372, Box 2, National Anthropological Archives, Smithsonian Institution.

34. Davis, *Hand Talk*, 15.

35. Gertrude Bonnin (Zitkala-Ša), "Letter to the Chiefs and Headmen of the Tribes," 197.

36. Mallery, *Introduction to the Study of Sign Language among the North American Indians*, 37.

37. Mallery, "Sign-Language of the North American Indians," 3–4.

38. Mallery, *Introduction to the Study of Sign Language among the North American Indians*, 58.

39. Ibid., iii.

40. Richard Dodge to Garrick Mallery, January 12, 1880, Garrick Mallery Collection on Sign Language and Pictography, Box 2, National Anthropological Archives, Smithsonian Institution.

41. Mallery, *Introduction to the Study of Sign Language among the North American Indians*, 64–65; emphasis added.

42. Mallery, "Sign Language among North American Indians," 397; my translation.

43. See Krentz, "Camera as Printing Press," 51, and Krentz, *Writing Deafness*, 24.

44. Burnet, *Tales of the Deaf and Dumb*, 24. Quoted in Krentz, "Camera as Printing Press," 51.

45. Tylor, *Researches into the Early History of Mankind and the Development of Civilization*, 33.

46. Farnell, "Ethno-graphics and the Moving Body," 938.

47. Dunbar, "On the Language of Signs among Certain North American Indians," 4.

48. Mallery, *Introduction to the Study of Sign Language among the North American Indians*, 22–23.

49. Mallery, *A Collection of Gesture-Signs and Signals of the North American Indians*, 184.

50. Mallery, "Sign Language among North American Indians," 397. For a contemporaneous account of illustration as a solution to the thick description problem, see W. P. Clark, *Indian Sign Language with Brief Explanatory Notes*: "Could this work have been illustrated, it would have added greatly to the facility of understanding and making the gestures, for it is extremely difficult to describe the most simple movements of the hands in space, so that a person who had never seen the movements would, by following the descriptions, make the correct motions. To this part of the work I have given great care, have devoted much time and thought, and if the directions contained in the brief descriptions are carried out, I am confident that most of the signs will be made in such a manner as to be readily recognized by those conversant with the language. In fact, nearly all of the descriptions have been tested and found to contain these essential elements" (15). Also a military man, Clark compiled a less successful encyclopedia of PISL during the early 1880s, completely independent of Mallery's efforts at the Bureau of Ethnology.

51. Mallery, *Introduction to the Study of Sign Language among the North American Indians*, 7.

52. Ibid., 72.

53. Mallery, "Sign Language among North American Indians," 395–96.

54. Ibid., 396.

55. Mallery, *Introduction to the Study of Sign Language among the North American Indians*, 4. Here it is worth mentioning Mallery's later publications on the subject of Indian pictography, which he saw as a definitive evolutionary link between sign language and phonetic writing. See Mallery, "Pictographs of the North American Indians," 5–256, and Mallery, "Picture-Writing of the American Indians," 3–822. Mallery's fascinating theories of pictography lie beyond the scope of my analysis in this chapter. Yet it is important to note that they have occasioned one of the only extant critical accounts of his work; see Kolodny, "Fictions of American Prehistory," 693–721.

56. Mallery, *Introduction to the Study of Sign Language Among the North American Indians*, 4–5; emphasis added. John Wesley Powell's "Report of the Director" in the *Fourteenth Annual Report of the Bureau of Ethnology to the Secretary of the Smithsonian Institution*, xxxi–xxxii, articulates similar ideas.

57. See Prodger, *Time Stands Still*, and Solnit, *River of Shadows*.

58. See Tosi, *Cinema before Cinema*.

59. Musser, *Emergence of Cinema*, 54–105; Braun, *Picturing Time*; and Gunning, "Never Seen This Picture Before," 222–74.

60. On Étienne-Jules Marey's photographic breakthroughs, see Doane, *Emergence of Cinematic Time*, 33–68.

61. Muybridge, *Descriptive Zoopraxography*, 2–3.

62. Ibid., 7.

63. On the influence of Muybridge's instantaneous photography on popular understandings of time, see Kern, *Culture of Time and Space*, 10–35, and Canales, *A Tenth of a Second*, 117–53.

64. On Muybridge's oft-overlooked images of the Modoc War, see Palmquist, "Imagemakers of the Modoc War," 206–41.

65. See "The Last of the Modocs," 532–34. Martha Sandweiss comments more fully on Muybridge's staging practices in *Print the Legend*, 243–44.

66. John Wesley Powell to Eadweard J. Muybridge, May 1887, Records of the Bureau of American Ethnology, Series 1 (Letters Received, 1879–87), Box 80.

67. Eadweard J. Muybridge to John Wesley Powell, March 1888, Records of the Bureau of American Ethnology, Series 1 (Letters Received, 1879–87), Box 80.

68. Eadweard J. Muybridge to John Wesley Powell, March 1, 1894, Records of the Bureau of American Ethnology, Series 1 (Letters Received, 1879–87), Box 115.

69. See Muybridge, *Animal Locomotion*, plates 532–36.

70. Mallery, *Introduction to the Study of Sign Language among North American Indians*, 65.

71. Mallery, "Sign Language among North American Indians," 396.

72. Ibid.

73. Scott, "Sign Language of the Plains Indian," 58. See also Bazin, "Ontology of the Photographic Image," 9.

74. Scott, "Sign Language of the Plains Indian," 66–67.

75. Ibid., 67.

76. Harrington, "American Indian Sign Language," 132.

77. Hugh Lenox Scott to Jesse Walter Fewkes, May 12, 1922, Records of the Bureau of American Ethnology, Series 1 (Letters Received, 1909–49), Box 218: "It is my opinion that it will be a great loss to posterity, if pictorial and other records of the sign language of the Plains Indians are not obtained before it is too late. . . . If I were to be in contact . . . with an old sign talker [from the] Sioux, Arapaho, Cheyenne, Crow, and Blackfoot, I believe that we could put anything on the screen that would be really true. I suggest that [we gather a] number of members of widely spread tribes in order to prove the unity and intertribal character of the language which can only be done in this way. . . . It would require a plan of what it is desired to put on the screen and possibly an English-language vocabulary it is desired to interpret in the sign language and a narrative conversation to be rendered on the screen with questions and answers to show the manner in which the different elements are combined in practical use from which grammatical and other deductions can be drawn and show the scope and quality as well as what the language is capable of expressing." On the 1930 Browning Sign Language Council, see Davis, *Hand Talk,* 72–84.

78. Extant versions of Scott's *Indian Sign Language* (1930) are currently held in the Smithsonian Institution Archives, Accession 05-143, Motion Pictures circa 1927–50, Boxes 3–4, Film 106-13, Smithsonian Institution.

79. Unlike Mallery, Scott was actually fluent in several different dialects of PISL. Many Plains Indian tribes in fact referred to him as *Mole-I-Gu-Op,* or "One Who Talks with His Hands." Davis, *Hand Talk,* 75.

80. The only extant account of Sanderville's life is Ewers, "Richard Sanderville, Blackfoot Indian Interpreter," 117–26.

81. See "Scott and Sanderville Movie" Vertical File, National Anthropological Archives, Smithsonian Institution. In e-mail correspondence with the author on August 23, 2011, Sanderville's grandson, James Mountain Chief Sanderville, speculated that Sanderville may have been unfairly barred from appearing onscreen because he wasn't a "full-blooded" Indian.

82. John G. Carter to M. W. Stirling, July 16, 1934, Records of the Bureau of American Ethnology "BAE Letters Received and Sent, 1909–1950," Box 76. The Smithsonian Archives currently holds fifty-four minutes of Scott's experimental "cinematic dictionary" footage under the title *Dictionary of Indian Sign Language* (1930/1931), Smithsonian Institution Archives, Accession 05-143, Motion Pictures circa 1927–50, Boxes 4–6, Film 106-14, Smithsonian Institution. The film depicts Scott demonstrating various PISL signs, with each demonstration preceded by a title card that identifies the sign in question.

83. Quoted in Ewers, "Richard Sanderville, Blackfoot Indian Interpreter," 121.

84. Richard Sanderville, "Contributions to *Dictionary of Indian Sign Language,*" Smithsonian Institution Archives, Accession 05-143, Motion Pictures circa 1927–50,

Box 24, Film 106-25, Smithsonian Institution, contains the only footage from Sander-ville's Bureau of Ethnology residence still in existence. However, correspondence surrounding his visit to Washington suggests that he filmed more than 350 signs and idioms for the dictionary while there. See C. G. Abbot to Cyrus H. McCormick, May 26, 1934, Records of the Bureau of American Ethnology, Series 1 (Letters Received, 1909–1949), Box 218, and John G. Carter to M. W. Stirling, July 16, 1934, Records of the Bureau of American Ethnology, "BAE Letters Received and Sent, 1909–1950," Box 76.

85. See Schuchman, *Hollywood Speaks*; Bauman, "Redesigning Literature," 34–47; and Krentz, "Camera as Printing Press," 51–70.

86. Krentz, "Camera as Printing Press," 51. Krentz's argument here obviously builds on Benedict Anderson's classic thesis on the relationship between print culture and nationalism in *Imagined Communities*.

87. Turner, *Frontier in American History*, 1–38.

88. My thinking here is influenced as much by Philip Rosen's discussion of film's inherent "pastness" in *Change Mummified* as by Johannes Fabian's account of anthropological time in *Time and the Other*. For Fabian, the production of anthropological knowledge entails a "denial of coevalness . . . a persistent and systematic tendency to place the referent(s) of anthropology in a time other than the present of the producer of anthropological discourse," thereby freezing the ethnographic other in an implied past (31). In a way, Rosen reads film similarly. As he argues in *Change Mummified*, filmed images are necessarily "past" because the cinema is itself an *indexical* media—it captures and displays as "present" profilmic events that have occurred at some point in history: "Photographic and filmic images have normally been apprehended as indexical traces, for their spatial field and the objects depicted were in the camera's 'presence' at some point prior to the actual reading of the sign. The indexical trace is a matter of pastness. This already makes it appear that the image is in some way 'historical.' The spectator is supposed to read pastness in the image, not only a past as a signified (as in, say, a historical painting), but also a past of the signifier, which is in turn that of a signifier-referent relation as a production" (20). "Pastness" is thus inherently central both to the cinema and to anthropological discourse.

89. On the trope of cinema as a "universal" language, see Hansen, *Babel and Babylon*, 16.

3. Originals and Aboriginals

1. Cable, *The Grandissimes*, 145. Further references to *The Grandissimes* are to this edition and will be cited parenthetically in the text.

2. Cable's final draft copy actually omitted his eventual admission of phonographic inadequacy—the original line merely reads, "ah! but type is an inadequate thing." Yet his editor at Scribner's quipped in the margins of the page that "even the phonograph" was insufficient for the task at hand, apparently in lighthearted reference to the complexity of the novel's orthographical system. Cable, seemingly tickled, followed suit. See "Printer's Copy of *The Grandissimes*," George Washington Cable Papers, MS Am 1288.4, Houghton Library, Harvard University, 261.

3. "*Old Creole Days* and Other Novels," 44.

4. "Madame Delphine," 259. It was not at all uncommon for Cable's readers to report that they actually read and imitated his written dialect aloud. William Dean Howells admitted in a letter to Cable that he and his wife often imitated the Creole dialect represented in *The Grandissimes* at home. In another letter dated March 7, 1882, Howells reported, "Yesterday I was at Mark Twain's and we read aloud from the Grandissimes. . . . Clemens and I went about talking Creole all day." See Turner, *George W. Cable*, 99, 122.

5. See, among many examples, "*The Grandissimes*," 153, which deems Cable's orthography accurate but ultimately "tedious by [its] excess." Edmund Wilson's 1929 appraisal of Cable's work, "Citizen of the Union," perhaps best captures this common response, which persisted well into the twentieth century: "Though Cable had a most remarkable, an almost unexcelled ear for human speech, though he reported it with the most scrupulous accuracy, he did little to make it attractive. . . . [He] studies the different varieties of the French, Spanish, and Negro Creole dialects and the language of the Acadians, both English and French, with scholarly exactitude that must be as valuable to the phonetician as it is forbidding to the ordinary reader. This rendering, with pitiless apostrophes, of these special pronunciations was complained of even in the period of Cable's greatest popularity, and it constitutes a formidable obstacle to appreciating him today." Wilson, *Shores of Light*, 417.

6. Jones, *Strange Talk*, 122–24.

7. What I am calling "hearing loss" here draws on theoretical debates about the relationship between speech and writing in poststructuralist theory and media theory; see Derrida, *Of Grammatology*, and Ong, *Orality and Literacy*. This chapter seeks to recontextualize these debates by examining a moment in American literary and intellectual history when the divide between sound and text, speech and writing, for many became a problem of cultural knowledge. A number of scholars working in African American literary studies have complicated these issues in especially valuable ways, and the trajectory of this chapter is indebted to their efforts: see Gates, *Signifying Monkey*, and, more recently, Mackey, *Discrepant Engagement*, 265–86; Edwards, "Seemingly Eclipsed Window of Form," 580–601; Moten, *In the Break*; and Weheliye, *Phonographies*. My thinking here is also in line with the work of Christopher Krentz's *Writing Deafness*, which examines hidden ideas about hearing and deafness that pervade nineteenth-century U.S. print culture.

8. Kittler, *Discourse Networks*, 229. See also Kittler, *Gramophone, Film, Typewriter*, 1–19.

9. "Edison Phonograph," 748.

10. Kittler, *Gramophone, Film, Typewriter*, 14.

11. On the rush to document difference in the nineteenth century, see Elliott, *Culture Concept*, and Evans, *Before Cultures*. On race and the culture of the phonograph more generally, see Weheliye, *Phonographies*; Biers, "Syncope Fever," 99–125; and Goble, *Beautiful Circuits*, 149–224.

12. Clifford, "Partial Truths," 1–26.

13. Edison, "Phonograph and Its Future," 527, 530.

14. For discussions of phonographic "fidelity" and its social construction, see Thompson, "Machines, Music, and the Quest for Fidelity," 131–71; Gitelman, *Scripts, Grooves, and Writing Machines,* 148–83; and Sterne, *Audible Past,* 215–86.

15. Ellison, *Invisible Man,* 581.

16. Cable, "My Politics," 14.

17. Quoted in Ekström, *George Washington Cable,* 164. The artist Joseph Pennell, who later worked to illustrate Cable's *The Creoles of Louisiana* (1884), provided this diagnosis. Pennell's statement notwithstanding, Kenneth W. Warren has demonstrated that there may have been more to Cable's racial politics than meets the eye. See Warren, *Black and White Strangers,* 48–70.

18. Cable, "My Politics," 2–3.

19. Ibid., 8–9. See Cable, "Freedman's Case in Equity," 409–18; Cable, "Silent South," 674–91; and Cable, "Negro Question in the United States," 443–68. All of these essays are reprinted in Cable, *Negro Question.*

20. Early drafts of *The Grandissimes* contained extended narrative dialogues that discussed slavery and its legacy, in addition to even more direct authorial asides. However, Cable's editors ended up striking what they deemed to be overly didactic passages from the novel's galley proofs. See "Printer's Copy of *The Grandissimes.*"

21. Cable, "My Politics," 11.

22. Ladd, "An Atmosphere of Hints and Allusions," 64.

23. Ekström, *George Washington Cable,* 67–69.

24. Hearn, "Creole *Patois,*" 146. On Cable's "revolutionary" interest in linguistic hybridity, see Jones, *Strange Talk,* 98–133.

25. Evans, "French-English Literary Dialect in *The Grandissimes,*" 210–22.

26. Quoted in Turner, *Critical Essays on George W. Cable,* 116. Cable's relationship to the history of Congo Square—and the folk myth of the "outlaw slave" Bras-Coupé that evolved out of it—is noteworthy, if vexed. Although he may have based "The Story of Bras-Coupé" on ethnographic research, this did not stop him from altering the local legend in crucial ways to suit his (and his editors') narrative demands. For the most part, this involved softening the figure of Bras-Coupé and minimizing the state's role in his eventual capture. See Wagner, "Disarmed and Dangerous," 117–51.

27. Quoted in Bikle, *George W. Cable,* 59.

28. See Cable, "Dance in Place Congo," 517–32, and Cable, "Creole Slave Songs," 807–28. The line of influence between Cable's Congo Square essays and more celebrated studies of black music, such as James Weldon Johnson's *The Book of American Negro Spirituals* (1925), runs through Henry Krehbiel's seminal *Afro-American Folksongs* (1914), which borrows from Cable's transcriptions freely. The traffic of musical material between Cable, Hearn, and Krehbiel is a subject that deserves a study of its own. The three worked closely together during the 1870s and 1880s. Krehbiel's arrangements for the songs "Miché Bainjo," "Quill Tune," "Ma Mourri," "Aurore Pradère," "Bon D'Je," and "Criole Candjo," for instance, are included in the texts of Cable's Congo Square essays. Hearn also made use of Krehbiel's early transcriptions in his ethnographic account of Afro-Creole culture in Martinique; see Hearn, *Two Years in the French West Indies,* 331–38. Furthermore, Hearn may have also borrowed

Cable's techniques for including slave songs in the context of fictional narration in his novel *Youma*—my thanks go to Werner Sollors for pointing out this connection to me. See Wagner, "Disarmed and Dangerous," 136–42, for an account of Cable's rather curious influence on early jazz historiography.

29. Hearn, *Creole Sketches*, 117, 120.

30. Lafcadio Hearn to Henry Krehbiel [1881], Edward Larocque Tinker Papers, bMS Am 2196, File 38, Houghton Library, Harvard University. This letter is also noteworthy in that it connects Cable's effort to transcribe Afro-Creole slave songs to the nineteenth-century debates about musical "partials" that I discuss later on in this chapter. "I was a little disappointed, although I was also much delighted, with parts of Cable's 'Grandissimes,'" Hearn wrote to Krehbiel. "He [Cable] did not follow out his first plan; as he told me he was going to do: vis., to scatter about 50 Creole songs through the work, with the music in the shape of notes at the end. There are only a few ditties published; and as the Creole music deals in fractions of tones, Mr. Cable failed to write it properly. He is not enough of a musician, I fancy, for that."

31. Hearn, *Creole Sketches*, 123.

32. Herskovits, *Myth of the Negro Past*, 246. Quoted in Jones, *Strange Talk*, 117–18. On the history of anthropology and African American life in the United States—a history in which figures like Cable and Hearn are often omitted—see Baker, *From Savage to Negro*, and Baker, *Anthropology and the Racial Politics of Culture*.

33. Jones, *Strange Talk*, 99. Aside from Jones's excellent study of nineteenth-century dialect writing, see, especially, Bridgeman, *Colloquial Style in America*; Gates, *Figures in Black*, 167–95; Brodhead, *Cultures of Letters*, 177–210; and Sundquist, *To Wake the Nations*, 271–454.

34. Elliott, *Culture Concept*, 65.

35. Evans, "French-English Literary Dialect in *The Grandissimes*," 216–17.

36. Quoted in ibid., 217–18.

37. Cable, "'Negro English' in Literature," 68. Signed under the acronym G. W. C. (George Washington Cable), the letter occasioned a defensive response from Page himself; see Page, "Mr. Page's Negro Dialect," 79. Still unsatisfied, Cable sent in a hostile rejoinder a few weeks later; see Cable, "A Protest against Dialect," 83.

38. Cable, "A Protest against Dialect," 83.

39. Jones, *Strange Talk*, 117–33.

40. Cable, *Creoles of Louisiana*, 317–18.

41. Ibid., 318–19.

42. Cable, "Creole Slave Songs," 808. See Jones, *Strange Talk*, 115–33, for more on the difficulty of translating the meaning of the Creole slave melodies in Cable's work.

43. On the transition from "armchair" ethnography to participant observation, see Stocking, "Ethnographic Sensibility of the 1920s," 208–9. There is also something to be said here about Frowenfeld's German ancestry, a minor narrative detail that Cable drives home throughout the novel, somewhat unnecessarily. My sense is that this may have had to do with the fact that in Cable's time, American anthropological thought was largely a German import, from the philosopher J. G. Herder all the

way down to Franz Boas, who was, of course, Cable's contemporary. On the relationship between participant observation and social marginality, see Liss, "Patterns of Strangeness," 114–30.

44. In *Shaping of American Anthropology*, vi, Stocking argues that the alternating sounds thesis contains "in germ most of Boasian anthropology."

45. Boas, "On Alternating Sounds," 52.

46. Ibid., 51.

47. Powell, *Introduction to the Study of Indian Languages*, 12.

48. Stocking, *Race, Culture, and Evolution*, 158–59.

49. Brinton, "Earliest Form of Human Speech," 408.

50. Boas, "On Alternating Sounds," 51.

51. Here Boas was building on what was then the cutting edge in research on linguistic psychology, especially the work of G. Stanley Hall and his student Sara E. Wiltse, who had completed a series of experiments suggesting that humans can only process and understand "new" perceptual sensations with reference to sensations that are already familiar. See "Sound-Blindness," 244–45, and Wiltse, "Psychological Literature: II: Experimental," 702–5. George Stocking has pointed out that the work of Horatio Hale may have also provided inspiration to Boas while he was formulating the alternating sounds thesis; see Stocking, *Ethnographer's Magic*, 66. In an 1884 essay for the *Journal of the Royal Anthropological Institute*, Hale recounts an accidental discovery he made while working with Alexander Melville Bell, whom we encountered in chapter 1. Hale and Bell were simultaneously recording the words of an Iroquois informant, and at several points in their transcriptions, Hale rendered as an *r* a sound that Bell rendered as an *l*. This led Hale to conclude that phonetic variations may in fact be the result of mishearing rather than misspeaking. See Hale, "On Some Doubtful or Intermediate Articulations," 233–43. Stocking, however, claims that Hale's influence on Boas's understanding was minimal. More likely, the discussion of the alternating sounds phenomenon in Powell's *Introduction to the Study of Indian Languages* provided Boas, a longtime correspondent of the Bureau of Ethnology, with the impetus for the 1889 essay.

52. Boas, "On Alternating Sounds," 52; emphasis added.

53. Ibid., 47.

54. Boas, *Introduction to the Handbook of American Indian Languages*, 12–13. Ruth Benedict made virtually the same claim in the 1930s, demonstrating just how irrevocably Boas's idea of sound-blindness influenced the diffusion of cultural relativism during the twentieth century: "A great deal of our misunderstanding of languages unrelated to our own has arisen from our attempts to refer alien phonetic systems back to ours as a point of reference. . . . We have a *d* and an *n*. They may have an intermediate sound which, if we fail to identify it, we write now *d* and now *n*, introducing distinctions which do not exist." See Benedict, *Patterns of Culture*, 23–24.

55. See Sundquist, *To Wake the Nations*, 294–323, and Radano, *Lying Up a Nation*, 164–229. Both here and subsequently, I am especially indebted to Radano's argument.

56. *Fugitive* is, as I noted earlier, the term that Thomas Edison uses to describe the perceived evanescence of sound prior to the invention of the phonograph. But I also

use the term here in the spirit of Nathaniel Mackey's idea of "fugitivity"—the resistance of minority cultural production, especially music, to mainstream appropriation. See Mackey, *Discrepant Engagement,* 268–70, and Mackey, *Paracritical Hinge,* 187.

57. Harrison, "Negro English," 232.

58. Ibid.

59. Harrison, "Creole Patois of Louisiana," 285–96. Cable cites this essay in the text of "Creole Slave Songs," 807.

60. Higginson, "Negro Spirituals," 685.

61. Brown, "Songs of the Slaves," 623.

62. Sundquist, *To Wake the Nations,* 310–11. Although this conjuncture points to the oft-discussed fluidities between spoken and musical forms in many non-European expressive traditions, it also reflects the fact that linguistic anthropology and early ethnomusicology developed in close intellectual proximity. A long line of figures in the United States (from Cable and Boas to twentieth-century language theorists such as Edward Sapir) in fact worked with linguistic and musical material simultaneously. See, for instance, Boas, "Eskimo Tales and Songs," 123–31, the first of several articles on Inuit Eskimo music that Boas would produce in his lifetime and an essay that likely played a role in the formulation of the alternating sounds thesis. See also Sapir, "Song Recitative in Paiute Mythology," 455–72. Sapir wrote about Paiute music throughout his early career in linguistics.

63. Garrison, "Songs of the Port Royal 'Contrabands,'" 10. Nineteenth-century attempts to reproduce birdsong in writing represent a strangely crucial subplot to this story. Unfortunately, the matter exceeds the scope of my argument here. Suffice it to say, Cable was renowned for his ability to transcribe birdsong—a fact that biographers often bring up in conjunction with the purported "true-to-life" fidelity of his orthographical system. As Cable's daughter recalled after her father's death, "one of his [Cable's] chief pleasures . . . had been to put into musical notation certain of the bird-songs, particularly that of the mockingbird; for he had a keenly correct musical ear, doubtless inherited, as was his clear tenor voice, from his father." Bikle, *George W. Cable,* 78.

64. Allen et al., *Slave Songs of the United States,* iv–v.

65. Radano, *Lying Up a Nation,* 186.

66. Fletcher, *A Study of Omaha Indian Music,* 7.

67. Ibid.

68. Boas, *Ethnography of Franz Boas,* 37.

69. Radano, *Lying Up a Nation,* 189.

70. On "audio–racial imagination," see Kun, *Audiotopia,* 25.

71. Quoted in Bikle, *George W. Cable,* 48.

72. Wagner, "Disarmed and Dangerous," 130.

73. Cable, "Creole Slave Songs," 825–26. As Gavin Jones has pointed out, the "mountains" *(montagne)* in all versions of this song contain an important, if heavily veiled, allusion to the San Domingo slave rebellion of 1791. See Jones, *Strange Talk,* 128.

74. Hearn, "The Creole *Patois,*" 151.

75. Boas's alternating sounds essay has been proposed as an important context both for the regional realist tradition of dialect writing, in general (see Sundquist, *To Wake the Nations*, 5–7, 312–13), and for Cable's work, in particular (see Wagner, "Disarmed and Dangerous," 130).

76. On "media relations" in literary history, see North, *Camera Works*, 187.

77. Boas, "Aims of Ethnology," 636. For more on Boas's ideas about solving problems of auditory subjectivity, see Boas, "Mythology and Folk-Tales of the North American Indians," 452.

78. Shelemay, "Recording Technology, the Record Industry, and Ethnomusicological Scholarship," 277–92.

79. Brady, *A Spiral Way*, 69. Ethnographic experiments with the phonograph weren't limited to the preservation of human language. The philologist R. L. Garner also used the Edison phonograph to document the protolinguistic sounds of monkeys around this same time. See Radick, "R. L. Garner and the Rise of the Edison Phonograph in Evolutionary Philology," 175–206. On audio ethnography's relationship to nineteenth-century ideas about death and cultural preservation, also see Sterne, *Audible Past*, 287–334.

80. Fewkes, "On the Use of the Phonograph in the Study of the Languages of American Indians," 268–69.

81. Fewkes, "A Contribution to Passamaquoddy Folk-Lore," 257.

82. On the popular response to the phonograph, see Kittler, *Gramophone, Film, Typewriter*, 21–114; Gitelman, *Scripts, Grooves, and Writing Machines*, 62–96; and Picker, *Victorian Soundscapes*.

83. Sterne, *Audible Past*, 246–86.

84. Edison, "Phonograph and Its Future," 527.

85. Sterne, *Audible Past*, 298–301.

86. On sound fidelity in the age of digital reproduction, see Sterne, *MP3*, esp. 128–47.

87. Edison, "Phonograph and Its Future," 534. The phonograph wouldn't take off in the realm of popular music and mass entertainment until the mid- to late 1890s. On the phonograph's transition from business machine to mass entertainment, see Gelatt, *Fabulous Phonograph*; Kenney, *Recorded Music in American Life*; and Millard, *America on Record*.

88. Edison, "Perfected Phonograph," 642.

89. For more on this, see Gitelman, "Souvenir Foils," 157.

90. Preece and Stroh, "Studies in Acoustics," 358–59. Preece made a similar claim that "musical notes always come out a little clearer than articulate speech" in a collection of essays on the phonograph published around the same time. See Preece, *Phonograph*, 5.

91. Quoted in Gelatt, *Fabulous Phonograph*, 31.

92. "Accuracy of the Phonograph in Acoustics," 87.

93. For more detailed accounts of Fewkes's biography, see Hough, "Jesse Walter Fewkes," 92–97; Tozzer, "Jesse Walter Fewkes," 535–36; and Hinsley, "Ethnographic Charisma and Scientific Routine," 53–69.

94. Brady, *A Spiral Way*, 129–30.

95. Mary E. Dewey, "Account of Zuni Visit to Mary Hemenway House, Summer 1886," Hemenway Southwest Expedition Records (1886–1914), Box 9, Peabody Museum of Archaeology and Ethnology, Harvard University.

96. J. Walter Fewkes to Mary Hemenway, March 15, 1890, Hemenway Southwest Expedition Records (1886–1914), Box 9.

97. Brady, *A Spiral Way*, 56–58.

98. Fewkes, "On the Use of the Phonograph in the Study of the Languages of American Indians," 267. Fewkes also published his initial findings with the phonograph as "Use of the Phonograph in the Study of the Languages of American Indians" in *The American Naturalist* in May 1890. See also Fewkes, "A Contribution to Passamaquoddy Folk-Lore," 256–80, and Fewkes, "Additional Studies of Zuñi Songs and Rituals with the Phonograph," 1094–98.

99. Fewkes, "On the Use of the Phonograph in the Study of the Languages of American Indians," 267–68.

100. See Brady, *A Spiral Way*, 42–43.

101. Fewkes, "A Contribution to Passamaquoddy Folk-Lore," 256.

102. Daston and Galison, *Objectivity*, 121.

103. Boas, "Introduction to the *International Journal of American Linguistics*," 200.

104. Fewkes, "A Contribution to Passamaquoddy Folk-Lore," 257.

105. According to Erika Brady, one reason for the scarcity of early ethnographic recordings today is the fact that they were often discarded after written transcriptions were derived from them. Brady, *A Spiral Way*, 62.

106. Fewkes, "A Contribution to Passamaquoddy Folk-Lore," 257, 277–78.

107. Fewkes's position was also echoed by Otto Abraham and E. M. von Hornbostel, the architects of turn-of-the-century phonographic ethnography in Germany. In 1904, Abraham and Hornbostel praised the phonograph's ability to enable the ethnographer to listen repeatedly and study auditory artifacts outside of the "distracting" physical spectacle of "native performance." Shelemay, "Recording Technology, the Record Industry, and Ethnomusicological Scholarship," 280. See also Wead, "Study of Primitive Music," 75–79, which similarly attempts to reconcile the study of Native American and African American music with Boas's alternating sounds thesis.

108. See Frisbie, *Music and Dance Research of the Southwestern United States Indians*; Levine, *Writing American Indian Music*; and Pisani, *Imagining Native America in Music*.

109. Gilman, "Zuñi Melodies," 68. Gilman's ideas here seem to anticipate the film theorist Michel Chion's landmark writings on "reduced listening." See Chion, *Audio-Vision*, 29–33.

110. Gilman, "Zuñi Melodies," 89. See also Gilman, "On Some Psychological Aspects of the Chinese Musical System," 57: "The invention of the phonograph bids fair to render the practice of music among non-European peoples as accessible to study as their ideas about the act have hitherto been. Whenever a phonographic cylinder can be exposed to a musical performance a close copy of the original texture of tone is fixed in a form which admits of subsequent examination of the most careful kind whenever and wherever desired."

111. See Fillmore, "Zuni Music as Translated by Mr. Benjamin Ives Gilman," and Fillmore, "What Do Indians Mean to Do When They Sing, and How Far Do They Succeed?," 138–42. For a more moderate response to Gilman's work, see Fletcher, "*Hopi Songs* by Benjamin Ives Gilman," 977–79.

112. Gilman, *Hopi Songs,* 8–9.

113. Ibid., 7.

114. Gilman, "Science of Exotic Music," 535.

115. Gilman, *Hopi Songs,* 31.

116. Adorno, "Form of the Phonograph Record," 277.

117. Ellison, *Invisible Man,* 443.

118. Adorno, "Form of the Phonograph Record," 279–80. More generally, see Lastra, *Sound Technology and the American Cinema,* 123–53, for an account of Adorno, Frankfurt School theory, and the problem of sound reproduction.

119. Including a comprehensive list of sources here is basically impossible. On the race and gender biases reflected in the photographic image, see, among scores of other studies, Wexler, *Tender Violence,* and Smith, *Photography on the Color Line.*

120. The image first appeared in *Profitable Advertising,* April 1909, 1128. It was likely reproduced in a variety of publications in the period.

121. Adorno, "Curves of the Needle," 273.

122. See Marx, *Machine in the Garden.*

123. This connection was especially powerful in the early history of the phonograph, which evolved against the backdrop of the "Golden Age" of Western imperialism in important ways. Ethnography is only one use for the device that links up with the history of global empire. As early as 1895, explorers began taking phonographs and gramophones on expeditions to colonial Africa and South America to help "win over" native populations. See Pietz, "Phonograph in Africa," 263–85, and Taussig, *Mimesis and Alterity.* For more general treatments of the colonial dimensions of modern technological advancement, see Adas, *Machines as the Measure of Men,* and, more recently, Larkin, *Signal and Noise.*

124. Miller, *Segregating Sound,* 167–71.

125. Taussig, *Mimesis and Alterity,* 208.

126. Deloria, *Indians in Unexpected Places,* 136–82. Allakariallak, the Inuit actor who played Nanook in Flaherty's film, was in fact familiar with sound recording technology. Like many of the scenes in *Nanook of the North,* his encounter with the gramophone was staged at Flaherty's suggestion.

4. Race, Empire, and the Skin of the Ethnographic Image

1. Mead, *Blackberry Winter,* 137; emphasis original.

2. Mead, *Coming of Age in Samoa,* xxvi.

3. Mead, *Letters from the Field,* 50. Mead mentions issues of *Asia* in an early letter from Samoa dated September 27, 1925. See ibid., 25. For more on Mead's creative uses of Robert and Frances Flaherty's Samoan photographs, see Mead, *Blackberry Winter,* 154, and Nordström, "Photography of Samoa," 35.

4. Flaherty, "Setting Up House and Shop in Samoa," 639–52. Given that Mead first mentions *Asia* in a letter composed in September 1925, the photographs in this article are the most likely candidates for the photographs Mead used. A May 1925 article written by Louis D. Froelick, *Asia*'s editor in chief, also includes a series of Flaherty's Samoan photographs. All of them follow the same visual conventions. See Froelick, "Moana of the South Seas," 389–400.

5. As I noted in my introductory chapter, Anglophone uses of the term *documentary* date back to the early decades of the nineteenth century. With few exceptions, however, critical accounts of the documentary genre's history typically cite John Grierson's classic review of *Moana*, written anonymously for the New York *Sun* in February 1926, as an inaugural landmark: "The golden beauty of primitive beings, of a South Sea Island that is an earthly paradise, is caught and imprisoned in Robert J. Flaherty's *Moana* . . . . Of course *Moana*, being a visual account of events in the daily life of a Polynesian youth and his family, has documentary value." Grierson, "Flaherty's Poetic *Moana*," 25.

6. Flaherty, "Film: Language of the Eye," 36. On the popularization of the anthropological "culture concept" in the United States during the 1920s and 1930s, see, in particular, Hegeman, *Patterns for America*.

7. The media historian Erik Barnouw, whose father enjoyed regular correspondence with Flaherty throughout the 1920s, begins his landmark *Documentary: A History of the Non-fiction Film* with the Lumière tradition of turn-of-the-century "actuality" cinema (1–51). Yet for Barnouw, it isn't until Flaherty's films begin to appear in the 1920s that the modern documentary style actually finds its true form. Barnouw's assessment reflected decades of film history that had identified Flaherty as, sui generis, the sole progenitor of modern "naturalistic filmmaking." See Gray, "Robert Flaherty and the Naturalistic Documentary," 41–48, and Van Dongen, "Robert J. Flaherty," 13–14, as well as some of the early career retrospectives that appeared immediately following Flaherty's death. The most notable of these is Griffith, *World of Robert Flaherty*.

Yet as early as the 1930s, film historians and nonfiction filmmakers themselves were already beginning to express doubts about the legitimacy of such appraisals. For instance, John Grierson's opening move in "First Principles of Documentary" (1932) was to distance the burgeoning international documentary movement from Flaherty's seemingly "escapist" leanings, and subsequent generations of *vérité* filmmakers openly condemned projects like *Nanook, Moana*, and Flaherty's later *Man of Aran* (1934) for their naked distortions of cultural reality. See Grierson, "First Principles of Documentary," 145–46. By the late 1970s and early 1980s, the idea that the "Flaherty myth" of documentary genesis needed to be debunked had become something of a critical commonplace. See, among others, Corliss, "Robert Flaherty," 230–38; Ruby, "Aggie Must Come First," 66–73; Ruby, "A Reexamination of the Early Career of Robert J. Flaherty," 431–58; Custen, "(Re)framing of Robert Flaherty," 87–94; Winston, "White Man's Burden," 58–60; Barsam, *Vision of Robert Flaherty*; Marks, "Ethnography and Ethnographic Film," 339–47; Langer, "Rethinking Flaherty," 239–55; Langer, "Flaherty's Hollywood Period," 38–57; Winston, "Documentary," 70–86;

and Raheja, "Reading Nanook's Smile," 1159–85. More recently, critical "demystifications" of Flaherty's work have advanced alongside a wholesale reevaluation of documentary cinema's visual history, which increasingly appears to encompass a heterogeneous set of representational practices that took shape well before the arrival of motion picture technology: "magic lantern" projections and illustrated travel lectures; ethnographic photographs, chronophotographic studies, and museum exhibitions; "detective" pictures, cartes de visite, and postcards; even life-group villages at world's fairs and window displays at department stores. See Musser, "Travel Genre in 1903–1904," 123–32; Barber, "Roots of Travel Cinema," 68–84; Winston, "Documentary Film as Scientific Inscription," 37–57; Gunning, "Embarrassing Evidence," 46–64; Rony, *Third Eye*; Grimshaw, *Ethnographer's Eye*, 44–56; Oksiloff, *Picturing the Primitive*; Amad, "Cinema's 'Sanctuary,'" 138–59; Rosen, *Change Mummified*, 225–63; Nichols, "Documentary Film and the Modernist Avant-Garde," 580–610; Griffiths, *Wondrous Difference*; and many of the essays included in Ruoff, *Virtual Voyages*.

8. Flaherty has been the subject of several biographies: see Calder-Marshall, *Innocent Eye*; Rotha, *Robert J. Flaherty*; and Christopher, *Robert and Frances Flaherty*. My brief account here draws mostly on Christopher's recent treatment, which integrates narrative biography with Robert and Frances Flaherty's letters and diary entries.

9. The essays collected in Danzker's *Robert Flaherty, Photographer/Filmmaker* shed crucial light onto Flaherty's oft-overlooked experiments with still photography during the 1910s.

10. Flaherty, *Odyssey of a Film-Maker*, 13.

11. See the assorted reviews of *Nanook* compiled in the Robert Joseph Flaherty Papers (1884–1970), Rare Book and Manuscript Library, Columbia University, Box 21, Reel 3.

12. Quoted in Calder-Marshall, *Innocent Eye*, 97.

13. As Elizabeth Edwards has pointed out, "re-enactment was not an unconsidered mode of [ethnographic] illustration. Rather, it was integrally linked to historically specific notions of intellectual validity, objectivity, and scientific method." Edwards, *Raw Histories*, 158. See also Griffiths, *Wondrous Difference*, 216–27.

14. Quoted in Christopher, *Robert and Frances Flaherty*, 232.

15. Ibid., 385.

16. Aside from a few scattered references in survey histories of nonfiction film, *Moana* has received scant critical attention. The lone exception here is Jeffrey Geiger's excellent chapter "Searching for *Moana*: Frances Hubbard and Robert J. Flaherty in Samoa," in Geiger, *Facing the Pacific*, 118–59. Geiger's work has been an immense help in clarifying my thinking here.

There are a variety of reasons why *Moana* has languished in comparison to more canonical Flaherty films like *Nanook of the North* and *Louisiana Story* (1948). Most important, perhaps, is the fact that very few prints of *Moana* remain in existence. The majority of the research for this chapter was conducted with reference to a 16mm print owned by the Harvard Film Archive, transferred from a 35mm original during the 1940s. My thanks go to Liz Coffey and Amy Sloper for their generous help on this front.

17. Quoted in Rotha, *Robert J. Flaherty*, 7.

18. Quoted in Barsam, *Vision of Robert Flaherty*, 39; emphasis original.

19. On myths and stereotypes of the South Seas, see Smith, *European Vision and the South Pacific*, and, more recently, Geiger, *Facing the Pacific*.

20. Salesa, "Samoan Half-Castes and Some Frontiers of Comparison," 72.

21. On U.S. foreign policy in the age of the "Open Door" doctrine, see Williams, *Tragedy of American Diplomacy*, 18–90.

22. See Kennedy, *Samoan Tangle*, as well as Heffer, *The United States and the Pacific*, 192–95.

23. Rony, *Third Eye*, 99–128. See also Limbrick, *Making Settler Cinemas*, 137–42. Limbrick demonstrates that the taxidermic impulse is common in so-called settler cinemas of colonial encounter. On the relationship between cinema and taxidermy more generally, see Haraway, "Teddy Bear Patriarchy," 237–91; Alvey, "Cinema as Taxidermy," 23–45; and Wakeham, *Taxidermic Signs*.

24. Balikci, "Anthropology, Film, and the Arctic Peoples," 7. *Nanook's* international popularity sparked, among many other notable fads, a craze for ice cream bars (the Eskimo Pie was first marketed in the United States around the same time), and 1922 also witnessed the release of "Nanook," a popular song featuring the refrain, "Ever loving Nanook / Though you don't read a book / But oh how you can love / And thrill me like the Twinkling Northern Lights above." Barnouw, *Documentary*, 43.

Ironically, Paramount/Famous Players-Lasky, which rushed to back *Moana*, was the first of several Hollywood production companies to balk on the distribution of Flaherty's first film. As Paul Rotha explains, "it was wholly in Hollywood's character for the major distributing company that had spurned the first offer of *Nanook* to offer Flaherty the chance to produce his next film. A major reason was that Jesse L. Lasky, production head of Famous Players-Lasky, the studio end of Paramount Pictures Corporation, was fascinated by exploration. . . . A second reason may have been that Paramount, like other American distributors, was finding that the overseas markets for its films were becoming very remunerative." Rotha, *Robert J. Flaherty*, 51. In addition to backing *Moana*, Paramount also worked to fund and distribute Ernest Schoedsack and Merian C. Cooper's classic travel film *Grass* (1925), which followed certain aspects of the *Nanook* formula; see Naficy, "Lured by the East," 117–38.

25. Quoted in Rotha, *Robert J. Flaherty*, 52. Flaherty offers a slight variation on this story in "Film: Language of the Eye," 34.

26. Geiger, *Facing the Pacific*, 74–75. On O'Brien's work and popularity in the early 1920s, see chapter 2 in the same volume, "Idylls and Ruins: Frederick O'Brien in the Marquesas," 74–117. Flaherty worked briefly with W. S. Van Dyke on the film version of O'Brien's narrative, released in 1928.

27. Quoted in ibid., 74.

28. Quoted in Rotha, *Robert J. Flaherty*, 52.

29. Articles in *National Geographic* often referred to Samoa as a "foster-child" territory during the 1910s and 1920s, paternalistically figuring the United States as a benevolent "foster-parent." See, for instance, Quinn, "America's South Sea Soldiers," 274.

30. The Flahertys in fact unknowingly arrived in the South Seas amid tremendous political upheaval. Anticolonial unrest and cultural nationalism emerged in western Samoa during the 1920s, mostly in response to widespread dissatisfaction with New Zealand's colonial administration, which had failed to take steps to quarantine the devastating Spanish flu pandemic of 1918. From 1918 to 1919 alone, the influenza virus killed 22 percent of the native population under New Zealand's jurisdiction. American Samoa, by contrast, suffered comparatively few casualties. Meleisea, *Change and Adaptations in Western Samoa*, 29–49.

31. On "Samoan mobility," see Salesa, "'Travel Happy' Samoa," 171–88.

32. Levi-Strauss, *Tristes Tropiques*, 41.

33. Flaherty, "Setting Up House and Shop in Samoa," 639.

34. Griffith, *World of Robert Flaherty*, 52. Frances's rhetoric here falls directly in line with what Johannes Fabian regards as one of the epistemological hallmarks of late-nineteenth- and early-twentieth-century anthropology: the "denial of coevalness." See Fabian, *Time and Other*, 1–35.

35. "*Moana of the South Seas*, 1925: Correspondence," Robert Joseph Flaherty Papers (1884–1970), Box 23, Reel 14. The "Nanook of the South" title was scrapped soon thereafter (replaced first by "Moana of the South" and finally *Moana: A Romance of the Golden Age*), but as late as 1928, Flaherty was lobbying Hollywood production companies to back a film about Acoma Indians in the U.S. Southwest titled "Nanook of the Desert." The project was eventually dropped during the early stages of filming. Langer, "Rethinking Flaherty," 243.

36. "*Moana of the South Seas*: Publicity Materials," Robert Joseph Flaherty Papers (1884–1970), Box 26, Reel 15.

37. Flaherty, "Setting Up House and Shop in Samoa," 648.

38. Flaherty, "A Search for Animal and Sea Sequences," 954–63, 1000–1004.

39. Rony, *Third Eye*, 115.

40. "*Moana*: The Intimate Drama of Life," X4.

41. Robert Flaherty to Louis D. Froelick, June 1925, Robert Joseph Flaherty Papers (1884–1970), Box 23, Reel 14.

42. Geiger, *Facing the Pacific*, 145.

43. Flaherty, "Camera's Eye," 346. Quoted in Rony, *Third Eye*, 141. This idea was widespread in the late nineteenth century, but it came under increasing scrutiny during the 1910s and 1920s, while the Flahertys were working in Nunavik and Safune. On visual anthropology's corporeal fascination, see Hansen et al., "Pornography, Ethnography, and the Discourses of Power," 220: "In ethnographic practice, the body is an instrument of cultural performance. Sometimes presented holistically, sometimes fragmentarily, and often naked (or nearly so), the body is where culture comes to life. Individual physical actions give a literal embodiment to culture." Accurate as these sorts of accounts are, Alison Griffiths has noted that they may not hold true for early-twentieth-century visual ethnography. During this period, anthropologists in the United States and Europe in fact expressed considerable skepticism as to whether culture's deep structures of belief were actually visible in embodied performance. This was one important reason why anthropologists were relatively slow to

incorporate motion picture technology—a technology that in many ways only captures visible surfaces—into ethnographic fieldwork. Griffiths, *Wondrous Difference*, xxi. I discuss this issue in greater detail in chapter 5.

44. Robert Flaherty to Jesse L. Lasky, November 28, 1923, Robert Joseph Flaherty Papers (1884–1970), Box 23, Reel 14: "In another package I am sending you a color plate (an autochrome) of Taioa, one of my characters, and also one of Ta'avale, another character. These plates might give you some idea of the picturable quality of the people with whom I am working. . . . My [panchromatic] motion picture portraits of the characters will have as good color values as these autochromes, since red and its variations (the predominating color of my portraits) is one that the color systems handle best—I might say, correctly. . . . Besides the autochromes, I am sending some portraits to show you how by the use of a heavy filter and panchromatic film I have taken care of the flesh tones of the face. The Samoan complexion is reddish-brown, which photographed on the ordinary orthochromatic film comes out very dark—hopelessly so. They look like Negroes, as indeed they have in any travel films I have seen of the South Seas." The autochrome is an important photographic technology in the evolution of salvage ethnography. I address its invention and use in ethnographic contexts in chapter 5.

45. Bordwell et al., *Classical Hollywood Cinema*, 281.

46. Ibid., 282.

47. Ibid., 284.

48. "The Log of a Great Picture," 10. Quoted in Bordwell et al., *Classical Hollywood Cinema*, 283.

49. *Eastman Panchromatic Negative Film for Motion Pictures*, 5. Quoted in Bordwell et al., *Classical Hollywood Cinema*, 284. See also Blair, "Development of the Motion Picture Raw Film Industry," 53: "[Panchromatic film is] invaluable when photographing colored sets or costumes and for accurately rendering flesh tints in close-ups."

50. The Flahertys frequently misidentified *Moana* as "the first film ever to be made wholly on panchromatic stock." See "Autobiographical Writings," Robert Joseph Flaherty Papers (1884–1970), Box 48, Reel 27.

51. Salt, *Film Style and Technology*, 181.

52. Flaherty, "Setting Up House and Shop in Samoa," 711.

53. Salt, *Film Style and Technology*, 256.

54. Bordwell et al., *Classical Hollywood Cinema*, 281.

55. Rotha, *Film till Now*, 134.

56. Rotha, *Celluloid*, 18. Here is Rotha on the virtues of panchromatic film stock: "I have explained at length in 'The Film Till Now' why colour is unnecessary in the dramatic theatrical film and how it definitely diminishes appeal. These reasons, I think, make clear to a large extent . . . how for aesthetic reasons colour is a white elephant to the cinematic medium. . . . Only on the rarest occasions and then purely for a decorative purpose, such as in posters, cartoon and abstract films, can I visualize colour in the cinema. . . . Realistic colour in its limited forms as we see it in films to-day is quite without use to a creative director. It is not accurate realism of colour which is desirable but the ability to be able to suggest colour. . . . Of particular

interest in this connection is Flaherty's *Moana,* the first film to be photographed in its entirety on panchromatic stock. After making many experiments at all times of the day, Flaherty found that if he did all his shooting before ten o'clock in the morning and between four and half-past six in the evening, the low angle of the sun produced not only a wonderful stereoscopic effect but suggested a broad range of greens and browns on the screen. By being photographed in this way, *Moana* possessed a beautiful golden quality as if the whole landscape had been drenched in sun, while the trees and figures stood out in amazing relief. No further device for obtaining colour reproduction could have been desired" (18).

57. Valentine, "Make-Up and Set Painting Aid New Film," 54. Quoted in Dyer, *White,* 93.

58. Bazin, "Evolution of the Language of Cinema," 30. The massive influence of Bazin's account of deep focus cinematography does much to explain why panchromatic technology remains so marginal in historical accounts of cinematic realism.

59. Here I diverge from Jean-Louis Comolli's discussion of the relationship between panchromatic film and deep focus cinematography in "Machines of the Visible." In the context of a much more complicated discussion about theories of cinematic realism, Comolli argues that the shift to panchro during the mid-1920s marked a moment in which "the 'realism' of the cinematic image" was effectively realigned "with that of the photographic image." See Comolli, "Machines of the Visible," 131. As I demonstrate later, however, the Flahertys' interest in panchro was as much about creating a kind of tactile "liveness" to the cinematic experience as it was about bringing out the medium's baseline photographic qualities.

60. Flaherty, "Handling of Motion Picture Film under Various Climatic Conditions." http://astro.temple.edu/~ruby/wava/Flaherty/handling.html.

61. Dyer, *White,* 89–90.

62. Flaherty, "Setting Up House and Shop in Samoa," 711.

63. "*Moana of the South Seas,* 1925: Correspondence," Robert Joseph Flaherty Papers (1884–1970), Box 23, Reel 14; Flaherty, "Filming Real People," 97.

64. Auslander, *Liveness,* 10–72. Auslander's terminology has special applicability here because, as he notes, the phenomenon of the "live" is a product of a "mediatized culture." By definition, there is no such thing as "liveness" without the existence of the media technology.

65. Flaherty, "Handling of Motion Picture Film under Various Climatic Conditions."

66. Cripps, *Slow Fade to Black,* 127–28. *Tabu,* F. W. Murnau's 1931 collaboration with Flaherty, is another important film in this tradition.

67. See also Geiger, *Facing the Pacific,* 141.

68. Robert Flaherty to Adriaan J. Barnouw, September 9, 1926, Robert Joseph Flaherty Papers (1884–1970), Box 7, Reel 3. In context, Flaherty's comments resemble more public statements that his wife made in press releases and magazine articles about the aesthetically "unpleasing" look of black skin on the silver screen.

69. Flaherty, "Fa'a Samoa," 1085.

70. Tcherkézoff, "A Long and Unfortunate Voyage," 175–96. For a fascinating take on the uses of these racial distinctions in American race science, see Fabian, *Skull Collectors,* 121–62.

71. Tcherkézoff, "A Long and Unfortunate Voyage," 186. The idea of Polynesians as "Caucasian" actually dates back to the 1590s, well before the rise of modern race science, when Spanish explorers reached the Marquesas and were surprised to find islanders who seemed to look just like they did. Because of the region's extraordinary linguistic and cultural diversity, visitors to the Pacific—from early European explorers to nineteenth-century anthropologists to twentieth-century writers—subsequently rooted their ideas about Pacific racial variation in skin color and physiognomy, even though this mode of racial identification largely fell out of favor by the end of the nineteenth century.

72. In the U.S. context, the most obvious point of comparison here is the case of the Philippines, which involved a much different set of racial formations and, as a result, engendered a much different system of imperial intervention and colonial governance. See Kramer, *Blood of Government*.

73. Geiger, *Facing the Pacific*, 59.

74. See Jacobson, *Whiteness of a Different Color*.

75. *United States v. Bhagat Singh Thind*, 261 U.S. 204, 211 (1923): "The word 'Caucasian' is in scarcely better repute [than the term *Aryan*]. It is, at best, a conventional term, with an altogether fortuitous origin which, under scientific manipulation, has come to include far more than the unscientific mind suspects. According to [Augustus Henry] Keane, for example . . . it includes not only the Hindu, but some of the Polynesians (that is, the Maori, Tahitians, Samoans, Hawaiians, and others), the Hamites of Africa, upon the ground of the Caucasic cast of their features, though in color they range from brown to black. We venture to think that the average well informed white American would learn with some degree of astonishment that the race to which he belongs is made up of such heterogeneous elements." http://supreme.justia.com/cases/federal/us/261/204/case.html#F1.

76. Murphy, "Romance of Science in Polynesia," 377.

77. Rogers, *Sex and Race*, 72.

78. Ibid.

79. Ibid., 74.

80. The Flahertys were hardly the first to use tattooing practices among Polynesian peoples as a way to showcase the possibilities and limitations of new photographic and cinematographic technologies. In a 1919 article *National Geographic Magazine* titled "A Vanishing People of the South Seas: The Tragic Fate of the Marquesan Cannibals, Noted for Their Warlike Courage and Physical Beauty," the photographer John W. Church complained of his camera's inability to capture the tattoos that adorned the skins of "cannibal" villagers in the Marquesas: "Had I not unfortunately lost the color screen of my camera, I would be able to show photographically some of the really beautiful [tattooing] work done with the bone needle. The ordinary lens of the camera will not reproduce the blue figures on brown skin, so I am without photographic confirmation of their skill in an art for which they have been famous throughout the South Seas." Church, "A Vanishing People of the South Seas," 291. On Western ideas about tattooing, see, among many sources, Cassuto, *Inhuman Race*, 168–216; Cheng, "Skin Deep," 35–78; and Cheng, "Skin, Tattoos, and Susceptibility," 98–119.

81. Flaherty, "Fa'a Samoa," 1097–98.

82. Geiger, *Facing the Pacific*, 154.

83. See Calder-Marshall, *Innocent Eye*, 113–14; Barsam, *Vision of Robert Flaherty*, 36–37; Geiger, *Facing the Pacific*, 154.

84. Prins, "Visual Media and the Primitivist Perplex," 61–62. Elsewhere, Prins has labeled this relationship the "paradox of primitivism"; see Prins, "Paradox of Primitivism," 243–66.

85. Flaherty, "Film: Language of the Eye," 30.

86. Calder-Marshall, *Innocent Eye*, 119–20.

87. Griffiths, *Wondrous Difference*, 216–18.

88. "*Moana*: The Intimate Drama of Life," X4.

89. Marks, *Skin of the Film*, xi. See also Barker, *Tactile Eye*, 23–68.

90. Grierson, "Flaherty's Poetic *Moana*," 25.

91. Heming, "Review of *Moana*," Robert Joseph Flaherty Papers (1884–1970), Box 25, Reel 15.

92. "*Moana of the South Seas*, 1925: Articles," Robert Joseph Flaherty Papers (1884–1970), Box 25, Reel 15.

93. C. Grant La Farge to Robert Flaherty, October 22, 1925, Robert Joseph Flaherty Papers (1884–1970), Box 23, Reel 14.

94. Rockwell Kent to Robert Flaherty, October 11, 1925, Robert Joseph Flaherty Papers (1884–1970), Box 23, Reel 14; emphasis original.

95. Geiger, *Facing the Pacific*, 136–45. Geiger's use of the term *scopic pleasure* draws on Laura Mulvey's classic theories of spectator identification. See Mulvey, "Visual Pleasure and Narrative Cinema," 6–18.

96. Quoted in Cripps, *Slow Fade to Black*, 133. See also Rotha, *Robert J. Flaherty*, 72. Scholars have made similar arguments about the unnecessary uses of nudity in *Nanook of the North*; see Marcus, "*Nanook of the North* as Primal Drama," 213.

97. Stewart, *Migrating to the Movies*, 37.

5. Local Colors

1. Clatworthy, "Western Views in the Land of the Best," 405–20.

2. Ibid., 417.

3. Franklin L. Fisher to Fred Payne Clatworthy, May 15, 1923, National Geographic Society Archives, Lecture Series 1922–1923/1923–1924, Box 34, Fred Payne Clatworthy (11–57.355), National Geographic Museum, Washington, D.C.

4. Clatworthy, "Western Views in the Land of the Best," 418.

5. Franklin L. Fisher to Fred Payne Clatworthy, May 15, 1923, National Geographic Society Archives, Lecture Series 1922–1923/1923–1924, Box 34, Fred Payne Clatworthy (11–57.355).

6. Goetzmann, *Exploration and Empire*, 57.

7. Dellenbaugh, *North-Americans of Yesterday*, vi. See also Dellenbaugh, *A Canyon Voyage*.

8. Franklin L. Fisher to Fred Payne Clatworthy, May 15, 1923, National Geographic Society Archives, Lecture Series 1922–1923/1923–1924, Box 34, Fred Payne Clatworthy (11–57.355).

9. Ibid.

10. Ibid.; emphasis added.

11. Edwards, "Salvaging Our Past," 83.

12. The body of critical literature on early color photography is small and somewhat limited, and scholars have rarely made mention of ethnographic or documentary photography in color prior to 1930. See, for instance, Roumette, *Early Color Photography*; Howard, "Autochromes," 42–58; Wood, *Art of the Autochrome*; and Wood, *Photographic Arts*, 21–31. The primary exceptions here are Vesilind, "*National Geographic* and Color Photography," which the archivists at the National Geographic Society generously let me consult in preparation for this chapter; Boulouch, "Documentary Use of the Autochrome in France," 143–45; and Amad, *Counter-Archive*, 55–61. Boulouch and Amad both examine the uses of autochrome photography in Albert Kahn's *Archives de la Planète* documentary project during the 1910s. Joshua Yumibe's *Moving Color* has recently redressed the dearth of scholarly materials on early color cinema.

13. See the appendix to Edwards, *Anthropology and Photography*, 267. In general, histories of ethnographic photography have focused on British anthropologists and photographers in the late nineteenth and early twentieth centuries. See Edwards, *Raw Histories*; Pinney, *Photography and Anthropology*; and Edwards, "Tracing Photography," 159–89. The primary exception to this rule is the extensive body of work on the American photographer Edward S. Curtis; see, among others, Gidley, *Edward S. Curtis and the North American Indian,* and Wakeham, *Taxidermic Signs,* 87–128. In part, my interest in examining ethnographic color photography at *National Geographic* represents an attempt to push the scholarly conversation beyond these two main fields of inquiry.

14. On photography's relationship to primitivism and exoticism in *National Geographic*, see Pauly, "The World and All That Is in It," 528–31; Lutz and Collins, *Reading National Geographic*; Steet, *Veils and Daggers*; Schulten, *Geographical Imagination in America,* 156–63; Rothenberg, *Presenting America's World,* 69–97; and Hawkins, *American Iconographic,* 8–101.

15. Clatworthy, "Sixty Years in Photography," 2.

16. Wood, *Art of the Autochrome,* 2–3; Ball, *Bright Earth,* 286–97.

17. Steichen, "Color Photography," 13.

18. Wood, *Art of the Autochrome,* 1–2. See "A New Method for the Production of Photographs in Colours," 605, for an early announcement of the initial public demonstrations of the autochrome.

19. Hammond, "Impressionist Theory and the Autochrome," 97. On the origins of turn-of-the-century theories of color, see Crary, *Techniques of the Observer,* 67–96.

20. For more on the unpredictable social lives of new media, see the essays collected in Thorburn and Jenkins, *Rethinking Media Change,* and in Gitelman and Pingree, *New Media.*

21. Stieglitz, "New Color Photography," 124, 126.

22. For more on the autochrome's role in the Photo-Secession, see Wood, *Art of the Autochrome,* 9–37. According to Mark Jacobs, owner and curator of the largest private collection of early color photographs in the United States, French publications

managed to reproduce the autochrome much earlier than *Camera Work* (telephone interview with author, July 2013). The earliest known print reproduction of an autochrome appeared just a few days after the Lumières unveiled the technology; the publication was timed as an advertisement for the invention. Richard Watson Gilder's *Century* magazine produced the first print reproduction of an autochrome in the United States, though his commitment to the technology never went beyond that.

23. "Color Photo Proves True," II8.

24. "Paintings' Colors Caught by Camera," 3.

25. "First Photograph in Colors of a Living Woman to Be Taken in America," 8A.

26. McFarland, "Real Color Photography Is Now a Fact," 1122. Photographers had so many difficulties with the autochrome that the *British Journal of Photography*'s monthly color supplement began running a series of articles on overcoming the challenges of the process. See, for instance, "Methods of Control in the Development of Autochrome Plates," 90–92, and "Recent Recommendation in the Autochrome Process," 93.

27. Lumière, "Lumière's Autochrome Plates," 36.

28. Quoted in Lester, "Travel and Early Colour," 27.

29. Eskilson, "Color and Consumption," 17. Eskilson has used the phrase *chromatic revolution* to describe the period between 1914 and 1934, which witnessed watershed advances in modern color media, both in terms of avant-garde art practice and mass-market consumer production. On the relationship between color and culture in this period more generally, see Gaskill, "Vibrant Environments."

30. Lumière, "Lumière's Autochrome Plates," 26; emphasis original.

31. de Vies, "Autochrome Work in Tropical Africa," 236.

32. See Lumière, "Lumière's Autochrome Plates," 51: "The Autochrome plates are comparatively slow, and it is not possible, therefore, to use them for instantaneous work in the strictest sense of this word; it is necessary, therefore, for the camera to be supported on a stand or other support so that time exposures may be given." For competing figures on autochrome exposure time, see Boulouch, "Documentary Use of the Autochrome in France," 143, and Amad, *Counter-Archive*, 56.

33. Steiglitz offered the following advice to amateur autochromists: "Begin with photographing still-life. At this season of the year [winter] the light is weakest, and the exposure of autochromes is 20 to 30 times as long as that on Seed 26x plates. Autochromes also cost about 15 times as much as those plates, so failures are expensive trials. In portraits you are apt to underexpose for fear of the subject moving so plates are wasted. Hence begin experiments with still-life." Stieglitz, "Autochrome Plate," 1.

34. Amad, *Counter-Archive*, 55.

35. "Duplicates of Autochromes by Contact Printing and Copying," 81. The *British Journal of Photography* explained the reproduction problem as a function of the material disparities between the technology of the autochrome and the printing processes then in existence: "There are many difficulties in the way of obtaining positive prints from negatives, or positive copies from positives, by ordinary printing or copying methods. In a copy made from a positive on a linear screen-plate the colours

must be degraded to the extent of two-thirds black, while in working from a negative they are diluted by two-thirds of grey. In the case of the Powrie Warner process the trouble is got over by the angling system of printing, but with the Autochrome plate no similar remedy can be applicable on account of the irregularity of the distribution of the starch grains and of their aggregates. Owing to this irregularity neither can the effects produced be uniformly the same. . . . The extent of the degradation is thus purely a matter of chance with the Autochrome. . . . The most useful method of reproduction would be one of printing by contact, but my experiments show that such a method is hardly practicable."

36. Wood, *Art of the Autochrome,* 9–37.

37. Stieglitz, "New Color Photography—a Bit of History," 124–25.

38. Stieglitz, "Editor's Note," 48: "In this issue of *Camera Work* we had hoped to announce definitely the date of publication of our Color Number. An unfortunate chain of circumstances has prevented the firm of Bruckmann, of Munich, from keeping their promise to let us have complete editions before December first. Word has reached us that the firm has had much trouble in the making of the reproductions. . . . It must be remembered that to reproduce these transparencies with any adequate degree of quality and precision is still a matter of initial experiment. The realization of this fact bridles our impatience." Remarkably, photographers were expressing similar sentiments over a decade later, even going so far as to claim that the problem of print reproduction was limiting the autochrome's public exposure. See Davidson, "Future of Color-Photography," 84: "Although it is twelve years since the autochrome process was introduced, there are numberless photographers who have never seen one. Widespread familiarity with the results of this process may have to await the development of the printing-press, for at present the cost of three-color half-tones is excessive for magazines of limited circulation, and photographic magazines are unable to even consider three-color reproduction."

39. Steichen, "Color Photography," 24. On the printing process used to reproduce Steichen's autochromes in *Camera Work,* see the editor's note that Stieglitz appended to Steichen's article: "This number of *Camera Work* contains but three illustrations, and these are reproductions by the four-color half-tone process of Lumière autochromes, the originals of which were done by Steichen, and are amongst the very earliest experiments in this new color process. The edition is by the firm of Bruckmann, of Munich, Germany, who are celebrated for the excellence of their color printing and work generally. These plates represent Bruckmann's first attempts in reproducing from Lumière polychrome screen transparencies and, of necessity, fall short of their anticipations and ours."

40. Ibid.

41. Wood, *Art of the Autochrome,* 29.

42. See "Announcement," i. Early members of the NGS associated with the Bureau of Ethnology include Gerard Fowke, G. K. Gilbert, H. W. Henshaw, Washington Matthews, W. J. McGee, and Lester F. Ward; see "Members of the Society," 94–98.

43. Schulten, *Geographical Imagination in America,* 153. Scholarly accounts of the rise of *National Geographic* represent a veritable cottage industry in the field of American

studies. See Pauly, "The World and All That Is in It"; Abramson, *National Geographic*; Bryan, *National Geographic Society*; Lutz and Collins, *Reading National Geographic*; Bloom, "Constructing Whiteness," 15–32; Steet, *Veils and Daggers*; Schulten, *Geographical Imagination in America*, 45–68, 148–75; Poole, *Explorers House*; Rothenberg, *Presenting America's World*; and Hawkins, *American Iconographic*. On magazines and mass culture in twentieth-century America more broadly, see Schneirov, *Dream of a New Social Order*, and Ohmann, *Selling Culture*.

44. Schulten, *Geographical Imagination in America*, 153.

45. Tuason, "Ideology of Empire," 34–53; Schulten, *Geographical Imagination in America*, 45–68.

46. Schulten, *Geographical Imagination in America*, 52–53.

47. La Gorce, *Story of the Geographic*, n.p.

48. On the history of halftone printing, see Taft, *Photography and the American Scene*, 435–50.

49. Ohmann, *Selling Culture*, 234–35.

50. Grosvenor, *National Geographic Society and Its Magazine*, 37. Twenty years later, Franklin Fisher would estimate that the ratio of illustrations to text was as high as 3 to 1. See Franklin L. Fisher to W. P. Appleford, May 31, 1927, National Geographic Society Archives, Franklin Price Knott File (503-8-5-2460).

51. La Gorce, *Story of the Geographic*, n.p.

52. Abramson, *National Geographic*, 61. On Levy and the development of halftone screen printing processes, see Tebbel, *A History of Book Publishing in the United States*, 2:665–66, and Last, *Color Explosion*, 25–27. On halftones in color, see Twyman, "Illustration Revolution," 132–35.

53. Lutz and Collins, *Reading National Geographic*, 131–33. On hand coloring and other "applied" color processes in the motion picture industry, see Yumibe, *Moving Color*, 37–75.

54. Vesilind, "*National Geographic* and Color Photography," 22.

55. Ibid., 31, 34.

56. Grosvenor, "Land of the Best," 379–405.

57. Knott, "Artist Adventures on the Island of Bali," 326.

58. Franklin Price Knott to Franklin L. Fisher, November 10, 1929, National Geographic Society Archives, Franklin Price Knott File (503-8-5-2460).

59. For more on the Indians-as-landscape trope in American art and letters, see Mitchell, *Witnesses to a Vanishing America*, 90–91.

60. Grosvenor, "Land of the Best," 392.

61. Ibid., 403.

62. Ibid., 398.

63. See Hawkins, *American Iconographic*, 76–87, for a detailed discussion of the tension between "straight" and "pictorial" photographic styles in *National Geographic*. On the straight photography–pictorial photography split in American visual culture more generally, see Trachtenberg, *Reading American Photographs*, 164–230.

64. Lutz and Collins, *Reading National Geographic*, 87–95.

65. Grosvenor, "Report of the Director and Editor of the National Geographic Society for the Year 1914," 319.

66. La Gorce, *Story of the Geographic*, n.p.

67. Banta and Hinsley, *From Site to Sight*, 11.

68. See Edwards, *Anthropology and Photography*, 4; Grimshaw, *Ethnographer's Eye*, 54; and Morton, "Initiation of Kamanga," 119. Alison Griffiths has also pointed out that early-twentieth-century anthropologists began to doubt the value of motion pictures for the exact same reasons. See Griffiths, *Wondrous Difference*, xxv–xxvi.

69. Poole, "An Excess of Description," 163–64.

70. Even here anthropology's rejection of visual information may be overstated. Anthropologists continued to produce images, both still and moving, throughout the early decades of the twentieth century, and they often trained their cameras on the body's physiognomic surfaces to collect ethnographic information. In the 1910s, for instance, Franz Boas wanted to reproduce autochrome photographs in his written studies to help illustrate variations in eye and hair color among immigrant populations living in the United States. See Franz Boas to Albert Jenks, March 23, 1908, and to W. W. Husband, July 27, 1910, Franz Boas Papers (MSS60202), Manuscript Division, Library of Congress, Washington, D.C., Reel 9; Reel 11. Many thanks go to my colleague Katherine Benton-Cohen for bringing this to my attention and for sharing her detailed notes from the Boas Papers. On Boas's interest in eye color, see Miller, "Seeing Eyes, Reading Bodies," 123–41.

71. Dudley, "Material Visions," 51–57. See Hutchinson, *Indian Craze*, for an extended examination of America's interest in Indian handcrafts and art objects in this same period.

72. Grosvenor, *National Geographic Society and Its Magazine*, 63.

73. Grosvenor, "Land of the Best," 396.

74. Ibid., 385.

75. Ibid., 393.

76. Ibid., 397.

77. See Batchelor, *Chromophobia*, and Taussig, *What Color Is the Sacred?*

78. Bryan, *National Geographic Society*, 294–95, and Lutz and Collins, *Reading National Geographic*, 31–32. The practice of shooting certain colors to maximize the chromatic brilliance of the printed product later became known (somewhat derisively) as the "red shirt school" of color photography. Historians often associate this style with the early adopters of Kodachrome film at *National Geographic* in the 1930s, but it has roots in the magazine's uses of the autochrome in the 1910s.

79. Quoted in Howard, "Autochromes," 42.

80. Williams, *Television*, 7.

81. "Fred Payne Clatworthy: Landscape Photographer," 422.

82. Gilbert Grosvenor to Fred Payne Clatworthy, November 25, 1914, National Geographic Society Archives, Lecture Series 1922–1923/1923–1924, Box 34, Fred Payne Clatworthy (11-57.355).

83. See "Our National Parks in Color," 511–19.

84. Clatworthy's self-published promotional pamphlet describes his autochrome lectures in this way: "The pictures shown by Mr. Clatworthy are original Lumière plates which portray the natural colors of the scenes presented, untouched by hand. These autochromes are 5x7 glass plates, projected on a sateen screen by means of a special lantern filled with a powerful nitrogen lamp. The result is a remarkable brilliancy and stereoscopic effect, with a truthful rendering of the colors of nature. Mr. Clatworthy furnishes his own screen and lantern and prefers to operate it himself, owing to the great value of the plates. About eighty slides are shown with each talk and the time consumed is a little over one hour, making with perhaps another musical feature, a delightful evening's entertainment." See "Fred Payne Clatworthy, Landscape Photographer, Traveler and Artist, Specialist in Natural Color Photography: Autochrome Talks on the Scenic Beauties of the Western United States" (circa 1922), National Geographic Society Archives, Lecture Series 1922–1923/1923–1924, Box 34, Fred Payne Clatworthy (11-57.355).

85. Fred Payne Clatworthy to Union Steamship Company of New Zealand, January 30, 1928, Fred Payne Clatworthy Collection (MSS #1794), Box 2, File Folder 88, History Colorado Museum, Denver.

86. Wood, *Photographic Arts*, 26; Fred Payne Clatworthy, "Something Different: The Clatworthy Lectures Using Natural Color Pictures," Fred Payne Clatworthy Collection (MSS #1794), Box 2, File Folder 92.

87. Fred Payne Clatworthy to Franklin L. Fisher, May 21, 1923, National Geographic Society Archives, Lecture Series 1922–1923/1923–1924, Box 34, Fred Payne Clatworthy (11-57.355).

88. On nineteenth-century traditions of western landscape and Indian photography, see Sandweiss, *Print the Legend*, 155–273.

89. Clatworthy, "Sixty Years in Photography," 2.

90. Retouching was actually an important part of Clatworthy's photographic practice. As autochrome collector and Clatworthy expert Mark Jacobs pointed out to me (telephone interview with author, July 2013), Clatworthy tended to shoot both black-and-white photographs and autochromes simultaneously. He used the black-and-white versions as templates for hand-painted color postcards that he sold in his Estes Park, Colorado, gallery and store.

91. Fred Payne Clatworthy to Franklin L. Fisher, September 17, 1923, National Geographic Society Archives, Lecture Series 1922–1923/1923–1924, Box 34, Fred Payne Clatworthy (11-57.355).

92. See Franklin L. Fisher to Fred Payne Clatworthy, June 17, 1924, National Geographic Society Archives, Lecture Series 1922–1923/1923–1924, Box 34, Fred Payne Clatworthy (11-57.355): "After the fullest consideration of the autochromes which we tentatively selected from the collection you showed here this spring, we have decided that there are not enough subjects with sufficient color in them to make a full sixteen-page series for The Geographic. Therefore, it has been decided to wait until next year and add to those we like any new subjects which you may obtain in the meantime. We are therefore sending you all of the 24 autochromes, carefully packed, via American Express, today and trust that they will reach you safely. The ones we

like have been indicated by a red mark across the corner. The others are also good subjects but we are afraid that their delicate colors will not reproduce satisfactorily."

93. Clatworthy, "Photographing the Marvels of the West in Colors," 718.

94. Clatworthy, "Scenic Glories of Western United States," 224.

95. Ibid., 227.

96. Wakeham, *Taxidermic Signs,* 33.

97. Clatworthy, "Photographing the Marvels of the West in Colors," 719.

98. Clatworthy, "Sixty Years in Photography," 2.

99. Clatworthy, "Photographing the Marvels of the West in Colors," 719.

100. W. B. Starr to Valentine Wilson, February 6, 1928, Fred Payne Clatworthy Collection (MSS #1794), Box 1, File Folder 28. For Clatworthy's itinerary in New Zealand, see "New Zealand Scenery," 12, and "Mr. Clatworthy Develops New Autochromes," 1.

101. Fred Payne Clatworthy to Franklin L. Fisher, June 16, 1928, Fred Payne Clatworthy Collection (MSS #1794), Box 1, File Folder 82.

102. Prior to Clatworthy's trip to New Zealand, *National Geographic* only had the occasion to publish hand-painted monochrome photographs of the Pacific region. See Grosvenor, "Hawaiian Islands," 115–238, and Murphy, "Romance of Science in Polynesia," 355–426.

103. Fred Payne Clatworthy to A. H. Messenger, August 3, 1928, Fred Payne Clatworthy Collection (MSS #1794), Box 1, File Folder 28.

104. Most of the surviving autochromes from New Zealand are held in the Mark Jacobs Photography Collection in Madison, Wisconsin. My thanks go to Mr. Jacobs for generously sharing hundreds of his digitized Clatworthy autochromes with me.

105. See Steichen, "Color Photography," 18–19: "It is strange how little people seem to realize that colors change, and change drastically, according to the intensity of the light. . . . For instance, bright orange seen in a very weak light assumes a brownish tone, yellow takes on a decided olive greenish cast, and vermillion loses its orange tone, and looks a purer red. In fact the whole tendency is towards blue; which tendency is then further exaggerated on the Autochrome plate. A portrait photographed indoors on a dull, gray day has a cold, bluish tone predominating; outdoors the result is sometimes so blue that one imagines the plate to have been exposed without a screen. . . . The tendency of the plate is to exaggerate these effects."

106. Franklin L. Fisher to Franklin Price Knott, November 18, 1929, National Geographic Society Archives, Franklin Price Knott File (503-8-5-2460).

107. See Lewis H. Southwick to Gilbert Grosvenor, July 18, 1928, and Gerald Thorne to National Geographic Society, July 18, 1928, Fred Payne Clatworthy Collection (MSS #1794), Box 1, File Folder 82.

108. Franklin L. Fisher to Gerald Thorne, July 20, 1928, Fred Payne Clatworthy Collection (MSS #1794), Box 1, File Folder 82.

109. Wood, *Photographic Arts,* 26.

110. Adams and Clatworthy, "A Sunshine Land of Fruits, Movies, and Sport," 545–92.

111. See Clatworthy, "Sixty Years in Photography," 2–3.

112. Franklin L. Fisher to Frederick S. Dellenbaugh, May 14, 1923, National Geographic Society Archives, Lecture Series 1922–1923/1923–1924, Box 34, Fred Payne Clatworthy (11-57.355).

113. Fred Payne Clatworthy to Franklin L. Fisher, May 21, 1923, National Geographic Society Archives, Lecture Series 1922–1923/1923–1924, Box 34, Fred Payne Clatworthy (11-57.355).

114. Mark Jacobs, e-mail correspondence with author, July 2013.

115. Clifford, "Partial Truths," 10.

Postscript

1. Levine and Leavitt's synopsis of the Language Keepers project can be found at http://www.languagekeepers.org/.

2. http://www.pmportal.org/.

3. http://www.languagekeepers.org/.

4. See http://www.pmportal.org/about-language-keepers: "Today, this methodology has evolved into a community documentation resource to include the Passamaquoddy–Maliseet Language Portal. The Portal now integrates dictionary development with media archives of Passamaquoddy language and culture, including public access and feedback functions; and a resource that encourages language use, language learning, research, and continuing documentation. The Portal has stimulated the training of indigenous filmmakers in IT skills as well as transcription and translation. Language Keepers offers this training."

5. See http://www.pmportal.org/videos/lets-all-sing. Aside from the documentation provided in the online Passamaquoddy–Maliseet Language Portal, my account of *Let's All Sing* in the paragraphs that follow draws on my own e-mail correspondence and telephone conversations with Language Keepers producer Ben Levine in July 2013. Levine filmed the proceedings on September 22, 2010. For firsthand accounts of the abuse many Passamaquoddy–Maliseet speakers endured for using their language in public, see the short films *If You Can't Read You Get Beaten* and *The Nun Would Always Tell Me, "Don't Speak Passamaquoddy"* on the Passamaquoddy–Maliseet Language Portal.

6. Jesse Walter Fewkes, "Passamaquoddy Diary: A Trip to Calais, Maine, for the Purpose of Experimenting with the Phonograph as an Instrument to Preserve the Ancient Language of That Tribe: March 16–19, 1890," Jesse Walter Fewkes Collection, American Folklife Center. Fewkes's recording of the Passamaquoddy trading song, performed either by Peter Selmore or Noel Josephs, is available at the Library of Congress's American Folklife Center. See Passamaquoddy Indian Music and Spoken Word, Reel 4260 (Box 3, Cylinder 1), Jesse Walter Fewkes Collection, American Folklife Center.

7. Fewkes, "A Contribution to Passamaquoddy Folk-Lore," 246. Here is how Fewkes describes the Passamaquoddy "Trade Dance" in his 1890 essay for *The Journal of American Folklore*—note the suggestion of its imminent obsolescence: "The participants, one or more in number, go to the wigwam of another person, and when near the entrance sing a song. The leader then enters, and, dancing about, sings at the

same time a continuation of the song he sang at the door of the hut. He then points out some object in the room which he wants to buy, and offers a price for it. The owner is obliged to sell the object pointed out, or to barter something of equal value. The narrator [Peter Selmore] remembers that the dress of the participants was similar to that of the Indians of olden times. He remembers, in the case of women, that they wore the variegated, pointed cap covered with beads, the loose robe, and leggings. The face of the participant was painted, or daubed black with paint or powder. . . . The singer [Selmore, again] told me, and I can well believe it, that the song is very ancient. I have little doubt that in this ceremony we have a survival of dances of the olden times" (263–64).

8. Wakeham, *Taxidermic Signs*, 155.

9. On the reinterpretation of ethnographic documents in the contemporary moment, especially photographs, see Horse Capture, foreword to *Native Nations*; Sandweiss, *Print the Legend*, 264–72; Peers and Brown, "Just by Bringing These Photographs," 265–80; and Edwards, "Tracing Photography," 177–86.

10. On the history and influence of the FCP in Native American communities across the United States, see Gray, "Early Ethnographic Recordings in Today's Indian Communities," 49–55; Gray, "Songs Come Home," 32–35; and Gray, "Returning Music to the Makers," 42–44.

11. Gray, "Returning Music to the Makers," 43; emphasis original.

12. Wayne Newell and Blanche Sockabasin, "Traditional Passamaquoddy Music from Maine," Library of Congress, Washington, D.C., September 16, 2009. An online recording of this performance is available at http://www.loc.gov/. For Fewkes's original account of the Passamaquoddy snake dance and snake song, see his "A Contribution to Passamaquoddy Folk-Lore," 260–63.

13. Gilman, *Hopi Songs*, 7.

14. See Paton, "Whispers in the Stacks," 274–80, and Paton, "Preservation Re-recording of Audio Recordings in Archives," 188–219, for accounts of the physical instability of early sound recordings. See Sterne, *Audible Past*, 325–33, for a more general discussion of sound recording and the problem of material permanence.

15. Paton, "Whispers in the Stacks," 276–77.

16. Ibid, 277.

17. Judith Gray, e-mail conversation with author, September 2013.

18. See Paton, "Preservation Re-recording of Audio Recordings in Archives," 193–95, for more on magnetic tape instability.

19. On contemporary efforts to reconstruct early sound recordings using digital image processing and three-dimensional optical metrology, see http://www.firstsounds.org/. See also Ernst, *Digital Memory and the Archive*, 126–28, 181–83, for a brief theoretical discussion of the importance of these efforts to the afterlife of the salvage ethnographic enterprise (and to media-archaeological knowledge more generally).

20. On the future obsolescence of today's digital sound formats, see Sterne, *MP3*, 227–30.

21. On the range of available solutions to the problem of film deterioration, see Hincha, "Crisis in Celluloid," 125–35, and Crofts, "Digital Decay," 21–29, among other

works. For accounts of the relationship between the material instability of the cinematic archive and the writing of film history, see Usai, "Unfortunate Spectator," 173–74; Usai, *Death of Cinema*; and Rodowick, *Virtual Life of Film*, 19–24.

22. Grierson, "Flaherty's Poetic *Moana*," 25.

23. See Sterne, *Audible Past*, 325–33; Chun, "Enduring Ephemeral," 184–203; and Ernst, *Digital Memory and the Archive*, 81–94.

24. See Slade, *Made to Break*, and Sterne, "Out with the Trash," 16–31.

25. The narrative of the disappearance of the analog is now so pervasive as to render any effort at citation insufficient. Notable scholarly works in the fields of media studies and cultural studies that use this narrative as a point of departure and an object of critique include Liu, "'Transcendental Data," 49–84; Hayles, *My Mother Was a Computer*; Stewart, *Framed Time*; Rodowick, *Virtual Life of Film*; Rombes, *Cinema in the Digital Age* ; Sterne, *MP3*; and Hoberman, *Film after Film*.

26. See Bolter and Grusin, *Remediation*, 2–50, and Manovich, *Language of New Media*. Analog devices and formats will only disappear completely, for example, if we fail to adhere to the canonical theory of "remediation," which posits that media cannot be created or destroyed, they can only change form—a sort of second law of thermodynamics for new media studies.

27. O'Brien and Walton, "Hand Talk—Preserving a Language Legacy."

BIBLIOGRAPHY

Archival Collections

Bureau of American Ethnology Records. National Anthropological Archives, Smithsonian Institution. Suitland, Md.

Dibner Library of the History of Science and Technology, Smithsonian Institution. Washington, D.C.

Eadweard Muybridge Collection. University of Pennsylvania Archives. Philadelphia, Pa.

Edward Larocque Tinker Papers (bMS Am 2196). Houghton Library, Harvard University. Cambridge, Mass.

Franz Boas Papers, 1878–1943 (MSS60202). Manuscript Division, Library of Congress. Washington, D.C.

Fred Payne Clatworthy Collection (MSS 1794). History Colorado Museum. Denver, Colo.

Garrick Mallery Papers (MS 2372, Boxes 1–12). National Anthropological Archives, Smithsonian Institution. Suitland, Md.

George Washington Cable Papers (MS Am 1288.4). Houghton Library, Harvard University. Cambridge, Mass.

Harvard Film Archive, Harvard University. Cambridge, Mass.

Hemenway Southwest Expedition Records (1886–1914). Peabody Museum of Archaeology and Ethnology, Harvard University. Cambridge, Mass.

Hugh Lenox Scott Collection (MS 2932). National Anthropological Archives, Smithsonian Institution. Suitland, Md.

Jesse Walter Fewkes Collection. American Folklife Center, Library of Congress. Washington, D.C.

John Peabody Harrington Papers. National Anthropological Archives, Smithsonian Institute. Suitland, Md.

Mark Jacobs Photography Collection. Madison, Wis.

National Geographic Society Archives. National Geographic Museum. Washington, D.C.

Robert Joseph Flaherty Papers (1884–1970). Rare Book and Manuscript Library, Columbia University. New York, N.Y.

Smithsonian Motion Picture Collection (circa 1927–1950). Smithsonian Institution Archives. Washington, D.C.

Books and Articles

Abramson, Howard S. *National Geographic: Behind America's Lens on the World*. New York: Crown, 1987.

"Accuracy of the Phonograph in Acoustics." *Phonogram* 1, no. 4 (1891): 87.

Acland, Charles R., ed. *Residual Media*. Minneapolis: University of Minnesota Press, 2007.

Adams, Clifton, and Fred Payne Clatworthy. "A Sunshine Land of Fruits, Movies, and Sport." *National Geographic Magazine* 66, no. 5 (1934): 545–92.

Adas, Michael. *Machines as the Measure of Men: Science, Technology, and Ideologies of Western Dominance*. Ithaca, N.Y.: Cornell University Press, 1989.

Adorno, Theodor W. "The Curves of the Needle." 1927. In Adorno, *Essays on Music*, 271–76.

———. *Essays on Music*. Edited by Richard Leppert and translated by Susan H. Gillespie. Berkeley: University of California Press, 2002.

———. "The Form of the Phonograph Record." 1934. In Adorno, *Essays on Music*, 277–82.

Allen, William Francis, Charles Packard Ware, and Lucy McKim Garrison. *Slave Songs of the United States*. New York: A. Simpson, 1867.

Alvey, Mark. "The Cinema as Taxidermy: Carl Akeley and the Preservative Obsession." *Framework* 48, no. 1 (2007): 23–45.

Amad, Paula. "Cinema's 'Sanctuary': From Pre-documentary to Documentary Film in Albert Kahn's *Archives de la Planète* (1908–1931)." *Film History* 13, no. 2 (2001): 138–59.

———. *Counter-Archive: Film, the Everyday, and Albert Kahn's Archives de la Planète*. New York: Columbia University Press, 2010.

Anderson, Benedict. *Imagined Communities: Reflections on the Origin and Spread of Nationalism*. 1983. Reprint, London: Verso, 1991.

Andresen, Julie Tetel. *Linguistics in America, 1769–1924: A Critical History*. New York: Routledge, 1990.

Andrew, Dudley. *The Major Film Theories: An Introduction*. New York: Oxford University Press, 1976.

———, ed. *Opening Bazin: Postwar Film Theory and Its Afterlife*. New York: Oxford University Press, 2011.

"Announcement." *National Geographic Magazine* 1, no. 1 (1888): i–ii.

Auslander, Philip. *Liveness: Performance in a Mediatized Culture*. 2nd ed. London: Routledge, 2008.

Baker, Lee D. *Anthropology and the Racial Politics of Culture*. Durham, N.C.: Duke University Press, 2010.

———. *From Savage to Negro: Anthropology and the Construction of Race, 1896–1954*. Berkeley: University of California Press, 1998.

Balikci, Asen. "Anthropology, Film, and the Arctic Peoples." *Anthropology Today* 5, no. 2 (1989): 4–10.

Ball, Phillip. *Bright Earth: Art and the Invention of Color*. New York: Farrar, Straus, and Giroux, 2001.

Banks, Marcus, and Jay Ruby, eds. *Made to Be Seen: Perspectives on the History of Visual Anthropology*. Chicago: University of Chicago Press, 2011.

Banta, Melissa, and Curtis M. Hinsley. *From Site to Sight: Anthropology, Photography, and the Power of Imagery*. Cambridge, Mass.: Peabody Museum Press/Harvard University Press, 1986.

Barber, X. Theodore. "The Roots of Travel Cinema: John L. Stoddard, E. Burton Holmes, and the Nineteenth-Century Illustrated Travel Lecture." *Film History* 5, no. 1 (1993): 68–84.

Barker, Jennifer M. *The Tactile Eye: Touch and the Cinematic Experience*. Berkeley: University of California Press, 2009.

Barnouw, Erik. *Documentary: A History of the Non-fiction Film*. 2nd rev. ed. New York: Oxford University Press, 1993.

Barsam, Richard. *The Vision of Robert Flaherty: The Artist as Myth and Filmmaker*. Bloomington: Indiana University Press, 1988.

Batchelor, David. *Chromophobia*. London: Reaktion Books, 2000.

Bauman, H-Dirksen L. "Redesigning Literature: The Cinematic Poetics of ASL Poetry." *Sign Language Studies* 4, no. 1 (2003): 34–47.

Baynton, Douglas C. *Forbidden Signs: American Culture and the Campaign against Sign Language*. Chicago: University of Chicago Press, 1996.

———. "Out of Sight: The Suppression of American Sign Language." In Sollors, *Multilingual America*, 367–69.

———. "Savages and Deaf-Mutes: Evolutionary Theory and the Campaign against Sign Language." In *Anthropology and Human Movement: Searching for Origins*, edited by Drid Williams, 39–74. Lanham, Md.: Scarecrow Press, 2000.

Bazin, André. "The Evolution of the Language of Cinema." In Bazin, *What Is Cinema?*, 1:23–40.

———. "The Ontology of the Photographic Image." In Bazin, *What Is Cinema?*, 1:9–16.

———. *What Is Cinema?* Vol. 1. Translated by Hugh Gray. Berkeley: University of California Press, 2007.

Bell, Alexander Melville. *Visible Speech: The Science of Universal Alphabetics; or, Self-Interpreting Physiological Letters, for the Writing of All Languages in One Alphabet, Illustrated by Tables, Diagrams, and Examples*. London: Simpkin, Marshall, 1867.

Bender, Margaret. *Signs of Cherokee Culture: Sequoyah's Syllabary in Eastern Cherokee Life*. Chapel Hill: University of North Carolina Press, 2002.

Benedict, Ruth. *Patterns of Culture*. 1934. Reprint, Boston: Mariner Books, 2005.

Benjamin, Walter. "Theses on the Philosophy of History." In *Illuminations*, edited by Hannah Arendt, translated by Harry Zohn, 253–64. New York: Schocken Books, 1968.

Berkhofer, Robert F., Jr. *The White Man's Indian: Images of the American Indian from Columbus to the Present*. New York: Vintage Books, 1978.

Bernardi, Daniel, ed. *The Birth of Whiteness: Race and the Emergence of U.S. Cinema*. New Brunswick, N.J.: Rutgers University Press, 1996.

Bieder, Robert E. *Science Encounters the Indian, 1820–1880: The Early Years of American Ethnology*. Norman: University of Oklahoma Press, 1986.

Biers, Katherine. "Syncope Fever: James Weldon Johnson and the Black Phonographic Voice." *Representations* 96 (Fall 2006): 99–125.

Bikle, Lucy Leffingwell Cable. *George W. Cable: His Life and Letters*. New York: Charles Scribner's Sons, 1928.

Biolsi, Thomas, and Larry J. Zimmerman, eds. *Indians and Anthropologists: Vine Deloria, Jr., and the Critique of Anthropology*. Tucson: University of Arizona Press, 1997.

Blair, George A. "The Development of the Motion Picture Raw Film Industry." *Annals of the American Academy of Political and Social Science* 128 (1926): 50–53.

Bloom, Lisa. "Constructing Whiteness: Popular Science and *National Geographic* in the Age of Multiculturalism." *Configurations* 2, no. 1 (1994): 15–32.

Boas, Franz. "The Aims of Ethnology." In Boas, *Race, Language, and Culture*, 626–38.

———. "Eskimo Tales and Songs." *Journal of American Folk-Lore* 2, no. 5 (1889): 123–31.

———. *The Ethnography of Franz Boas: Letters and Diaries of Franz Boas Written on the Northwest Coast from 1886 to 1931*. Edited by Ronald P. Rohner. Chicago: University of Chicago Press, 1969.

———. "Ethnological Problems in Canada." In Boas, *Race, Language, and Culture*, 331–42.

———. *Introduction to the Handbook of American Indian Languages*. 1911. Edited by Preston Holder. Reprint, Lincoln: University of Nebraska Press, 1966.

———. "Introduction to the *International Journal of American Linguistics*." In Boas, *Race, Language, and Culture*, 199–210.

———. "Mythology and Folk-Tales of the North American Indians." In Boas, *Race, Language, and Culture*, 451–90.

———. "On Alternating Sounds." *American Anthropologist* 2, no. 1 (1889): 47–54.

———. *Race, Language, and Culture*. Chicago: University of Chicago Press, 1941.

Bolter, Jay David, and Richard Grusin. *Remediation: Understanding New Media*. Cambridge, Mass.: MIT Press, 1999.

Bonnin, Gertrude (Zitkala-Ša). "Letter to the Chiefs and Headmen of the Tribes." *American Indian Magazine* 6, no. 4 (1919): 196–97.

Bonvillian, John D., Vicky L. Ingram, and Brendan M. McCleary. "Observations on the Use of Manual Signs and Gestures in the Communicative Interactions between Native Americans and Spanish Explorers of North America: The Accounts of Bernal Díaz del Castillo and Álvar Núñez Cabeza de Vaca." *Sign Language Studies* 9, no. 2 (2009): 132–65.

Boone, Elizabeth Hill, and Walter D. Mignolo, eds. *Writing without Words: Alternative Literacies in Mesoamerica and the Andes*. Durham, N.C.: Duke University Press, 1994.

Bordwell, David, Janet Staiger, and Kristin Thompson. *The Classical Hollywood Cinema: Film Style and Mode of Production to 1960*. New York: Columbia University Press, 1985.

Boudinot, Elias. "Invention of a New Alphabet." In *Cherokee Editor: The Writings of Elias Boudinot*, edited by Theda Perdue, 48–63. Athens: University of Georgia Press, 1983.

Boulouch, Nathalie. "The Documentary Use of the Autochrome in France." *History of Photography* 18, no. 2 (1994): 143–45.

Brady, Erika. *A Spiral Way: How the Phonograph Changed Ethnography*. Jackson: University Press of Mississippi, 1999.

Brantlinger, Patrick. *Dark Vanishings: Discourse on the Extinction of Primitive Races, 1800–1930*. Ithaca, N.Y.: Cornell University Press, 2003.

Braun, Marta. *Picturing Time: The Work of Étienne-Jules Marey (1830–1904)*. Chicago: University of Chicago Press, 1992.

Bridgeman, Richard. *The Colloquial Style in America*. New York: Oxford University Press, 1966.

Brinton, Daniel Garrison. "American Languages, and Why We Should Study Them." *Pennsylvania Magazine of History and Biography* 9, no. 1 (1885): 15–35.

———. "The Earliest Form of Human Speech, as Revealed by American Tongues." 1888. In *Essays of an Americanist*, 390–409. Philadelphia: Porter and Coates, 1890.

Brodhead, Richard H. *Cultures of Letters: Scenes of Reading and Writing in Nineteenth-Century America*. Chicago: University of Chicago Press, 1993.

Brooks, Lisa. "Characters Cut in the Trees: Sequoyah Demonstrates His Syllabary to the Cherokee Council." In *A New Literary History of America*, edited by Greil Marcus and Werner Sollors, 160–64. Cambridge, Mass.: Belknap Press, 2009.

———. *The Common Pot: The Recovery of Native Space in the Northeast*. Minneapolis: University of Minnesota Press, 2008.

Brown, John Mason. "Songs of the Slaves." *Lippincott's Magazine* 2 (1868): 617–23.

Bryan, C. D. B. *The National Geographic Society: 100 Years of Adventure and Discovery*. New York: Harry N. Abrams, 1987.

Burnet, John R. *Tales of the Deaf and Dumb*. Newark, N.J.: Benjamin Olds, 1835.

Cable, George Washington. *The Creoles of Louisiana*. New York: Charles Scribner's Sons, 1884.

———. "Creole Slave Songs." *Century Illustrated Magazine* 31, no. 6 (1886): 807–28.

———. "Dance in Place Congo." *Century Illustrated Magazine* 31, no. 4 (1886): 517–32.

———. "The Freedman's Case in Equity." *Century Magazine* 29 (January 1885): 409–18.

———. *The Grandissimes: A Story of Creole Life*. 1880. Reprint, New York: Penguin Books, 1988.

———. "My Politics." In Cable, *The Negro Question*, 1–25.

———. "'Negro English' in Literature." *The Critic*, April 18, 1885, 68.

———. *The Negro Question: A Selection of Writings on Civil Rights in the South*. Edited by Arlin Turner. New York: Norton Library, 1968.

———. "The Negro Question in the United States." *Contemporary Review* 53 (March 1888): 443–68.

————. "A Protest against Dialect." *The Critic,* August 1, 1885, 83.

————. "The Silent South." *Century Magazine* 30 (September 1885): 674–91.

Calder-Marshall, Arthur. *The Innocent Eye: The Life of Robert J. Flaherty.* London: W. H. Allen, 1963.

Campbell, Lyle. *American Indian Languages: The Historical Linguistics of Native America.* New York: Oxford University Press, 1997.

Canales, Jimena. *A Tenth of a Second: A History.* Chicago: University of Chicago Press, 2009.

Cassuto, Leonard. *The Inhuman Race: The Racial Grotesque in American Literature and Culture.* New York: Columbia University Press, 1997.

Cheng, Anne Anlin. "Skin Deep: Josephine Baker and the Colonial Fetish." *Camera Obscura* 69, no. 3 (2008): 35–78.

————. "Skin, Tattoos, and Susceptibility." *Representations* 108 (Fall 2009): 98–119.

Chion, Michel. *Audio-Vision: Sound on Screen.* Translated by Claudia Gorbman. New York: Columbia University Press, 1994.

Christopher, Robert J. *Robert and Frances Flaherty: A Documentary Life, 1883–1922.* Montreal: McGill-Queen's University Press, 2005.

Chun, Wendy Hui Kyong. "The Enduring Ephemeral, or The Future Is a Memory." In Huhtamo and Parikka, *Media Archaeology,* 184–203.

————. "Race and/as Technology; or, How to Do Things to Race." *Camera Obscura* 24, no. 70 (2009): 6–35.

Church, John W. "A Vanishing People of the South Seas: The Tragic Fate of the Marquesan Cannibals, Noted for Their Warlike Courage and Physical Beauty." *National Geographic Magazine* 36, no. 4 (1919): 275–306.

Clark, W. P. *The Indian Sign Language with Brief Explanatory Notes of the Gestures Taught Deaf-Mutes in Our Institutions for Their Instruction, and a Description of Some of the Peculiar Laws, Customs, Myths, Superstitions, Ways of Living, Code of Peace and War Signals of Our Aborigines.* Philadelphia: L. R. Hamersly, 1885.

Clatworthy, Fred Payne. "Photographing the Marvels of the West in Colors." *National Geographic Magazine* 53, no. 6 (1928): 694–719.

————. "Scenic Glories of Western United States." *National Geographic Magazine* 56, no. 2 (1929): 223–34.

————. "Sixty Years in Photography." *Denver Council of Camera Clubs Photogram,* November 1948, 2–3.

————. "Western Views in the Land of the Best." *National Geographic Magazine* 43, no. 4 (1923): 405–20.

Clifford, James. "Of Other Peoples: Beyond the 'Salvage' Paradigm." *Discussions in Contemporary Culture* 1 (1987): 120–30, 142–50.

————. "On Ethnographic Allegory." In Clifford and Marcus, *Writing Culture,* 98–121.

————. "Partial Truths." In Clifford and Marcus, *Writing Culture,* 1–26.

————. *The Predicament of Culture: Twentieth-Century Ethnography, Literature, and Art.* Cambridge, Mass.: Harvard University Press, 1988.

————. *Routes: Travel and Translation in the Late Twentieth Century.* Cambridge, Mass.: Harvard University Press, 1997.

Clifford, James, and George E. Marcus, eds. *Writing Culture: The Poetics and Politics of Ethnography.* Berkeley: University of California Press, 1986.

Cohen, Matt. *The Networked Wilderness: Communicating in Early New England.* Minneapolis: University of Minnesota Press, 2010.

Coleman, Beth. "Race as Technology." *Camera Obscura* 24, no. 70 (2009): 176–207.

"Color Photo Proves True: Lumière Plate a Success in First Tests Here." *Los Angeles Times,* February 9, 1908, II8.

Comolli, Jean-Louis. "Machines of the Visible." In *The Cinematic Apparatus,* edited by Teresa de Lauretis and Stephen Heath, 121–43. New York: St. Martin's Press, 1980.

Conn, Steven. *History's Shadow: Native Americans and Historical Consciousness in the Nineteenth Century.* Chicago: University of Chicago Press, 2004.

Cooper, Merian C. "Grass: A Persian Epic of Migration." *Asia* 24–25 (1924–25).

Corliss, Richard. "Robert Flaherty: The Man in the Iron Myth." In *Nonfiction Film Theory and Criticism,* edited by Richard Barsam, 230–38. New York: E. P. Dutton, 1976.

Corner, John. *The Art of Record: A Critical Introduction to Documentary.* Manchester, U.K.: Manchester University Press, 1996.

Crain, Patricia. *The Story of A: The Alphabetization of America from* The New England Primer *to* The Scarlet Letter. Stanford, Calif.: Stanford University Press, 2000.

Crary, Jonathan. *Techniques of the Observer: On Vision and Modernity in the Nineteenth Century.* Cambridge, Mass.: MIT Press, 1990.

Cripps, Thomas. *Slow Fade to Black: The Negro in American Film, 1900–1942.* 1977. Reprint, Oxford: Oxford University Press, 1993.

Crofts, Charlotte. "Digital Decay." *The Moving Image* 8, no. 2 (2008): 1–35.

Curtis, Edward S. *The North American Indian; Being a Series of Volumes Picturing and Describing the Indians of the United States and Alaska, Portfolio 1.* Cambridge: Edward S. Curtis, 1907.

———. "Vanishing Indian Types: The Tribes of the Northwest Plains." *Scribner's* 39 (June 1906): 657–71.

Custen, George F. "The (Re)framing of Robert Flaherty." *Quarterly Review of Film Studies* 7 (Winter 1982): 87–94.

Danzker, Jo-Anne Birnie, ed. *Robert Flaherty, Photographer/Filmmaker: The Inuit 1910–1922.* Vancouver: Vancouver Art Gallery, 1979.

Darwin, Charles. *The Descent of Man, and Selection in Relation to Sex.* 1871. Reprint, New York: Penguin Books, 2004.

Daston, Lorraine, and Peter Galison. *Objectivity.* New York: Zone Books, 2007.

Davidson, Winn W. "The Future of Color-Photography." *Photo-Era* 44, no. 2 (1920): 80–85.

Davis, Jeffrey E. *Hand Talk: Sign Language Among American Indian Nations.* Cambridge: Cambridge University Press, 2010.

Deger, Jennifer. *Shimmering Screens: Making Media in an Aboriginal Community.* Minneapolis: University of Minnesota Press, 2006.

Dellenbaugh, Frederick S. *A Canyon Voyage: The Narrative of the Second Powell Expedition Down the Green-Colorado River from Wyoming, and the Explorations on Land, in the Years 1871 and 1872.* New York: G. P. Putnam's Sons, 1908.

――――. *The North-Americans of Yesterday: A Comparative Study of North-American Indian Life Customs, and Products, on the Theory of the Ethnic Unity of the Race.* New York: G. P. Putnam's Sons, 1900.

Deloria, Philip J. *Indians in Unexpected Places.* Lawrence: University Press of Kansas, 2004.

Derrida, Jacques. *Of Grammatology.* Translated by Gayatri Chakravorty Spivak. Baltimore: The Johns Hopkins University Press, 1976.

――――. "Plato's Pharmacy." In *Dissemination,* translated by Barbara Johnson, 61–84. Chicago: University of Chicago Press, 1981.

de Vies, Guilliam. "Autochrome Work in Tropical Africa." *Amateur Photographer and Photography* 49 (March 24, 1920): 236.

Dippie, Brian W. *The Vanishing American: White Attitudes and U.S. Indian Policy.* Middletown, Conn.: Wesleyan University Press, 1982.

Dixon, Joseph Kossuth, and Rodman Wanamaker. *The Vanishing Race: The Last Great Indian Council.* Garden City, N.Y.: Doubleday, Page, 1913.

Doane, Mary Ann. *The Emergence of Cinematic Time: Modernity, Contingency, the Archive.* Cambridge, Mass.: Harvard University Press, 2002.

Draper, William R. "The Last of the Red Race." *Cosmopolitan* 32, no. 3 (1902): 244–46.

Dudley, Sandra. "Material Visions: Dress and Textiles." In Banks and Ruby, *Made to Be Seen,* 45–73.

Dunbar, William. "On the Language of Signs among Certain North American Indians." *Transactions of the American Philosophical Society* 6, no. 1 (1809): 1–8.

"Duplicates of Autochromes by Contact Printing and Copying." *Colour Photography: Supplement to the British Journal of Photography,* November 1, 1907, 81.

Duponceau, Peter Stephen. "English Phonology; or, An Essay towards an Analysis and Description of the Component Sounds of the English Language." *Transactions of the American Philosophical Society, New Series* 1 (1818): 228–64.

Duranti, Alessandro. "Language as Culture in U.S. Anthropology: Three Paradigms." *Cultural Anthropology* 44, no. 3 (2003): 323–47.

Dyer, Richard. *White.* New York: Routledge, 1997.

Eastman Panchromatic Negative Film for Motion Pictures. Rochester, N.Y.: Eastman Kodak, 1925.

"The Edison Phonograph." *Popular Science Monthly,* April 1878, 748–49.

Edison, Thomas A. "The Perfected Phonograph." *North American Review,* June 1888, 641–50.

――――. "The Phonograph and Its Future." *North American Review,* June 1878, 527–36.

Edwards, Brent Hayes. "The Seemingly Eclipsed Window of Form: James Weldon Johnson's Prefaces." In *The Jazz Cadence of American Culture,* edited by Robert G. O'Meally, 580–601. New York: Columbia University Press, 1998.

Edwards, Elizabeth, ed. *Anthropology and Photography, 1860–1920.* New Haven, Conn.: Yale University Press, 1992.

――――. *Raw Histories: Photographs, Anthropology, and Museums.* Oxford: Berg Press, 2001.

――――. "Salvaging Our Past: Photography and Survival." In Morton and Edwards, *Photography, Anthropology, and History,* 67–87.

————. "Talking Visual Histories." In *Museums and Source Communities: A Routledge Reader,* edited by Laura Peers and Alison K. Brown, 83–99. London: Routledge, 2003.

————. "Tracing Photography." In Banks and Ruby, *Made to Be Seen,* 159–89.

Ekström, Kjell. *George Washington Cable: A Study of His Early Life and Work.* Cambridge, Mass.: Harvard University Press, 1950.

Elliott, Michael A. *The Culture Concept: Writing and Difference in the Age of Realism.* Minneapolis: University of Minnesota Press, 2002.

Ellison, Ralph. *Invisible Man.* 1952. Reprint, New York: Vintage International, 1995.

Elsaesser, Thomas, ed. *Early Cinema: Space, Frame, Narrative.* London: BFI, 1990.

————. "The New Film History as Media Archaeology." *Cinémas* 14, nos. 2–3 (2004): 75–117.

Ernst, Wolfgang. *Digital Memory and the Archive.* Edited by Jussi Parikka. Minneapolis: University of Minnesota Press, 2013.

Eskilson, Stephen. "Color and Consumption." *Design Issues* 18, no. 2 (2002): 17–29.

Evans, Brad. *Before Cultures: The Ethnographic Imagination in American Literature.* Chicago: University of Chicago Press, 2005.

Evans, William. "French–English Literary Dialect in *The Grandissimes.*" *American Speech* 46 (Autumn–Winter 1971): 210–22.

Ewers, John C. "Richard Sanderville, Blackfoot Indian Interpreter." In *American Indian Intellectuals,* edited by Margot Liberty, 117–26. St. Paul, Minn.: West, 1977.

Fabian, Ann. *The Skull Collectors: Race, Science, and America's Unburied Dead.* Chicago: University of Chicago Press, 2010.

Fabian, Johannes. *Time and Other: How Anthropology Makes Its Object.* 1983. Reprint, New York: Columbia University Press, 2002.

Farnell, Brenda M. *Do You See What I Mean? Plains Indian Sign Talk and the Embodiment of Action.* Austin: University of Texas Press, 1995.

————. "Ethno-graphics and the Moving Body." *Man* 29, no. 4 (1994): 929–74.

Fewkes, Jesse Walter. "Additional Studies of Zuñi Songs and Rituals with the Phonograph." *American Naturalist* 24, no. 287 (1890): 1094–98.

————. "A Contribution to Passamaquoddy Folk-Lore." *Journal of American Folklore* 3, no. 11 (1890): 257–80.

————. "A Few Summer Ceremonials at Zuñi Pueblo." *Journal of American Ethnology and Archaeology* 1 (1891): 1–61.

————. "On the Use of the Phonograph in the Study of the Languages of American Indians." *Science* 15, no. 378 (1890): 267–69.

————. "The Use of the Phonograph in the Study of the Languages of American Indians." *American Naturalist* 24, no. 281 (1890): 495–96.

Filene, Benjamin. *Romancing the Folk: Public Memory and American Roots Music.* Chapel Hill: University of North Carolina Press, 2000.

Fillmore, John Comfort. "What Do Indians Mean to Do When They Sing, and How Far Do They Succeed?" *Journal of American Folklore* 8, no. 29 (1895): 138–42.

————. "The Zuni Music as Translated by Mr. Benjamin Ives Gilman." *Music* 5 (November–April 1893–94): 39–46.

"First Photograph in Colors of a Living Woman to Be Taken in America." *Chicago Daily Tribune*, January 5, 1908, 8A.

Flaherty, Frances Hubbard. "The Camera's Eye." In *Spellbound in Darkness: A History of the Silent Film*, edited by George C. Pratt, 344–47. Rochester, N.Y.: University of Rochester Press, 1966.

———. "Fa'a Samoa: The Old, Primitive Polynesian Life—a Fleeting Ghost—Caught for the American Screen." *Asia* 25, no. 12 (1925): 1085–90, 1096–1100.

———. *The Odyssey of a Film-Maker: Robert Flaherty's Story.* Urbana, Ill.: Beta Phi Mu, 1960.

———. "A Search for Animal and Sea Sequences: Wherein 'Natural Drama' Goes Under and 'Fa'a Samoa' Comes Out on Top." *Asia* 25, no. 11 (1925): 954–63, 1000–1004.

———. "Setting Up House and Shop in Samoa: The Struggle to Find Screen Material in the Lyric Beauty of Polynesian Life." *Asia* 25, no. 8 (1925): 638–50, 709–11.

Flaherty, Robert J. "Film: Language of the Eye." *Theater Arts* 36, no. 5 (1951): 30–36.

———. "Filming Real People." In *The Documentary Tradition: From Nanook to Woodstock*, edited by Lewis Jacobs, 97–98. New York: Hopkinson and Blake, 1971.

———. "The Handling of Motion Picture Film under Various Climatic Conditions." *Transactions of the Society of Motion Picture Engineers* 26 (May 1926): 85–93. http://astro.temple.edu/~ruby/wava/Flaherty/handling.html.

Fletcher, Alice Cunningham. "*Hopi Songs* by Benjamin Ives Gilman." *Science* 29, no. 755 (1909): 977–79.

———. *A Study of Omaha Indian Music.* 1893. Edited by Helen Myers. Reprint, Lincoln: University of Nebraska Press, 1994.

Fletcher, Robert. *Brief Memoirs of Colonel Garrick Mallery, U.S.A., Who Died October 24, 1894.* Washington, D.C.: Judd and Detweiler, 1895.

"Fred Payne Clatworthy: Landscape Photographer." *Art and Progress* 5, no. 12 (1914): 422–26.

Freeman, Derek. *Margaret Mead and Samoa: The Making and Unmaking of an Anthropological Myth.* Cambridge, Mass.: Harvard University Press, 1983.

Frisbie, Charlotte J. *Music and Dance Research of the Southwestern United States Indians: Past Trends, Present Activities, and Suggestions for Future Research.* Detroit, Mich.: Information Coordinators, 1977.

Froelick, Louis D. "Moana of the South Seas: One of Seven Immortals in a Radiant Land of Morning Light." *Asia* 25, no. 5 (1925): 389–400.

Gaines, Jane M., and Michael Renov, eds. *Collecting Visible Evidence.* Minneapolis: University of Minnesota Press, 1999.

Gallaudet, Thomas H. "On the Natural Language of Signs; and Its Value and Uses in the Instruction of the Deaf and Dumb. Part I." *American Annals of the Deaf and Dumb* 1, no. 1 (1847): 55–60.

———. "On the Natural Language of Signs; and Its Value and Uses in the Instruction of the Deaf and Dumb. Part II." *American Annals of the Deaf and Dumb* 1, no. 2 (1848): 79–93.

Garrison, Lucy McKim. "Songs of the Port Royal 'Contrabands.'" 1862. In *The Social Implications of Early Negro Music in the United States,* edited by Bernard Katz, 9–10. New York: Arno Press, 1969.

Gaskill, Nicholas. "Vibrant Environments: The Feel of Color from the White Whale to the Red Wheelbarrow." PhD diss., University of North Carolina at Chapel Hill, 2010.

Gates, Henry Louis, Jr. *Figures in Black Words, Signs, and the "Racial" Self.* New York: Oxford University Press, 1987.

———. *The Signifying Monkey: A Theory of African-American Literary Criticism.* New York: Oxford University Press, 1989.

Geiger, Jeffrey. *Facing the Pacific: Polynesia and the U.S. Imperial Imagination.* Honolulu: University of Hawai'i Press, 2007.

Gelatt, Roland. *The Fabulous Phonograph, 1877–1977.* New York: Macmillan, 1977.

Gibbs, George. *Instructions for Research Relative to the Ethnology and Philology of America.* Washington, D.C.: Smithsonian Institution, 1863.

———. "On the Language of the Aboriginal Indians of America." In *Annual Report of the Smithsonian Institution for 1870,* 364–67. Washington, D.C.: Government Printing Office, 1871.

Gidley, Mick. *Edward S. Curtis and the North American Indian, Incorporated.* New York: Cambridge University Press, 1998.

Gilbert, G. K. "John Wesley Powell." *Science* 16, no. 406 (1902): 561–67.

Gilder, Richard Watson. "The Recording Tendency and What It Is Coming To." *Century Illustrated Magazine* 53, no. 4 (1897): 634–35.

Gilman, Benjamin Ives. *Hopi Songs.* Boston: Houghton Mifflin, 1908.

———. "On Some Psychological Aspects of the Chinese Musical System." *Philosophical Review* 1, no. 1 (1892): 54–78.

———. "The Science of Exotic Music." *Science* 30, no. 722 (1909): 532–35.

———. "Zuñi Melodies." *Journal of American Ethnology and Archaeology* 1 (1891): 63–91.

Ginsburg, Faye. "Culture/Media: A (Mild) Polemic." *Anthropology Today* 10, no. 2 (1994): 5–15.

———. "Indigenous Media: Faustian Contract or Global Village." *Cultural Anthropology* 6, no. 1 (1991): 92–112.

Gitelman, Lisa. *Always Already New: Media, History, and the Data of Culture.* Cambridge, Mass.: MIT Press, 2006.

———. *Scripts, Grooves, and Writing Machines: Representing Technology in the Edison Era.* Stanford, Calif.: Stanford University Press, 1999.

———. "Souvenir Foils: On the Status of Print at the Origin of Recorded Sound." In Gitelman and Pingree, *New Media, 1740–1915,* 157–74.

Gitelman, Lisa, and Geoffrey B. Pingree, eds. *New Media, 1740–1915.* Cambridge, Mass.: MIT Press, 2003.

Goble, Mark. *Beautiful Circuits: Modernism and the Mediated Life.* New York: Columbia University Press, 2010.

Goetzmann, William H. *Exploration and Empire: The Explorer and the Scientist in the Winning of the American West.* 1966. Reprint, New York: History Book Club, Francis Parkman Prize Edition, 2006.

Goody, Jack. *The Domestication of the Savage Mind*. Cambridge: Cambridge University Press, 1977.

———. *The Interface between the Written and the Oral*. Cambridge: Cambridge University Press, 1987.

Graham, Andrew Jackson. *Exhibits of the State of the Phonographic Art with Reference to the Copyright Case of Graham v. Pitman*. New York: A. J. Graham, 1864.

"The Grandissimes." *Harper's Magazine*, December 1880, 153.

Gray, Edward G. *New World Babel: Languages and Nations in Early America*. Princeton, N.J.: Princeton University Press, 1999.

Gray, Hugh. "Robert Flaherty and the Naturalistic Documentary." *Hollywood Quarterly* 5, no. 1 (1950): 41–48.

Gray, Judith. "Early Ethnographic Recordings in Today's Indian Communities: Federal Agencies and the Federal Cylinder Project." In *Songs of Indian Territory: Native American Music Traditions of Oklahoma*, edited by Willie Smyth, 49–55. Oklahoma City: Center of the American Indian, 1989.

———. "Returning Music to the Makers: The Library of Congress, American Indians, and the Federal Cylinder Project." *Cultural Survival Quarterly* 20, no. 4 (1996): 42–44.

———. "The Songs Come Home—The Federal Cylinder Project." *Cultural Resource Management* 14, no. 5 (1994): 32–35.

Grierson, John. "First Principles of Documentary." In *Grierson on Documentary*, edited by Forsyth Hardy, 145–56. Berkeley: University of California Press, 1966.

———. "Flaherty's Poetic *Moana*." In *The Documentary Tradition: From Nanook to Woodstock*, edited by Lewis Jacobs, 25–26. New York: Hopkinson and Blake, 1971.

Griffith, Richard. *The World of Robert Flaherty*. New York: Duell, Sloan, and Pearce, 1953.

Griffiths, Alison. *Wondrous Difference: Cinema, Anthropology, and Turn-of-the-Century Visual Culture*. New York: Columbia University Press, 2002.

Grimshaw, Anna. *The Ethnographer's Eye: Ways of Seeing in Anthropology*. New York: Cambridge University Press, 2001.

Grosvenor, Gilbert H. "The Hawaiian Islands: America's Strongest Outpost of Defense—The Volcanic and Floral Wonderland of the World." *National Geographic Magazine* 45, no. 2 (1924): 115–238.

———. "The Land of the Best." *National Geographic Magazine* 29, no. 4 (1916): 379–405.

———. *The National Geographic Society and Its Magazine*. Washington, D.C.: National Geographic Society, 1957.

———. "Report of the Director and Editor of the National Geographic Society for the Year 1914." *National Geographic Magazine* 27, no. 3 (1915): 318–20.

Gruber, Jacob W. "Ethnographic Salvage and the Shaping of Anthropology." *American Anthropologist* 72, no. 6 (1970): 1289–99.

Guillory, John. "Genesis of the Media Concept." *Critical Inquiry* 36, no. 2 (2010): 321–62.

Gunning, Tom. "Embarrassing Evidence: The Detective Camera and the Documentary Impulse." In Gaines and Renov, *Collecting Visible Evidence*, 46–64.

———. "Never Seen This Picture Before: Muybridge in Multiplicity." In Prodger, *Time Stands Still: Muybridge and the Instantaneous Photography Movement*, 222–74.

Hale, Horatio. "On Some Doubtful or Intermediate Articulations." *Journal of the Royal Anthropological Institute* 14 (1884): 233–43.

Haller, John S., Jr. "Race and the Concept of Progress in Nineteenth-Century American Ethnology." *American Anthropologist* 73, no. 3 (1971): 710–24.

Hammond, Anne. "Impressionist Theory and the Autochrome." *History of Photography* 15, no. 2 (1991): 96–100.

Hansen, Christine, Catherine Needham, and Bill Nichols. "Pornography, Ethnography, and the Discourses of Power." In Nichols, *Representing Reality: Issues and Concepts in Documentary*, 201–28.

Hansen, Miriam. *Babel and Babylon: Spectatorship in American Silent Film*. Cambridge, Mass.: Harvard University Press, 1991.

Haraway, Donna. "Teddy Bear Patriarchy: Taxidermy in the Garden of Eden, New York City, 1908–1936." In *Cultures of United States Imperialism*, edited by Amy Kaplan and Donald E. Pease, 237–91. Durham, N.C.: Duke University Press, 1993.

Harrington, John P. "The American Indian Sign Language." In Umiker-Sebeok and Sebeok, *Aboriginal Sign Languages of the Americas and Australia*, 2:109–42.

———. "Visible Speech." *International Journal of American Linguistics* 14, no. 2 (1949): 134–35.

Harrison, James A. "The Creole Patois of Louisiana." *Journal of American Philology* 3, no. 11 (1882): 285–96.

———. "Negro English." *Anglia* 7, no. 3 (1884): 232–79.

Hawkins, Stephanie L. *American Iconographic: National Geographic, Global Culture, and the Visual Imagination*. Charlottesville: University of Virginia Press, 2010.

Hayles, N. Katherine. *My Mother Was a Computer: Digital Subjects and Literary Texts*. Chicago: University of Chicago Press, 2005.

Hearn, Lafcadio. "The Creole *Patois*." In *An American Miscellany: Articles and Stories Now First Collected by Albert Mordell*, edited by Albert Mordell, 144–53. Vol. 2. New York: Dodd, Mead, 1925.

———. *Creole Sketches*. Edited by Charles Woodward Hutson. Boston: Houghton Mifflin, 1924.

———. *Two Years in the French West Indies*. 1890. Reprint, New York: Interlink Books, 2001.

———. *Youma: The Story of a West-Indian Slave*. New York: Harper and Brothers, 1890.

Heffer, Jean. *The United States and the Pacific: History of a Frontier*. 1995. Translated by W. Donald Wilson. Notre Dame, Ind.: University of Notre Dame Press, 2001.

Hegeman, Susan. *Patterns for America: Modernism and the Concept of Culture*. Princeton, N.J.: Princeton University Press, 1999.

Herskovits, Melville J. *The Myth of the Negro Past*. 1941. Reprint, New York: Beacon Books, 1958.

Higginson, Ella. *The Vanishing Race and Other Poems*. Bellingham, Wash.: C. M. Sherman, 1911.

Higginson, Thomas Wentworth. "Negro Spirituals." *Atlantic Monthly,* June 1867, 685–94.

Hincha, Richard. "Crisis in Celluloid: Color Fading and Film Base Deterioration." *Archival Issues* 17, no. 2 (1992): 125–35.

Hinsley, Curtis. "Ethnographic Charisma and Scientific Routine: Cushing and Fewkes in the American Southwest, 1879–1893." In *Observers Observed: Essays on Ethnographic Fieldwork,* edited by George W. Stocking Jr., 53–69. Madison: University of Wisconsin Press, 1983.

———. *Savages and Scientists: The Smithsonian Institution and the Development of American Anthropology, 1846–1910.* Washington, D.C.: Smithsonian Institution Press, 1981.

Hoberman, J. *Film after Film, or, What Became of 21st-Century Cinema?* London: Verso, 2012.

hooks, bell. *Black Looks: Race and Representation.* Boston: South End Press, 1992.

Horse Capture, George P. Foreword to *Native Nations: First Americans as Seen by Edward S. Curtis,* edited by Christopher Cardozo. Boston: Bullfinch Press, 1993.

Hough, Walter. "Jesse Walter Fewkes." *American Anthropologist* 33, no. 1 (1931): 92–97.

Howard, April. "Autochromes." *Darkroom Photography,* July 1989, 42–58.

Hrdlička, Aleš. "The Vanishing Indian." *Science* 46, no. 1185 (1917): 266–67.

Huhtamo, Erkki, and Jussi Parikka, eds. *Media Archaeology: Approaches, Applications, and Implications.* Berkeley: University of California Press, 2011.

Hutchinson, Elizabeth. *The Indian Craze: Primitivism, Modernism, and Transculturation in American Art, 1890–1915.* Durham, N.C.: Duke University Press, 2009.

Innis, Harold A. *The Bias of Communication.* 1951. Reprint, Toronto: University of Toronto Press, 2008.

———. *Empire and Communications.* 1950. Reprint, Lanham, Md.: Rowman and Littlefield, 2007.

"An Interesting Session Yesterday: Edison, the Modern Magician, Unfolds the Mysteries of the Phonograph." *Washington Star,* April 19, 1878.

Jacobson, Matthew Frye. *Whiteness of a Different Color: European Immigrants and the Alchemy of Race.* Cambridge, Mass.: Harvard University Press, 1998.

James, Edwin. *Account of an Expedition from Pittsburgh to the Rocky Mountains.* Philadelphia: H. C. Carey and I. Lea, 1823.

Jefferson, Thomas. *Notes on the State of Virginia.* 1787. In *The Portable Thomas Jefferson,* edited by Merrill D. Peterson, 23–232. New York: Penguin Books, 1975.

Johnson, Walter. "On Agency." *Journal of Social History* 37, no. 1 (2003): 113–23.

Jones, Gavin. *Strange Talk: The Politics of Dialect Literature in Gilded Age America.* Berkeley: University of California Press, 1999.

Joyrich, Lynne. "Bringing Race and Media Technologies into Focus." *Camera Obscura* 24, no. 70 (2009): 1–5.

Kaplan, Amy. *The Anarchy of Empire in the Making of U.S. Culture.* Cambridge, Mass.: Harvard University Press, 2002.

Kendon, Adam. *Gesture: Visible Action as Utterance.* New York: Cambridge University Press, 2004.

Kennedy, Paul. *The Samoan Tangle: A Study in Anglo-German-American Relations, 1878–1900*. New York: Barnes and Noble, 1974.

Kenney, William Howland. *Recorded Music in American Life: The Phonograph and Popular Memory, 1890–1945*. New York: Oxford University Press, 1999.

Kern, Stephen. *The Culture of Time and Space, 1880–1918*. Cambridge, Mass.: Harvard University Press, 1983.

Kittler, Friedrich. *Discourse Networks, 1800/1900*. Translated by Michael Metteer with Chris Cullens. Stanford, Calif.: Stanford University Press, 1990.

———. *Gramophone, Film, Typewriter*. Translated by Geoffrey Winthrop-Young and Michael Wutz. Stanford, Calif.: Stanford University Press, 1999.

———. *Optical Media: Berlin Lectures 1999*. Translated by Anthony Enns. Cambridge, Mass.: Polity Press, 2010.

Knapp, Samuel L. *Lectures on American Literature, with Remarks on Some Passages of American History*. New York: Elam Bliss, 1829.

Knott, Franklin Price. "Artist Adventures on the Island of Bali." *National Geographic Magazine* 53, no. 3 (1928): 326–47.

Kolodny, Annette. "Fictions of American Prehistory: Indians, Archaeology, and National Origins Myths." *American Literature* 75, no. 4 (2003): 693–721.

Kramer, Michael P. *Imagining Language in America: From the Revolution to the Civil War*. Princeton, N.J.: Princeton University Press, 1992.

Kramer, Paul A. *The Blood of Government: Race, Empire, the United States, and the Philippines*. Chapel Hill: University of North Carolina Press, 2006.

Krehbiel, Henry. *Afro-American Folksongs: A Study in Racial and National Music*. New York: G. Schirmer, 1914.

Krentz, Christopher B. "The Camera as Printing Press: How Film Has Influenced ASL Literature." In *Signing the Body Poetic: Essays on American Sign Language Literature*, edited by H-Dirksen L. Bauman, Jennifer L. Nelson, and Heidi M. Rose, 51–70. Berkeley: University of California Press, 2006.

———. *Writing Deafness: The Hearing Line in Nineteenth-Century American Literature*. Chapel Hill: University of North Carolina Press, 2007.

Kroeber, Alfred L., and Clyde Kluckhohn. *Culture: A Critical Review of Concepts and Definitions*. Cambridge, Mass.: Peabody Museum of American Archaeology and Ethnology, 1952.

Kun, Josh. *Audiotopia: Music, Race, and America*. Berkeley: University of California Press, 2005.

Ladd, Barbara. "'An Atmosphere of Hints and Allusions': Bras-Coupé and the Context of Black Insurrection in *The Grandissimes*." *Southern Quarterly* 29, no. 3 (1991): 63–76.

La Gorce, John Oliver. *The Story of the Geographic*. Washington, D.C.: James William Bryan Press, 1915.

Lamothe, Daphne. *Inventing the New Negro: Narrative, Culture, and Ethnography*. Philadelphia: University of Pennsylvania Press, 2008.

Langer, Mark. "Flaherty's Hollywood Period: The Crosby Version." *Wide Angle* 20 (1998): 38–57.

———. "Rethinking Flaherty: Acoma and Hollywood." *Wide Angle* 17 (1995): 239–55.

Larkin, Brian. *Signal and Noise: Media, Infrastructure, and Urban Culture in Nigeria.* Durham, N.C.: Duke University Press, 2007.

Last, Jay T. *The Color Explosion: Nineteenth-Century American Lithography.* Santa Ana, Calif.: Hillcrest Press, 2005.

"The Last of the Modocs." *Harper's Weekly,* June 21, 1873, 532–34.

Lastra, James. *Sound Technology and the American Cinema: Perception, Representation, Modernity.* New York: Columbia University Press, 2000.

Lepore, Jill. *A Is for American: Letters and Other Characters in the Newly United States.* New York: Alfred A. Knopf, 2002.

———. "Wigwam Words." *American Scholar* 70 (Winter 2001): 97–108.

Lester, Peter. "Travel and Early Colour." *Photography,* March 1992, 24–27.

Levine, Victoria Lindsay. *Writing American Indian Music: Historic Transcriptions, Notations, and Arrangements.* Middleton, Conn.: American Musicological Society/A-R Editions, 2002.

Levi-Strauss, Claude. *Tristes Tropiques.* 1955. Translated by John and Doreen Weightman. Reprint, New York: Penguin Books, 1992.

Limbrick, Peter. *Making Settler Cinemas: Film and Colonial Encounters in the United States, Australia, and New Zealand.* New York: Palgrave Macmillan, 2010.

Liss, Julia E. "Patterns of Strangeness: Franz Boas, Modernism, and the Origins of Anthropology." In *Prehistories of the Future: The Primitivist Project and the Culture of Modernism,* edited by Elazar Barkan and Ronald Bush, 114–30. Stanford, Calif.: Stanford University Press, 1995.

Liu, Alan. "Transcendental Data: Toward a History and Aesthetics of the New Encoded Discourse." *Critical Inquiry* 31, no. 1 (2004): 49–84.

"The Log of a Great Picture." *American Cinematographer,* November 1921, 10.

Lott, Eric. *Love and Theft: Blackface Minstrelsy and the American Working Class.* New York: Oxford University Press, 1993.

Luciano, Dana. *Arranging Grief: Sacred Time and the Body in Nineteenth-Century America.* New York: New York University Press, 2007.

Lumière, Auguste. "Lumière's Autochrome Plates: Instructions for Their Use." [1904]. In *Early Experiments with Direct Color Photography: Three Texts,* edited by Robert Sobieszek, 1–36. New York: Arno Press, 1979.

Lutz, Catherine A., and Jane L. Collins. *Reading National Geographic.* Chicago: University of Chicago Press, 1993.

Mackey, Nathaniel. *Discrepant Engagement: Dissonance, Cross-Culturality, and Experimental Writing.* Tuscaloosa: University of Alabama Press, 1993.

———. *Paracritical Hinge: Essays, Talks, Notes, Interviews.* Madison: University of Wisconsin Press, 2005.

"Madame Delphine." *Literary World* 12, no. 16 (1881): 259.

Maddox, Lucy. *Removals: Nineteenth-Century American Literature and the Politics of Indian Affairs.* New York: Oxford University Press, 1991.

Makagon, Daniel, and Mark Neumann. *Recording Culture: Audio Documentary and the Ethnographic Experience.* Los Angeles, Calif.: Sage, 2009.

Mallery, Garrick. "A Calendar of the Dakota Nation." *Bulletin of the U.S. Geological and Geographical Survey of the Territories* 3 (1877): 4–25.

———. *A Collection of Gesture-Signs and Signals of the North American Indians with Some Comparisons.* Washington, D.C.: U.S. Government Printing Office, 1880.

———. "The Former and Present Number of Our Indians." In *Proceedings of the American Association for the Advancement of Science: Twenty-Sixth Meeting, Held at Nashville, Tenn., August 1877,* edited by Frederick W. Putnam, 340–66. Salem, Mass.: Permanent Secretary, 1878.

———. "The Gesture Speech of Man." 1881. In Umiker-Sebeok and Sebeok, *Aboriginal Sign Languages of the Americas and Australia,* 1:407–37.

———. *Introduction to the Study of Sign Language among the North American Indians as Illustrating the Gesture Speech of Mankind.* Washington, D.C.: U.S. Government Printing Office, 1880.

———. "Pictographs of the North American Indians: A Preliminary Paper." In *The Fourth Annual Report of the Bureau of Ethnology to the Secretary of the Smithsonian Institution, 1882–1883,* edited by J. W. Powell, 5–256. Washington, D.C.: U.S. Government Printing Office, 1886.

———. "Picture-Writing of the American Indians." In *The Tenth Annual Report of the Bureau of Ethnology to the Secretary of the Smithsonian Institution, 1888–1889,* edited by J. W. Powell, 3–822. Washington, D.C.: U.S. Government Printing Office, 1893.

———. "Sign Language among North American Indians Compared with That among Other Peoples and Deaf-Mutes." In *The First Annual Report of the Bureau of Ethnology to the Secretary of the Smithsonian Institution, 1879–1880,* edited by J. W. Powell, 263–552. Washington, D.C.: U.S. Government Printing Office, 1881.

———. "The Sign-Language of the North American Indians." *American Annals of the Deaf and Dumb* 25, no. 1 (1880): 1–21.

Manovich, Lev. *The Language of New Media.* Cambridge, Mass.: MIT Press, 2001.

Marcus, Alan. "*Nanook of the North* as Primal Drama." *Visual Anthropology* 19, nos. 3–4 (2006): 201–22.

Marks, Dan. "Ethnography and Ethnographic Film: From Flaherty to Asch and After." *American Anthropologist* 97, no. 2 (1995): 339–47.

Marks, Laura U. *The Skin of the Film: Intercultural Cinema, Embodiment, and the Senses.* Durham, N.C.: Duke University Press, 2000.

Marvin, Carolyn. *When Old Technologies Were New: Thinking about Electric Communication in the Late Nineteenth Century.* New York: Oxford University Press, 1988.

Marx, Leo. *The Machine in the Garden: Technology and the Pastoral Ideal in America.* 1964. Reprint, New York: Oxford University Press, 2000.

Maurice, Alice. *The Cinema and Its Shadow: Race and Technology in Early Cinema.* Minneapolis: University of Minnesota Press, 2013.

McFarland, J. Horace. "Real Color Photography Is Now a Fact: The How and Why of the New Lumière Autochrome Process, and Its Great Commercial Possibilities." *Profitable Advertising,* April 1909, 1119–26.

McLuhan, Marshall. *The Gutenberg Galaxy: The Making of Typographic Man.* 1962. Reprint, Toronto: University of Toronto Press, 2002.

————. *Understanding Media: The Extensions of Man.* 1964. Reprint, Cambridge, Mass.: MIT Press, 1994.

McLuhan, Marshall, and Quentin Fiore. *The Medium Is the Massage.* New York: Random House, 1967.

Mead, Margaret. *Blackberry Winter: My Earlier Years.* New York: Simon and Schuster, 1972.

————. *Coming of Age in Samoa: A Psychological Study of Primitive Youth for Western Civilization.* 1928. Reprint, New York: Perennial Classics, 2001.

————. *Letters from the Field, 1925–1975.* Edited by Ruth Nanda Anshen. New York: Harper and Row, 1977.

Meleisea, Malama. *Change and Adaptations in Western Samoa.* Christchurch, New Zealand: Macmillan Brown Centre for Pacific Studies, University of Canterbury, 1992.

"Members of the Society." *National Geographic Magazine* 1, no. 1 (1888): 94–98.

"Methods of Control in the Development of Autochrome Plates." *Colour Photography: Supplement to the British Journal of Photography,* December 6, 1907, 90–92.

Mignolo, Walter D. *The Darker Side of the Renaissance: Literacy, Territoriality, and Colonization.* Ann Arbor: University of Michigan Press, 1995.

Millard, Andre. *America on Record: A History of Recorded Sound.* 2nd ed. New York: Cambridge University Press, 2005.

Miller, Karl Hagstrom. *Segregating Sound: Inventing Folk and Pop Music in the Age of Jim Crow.* Durham, N.C.: Duke University Press, 2010.

Miller, Thomas R. "Seeing Eyes, Reading Bodies: Visuality, Race, and Color Perception or a Threshold in the History of Human Sciences." In *Colors 1800/1900/2000: Signs of Ethnic Difference,* edited by Birgit Tautz, 123–41. Amsterdam: Rodopi Press, 2004.

Mitchell, Lee Clark. *Witnesses to a Vanishing America: The Nineteenth-Century Response.* Princeton, N.J.: Princeton University Press, 1981.

Mithun, Marianne. *The Languages of Native North America.* Cambridge: Cambridge University Press, 1999.

"*Moana*: The Intimate Drama of Life." *New York Times,* February 7, 1926, X4.

Mooney, James. "The Passing of the Indian." In *Proceedings of the Second Pan American Scientific Congress, Section 1: Anthropology,* 174–79. Washington, D.C.: Smithsonian Institution, 1909–10.

Morgan, Lewis Henry. *Ancient Society; or, Researches in the Lines of Human Progress from Savagery through Barbarism to Civilization.* 1877. Edited by Eleanor Burke Leacock. Reprint, Gloucester, U.K.: Peter Smith, 1974.

Morton, Christopher. "The Initiation of Kamanga: Visuality and Textuality in Evans-Pritchard's Zande Ethnography." In Morton and Edwards, *Photography, Anthropology, and History,* 119–42.

Morton, Christopher, and Elizabeth Edwards, eds. *Photography, Anthropology, and History: Expanding the Frame.* Farnham, U.K.: Ashgate, 2009.

Moten, Fred. *In the Break: The Aesthetics of the Black Radical Tradition.* Minneapolis: University of Minnesota Press, 2003.

"Mr. Clatworthy Develops New Autochromes." *Estes Park Trail*, June 8, 1928, 1.

Mulvey, Laura. "Visual Pleasure and Narrative Cinema." *Screen* 16, no. 3 (1975): 6–18.

Murphy, Robert Cushman. "The Romance of Science in Polynesia: An Account of Five Years of Cruising among the South Sea Islands, with Illustrations from Photographs by Rollo H. Beck." *National Geographic Magazine* 48, no. 4 (1925): 355–426.

Murray, Laura J. "Vocabularies of Native American Languages: A Literary and Historical Approach to an Elusive Genre." *American Quarterly* 53, no. 4 (2001): 590–623.

Musser, Charles. *Before the Nickelodeon Era: Edwin S. Porter and the Edison Manufacturing Company*. Berkeley: University of California Press, 1991.

———. *The Emergence of Cinema: The American Screen to 1907*. New York: Charles Scribner's Sons, 1990.

———. "The Travel Genre in 1903–1904: Moving towards Fictional Narrative." In Elsaesser, *Early Cinema*, 123–32.

Muybridge, Eadweard J. *Animal Locomotion: An Electro-photographic Investigation of Consecutive Phases of Animal Movements*. Philadelphia: J. B. Lippincott, 1887.

———. *Descriptive Zoopraxography; or, The Science of Animal Locomotion*. Philadelphia: University of Pennsylvania, 1893.

Naficy, Hamid. "Lured by the East: Ethnographic and Expedition Films About Nomadic Tribes—The Case of *Grass* (1925)." In Ruoff, *Virtual Voyages*, 117–38.

"A New Method for the Production of Photographs in Colours." *British Journal of Photography* 51 (July 1904): 605.

"New Zealand Scenery: Colour Photography by Expert." *Evening Post*, April 10, 1928, 12.

Nichols, Bill. "Documentary Film and the Modernist Avant-Garde." *Critical Inquiry* 27, no. 4 (2001): 580–610.

———. *Representing Reality: Issues and Concepts in Documentary*. Bloomington: Indiana University Press, 1991.

Nordström, Alison Devine. "Photography of Samoa: Production, Dissemination, and Use." In *Picturing Paradise: Colonial Photography of Samoa, 1875 to 1925*, edited by Casey Blanton, 11–40. Daytona Beach, Fla.: Southeast Museum of Photography, 1995.

North, Michael. *Camera Works: Photography and the Twentieth-Century Word*. New York: Oxford University Press, 2007.

O'Brien, Miles, and Marsha Walton. "Hand Talk—Preserving a Language Legacy." *Science Nation*, May 17, 2010. http://www.nsf.gov/news/special_reports/science_nation/indianhandtalk.jsp.

Ohmann, Richard. *Selling Culture: Magazines, Markets, and Class at the Turn of the Century*. New York: Verso, 1996.

Oksiloff, Assenka. *Picturing the Primitive: Visual Culture, Ethnography, and Early German Cinema*. New York: Palgrave, 2001.

"*Old Creole Days* and Other Novels." *Atlantic Monthly*, January 1880, 44–53.

Omi, Michael, and Howard Winant. *Racial Formation in the United States: From the 1960s to the 1990s*. 2nd ed. New York: Routledge, 1994.

Ong, Walter J. *Orality and Literacy: The Technologizing of the Word*. 1982. Reprint, New York: Routledge, 2002.

Ortner, Sherry. "Resistance and the Problem of Ethnographic Refusal." *Comparative Studies in Society and History* 37, no. 1 (1995): 173–93.

"Our National Parks in Color." *National Geographic Magazine* 37, no. 6 (1920): 511–19.

Pagden, Anthony. *The Fall of Natural Man: The American Indian and the Origins of Comparative Ethnology*. Cambridge: Cambridge University Press, 1982.

Page, Thomas Nelson. "Mr. Page's Negro Dialect." *The Critic*, July 4, 1885, 79.

"Paintings' Colors Caught by Camera: Famous Masterpieces Appear on Screen as They Are in Their Own Galleries." *New York Times*, January 27, 1913, 3.

Palmquist, Peter. "Imagemakers of the Modoc War: Louis Heller and Eadweard Muybridge." *Journal of California Anthropology* 4, no. 2 (1977): 206–41.

Parikka, Jussi. *What Is Media Archaeology?* Cambridge, Mass.: Polity Press, 2012.

Parker, Elizabeth Scott. "Samoa and Its People." *Cosmopolitan*, November 1888, 33–45.

Paton, Christopher Ann. "Preservation Re-recording of Audio Recordings in Archives: Problems, Priorities, Technologies, and Recommendations." *American Archivist* 61, no. 1 (1998): 188–219.

———. "Whispers in the Stacks: The Problem of Sound Recordings in Archives." *American Archivist* 53, no. 2 (1990): 274–80.

Pauly, Philip J. "The World and All That Is in It: The National Geographic Society, 1888–1918." *American Quarterly* 31, no. 4 (1979): 517–32.

Payne, John Howard. "The Cherokee Cause [1835]." *Journal of Cherokee Studies* 1, no. 1 (1976): 17–22.

Pedersen, Holger. *The Discovery of Language: Linguistic Science in the Nineteenth Century*. 1931. Translated by John Webster Spargo. Reprint, Bloomington: Indiana University Press, 1967.

Peers, Laura, and Alison K. Brown. "'Just by Bringing These Photographs . . .': On the Other Meanings of Anthropological Images." In Morton and Edwards, *Photography, Anthropology, and History*, 265–80.

Perdue, Theda. "The Sequoyah Syllabary and Cultural Revitalization." In *Perspectives on the Southeast: Linguistics, Archaeology, and Ethnohistory*, edited by Patricia B. Kwachka, 116–25. Athens: University of Georgia Press, 1994.

Picker, John M. *Victorian Soundscapes*. New York: Oxford University Press, 2003.

Pickering, John. *An Essay on a Uniform Orthography for the Indian Languages of North America*. Cambridge: Hilliard and Metcalf, 1820.

Pickering, Mary Orne. *Life of John Pickering*. Boston: John Wilson and Son, 1887.

Pietz, William. "The Phonograph in Africa: International Phonocentrism from Stanley to Sarnoff." In *Poststructuralism and the Question of History*, edited by Derek Attridge, Geoff Bennington, and Robert Young, 263–85. Cambridge: Cambridge University Press, 1987.

Pinney, Christopher. *Photography and Anthropology*. London: Reaktion Books, 2011.

Pisani, Michael V. *Imagining Native America in Music*. New Haven, Conn.: Yale University Press, 2005.

Poole, Deborah. "An Excess of Description: Ethnography, Race, and Visual Technologies." *Annual Review of Anthropology* 34 (2005): 159–79.

Poole, Robert M. *Explorers House: National Geographic and the World It Made.* New York: Penguin Press, 2004.

Powell, John Wesley. "The Cañons of the Colorado." *Scribner's Monthly* 9, nos. 3–5 (1875): 293–310, 394–410, 523–38.

———. "Competition as a Factor in Human Evolution." *American Anthropologist* 1, no. 4 (1888): 297–323.

———. "A Discourse on the Philosophy of the North American Indians." *Journal of the American Geographical Society of New York* 8 (1876): 251–68.

———, ed. *First Annual Report of the Bureau of Ethnology to the Secretary of the Smithsonian Institution, 1879–1880.* Washington, D.C.: Government Printing Office, 1881.

———. "From Barbarism to Civilization." *American Anthropologist* 1, no. 2 (1888): 97–123.

———. "From Savagery to Barbarism." *Transactions of the Anthropological Society of Washington* 3 (1883–85): 173–96.

———. "Human Evolution." *Transactions of the Anthropological Society of Washington* 2 (1882–83): 176–208.

———. *Indian Linguistic Families of America North of Mexico.* 1891. Edited by Preston Holder. Reprint, Lincoln: University of Nebraska Press, 1966.

———. *Introduction to the Study of Indian Languages: With Words, Phrases, and Sentences to be Collected.* 1877. Reprint, Washington, D.C.: Government Printing Office, 1880.

———. "An Overland Trip to the Grand Canyon." *Scribner's Monthly* 10, no. 6 (1875): 659–78.

———. "Physical Features of the Colorado Valley." *Popular Science Monthly* 7 (1875): 385–99, 531–92, 670–80.

———. "Report of the Director." In *The Fourteenth Annual Report of the Bureau of Ethnology to the Secretary of the Smithsonian Institution, 1892–1893,* edited by J. W. Powell, xxv–lxi. Washington, D.C.: U.S. Government Printing Office, 1896.

———. "Report of the Director" In *The Sixteenth Annual Report of the Bureau of Ethnology to the Secretary of the Smithsonian Institution, 1894–1895,* edited by J. W. Powell, xiii–cxix. Washington: U.S. Government Printing Office, 1897.

Pratt, Mary Louise. *Imperial Eyes: Travel Writing and Transculturation.* 2nd ed. New York: Routledge, 2008.

Preece, William Henry. *The Phonograph; or, Speaking and Singing Machine, Invented and Patented by Thomas Alva Edison: Full Description of Its Construction, Working, &c.* London: London Stereoscopic Company, 1878.

Preece, William Henry, and Augustus Stroh. "Studies in Acoustics. I. On the Synthetic Examination of Vowel Sounds." *Proceedings of the Royal Society of London* 28 (1878–79): 558–67.

"Preserving Indian Songs and Tales." *Phonogram* 1, no. 1 (1891): 12.

Prins, Harald E. L. "The Paradox of Primitivism: Native Rights and the Problem of Imagery in Cultural Survival Films." *Visual Anthropology* 9, nos. 3–4 (1997): 243–66.

———. "Visual Media and the Primitivist Perplex." In *Media Worlds: Anthropology on New Terrain*, edited by Faye D. Ginsburg, Lila Abu-Lughod, and Brian Larkin, 58–74. Berkeley: University of California Press, 2002.

Prodger, Philip. *Time Stands Still: Muybridge and the Instantaneous Photography Movement*. New York: Oxford University Press, 2003.

Pynchon, Thomas. *The Crying of Lot 49*. 1965. Reprint, New York: Perennial Classics, 1999.

Quinn, Lorena MacIntyre. "America's South Sea Soldiers." *National Geographic Magazine* 36, no. 9 (1919): 267–74.

Radano, Ronald. *Lying Up a Nation: Race and Black Music*. Chicago: University of Chicago Press, 2003.

Radick, Gregory. "R. L. Garner and the Rise of the Edison Phonograph in Evolutionary Philology." In Gitelman and Pingree, *New Media, 1740–1915*, 175–206.

Raheja, Michelle. "Reading Nanook's Smile: Visual Sovereignty, Indigenous Revisions of Ethnography, and *Atanarjuat (The Fast Runner)*." *American Quarterly* 59, no. 4 (2007): 1159–85.

———. *Reservation Reelism: Redfacing, Visual Sovereignty, and Representations of Native Americans in Film*. Lincoln: University of Nebraska Press, 2010.

Rasmussen, Birgit Brander. *Queequeg's Coffin: Indigenous Literacies and Early American Literature*. Durham, N.C.: Duke University Press, 2012.

"Recent Recommendation in the Autochrome Process." *Colour Photography: Supplement to the British Journal of Photography*, December 6, 1907, 93.

Renov, Michael, ed. *Theorizing Documentary*. New York: Routledge, 1993.

Rodowick, D. N. *The Virtual Life of Film*. Cambridge, Mass.: Harvard University Press, 2007.

Rogers, Joel A. *Sex and Race, Volume I: Negro-Caucasian Mixing in All Ages and All Lands*. 1941. Reprint, New York: Helga M. Rogers, 1967.

Rombes, Nicholas. *Cinema in the Digital Age*. London: Wallflower Press, 2009.

Rony, Fatimah Tobing. *The Third Eye: Race, Cinema, and Ethnographic Spectacle*. Durham, N.C.: Duke University Press, 1996.

Rosaldo, Renato. *Culture and Truth: The Remaking of Social Analysis*. Boston: Beacon Press, 1989.

Rosen, Phillip. *Change Mummified: Cinema, Historicity, Theory*. Minneapolis: University of Minnesota Press, 2001.

Rotha, Paul. *Celluloid: The Film To-Day*. London: Longmans, Green, 1931.

———. *The Film till Now: A Survey of the Cinema*. New York: Jonathan Cape and Harrison Smith, 1930.

———. *Robert J. Flaherty: A Biography*. Edited by Jay Ruby. Philadelphia: University of Pennsylvania Press, 1983.

Rothenberg, Tamar Y. *Presenting America's World: Strategies of Innocence in National Geographic Magazine, 1888–1945*. Burlington, Vt.: Ashgate, 2007.

Roumette, Sylvain. *Early Color Photography*. New York: Pantheon Books, 1986.

Round, Phillip H. *Removable Type: Histories of the Book in Indian Country, 1663–1880*. Chapel Hill: University of North Carolina Press, 2010.

Rousseau, Jean-Jacques. "Essay on the Origin of Languages." 1781. In *On the Origin of Language: Two Essays by Jean-Jacques Rousseau and Johann Gottfried Herder,* edited and translated by John H. Moran and Alexander Gode, 1–74. Chicago: University of Chicago Press, 1996.

Ruby, Jay. "'The Aggie Must Come First': The Demystification of Robert Flaherty." In Danzker, *Robert Flaherty, Photographer/Filmmaker,* 66–73.

———. "A Reexamination of the Early Career of Robert J. Flaherty." *Quarterly Review of Film Studies* 5 (Fall 1980): 431–58.

Ruoff, Jeffrey, ed. *Virtual Voyages: Cinema and Travel.* Durham, N.C.: Duke University Press, 2006.

Salesa, Damon. "Samoan Half-Castes and Some Frontiers of Comparison." In *Haunted by Empire: Geographies of Intimacy in North American History,* edited by Ann Laura Stoler, 71–93. Durham, N.C.: Duke University Press, 2006.

———. "'Travel Happy' Samoa: Colonialism, Samoan Migration, and a 'Brown Pacific.'" *New Zealand Journal of History* 37, no. 2 (2003): 171–88.

Salt, Barry. *Film Style and Technology: History and Analysis.* London: Starword, 1983.

Sandweiss, Martha A. *Print the Legend: Photography and the American West.* New Haven, Conn.: Yale University Press, 2002.

Sapir, Edward. "An Anthropological Survey of Canada." *Science* 34, no. 884 (1911): 789–93.

———. "Communication." *Encyclopedia of the Social Sciences* 4 (1931): 78–81.

———. "Song Recitative in Paiute Mythology." *Journal of American Folklore* 23, no. 90 (1910): 455–72.

Savage, Barbara Dianne. *Broadcasting Freedom: Radio, War, and the Politics of Race, 1938–1948.* Chapel Hill: University of North Carolina Press, 1999.

Schneirov, Matthew. *The Dream of a New Social Order: Popular Magazines in America, 1893–1914.* New York: Columbia University Press, 1994.

Schuchman, John S. *Hollywood Speaks: Deafness and the Film Entertainment Industry.* Urbana: University of Illinois Press, 1999.

Schulten, Susan. *The Geographical Imagination in America, 1880–1950.* Chicago: University of Chicago Press, 2001.

Scott, Hugh L. "The Sign Language of the Plains Indian." 1893. In Umiker-Sebeok and Sebeok, *Aboriginal Sign Languages of the Americas and Australia,* 2:53–67.

Shaul, D. Leedom. "Linguistic Natural History: John Wesley Powell and the Classification of American Languages." *Journal of the Southwest* 41, no. 2 (1999): 297–310.

Shelemay, Kay Kaufman. "Recording Technology, the Record Industry, and Ethnomusicological Scholarship." In *Comparative Musicology and Anthropology of Music: Essays on the History of Ethnomusicology,* edited by Bruno Nettl and Philip V. Bohlman, 277–92. Chicago: University of Chicago Press, 1991.

Shell, Marc, ed. *American Babel: Literatures of the United States from Abanaki to Zuni.* Cambridge, Mass.: Harvard University Press, 2002.

———. "Babel in America; or, The Politics of Language Diversity in the United States." *Critical Inquiry* 20, no. 1 (1993): 103–27.

Simpson, David. *The Politics of American English, 1776–1850*. New York: Oxford University Press, 1986.

Slade, Giles. *Made to Break: Technology and Obsolescence in America*. Cambridge, Mass.: Harvard University Press, 2007.

Smith, Bernard. *European Vision and the South Pacific, 1768–1850*. New York: Oxford University Press, 1960.

Smith, Shawn Michelle. *American Archives: Gender, Race, and Class in Visual Culture*. Princeton, N.J.: Princeton University Press, 1999.

———. *Photography on the Color Line: W. E. B. Du Bois, Race, and Visual Culture*. Durham, N.C.: Duke University Press, 2004.

Sollors, Werner, ed. *Multilingual America: Transnationalism, Ethnicity, and the Languages of American Literature*. New York: New York University Press, 1998.

Solnit, Rebecca. *River of Shadows: Eadweard Muybridge and the Technological Wild West*. New York: Viking, 2003.

"Sound-Blindness." *Science* 10, no. 250 (1887): 244–45.

Steet, Linda. *Veils and Daggers: A Century of National Geographic's Representation of the Arab World*. Philadelphia: Temple University Press, 2000.

Stegner, Wallace. *Beyond the Hundredth Meridian: John Wesley Powell and the Second Opening of the West*. 1954. Reprint, New York: Penguin Books, 1992.

Steichen, Eduard J. "Color Photography." *Camera Work* 22 (April 1908): 13–24.

Sterne, Jonathan. *The Audible Past: Cultural Origins of Sound Reproduction*. Durham, N.C.: Duke University Press, 2003.

———. *MP3: The Meaning of a Format*. Durham, N.C.: Duke University Press, 2012.

———. "Out with the Trash: On the Future of New Media." In Acland, *Residual Media*, 16–31.

Stewart, Garrett. *Framed Time: Toward a Postfilmic Cinema*. Chicago: University of Chicago Press, 2007.

Stewart, Jacqueline Najuma. *Migrating to the Movies: Cinema and Black Urban Modernity*. Berkeley: University of California Press, 2005.

Stieglitz, Alfred. "The Autochrome Plate." *Down-Town Topics* 6, no. 6 (1907): 1.

———. "Editor's Note." *Camera Work* 21 (January 1908): 48.

———. "The New Color Photography—a Bit of History." In *Camera Work: A Critical Anthology*, edited by Jonathan Green, 124–30. Millerton, N.Y.: Aperture, 1973.

Stirling, M. W. "John Peabody Harrington, 1884–1961." *American Anthropologist* 65, no. 2 (1963): 370–81.

Stocking, George W., Jr. *The Ethnographer's Magic and Other Essays in the History of Anthropology*. Madison: University of Wisconsin Press, 1992.

———. "The Ethnographic Sensibility of the 1920s and the Dualism of the Anthropological Tradition." In *Romantic Motives: Essays on Anthropological Sensibility*, edited by George W. Stocking Jr., 208–76. Madison: University of Wisconsin Press, 1989.

———. *Race, Culture, and Evolution: Essays in the History of Anthropology*. Chicago: University of Chicago Press, 1968.

———. *The Shaping of American Anthropology, 1883–1911: A Franz Boas Reader*. New York: Basic Books, 1974.

———. *Victorian Anthropology*. New York: Free Press, 1987.

Stott, William. *Documentary Expression and Thirties America*. New York: Oxford University Press, 1973.

Sundquist, Eric J. *To Wake the Nations: Race in the Making of American Literature*. Cambridge, Mass.: Belknap Press, 1993.

Taft, Robert. *Photography and the American Scene, 1839–1889: A Social History*. New York: Macmillan, 1942.

Tagg, John. *The Burden of Representation: Essays on Photographies and Histories*. Minneapolis: University of Minnesota Press, 1988.

Taussig, Michael. *Mimesis and Alterity: A Particular History of the Senses*. New York: Routledge, 1993.

———. *What Color Is the Sacred?* Chicago: University of Chicago Press, 2009.

Tawil, Ezra. *The Making of Racial Sentiment: Slavery and the Birth of the Frontier Romance*. New York: Cambridge University Press, 2006.

Tcherkézoff, Serge. "A Long and Unfortunate Voyage towards the 'Invention' of the Melanesia/Polynesia Distinction, 1595–1832." *Journal of Pacific History* 38, no. 2 (2003): 175–96.

Tebbel, John. *A History of Book Publishing in the United States*. Vol. 2. *The Expansion of an Industry, 1865–1919*. New York: R. R. Bowker, 1975.

Thompson, Emily. "Machines, Music, and the Quest for Fidelity: Marketing the Edison Phonograph in America, 1877–1925." *Musical Quarterly* 79, no. 1 (1995): 131–71.

Thorburn, David, and Henry Jenkins, eds. *Rethinking Media Change: The Aesthetics of Transition*. Cambridge, Mass.: MIT Press, 2003.

Tosi, Virgilio. *Cinema before Cinema: The Origins of Scientific Cinematography*. 1984. Translated by Sergio Angelini. Reprint, London: British Universities Film and Video Council, 2005.

Tozzer, Alfred M. "Jesse Walter Fewkes (1850–1930)." *Proceedings of the American Academy of Arts and Sciences* 70, no. 10 (1936): 535–36.

Trachtenberg, Alan. *Reading American Photographs: Images as History, Matthew Brady to Walker Evans*. New York: Hill and Wang, 1989.

———. *Shades of Hiawatha: Staging Indians, Making Americans, 1880–1930*. New York: Hill and Wang, 2004.

Tuason, Julie A. "The Ideology of Empire in *National Geographic Magazine*'s Coverage of the Philippines, 1898–1908." *Geographical Review* 89, no. 1 (1999): 34–53.

Turner, Arlin, ed. *Critical Essays on George W. Cable*. Boston: G. K. Hall, 1980.

———. *George W. Cable: A Biography*. Baton Rouge: Louisiana State University Press, 1966.

Turner, Frederick Jackson. *The Frontier in American History*. New York: Henry Holt, 1920.

Twyman, Michael. "The Illustration Revolution." In *The Cambridge History of the Book in Britain*, Vol. 4, *1830–1914*, edited by David McKitterick, 144–71. Cambridge: Cambridge University Press, 2009.

Tylor, Edward B. *Researches into the Early History of Mankind and the Development of Civilization*. London: John Murray, 1870.

Umiker-Sebeok, D. Jean, and Thomas A. Sebeok, eds. *Aboriginal Sign Languages of the Americas and Australia*. Vol. 1. *North America Classic Comparative Perspectives*. New York: Plenum Press, 1978.

———. *Aboriginal Sign Languages of the Americas and Australia*. Vol. 2. *The Americas and Australia*. New York: Plenum Press, 1978.

United States v. Bhagat Singh Thind, 261 U.S. 204, 211 (1923).

Uricchio, William. "Television, Film, and the Struggle for Media Identity." *Film History* 10, no. 2 (1998): 118–27.

Usai, Paulo Cherchi. *The Death of Cinema: History, Cultural Memory, and the Digital Dark Age*. London: BFI, 2001.

———. "The Unfortunate Spectator." *Sight and Sound* 56, no. 3 (1987): 170–74.

Valentine, Joseph. "Make-Up and Set Painting Aid New Film." *American Cinematographer*, February 1939, 54.

Van Dongen, Helen. "Robert J. Flaherty, 1884–1951." *Film Quarterly* 18, no. 4 (1965): 3–14.

Vesilind, Priit Juho. "*National Geographic* and Color Photography." MA thesis, Syracuse University, 1977.

Vizenor, Gerald. "Aesthetics of Survivance: Literary Theory and Practice." In *Survivance: Narratives of Native Presence*, edited by Gerald Vizenor, 1–24. Lincoln: University of Nebraska Press, 2008.

———. *Fugitive Poses: Native American Indian Scenes of Absence and Presence*. Lincoln: University of Nebraska Press, 2000.

Wagner, Bryan. "Disarmed and Dangerous: The Strange Career of Bras-Coupé." *Representations* 92 (Fall 2005): 117–51.

Wakeham, Pauline. *Taxidermic Signs: Reconstructing Aboriginality*. Minneapolis: University of Minnesota Press, 2008.

Walker, Willard B. "Native Writing Systems." In *Handbook of North American Indians*, vol. 17, *Languages*, edited by Ives Goddard, 155–84. Washington, D.C.: Smithsonian Institution, 1996.

Warren, Kenneth W. *Black and White Strangers: Race and American Literary Realism*. Chicago: University of Chicago Press, 1993.

Wead, Charles K. "The Study of Primitive Music." *American Anthropologist* 2, no. 1 (1900): 75–79.

Weheliye, Alexander G. *Phonographies: Grooves in Sonic Afro-Modernity*. Durham, N.C.: Duke University Press, 2005.

Wexler, Laura. *Tender Violence: Domestic Visions in an Age of U.S. Imperialism*. Chapel Hill: University of North Carolina Press, 2000.

Whitney, William Dwight. *Language and the Study of Language*. New York: Charles Scribner's Sons, 1867.

Williams, Raymond. *Keywords: A Vocabulary of Culture and Society*. Rev. ed. New York: Oxford University Press, 1985.

———. *Marxism and Literature*. New York: Oxford University Press, 1977.

———. *Television: Technology and Cultural Form*. New York: Schocken Books, 1974.

Williams, William Appleman. *The Tragedy of American Diplomacy*. 50th anniversary ed. New York and London: W. W. Norton, 2009.

Wilson, Edmund. *The Shores of Light: A Literary Chronicle of the Twenties and Thirties.* New York: Farrar, Straus, and Young, 1952.

Wiltse, Sara E. "Psychological Literature: II: Experimental." *American Journal of Psychology* 1, no. 4 (1888): 702–5.

Winston, Brian. *Claiming the Real: Documentary, Grierson, and Beyond.* 2nd ed. New York: Palgrave Macmillan, 2008.

———. "The Documentary Film as Scientific Inscription." In Renov, *Theorizing Documentary,* 37–57.

———. "Documentary: How the Myth Was Deconstructed." *Wide Angle* 21 (1999): 70–86.

———. "The White Man's Burden: The Example of Robert Flaherty." *Sight and Sound* 54 (Winter 1984–85): 58–60.

Wood, John. *The Art of the Autochrome: The Birth of Color Photography.* Iowa City: University of Iowa Press, 1993.

———. *The Photographic Arts.* Iowa City: University of Iowa Press, 1997.

Woodbury, Richard B., and Nathalie F. S. Woodbury. "The Rise and Fall of the Bureau of American Ethnology." *Journal of the Southwest* 41, no. 3 (1999): 283–96.

Worster, Donald. *A River Running West: The Life of John Wesley Powell.* New York: Oxford University Press, 2001.

Wundt, Wilhelm. *The Language of Gestures.* 1921. Reprint, Paris: Mouton, 1973.

Wurtzburg, Susan, and Lyle Campbell. "North American Indian Sign Language: Evidence of Its Existence before European Contact." *International Journal of American Linguistics* 61, no. 2 (1995): 153–67.

Yumibe, Joshua. *Moving Color: Early Film, Mass Culture, Modernism.* New Brunswick, N.J.: Rutgers University Press, 2012.

Zedeño, M. Nieves. "Preface: BAE Anthropology, Its Roots and Legacy." *Journal of the Southwest* 41, no. 3 (1999): 273–81.

Zielinski, Siegfried. *Deep Time of the Media: Toward an Archaeology of Hearing and Seeing by Technical Means.* Cambridge, Mass.: MIT Press, 2006.

Films

Contributions to *Dictionary of Indian Sign Language.* Directed by Richard Sanderville. 1934. Smithsonian Institution Archives, Accession 05-143, Smithsonian Institution, Motion Pictures circa 1927–50, Box 24, Film 106-25.

Dictionary of Indian Sign Language. Directed by Hugh Lenox Scott. [1931]. Smithsonian Institution Archives, Accession 05-143, Smithsonian Institution, Motion Pictures circa 1927–50, Boxes 4–6, Film 106-14.

Elephant Boy. VHS. Directed by Robert J. Flaherty. 1937. Beverly Hills, Calif.: MGM, 2000.

Grass: A Nation's Battle for Life. DVD. Directed by Ernest Shoedsack and Merian C. Cooper. 1925. Los Angeles, Calif.: Image Entertainment, 2000.

The Indian Sign Language. Directed by Hugh Lenox Scott. 1930. Smithsonian Institution Archives, Accession 05-143, Smithsonian Institution, Motion Pictures circa 1927–50, Boxes 3–4, Film 106-13.

Louisiana Story. DVD. Directed by Robert J. Flaherty. 1948. Chicago: Home Vision Entertainment, 2003.

Man of Aran. DVD. Directed by Robert J. Flaherty. 1934. Chicago: Home Vision Entertainment, 2003.

Moana: A Romance of the Golden Age. Directed by Robert J. Flaherty and Frances Hubbard Flaherty. Hollywood, Calif.: Paramount Pictures/Famous Players-Lasky, 1926.

Nanook of the North. DVD. Directed by Robert J. Flaherty. 1922. New York: Criterion, 1998.

Tabu: A Story of the South Seas. DVD. Directed by F. W. Murnau. 1931. Los Angeles, Calif.: Image Entertainment, 2000.

White Shadows in the South Seas. DVD. Directed by W. S. Van Dyke. 1928. Beverly Hills, Calif.: MGM, 2010.

INDEX

Page references in italics refer to illustrations.

BRIAN HOCHMAN is assistant professor of English at Georgetown University.